# Residential Design
# Using Autodesk® Revit® 2019

Daniel John Stine

Publications

**SDC Publications**
P.O. Box 1334
Mission, KS 66222
913-262-2664
www.SDCpublications.com
Publisher: Stephen Schroff

**Examination Copies**
Books received as examination copies are for review purposes only and may not be made available for student use. Resale of examination copies is prohibited.

**Electronic Files**
Any electronic files associated with this book are licensed to the original user only. These files may not be transferred to any other party.

**Trademarks**
**Autodesk®, AutoCAD®, Maya®, mental ray®, Revit®, 3ds Max®** are registered trademarks or trademarks of Autodesk, Inc., and/or its subsidiaries and/or affiliates in the USA and/or other countries. All other trademarks are trademarks of their respective holders.

**Disclaimer**
The author and publisher of this book have used their best efforts in preparing this book. These efforts include the development, research and testing of the material presented. The author and publisher shall not be liable in any event for incidental or consequential damages with, or arising out of, the furnishing, performance, or use of the material.

ISBN-13: 978-1-63057-187-0
ISBN-10: 1-63057-187-3

Printed and bound in the United States of America.

# FOREWORD

**To the Student:**

This book has been written with the assumption that the reader has no prior experience using Autodesk® Revit®. The intent of this book is to provide the student with a well-rounded knowledge of the architectural tools and techniques for use in both school and industry.

The book consists of a series of tutorials which primarily focus on the development of a single project. When you finish the book, you will have learned how to document and model all of the major architectural aspects of a residential project. This includes floor plans, interior and exterior elevations, wall and building sections, door and room finish schedules and organizing drawings on sheets for printing.

The exclusive online content contains several videos that supplement the book. Studying these videos along with the book will help the reader to better understand Autodesk Revit features. The book and videos will also help you prepare for the Autodesk Revit Architecture Certification Exam; see Appendix B for more information.

Be sure to check out the additional material included with the online content. There you will find a chapter introducing computers and on Autodesk Revit content creation.

**Errata:**
Please check the publisher's website from time to time for any errors or typos found in this book after it went to the printer. Simply browse to www.SDCpublications.com, and then navigate to the page for this book. Click the **View/Submit errata** link in the upper right corner of the page. If you find an error, please submit it so we can correct it in the next edition.

You may contact the publisher with comments or suggestions at service@SDCpublications.com.
*Please do not email with Revit questions unless they relate to a problem with this book.*

**To the Instructor:**

This book was designed for the architectural student using *Autodesk Revit 2019*. Note: a student can successfully work through this book using *Autodesk Revit Architecture 2019* as well. Throughout the book, the student develops a single family residence. The drawings start with the floor plans and develop all the way to photo-realistic renderings similar to the one on the cover of this book.

Throughout the book many Autodesk Revit architectural tools and techniques are covered while creating the house model. Also, in a way that is applicable to the current exercise, industry standards and conventions are covered. Access to the internet is required for some exercises.

Each chapter concludes with a self-exam and review questions. The answers to the self-exam questions are provided, but review question answers are not (they can only be found in the Instructor's Guide available from the publisher).

Since its initial release in 2005, this book has been updated every year for the latest version of Autodesk Revit. The printed text has always been available for the fall term.

An Instructor's Resource Guide is available for this book. It contains:
- Answers to the questions at the end of each chapter
- Example images of each exercise to be turned in (can be used to grade students' work)
- Outline of tools and topics to be covered in each lesson's lecture
- Suggestions for additional student work (for each lesson)
- Author's direct contact information

**About the Author:**
Daniel John Stine AIA, CSI, CDT, is a registered architect with over twenty years of experience in the field of architecture. He is the BIM Administrator at LHB, a 250-person full service design firm. In addition to providing training and support for four offices, Dan implemented BIM-based lighting analysis using ElumTools, early energy modeling using Autodesk Insight, virtual reality (VR) using the HTC Vive/Oculus Rift along with Fuzor & Enscape, Augmented Reality (AR) using the Microsoft Hololens, and the Electrical Productivity Pack for Revit (sold by CTC Express Tools). Dell, the world-renowned computer company, created a video highlighting his implementation of VR at LHB.

Dan has presented internationally on BIM in the USA, Canada, Ireland, Denmark, Australia and Singapore. He was ranked multiple times as a top-ten speaker by attendees at Autodesk University, RTC/BILT, Midwest University, AUGI CAD Camp, NVIDIA GPU Technology Conference, Lightfair, and AIA-MN Convention. By invitation, he spent a week at Autodesk's largest R&D facility in Shanghai, China to beta test and brainstorm new Revit features in 2016.

Committed to furthering the design profession, Dan teaches graduate architecture students at North Dakota State University (NDSU) and has lectured for interior design programs at NDSU, Northern Iowa State, and University of Minnesota, as well as Dunwoody's new School of Architecture in Minneapolis. As an adjunct instructor, Dan previously taught AutoCAD and Revit for twelve years at Lake Superior College. Dan is a member of the American Institute of Architects (AIA), Construction Specifications Institute (CSI), and Autodesk Developer Network (ADN), and is a Construction Document Technician (issued by CSI). He has presented live webinars for ElumTools, ArchVision, Revizto and NVIDIA. Dan writes about design on his blog, BIM Chapters, and in his textbooks published by SDC Publications:

- *Residential Design Using Autodesk Revit 2019*
- *Commercial Design Using Autodesk Revit 2019*
- *Design Integration Using Autodesk Revit 2019 (Architecture, Structure and MEP)*
- *Interior Design Using Autodesk Revit 2019 (with co-author Aaron Hansen)*
- *Residential Design Using AutoCAD 2019*
- *Commercial Design Using AutoCAD 2013*
- *Chapters in Architectural Drawing (with co-author Steven H. McNeill, AIA, LEED AP)*
- *Interior Design Using Hand Sketching, SketchUp and Photoshop (also with Steven H. McNeill)*
- *Google SketchUp 2013 for Interior Designers; Just the Basics*

**Social Media:**
Students can use social media, such as Twitter and LinkedIn to start developing professional contacts and knowledge. Follow the author on social media for new articles, tips and errata updates. Consider following the design firms and associations (AIA, CSI, etc.) in your area, this could give you an edge in an interview!

**Author's Blog:** http://bimchapters.blogspot.com/

Twitter
@DanStine_MN

LinkedIn
https://www.linkedin.com/in/danstinemn

**Thanks:**
I could not have done this without the support from my family: Cheri, Kayla and Carter.

Many thanks go out to SDC Publications for making this book possible!

# TABLE OF CONTENTS

Page

1. **Getting Started with Autodesk® Revit® 2019**
   1-1    What is Revit 2019?                                          1-1
   1-2    Overview of the Revit User Interface                         1-11
   1-3    Open, Save and Close a Revit Project                         1-26
   1-4    Creating a New Project                                       1-31
   1-5    Using Zoom and Pan to View Your Drawings                     1-33
   1-6    Using Revit's Help System                                    1-38
   1-7    Introduction to Autodesk 360                                 1-41
          *Self-Exam and Review Questions*

2. **Lake Cabin: FLOOR PLAN  (The Basics)**
   2-1    Walls                                                        2-1
   2-2    Doors                                                        2-5
   2-3    Windows                                                      2-7
   2-4    Roof                                                         2-9
   2-5    Annotation and Dimensions                                    2-11
   2-6    Printing                                                     2-15
          *Self-Exam and Review Questions*

3. **Overview of Linework and Modify Tools**
   3-1    Lines and Shapes                                             3-1
   3-2    Snaps                                                        3-15
   3-3    Edit Tools                                                   3-20
   3-4    Annotations                                                  3-33
          *Self-Exam and Review Questions*

4. **Drawing 2D Architectural Objects**
   4-1    Sketching Rectilinear Objects                                4-1
   4-2    Sketching Objects with Curves                                4-11
          *Self-Exam and Review Questions*

5. **FLOOR PLAN (First Floor)**
   5-1    Project Setup                                                5-1
   5-2    Exterior Walls                                               5-7
   5-3    Interior Walls                                               5-23
   5-4    Doors, Openings and Windows                                  5-35
   5-5    Adding a Fireplace                                           5-51
          *Self-Exam and Review Questions*

6. **FLOOR PLANS (Second Floor and Basement Plans)**
   6-1    View Setup and Enclosing the Shell                           6-1
   6-2    Adding the Interior Walls                                    6-6
   6-3    Adding Doors, Openings and Windows                           6-10
   6-4    Basement Floor Plan                                          6-15
   6-5    Stairs                                                       6-22
          *Self-Exam and Review Questions*

7. **ANNOTATION**
   7-1    Text                                                         7-2
   7-2    Dimensions                                                   7-16
   7-3    Tagging                                                      7-31
   7-4    Shared Parameters                                            7-39
   7-5    Keynoting                                                    7-46
   7-6    Adding Dimensions                                            7-55
          *Self-Exam and Review Questions*

### 8. ROOF
| | | |
|---|---|---|
| 8-1 | Roof Design Options (Style, Pitch and Overhang) | 8-1 |
| 8-2 | Gable Roof | 8-16 |
| 8-3 | Low Roof Elements | 8-24 |
| 8-4 | Skylights | 8-35 |
| | *Self-Exam and Review Questions* | |

### 9. FLOOR SYSTEMS AND REFLECTED CEILING PLANS
| | | |
|---|---|---|
| 9-1 | Floor Systems | 9-1 |
| 9-2 | Ceiling Systems (Susp. ACT and Gypsum Board) | 9-16 |
| 9-3 | Placing Light Fixtures | 9-31 |
| 9-4 | Annotations | 9-36 |
| | *Self-Exam and Review Questions* | |

### 10. ELEVATIONS
| | | |
|---|---|---|
| 10-1 | Creating and Viewing Exterior Elevations | 10-1 |
| 10-2 | Modifying the Project Model: Exterior Elevations | 10-9 |
| 10-3 | Creating and Viewing Interior Elevations | 10-16 |
| 10-4 | Modifying the Project Model: Interior Elevations | 10-22 |
| 10-5 | Design Options | 10-25 |
| | *Self-Exam and Review Questions* | |

### 11. SECTIONS
| | | |
|---|---|---|
| 11-1 | Specify Section Cutting Plane in Plan View | 11-1 |
| 11-2 | Modifying the Project Model in Section View | 11-7 |
| 11-3 | Wall Sections | 11-15 |
| 11-4 | Annotation and Detail Components | 11-25 |
| | *Self-Exam and Review Questions* | |

### 12. INTERIOR DESIGN
| | | |
|---|---|---|
| 12-1 | Bathroom Layouts | 12-1 |
| 12-2 | Kitchen Layout | 12-7 |
| 12-3 | Furniture | 12-20 |
| 12-4 | Adding Guardrails | 12-25 |
| | *Self-Exam and Review Questions* | |

### 13. SCHEDULES
| | | |
|---|---|---|
| 13-1 | Room and Door Tags | 13-1 |
| 13-2 | Generate a Door Schedule | 13-6 |
| 13-3 | Generate a Room Finish Schedule | 13-10 |
| | *Self-Exam and Review Questions* | |

### 14. SITE TOOLS & PHOTO-REALISTIC RENDERING
| | | |
|---|---|---|
| 14-1 | Site Tools | 14-1 |
| 14-2 | Creating an Exterior Rendering | 14-15 |
| 14-3 | Rendering an Isometric in Section | 14-28 |
| 14-4 | Creating an Interior Rendering | 14-35 |
| 14-5 | Adding People to the Rendering | 14-42 |
| | *Self-Exam and Review Questions* | |

### 15. CONSTRUCTION DOCUMENTS SET
| | | |
|---|---|---|
| 15-1 | Setting Up a Sheet | 15-1 |
| 15-2 | Sheet Index | 15-10 |
| 15-3 | Printing a Set of Drawings | 15-17 |
| | *Self-Exam and Review Questions* | |

### 16. INTRODUCTION TO PHASING AND WORKSHARING
| | | |
|---|---|---|
| 16-1 | Introduction to Phasing | 16-1 |
| 16-2 | Introduction to Worksharing | 16-10 |
| 16-3 | Phasing Exercise | 16-23 |
| 16-4 | Worksharing Exercise | 16-35 |
| | *Self-Exam and Review Questions* | |

### 17.  INTRODUCTION TO REVIT CONTENT CREATION

| | | |
|---|---|---|
| 17-1 | Basic Family Concepts | 17-1 |
| 17-2 | The Box: Creating the Geometry | 17-13 |
| 17-3 | The Box: Adding Parameters | 17-29 |
| 17-4 | The Box: Formulas and Materials | 17-45 |
| 17-5 | The Box: Family Types and Categories | 17-59 |
| | *Self-Exam & Review Questions* | |

## Exclusive Online Content: Bonus Chapters

Instructions for download on inside front cover of book

### 18.  INTRODUCTION TO COMPUTERS - 46 pages

| | |
|---|---|
| 18-1 | Computer Basics:  Terms and Functions |
| 18-2 | Overview of the Windows User Interface |
| 18-3 | File Management Introduction |
| | *Self-Exam & Review Questions* |

**Appendix A – ENGINEERING GRAPHICS**  - 38 pages

**Appendix B – AUTODESK REVIT CERTIFICATION EXAM**  - 10 pages

**Appendix C – ROOF STUDY WORKBOOK – DRAFT EDITION**  - 90 pages

**Appendix D – FINDING MISSING ELEMENTS IN REVIT**  - 24 pages

**Appendix E – INTRODUCTION TO HAND SKETCHING**  - 42 pages

## Exclusive Online Content: Videos

Each category below has several short videos, approximately 3-5 minutes long, in the online library for this book. These videos can be watched in order while working through this book, or they can be watched in any order as needed. Check back occasionally as new videos will be added – follow the author on Twitter for updates.

1. **User Interface**
2. **Walls**
3. **Doors and Windows**
4. **Stairs**
5. **Roofs**
6. **Floors**
7. **Ceilings**
8. **Elevations**
9. **Sections**
10. **Schedules**
11. **Rendering**
12. **Design Options**
13. **Sheets and Sheet Lists**
14. **Worksharing Introduction**
15. **Phases**
16. **Sweeps and Reveals**

**Notes:**

## Lesson 1
# Getting Started with Autodesk Revit 2019:

This chapter will introduce you to Autodesk® Revit® 2019. You will study the User Interface and learn how to open and exit a project and adjust the view of the drawing on the screen. It is recommended that you spend an ample amount of time learning this material, as it will greatly enhance your ability to progress smoothly through subsequent chapters.

## Exercise 1-1:
## What is Revit 2019?

## What is Autodesk Revit used for?

Autodesk Revit (Architecture, Structure and MEP) is the world's first fully parametric building design software. This revolutionary software, for the first time, truly takes architectural computer aided design beyond simply being a high-tech pencil. Revit is a product of Autodesk, makers of AutoCAD, Civil 3D, Inventor, 3DS Max, Maya and many other popular design programs.

Revit can be thought of as the foundation of a larger process called **Building Information Modeling** (BIM). The BIM process revolves around a virtual, information rich 3D model. In this model all the major building elements are represented and contain information such as manufacturer, model, cost, phase and much more. Once a model has been developed in Revit, third-party add-ins and applications can be used to further leverage the data. Some examples are Facilities Management, Analysis (Energy, Structural, Lighting), Construction Sequencing, Cost Estimating, Code Compliance and much more!

Revit can be an invaluable tool to designers when leveraged to its full potential. The iterative design process can be accomplished using special Revit features such as *Phasing* and *Design Options*. Material selections can be developed and attached to various elements in the model, where one simple change adjusts the wood from oak to maple throughout the project. The power of schedules may be used to determine quantities and document various parameters contained within content (this is the "I" in BIM, which stands for Information). Finally, the three-dimensional nature of a Revit-based model allows the designer to present compelling still images and animations. These graphics help to more clearly communicate the design intent to clients and other interested parties. This book will cover many of these tools and techniques to **assist** in the creative process.

## What is a parametric building modeler?

Revit is a program designed from the ground up using state-of-the-art technology. The term parametric describes a process by which an element is modified and an adjacent element(s) is automatically modified to maintain a previously established relationship. For example, if a wall is moved, perpendicular walls will grow, or shrink, in length to remain attached to the related wall. Additionally, elements attached to the wall will move, such as wall cabinets, doors, windows, air grilles, etc.

Revit stands for **Rev**ise **In**stantly; a change made in one view is automatically updated in all other views and schedules. For example, if you move a door in an interior elevation view, the floor plan will automatically update. Or, if you delete a door, it will be deleted from all other views and schedules.

A major goal of Revit is to eliminate much of the repetitive and mundane tasks traditionally associated with CAD programs allowing more time for design, coordination and visualization. For example, all sheet numbers, elevation tags and reference bubbles are updated automatically when changed anywhere in the project. Therefore, it is difficult to find a mis-referenced detail tag.

The best way to understand how a parametric model works is to describe the Revit project file. A single Revit file contains your entire building project. Even though you mostly draw in 2D views, you are actually drawing in 3D. In fact, the entire building project is a 3D model. From this 3D model you can generate 2D elevations, 2D sections and perspective views. Therefore, when you delete a door in an elevation view you are actually deleting the door from the 3D model from which all 2D views are generated and automatically updated.

Another way in which Revit is a parametric building modeler is that **parameters** can be used to control the size and shape of geometry. For example, a window model can have two *parameters* set up which control the size of the window. Thus, from a window's properties it is possible to control the size of the window without using any of the drawing modify tools such as *Scale* or *Move*. Furthermore, the *parameter* settings (i.e., width and height in this example) can be saved within the window model (called a *Family*). You could have the 2′ x 4′ settings saved as "Type A" and the 2′ x 6′ as "Type B." Each saved list of values is called a *Type* within the *Family*. Thus, this one double-hung window *Family* could represent an unlimited number of window sizes! You will learn more about this later in the book.

Window model size controlled by parameters *Width* and *Height*

## What Disciplines does Revit Support?

Revit supports **Architecture, Interior Design, Structure** and **MEP** (which stands for Mechanical, Electrical and Plumbing). There used to be three discipline specific versions of Revit and an all-in-one version—now there is just the all-in-one version. You can download the free 30-day trial from autodesk.com. Students may download a free 3-year version of Revit at www.autodesk.com/education.

Revit is not meant to support professional Civil design.

Revit model of an existing building, with architecture, structural, mechanical, plumbing and electrical all modeled.

*Image courteous of LHB, Inc.* *www.LHBcorp.com*

Now is as good a time as any to make sure the reader understands that Revit is not, nor has it ever been, backwards compatible. This means there is no *Save-As* back to a previous version of Revit. Also, an older version of Revit cannot open a file, project or content saved in a newer format. So, make sure you consider what version your school or employer is currently standardized on before upgrading any projects or content. Revit will automatically upgrade an older format when opened in a newer version of the software. This is a onetime process which can take several minutes.

3D model of lunch room created in *Interior Design Using Autodesk Revit 2019*

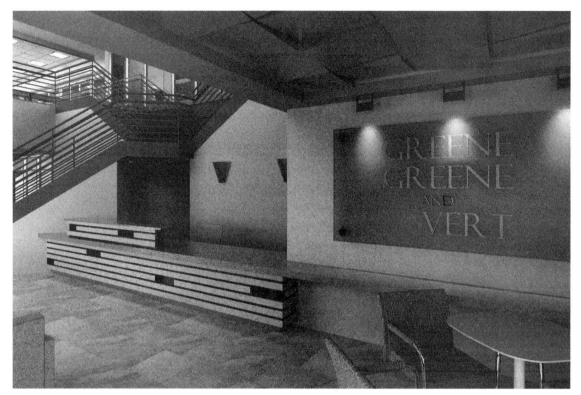

Lobby rendering from *Interior Design Using Autodesk Revit 2019*

## Why use Revit?

Many people ask the question, why use Revit versus other programs? The answer can certainly vary depending on the situation and particular needs of an individual or organization.

Generally speaking, this is why most companies use Revit:

- Many designers and drafters are using Revit to streamline repetitive drafting tasks and focus more on designing and detailing a project.
- Revit is a very progressive program and offers many features for designing buildings. Revit is constantly being developed and Autodesk provides incremental upgrades and patches on a regular basis; Revit 2019 was released about a year after the previous version.
- Revit was designed specifically for architectural design and includes features like:
  - *Autodesk Renderer* Photo Realistic Rendering
  - Phasing; model changes over time
  - Design Options; model changes during the same time period
  - Live schedules
  - Cloud Rendering via *Autodesk A360*
  - Conceptual Energy Analysis via *Autodesk A360*
  - Daylighting Analysis via *Autodesk A360*

# A few basic Revit concepts:

The following is meant to be a brief overview of the basic organization of Revit as a software application. You should not get too hung up on these concepts and terms as they will make more sense as you work through the tutorials in this book. This discussion is simply laying the groundwork so you have a general frame of reference on how Revit works.

The Revit platform has three fundamental types of elements:
- Model Elements
- Datum Elements
- View-Specific Elements

## Model Elements

Think of *Model Elements* as things you can put your hands on once the building has been constructed. They are typically 3D but can sometimes be 2D. There are two types of *Model Elements*:

- **Host Elements**: walls, floors, slabs, roofs, ceilings.

- **Model Components**; Stairs, Doors, Furniture, Casework, Beams, Columns, Pipes, Ducts, Light Fixtures, Model Lines, etc.

    o Some *Model Components* require a host before they can be placed within a project. For example, a window can only be placed in a host, which could be a wall, roof or floor depending on how the element was created. If the host is deleted, all hosted or dependent elements are automatically deleted.

**Model Elements**
*Windows & Doors; require a host*

**Host Elements**
*Roof, Wall & Floor*

**Model Elements**
*Stair & Washer/Dryer; do not require a host*

## Datum Elements

*Datum Elements* are reference planes within the building that graphically and parametrically define the location of various elements within the model. These are the three types of *Datum Elements,* all of which define 3D planes:

- **Grids**
  - o Typically laid out in a plan view to locate structural elements such as columns and beams, as well as walls. Grids show up in plan, elevation and section views. Moving a grid in one view moves it in all other views as it is the same element. (See the next page for an example of a grid in plan view.)

- **Levels**
  - o Used to define vertical relationships, mainly surfaces that you walk on. They only show up in elevation, section and 3D views. Most elements are placed relative to a *Level;* when the *Level* is moved those elements move with it (e.g., doors, windows, casework, ceilings). ***WARNING:*** *If a Level is deleted, those same "dependent" elements will also be deleted from the project!*

- **Reference Planes**
  - o These are similar to grids in that they show up in plan and elevation or sections. They do not have reference bubbles at the end like grids. Revit breaks many tasks down into simple 2D tasks which result in 3D geometry. *Reference Planes* are used to define 2D surfaces on which to work within the 3D model. They can be placed in any view, horizontally, vertically or at an angle.

## View-Specific Elements

As the name implies, the items about to be discussed only show up in the specific view in which they are created. For example, notes and dimensions added in the architectural floor plans will not show up in the structural floor plans. These elements are all 2D and are mainly communication tools used to accurately document the building for construction or presentations.

- **Annotation elements** (text, tags, symbols, dimensions)
  - Size automatically set and changed based on selected view scale

- **Details** (detail lines, filled regions, 2D detail components)

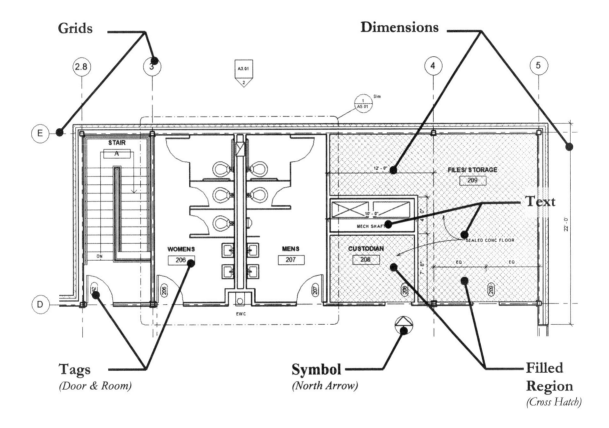

**Grids**

**Dimensions**

**Text**

**Tags**
*(Door & Room)*

**Symbol**
*(North Arrow)*

**Filled Region**
*(Cross Hatch)*

---

**File Types (and extensions):**

Revit has four primary types of files that you will work with as a Revit user. Each file type, as with any Microsoft Windows based program, has a specific three letter file name extension; that is, after the name of the file on your hard drive you will see a period and three letters. They are:

| | |
|---|---|
| .RVT | Revit project files; the file most used (also for backup files) |
| .RFA | Revit family file; loadable content for your project |
| .RTE | Revit template; a project starter file with office standards preset |
| .RFT | Revit family template; a family starter file with parameters |

The Revit platform has three fundamental ways in which to work with the elements (for display and manipulation):

- Views
- Schedules
- Sheets

The following is a cursory overview of the main ideas you need to know. This is not an exhaustive study on views, schedules and sheets.

## Views

*Views*, accessible from the *Project Browser*, is where most of the work is done while using Revit. Think of views as slices through the building, both horizontal (plans) and vertical (elevations and sections).

- **Plans**
  - A *Plan View* is a horizontal slice through the building. You can specify the location of the **cut plane** which determines if certain windows show up or how much of the stair is seen. A few examples are architectural floor plan, reflected ceiling plan, site plan, structural framing plan, HVAC floor plan, electrical floor plan, lighting [ceiling] plan, etc. The images below show this concept; the image on the left is the 3D BIM. The middle image shows the portion of building above the cut plane removed. Finally, the last image on the right shows the plan view in which you work and place on a sheet.

- **Elevations**
  - An "exterior" elevation is a vertical slice, but where the slice lies outside the floor plan as in the middle image below. Each elevation created is listed in the *Project Browser*. The image on the right is an example of a South exterior elevation view, which is a "live" view of the 3D model. If you select a window here and delete it, the floor plans will update instantly.

  - Similarly, an "interior" elevation is a vertical slice, but inside the building. This view is cropped at the perimeter of a given room.

- **Sections**
  - o Similar to elevations, sections are also vertical slices. However, these slices cut through the building. A section view can be cropped down to become a wall section or even look just like an elevation. The images below show the slice, the portion of building in the foreground removed, and then the actual view created by the slice. A setting exists, for each section view, to control how far into that view you can see. The example on the right is "seeing" deep enough to show the doors on the interior walls.

- **3D and Camera**
  - o In addition to the traditional "flattened" 2D views that you will typically work in, you are able to see your designs more naturally via 3D and Camera views. A 3D view is simply an orthogonal view of the project viewed from the exterior. A Camera view is a perspective view; cameras can be created both in and outside of the building. Like the 2D views, these 3D/Camera views can be placed on a sheet to be printed. Revit provides a number of tools to help explore the 3D view, such as Section Box, Steering Wheel, Temporary Hide and Isolate, and Render.

    The image on the left is a 3D view set to "shade mode" and has shadows turned on. The image on the right is a camera view set up inside the building; the view is set to "hidden line" rather than shaded, and the camera is at eyelevel.

## Schedules

Schedules are lists of information generated based on content that has been placed, or modeled, within the project. A schedule can be created, such as the door schedule example shown below, that lists any of the data associated with each door that exists in the project. Revit allows you to work directly in the schedule views. Any change within a schedule view is a change directly to the element being scheduled. Again, if a door were to be deleted from this schedule, that door would be instantly deleted from the project.

| | | | | | | | | DOOR AND FRAME SCHEDULE | | | | | |
|---|---|---|---|---|---|---|---|---|---|---|---|---|---|
| DOOR NUMBER | DOOR | | | | FRAME | | DETAIL | | | | FIRE RATING | HDWR GROUP | |
| | WIDTH | HEIGHT | MATL | TYPE | MATL | TYPE | HEAD | JAMB | SILL | GLAZING | | | |
| 1000A | 3' - 8" | 7' - 2" | WD | | HM | | 11/A8.01 | 11/A8.01 | | | | | |
| 1046 | 3' - 0" | 7' - 2" | WD | D10 | HM | F10 | 11/A8.01 | 11/A8.01 SIM | | | | 34 | |
| 1047A | 6' - 0" | 7' - 10" | ALUM | D15 | ALUM | SF4 | 6/A8.01 | 6/A8.01 | 1/A8.01 SIM | 1" INSUL | | 2 | CARD READER N. LEAF |
| 1047B | 8' - 0" | 7' - 2" | WD | D10 | HM | F13 | 12/A8.01 | 11/A8.01 SIM | | | 60 MIN | 85 | MAG HOLD OPENS |
| 1050 | 3' - 0" | 7' - 2" | WD | D10 | HM | F21 | 8/A8.01 | 11/A8.01 | | 1/4" TEMP | | 33 | |
| 1051 | 3' - 0" | 7' - 2" | WD | D10 | HM | F21 | 8/A8.01 | 11/A8.01 | | 1/4" TEMP | | 33 | |
| 1052 | 3' - 0" | 7' - 2" | WD | D10 | HM | F21 | 8/A8.01 | 11/A8.01 | | 1/4" TEMP | | 33 | |
| 1053 | 3' - 0" | 7' - 2" | WD | D10 | HM | F21 | 8/A8.01 | 11/A8.01 | | 1/4" TEMP | | 33 | |
| 1054A | 3' - 0" | 7' - 2" | WD | D10 | HM | F10 | 8/A8.01 | 11/A8.01 | | 1/4" TEMP | - | 34 | |
| 1054B | 3' - 0" | 7' - 2" | WD | D10 | HM | F21 | 8/A8.01 | 11/A8.01 | | 1/4" TEMP | - | 33 | |
| 1055 | 3' - 0" | 7' - 2" | WD | D10 | HM | F21 | 8/A8.01 | 11/A8.01 | | 1/4" TEMP | - | 33 | |
| 1056A | 3' - 0" | 7' - 2" | WD | D10 | HM | F10 | 9/A8.01 | 9/A8.01 | | | 20 MIN | 33 | |
| 1056B | 3' - 0" | 7' - 2" | WD | D10 | HM | F10 | 11/A8.01 | 11/A8.01 | | | 20 MIN | 34 | |
| 1056C | 3' - 0" | 7' - 2" | WD | D10 | HM | F10 | 20/A8.01 | 20/A8.01 | | | 20 MIN | 33 | |
| 1057A | 3' - 0" | 7' - 2" | WD | D10 | HM | F10 | 8/A8.01 | 11/A8.01 | | | 20 MIN | 34 | |
| 1057B | 3' - 0" | 7' - 2" | WD | D10 | HM | F30 | 9/A8.01 | 9/A8.01 | | 1/4" TEMP | 20 MIN | 33 | |
| 1058A | 3' - 0" | 7' - 2" | WD | D10 | HM | F10 | 9/A8.01 | 9/A8.01 | | | - | 33 | |

## Sheets

You can think of sheets as the pieces of paper on which your views and schedules will be printed. Views and schedules are placed on sheets and then arranged. Once a view has been placed on a sheet, its reference bubble is automatically filled out and that view cannot be placed on any other sheet. The setting for each view, called "view scale," controls the size of the drawing on each sheet; view scale also controls the size of the text and dimensions.

# Exercise 1-2:
# Overview of the Revit User Interface

Revit is a powerful and sophisticated program. Because of its powerful feature set, it has a measurable learning curve, though its intuitive design makes it easier to learn than other CAD or BIM based programs. However, like anything, when broken down into smaller pieces, we can easily learn to harness the power of Revit. That is the goal of this book.

This section will walk through the different aspects of the User Interface (UI). As with any program, understanding the user interface is the key to using the program's features.

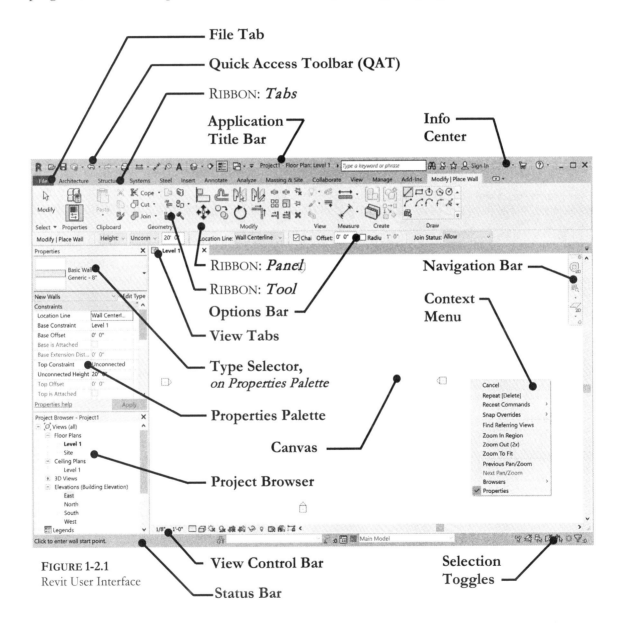

**FIGURE 1-2.1**
Revit User Interface

# The Revit User Interface:

*TIP: See the online videos for on the User Interface.*

## Application Title Bar

In addition to the *Quick Access Toolbar* and *Info Center*, which are all covered in the next few sections, you are also presented with the product name, version and the current **file-view** in the center. As previously noted already, the version is important as you do not want to upgrade unless you have coordinated with other staff and/or consultants; everyone must be using the same version of Revit. **Note:** the "R" icon on the left is not the same as in previous versions—the *Application Menu* has been replaced with the File Tab covered next.

## File Tab

Access to *File* tools such as *Save, Plot, Export* and *Print* (both hardcopy and electronic printing). You also have access to tools which control the Revit application as a whole, not just the current project, such as *Options* (see the end of this section for more on *Options*).

**Recent and Open Documents:**

These two icons (from the *File tab*) toggle the entire area on the right to show either the recent documents you have been in (icon on the left) or a list of the documents you currently have open.

In the *Recent Documents* list you click a listed document to open it. This saves time as you do not have to click *Open* → *Project* and browse for the document (*Document* and *Project* mean the same thing here). Finally, clicking the "Pin" keeps that project from getting bumped off the list as additional projects are opened.

In the *Open Documents* list the "active" project you are working in is listed first; clicking another project switches you to that open project.

The list on the left, in the *File Tab* shown above, represents three different types of buttons: *button*, *drop-down button* and *split button*. Save and Close are simply **buttons**. Save-As and Export are **drop-down buttons**, which means to reveal a group of related tools. If you click or hover your cursor over one of these buttons, you will get a list of tools on the right. Finally, **split buttons** have two actions depending on what part of the button you click on; hovering over the button reveals the two parts (see bottom image to the right). The main area is the most used tool; the arrow reveals additional related options.

*Button*

*Drop-down Button*

*Split Button*

## Quick Access Toolbar

Referred to as *QAT* in this book, this single toolbar provides access to often used tools (*Open*, *Save*, *Undo*, *Redo*, *Measure*, *Tag*, etc.). It is always visible regardless of what part of the *Ribbon* is active.

The *QAT* can be positioned above or below the *Ribbon* and any command from the *Ribbon* can be placed on it; simply right-click on any tool on the *Ribbon* and select *Add to Quick Access Toolbar*. Moving the *QAT* below the *Ribbon* gives you a lot more room for your favorite commands to be added from the *Ribbon*. Clicking the larger down-arrow to the far right reveals a list of common tools which can be toggled on and off.

Some of the icons on the *QAT* have a down-arrow on the right. Clicking this arrow reveals a list of related tools. In the case of *Undo* and *Redo*, you have the ability to undo (or redo) several actions at once.

## Ribbon – Architecture Tab

The *Architecture* tab on the *Ribbon* contains most of the tools the architect needs to model a building, essentially the things you can put your hands on when the building is done. The specific discipline versions of Revit omit some of the other discipline tabs.

Each tab starts with the *Modify* tool, i.e., the first button on the left. This tool puts you into "selection mode" so you can select elements to modify. Clicking this tool cancels the current tool and unselects elements. With the *Modify* tool selected you may select elements to view their properties or edit them. Note that the *Modify* tool, which is a button, is different than the *Modify* tab on the *Ribbon*.

The *Ribbon* has three types of buttons: *button, drop-down button* and *split*, as covered on the previous page. In the image above you can see the *Wall* tool is a **split button**. Most of the time you would simply click the top part of the button to draw a wall. Clicking the down-arrow part of the button, for the *Wall* tool example, gives you the option to draw a *Wall, Structural Wall, Wall by Face, Wall Sweep*, and a *Reveal.*

*TIP: The Model Text tool is only for placing 3D text in your model, not for adding notes!*

## Ribbon – Annotate Tab

To view this tab, simply click the label "Annotate" near the top of the *Ribbon.* This tab presents a series of tools which allow you to add notes, dimensions and 2D "embellishments" to your model in a specific view, such as a floor plan, elevation, or section. All of these tools are **view specific**, meaning a note added in the first floor plan will not show up anywhere else, not even another first floor plan: for instance, a first floor electrical plan.

Notice, in the image above, that the *Dimension* panel label has a down-arrow next to it. Clicking the down-arrow will reveal an **extended panel** with additional related tools.

Finally, notice the *Component* tool in the image above; it is a **split button** rather than a *drop-down button*. Clicking the top part of this button will initiate the *Detail Component* tool. Clicking the bottom part of the button opens the fly-out menu revealing related tools. Once you select an option from the fly-out, that tool becomes the default for the top part of the split button for the current session of Revit (see image to right).

## Ribbon – Modify Tab

Several tools which manipulate and derive information from the current model are available on the *Modify* tab. Additional *Modify* tools are automatically appended to this tab when elements are selected in the model (see *Modify Contextual Tab* on the next page).

> *TIP: Do not confuse the Modify tab with the Modify tool when following instructions in this book.*

## Ribbon – View Tab

The tools on the *View* tab allow you to create new views of your 3D model; this includes views that look 2D (e.g., floor plans, elevations and sections) as well as 3D views (e.g., isometric and perspective views).

The *View* tab also gives you tools to control how views look, everything from what types of elements are seen (e.g., Plumbing Fixture, Furniture or Section Marks) as well as line weights.

> *NOTE: Line weights are controlled at a project wide level but may be overridden.*

Finally, notice the little arrow in the lower-right corner of the *Graphics* panel. When you see an arrow like this you can click on it to open a dialog box with settings that relate to the panel's tool set (*Graphics* in this example). Hovering over the arrow reveals a tooltip which will tell you what dialog box will be opened.

## Ribbon – Modify Contextual Tab

The *Modify* tab is appended when certain tools are active or elements are selected in the model; this is referred to as a *contextual tab*. The first image below shows the *Place Wall* tab which presents various options while adding walls. The next example shows the *Modify Walls* contextual tab which is accessible when one or more walls are selected.

*Place Wall contextual tab – visible when the Wall tool is active.*

*Modify Walls contextual tab – visible when a wall is selected.*

## Ribbon – Customization

There is not too much customization that can be done to the *Ribbon*. One of the only things you can do is pull a panel off the *Ribbon* by clicking and holding down the left mouse button on the titles listed, e.g. "Link" or "Build", across the bottom. This panel can be placed within the *drawing window* or on another screen if you have a dual monitor setup.

The image above shows the *Build* panel, from the *Architecture* tab, detached from the *Ribbon* and floating within the drawing window. Notice that the *Insert* tab is active. Thus, you have constant access to the *Build* tools while accessing other tools. Note that the *Build* panel is not available on the *Architecture* tab as it is literally moved, not just copied.

When you need to move a detached panel back to the *Ribbon* you do the following: hover over the detached panel until the sidebars show up and then click the "Return panels to ribbon" icon in the upper right (identified in the image above).

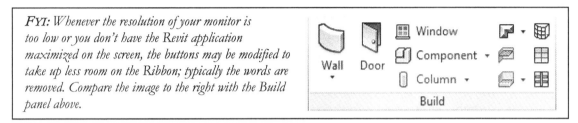

*FYI: Whenever the resolution of your monitor is too low or you don't have the Revit application maximized on the screen, the buttons may be modified to take up less room on the Ribbon; typically the words are removed. Compare the image to the right with the Build panel above.*

If you install an **add-in** for Revit on your computer, you will likely see a new tab appear on the Ribbon. Some add-ins are free while others require a fee. If an add-in only has one tool, it will likely be added to the catch-all tab called Add-Ins (shown in the image below).

This is not really customizing the User Interface, but in the Options dialog there are several adjustments one can make – such as turning off tabs and tools not used. However, turning off, for example, the electrical tools, in turn limits the number of electrical parameter types that can be created.

## Ribbon – States

The *Ribbon* can be displayed in one of four states:

- Full Ribbon (default)
- Minimize to Tabs
- Minimize to Panel Tiles
- Minimize to Panel Buttons

The intent of this feature is to increase the size of the available drawing window. It is recommended, however, that you leave the *Ribbon* fully expanded while learning to use the program. The images in this book show the fully expanded state. The images below show the other three options. When using one of the minimized options you simply hover (or click) your cursor over the Tab or Panel to temporarily reveal the tools.

*FYI:* Double-clicking on a Ribbon tab will also toggle the states.

*Minimize to Tabs*

*Minimize to Panel Tiles*

*Minimize to Panel Buttons*

## Ribbon – References in this Book

When the exercises make reference to the tools in the *Ribbon* a consistent method is used to eliminate excessive wording and save space. Take a moment to understand this so that things go smoothly for you later.

Throughout the textbook you will see an instruction similar to the following:

23. Select **Architecture** → **Build** → **Wall**

This means click the ***Architecture*** tab, and within the ***Build*** panel, select the ***Wall*** tool. Note that the *Wall* tool is actually a split button, but a subsequent tool was not listed so you are to click on the primary part of the button. Compare the above example to the one below:

23. Select **Architecture** → **Build** → **Wall** → **Structural Wall**

The above example indicates that you should click the down-arrow part of the *Wall* tool in order to select the *Structural Wall* option.

Thus the general pattern is this:

**Tab → Panel → Tool → drop-down list item**

*#1 Tab:* This will get you to the correct area within the *Ribbon*.

*#2 Panel:* This will narrow down your search for the desired tool.

*#3 Tool:* Specific tool to select and use.

*Drop-down list item:* This will only be specified for drop-down buttons and sometimes for split buttons.

The image below shows the order in which the instructions are given to select a tool; note that you do not actually click the panel title.

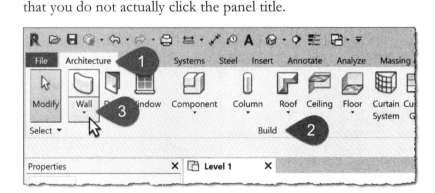

## Options Bar

This area dynamically changes to show options that complement the current operation. The *Options Bar* is located directly below the *Ribbon*. When you are learning to use Revit you should keep your eye on this area and watch for features and options appearing at specific times. The image below shows the *Options Bar* example with the *Wall* tool active.

## Properties Palette – Element Type Selector

*Properties Palette; nothing selected*

The *Properties Palette* provides instant access to settings related to the element selected or about to be created. When nothing is selected, it shows information about the current view. When multiple elements are selected, the common parameters are displayed.

The *Element Type Selector* is an important part of the *Properties Palette*. Whenever you are adding elements or have them selected, you can select from this list to determine how a wall to be drawn will look, or how a wall previously drawn should look (see lower left image). If a wall type needs to change, you never delete it and redraw it; you simply select it and pick a new type from the *Type Selector*.

The **Selection Filter** drop-down list below the *Type Selector* lets you know the type and quantity of the elements currently selected. When multiple elements are selected you can narrow down the properties for just one element type, such as *wall*. Notice the image below shows four walls are in the current selection set. Selecting **Walls (4)** will cause the *Palette* to only show *Wall* properties even though many other elements are selected (and remain selected).

The width of the *Properties Palette* and the center column position can be adjusted by dragging the cursor over that area. You may need to do this at times to see all the information. However, making the *Palette* too wide will reduce the useable drawing area.

*Type Selector; Wall tool active or a Wall is selected*

*Selection Filter; multiple elements selected*

The *Properties Palette* should be left open; if you accidentally close it you can reopen it by **View → Window → User Interface → Properties** or by typing **PP** on the keyboard.

## Project Browser

The *Project Browser* is the "Grand Central Station" of the Revit project database. All the views, schedules, sheets and content are accessible through this hierarchical list. The first image to the left shows the seven major categories; any item with a "plus" next to it contains sub-categories or items.

Double-clicking on a View, Legend, Schedule or Sheet will open it for editing; the current item open for editing is bold (**Level 1** in the example to the left). Right-clicking will display a pop-up menu with a few options such as *Delete* and *Copy*.

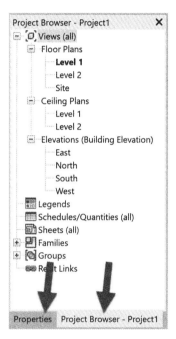

Right-click on *Views (all)*, at the top of the *Project Browser*, and you will find a **Search** option in the pop-up menu. This can be used to search for a *View, Family*, etc., a very useful tool when working on a large project with 100s of items to sift through.

Like the *Properties Palette*, the width of the *Project Browser* can be adjusted. When the two are stacked above each other, they both move together. You can also stack the two directly on top of each other; in this case you will see a tab for each at the bottom as shown in the second image to the left.

The *Project Browser* should be left open; if you accidentally close it by clicking the "X" in the upper right, you can reopen it by **View → Window → User Interface → Project Browser**.

The *Project Browser* and *Properties Palette* can be repositioned on a second monitor, if you have one, when you want more room to work in the drawing window.

## Status Bar

This area will display information, on the far left, about the current command or list information about a selected element. The right-hand side of the *Status Bar* shows the number of elements selected. The small funnel icon to the left of the selection number can be clicked to open the *Filter* dialog box, which allows you to reduce your current selection to a specific category; for example, you could select the entire floor plan, and then filter it down to just the doors. This is different than the *Selection Filter* in the *Properties Palette* which keeps everything selected.

On the *Status Bar*, the five icons on the right, shown in the image below, control how elements are selected. From left to right these are

- Select Links
- Select Underlay Elements
- Select Pinned Elements
- Select Elements by Face
- Drag Elements on Selection

Hover your cursor over an icon for the name and for a brief description of what it does. These are toggles that are on or off; **the red 'X' in the upper right of each icon means you cannot select that type of element within the model**. These controls help prevent accidentally moving or deleting things. Keep these toggles in mind if you are having trouble selecting something; you may have accidentally toggled one of these on.

Finally, the two drop-down lists towards the center of the *Status Bar* control **Design Options** and **Worksets** (see image on previous page). Design Options facilitate multiple design solutions in the same area, and *Worksets* relate to the ability for more than one designer to be in the model at a time.

## View Control Bar

This is a feature which gives you convenient access to tools which control each view's display settings (i.e., scale, shadows, detail level, graphics style, etc.). The options vary slightly between view types: 2D View, 3D view, Sheet and Schedule. The important thing to know is that these settings only affect the current view, the one listed on the *Application Title Bar*. All of these settings are available in the *Properties Palette*, but this toolbar cannot be turned off like the *Properties Palette* can.

## Context Menu

The *context menu* appears near the cursor whenever you right-click on the mouse (see image at right). The options on that menu will vary depending on what tool is active or what element is selected.

## Drawing Window

This is where you manipulate the Building Information Model (BIM). Here you will see the current view (plan, elevation or section), schedule or sheet. Any changes made are instantly propagated to the entire database.

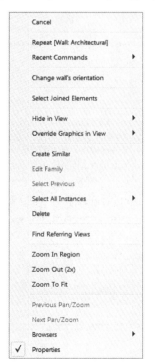

*Context menu example with a wall selected*

## Elevation Marker

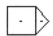

This item is not really part of the Revit UI but is visible in the drawing window by default via the various templates you can start with, so it is worth mentioning at this point. The four elevation markers point at each side of your project and ultimately indicate the drawing sheet on which you would find an elevation drawing of each side of the building. All you need to know right now is that you should draw your floor plan generally in the middle of the four elevation markers that you will see in each plan view; DO NOT delete them as this will remove the related view from the *Project Browser*.

## Revit Options

There are several settings, related to the *User Interface*, which are not tied to the current model. That is, these settings apply to the installation of Revit on your computer, rather than applying to just one model or file on your computer. A few of these settings will be briefly discussed here. It is recommended that you don't make any changes here right now.

Click on **Options** in the *File* tab. The options under File Locations tell Revit where to find templates and content. In the Hardware section you can verify your display driver information and compare with the "Supported Hardware" link. If Revit is crashing or exhibits strange behavior, it often relates to your graphics driver. You can bypass this problem by turning off *Use Hardware Acceleration*, but this will make Revit run slower when panning and zooming.

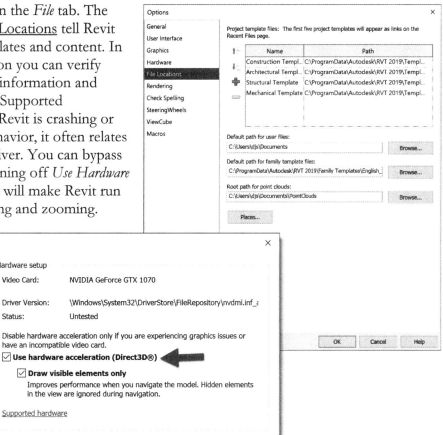

This concludes your brief overview of the Revit user interface. Many of these tools and operations will be covered in more detail throughout the book.

## Efficient Practices:

The *Ribbon* and menus are really helpful when learning a program like Revit; however, most experienced users rarely use them! The process of moving the mouse to the edge of the screen to select a command and then back to where you were is very inefficient, especially for those who do this all day long, five days a week. Here are a few ways experienced BIM operators work:

- Use the wheel on the mouse to Zoom (spin the wheel), Pan (press and hold the wheel button while moving the mouse) and Zoom Extents (double-clicking the wheel button). All this can be done while in another command; so, if you are in the middle of drawing walls and need to zoom in to see which point you are about to Snap to, you can do it without canceling the Line command and without losing focus on the area you are designing by having to click an icon near the edge of the screen.

- Revit conforms to many of the Microsoft Windows operating system standards. Most programs, including Revit, have several standard commands that can be accessed via keyboard shortcuts. Here are a few examples (press both keys at the same time):

  - Ctrl + S     Save         *(saves the current model)*
  - Ctrl + A     Select All    *(selects everything in text editor)*
  - Ctrl + Z     Undo        *(undoes the previous action)*
  - Ctrl + X     Cut          *(Cut to Windows clipboard)*
  - Ctrl + C     Copy        *(does not replace Revit's Copy tool)*
  - Ctrl + V     Paste       *(used to copy between models/views/levels)*
  - Ctrl + Tab   Change View   *(toggles between open views)*
  - Ctrl + P     Print       *(opens print dialog)*
  - Ctrl + N     New          *(create new project file)*
  - F7           Spelling     *(launch spell check feature)*
  - ENTER      Previous Command   *(repeat previous command)*

- If you recall, the *Open Documents* area, on the *File Tab,* lists all the views that are currently open on your computer. By clicking one of the names in the list you "switch" to that view. A shortcut is to press **Ctrl + Tab** to quickly cycle through the open drawings.

- Many Revit commands also have keyboard shortcuts. So, with your right hand on the mouse (and not moving from the "design" area), your left hand can type **WA** when you want to draw a Wall, for example. You can see all the

*Keyboard shortcuts dialog*

preloaded shortcuts and add new ones by clicking *View (tab)* → *User Interface (drop-down)* → *Keyboard Shortcuts*.

It should be noted that any customized keyboard shortcuts are specific to the computer you are working on, not the project. You can use the *Export* button (see image to right) to save the entire keyboard shortcuts list to a file, and then *Import* it into another computer's copy of Revit.

## View Tabs

Revit displays a tab for each open view. Clicking a tab is a quick way to switch between open views. Click the "X" in each view tab to close that view. Drag a tab to change its position. Tabs can also be pulled outside of the main Revit application window – even to a second monitor. In the second image below, the schedule could be filling a second computer screen while reviewing the same information in the floor plan.

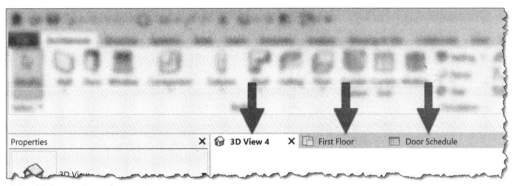

*View Tabs; one for each open view*

*View Tabs can be pulled outside of the main Revit application window, even to a second screen*

This concludes your brief overview of the Revit user interface. Many of these tools and operations will be covered in more detail throughout the book.

## Exercise 1-3:
## Open, Save and Close a Revit Project

To *Open* **Revit 2019**:

**Start → All Apps → Autodesk → Revit 2019**

Or double-click the Revit icon from your desktop.

This may vary slightly on your computer; see your instructor or system administrator if you need help.

# How to Open a Revit Project:

By default, Revit will open in the *Recent Files* window, which will display thumbnails of recent projects you have worked on. Clicking on the preview will open the project.

1. Click the **Open** link (see the image to the right).

You may click open under *Project* or on the *Quick Access Toolbar*.

FIGURE 1-3.1 Recent Files startup screen

Next you will open an existing Revit project file. You will select a sample file provided online at SDCpublications.com; see the inside front cover for more information.

2. Click the drop-down box at the top of the *Open* dialog (Figure 1-3.2). Browse to your downloaded files (provided files need to be downloaded from www.SDCpublications.com).

*TIP: If you cannot access the online sample files, you can substitute any Revit file you can find. Some sample files may be found here on your computer's hard drive:  C:\Program Files\Autodesk\Revit 2019\Samples, or via File (tab) → Open (fly-out) → Sample Files.*

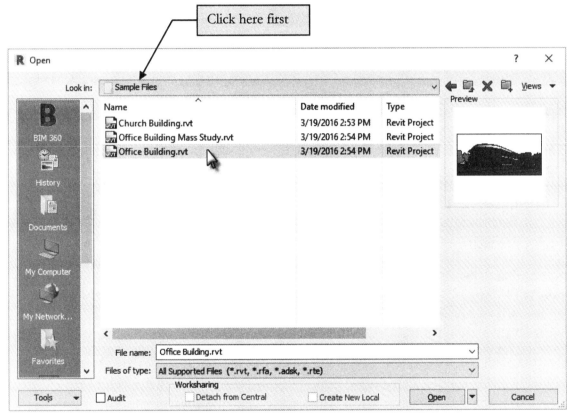

FIGURE 1-3.2 Open dialog; downloaded content from SDCpublications.com

3. Select the file named **Office Building.rvt** and click **Open**.

*FYI: Notice the preview of the selected file. This will help you select the correct file before taking the time to open it.*

The *Office Building.rvt* file is now open and the last saved view is displayed in the drawing window (Figure 1-3.3).

**FIGURE 1-3.3** Sample file "Office Building.rvt"

The *File Tab* lists the projects and views currently open on your computer (Figure 1-3.4).

4. Click **File Tab → Open Documents (icon)** (Figure 1-3.4).

Notice that the *Office Building.rvt* project file is listed. Next to the project name is the name of a view open on your computer (e.g., floor plan, elevation).

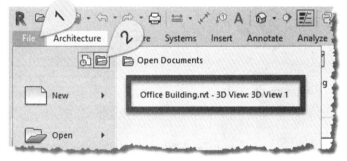

**FIGURE 1-3.4** File Tab: Open Documents view

Additional views will be added to the list as you open them. Each view has the project name as a prefix. The current view, the view you are working in, is always at the top of the list. You can quickly toggle between opened views from this menu by clicking on them.

You can also use the *Switch Windows* tool on the *View* tab; both do essentially the same thing.

# Opening Another Revit Project:

Revit allows you to have more than one project open at a time.

5. Click **Open** from the *Quick Access Toolbar*.

6. Per the instructions previously covered, browse the downloaded online files.

7. Select the file named **Church Building.rvt** and click **Open** (Figure 1-3.5).

> *TIP: If you cannot locate the online files, substitute one of the sample files.*

**FIGURE 1-3.5** Sample file "Church Building.rvt"

8. Click **Open Documents** from the *File Tab* (Figure 1-3.6).

Notice that the *Church Building.rvt* project is now listed along with a view: Floor Plan: Level 1.

Try toggling between projects by clicking on *Office Building.rvt – 3D View: 3D View 1.*

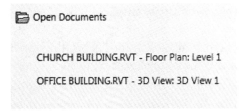

**FIGURE 1-3.6** Open Documents

## Close a Revit Project:

9. Select **File Tab** ➔ **Close**; click **No** if prompted to save.

This will close the current project/view. If more than one view is open for a project, only the current view will close. The project and the other opened views will not close until you get to the last open view.

10. Repeat the previous step to close the other project file.

If you made changes and have not saved your project yet, you will be prompted to do so before Revit closes the view. **Do not save at this time**. When all open project files are closed, you find yourself back in the *Recent Files* screen – which is where you started.

## Saving a Revit Project:

**At this time we will not actually save a project.**

To save a project file, simply select *Save* from the *Quick Access Toolbar*. You can also select *Save* from the *File Tab* or press *Ctrl + S* on the keyboard.

You should get in the habit of saving often to avoid losing work due to a power outage or program crash. Revit offers a reminder to save, this notification is based on the amount of time since your last save. The **Save Time Interval** is set in *Options*.

You can also save a copy of the current project by selecting **Save As** from the File Tab. Once you have used the *Save As* command you are in the new project file and the file you started in is then closed.

## Closing the Revit Program:

Finally, from the *File Tab* select **Exit Revit**. This will close any open projects/views and shut down Revit. Again you will be prompted to save, if needed, before Revit closes the view. **Do not save at this time**.

You can also click the "X" in the upper right corner of the *Revit Application* window.

## Exercise 1-4:
## Creating a New Project

Open **Autodesk Revit**.

## Creating a New Project File:

The steps required to set up a new Revit model project file are very simple. As mentioned earlier, simply opening the Revit program starts you in the *Recent Files* window.

To manually create a new project (maybe you just finished working on a previous assignment and want to start the next one):

1.  Select **File tab → New → Project**.

    *FYI: You can also select the* New *link in the* Recent Files *startup screen.*

After clicking *New → Project* you will get the ***New Project*** dialog box (Figure 1-4.1).

**FIGURE 1-4.1** New Project dialog box

The *New Project* dialog box lets you specify the template file you want to use, or not use a template at all. You can also specify whether you want to create a new project or template file.

2. Select the **Architectural Template** option in the drop-down list. Leave *Create new* set to **Project** (Figure 1-4.1).

3. Click **OK**. You now have a new unnamed/unsaved project file.

To name an unnamed project file you simply *Save*. The first time an unnamed project file is saved you will be prompted to specify the name and location for the project file.

4. Select **File Tab → Save** from the *Menu Bar*.

5. Specify a **name** and **location** for your new project file.
   *Your instructor may specify a location or folder for your files if in a classroom setting.*

# What is a Template File?

A template file allows you to start your project with specific content and certain settings preset the way you like or need them.

For example, you can have the units set to *Imperial* or *Metric*. You can have the door, window and wall families you use most loaded and eliminate other less often used content. Also, you can have your company's title block preloaded and even have all the sheets for a project set up.

A custom template is a must for design firms and contractors using Revit and will prove useful to the student as he or she becomes more proficient with the program.

---

**Be Aware:**
It will be assumed from this point forward that the reader understands how to create, open and save project files. Please refer back to this section as needed. If you still need further assistance, ask your instructor for help.

---

## Exercise 1-5:
## Using Zoom and Pan to View Your Drawings

Learning to *Pan* and *Zoom* in and out of a drawing is essential for accurate and efficient drafting and visualization. We will review these commands now so you are ready to use them with the first design exercise.

Open **Revit**.

You will select a sample file from the provided online files.

1. Select **Open** from the *Quick Access Toolbar*.

2. Browse to the **downloaded online files**.

3. Select the file named **Church Building.rvt** and click **Open** (Figure 1-5.1).

   *TIP: If you cannot locate the online files, substitute any of the training files that come with Revit, found at C:\Program Files\Autodesk\Revit 2019\Samples.*

**FIGURE 1-5.1** Church Building.rvt project

If the default view that is loaded is not **Floor Plan: Level 1**, double-click on **Level 1** under **Views\Floor Plans** in the *Project Browser*. Level 1 will be bold when it is the active or current view in the drawing window.

## Using Zoom and Pan Tools:

You can access the zoom tools from the ***Navigation Bar***, or the *scroll wheel* on your mouse.

The *Zoom* icon contains several *Zoom* related tools:
- The default (i.e., visible) icon is *Zoom in Region*, which allows you to window an area to zoom into.
- The *Zoom* icon is a **split button**.
- Clicking the down-arrow part of the button reveals a list of related *Zoom* tools.
- You will see the drop-down list on the next page.

### Zoom In

4.  Select the top portion of the *Zoom* icon (see image to right).

5.  Drag a window over your plan view (Figure 1-5.2).

Selection window: Pick two diagonal points, that is, two opposite corners to define the window.

**FIGURE 1-5.2** Zoom In window

You should now be zoomed in to the specified area (Figure 1-5.3).

**FIGURE 1-5.3** Zoom In results

## Zoom Out

6. Click the down-arrow next to the zoom icon (Figure 1-5.4). Select **Previous Pan/Zoom**.

You should now be back where you started. Each time you select this icon you are resorting to a previous view state. Sometimes you have to select this option multiple times if you did some panning and multiple zooms.

7. **Zoom** into a smaller area, and then **Pan**, i.e., adjusting the portion of the view seen, by holding down the scroll wheel button.

The Pan tool just changes the portion of the view you see on the screen; it does not actually move the model.

**FIGURE 1-5.4** Zoom Icon drop-down

Take a minute and try the other *Zoom* tools to see how they work. When finished, click **Zoom to Fit** before moving on.

*TIP:* *You can double-click the wheel button on your mouse to* Zoom Extents *in the current view.*

## Default 3D View:

Clicking on the *Default 3D View* icon, on the *QAT*, loads a 3D View. This allows you to quickly switch to a 3D view.

8. Click on the **Default 3D View** icon.

9. Go to the **Open Documents** listing in the *File Tab* and notice the *3D View* and the *Floor Plan* view are both listed at the bottom.

   *REMEMBER: You can toggle between views here.*

10. Click the **Esc** key to close the *File Tab*.

## ViewCube:

The *ViewCube* gives you convenient view control over the 3D view. This technology has been implemented in many of Autodesk's programs to make the process seamless for the user.

11. You should notice the **ViewCube** in the upper right corner of the drawing window (Figure 1-5.5). If not, you can turn it on by clicking *View → Windows → User Interface → ViewCube*.

   *TIP: The ViewCube only shows up in 3D views.*

Hovering your cursor over the *ViewCube* activates it. As you move about the *Cube* you see various areas highlight. If you click, you will be taken to that highlighted area in the drawing window. You can also click and drag your cursor on the *Cube* to "roll" the model in an unconstrained fashion. Clicking and dragging the mouse on the disk below the *Cube* allows you to spin the model without rolling. Finally, you have a few options in a right-click menu, and the **Home** icon, just above the *Cube*, gets you back to where you started if things get disoriented!

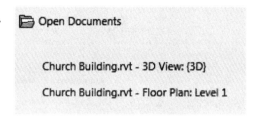

FIGURE 1-5.5 ViewCube

12. Give the *ViewCube* a try, then click the **Home** icon when you are done.

   *REMEMBER: The Home icon only shows up when your cursor is over the ViewCube.*

## Navigation Wheel:

Similar to the *ViewCube*, the *Navigation Wheel* aids in navigating your model. With the *Navigation Wheel* you can walk through your model, going down hallways and turning into rooms. Revit has not advanced to the point where the doors will open for you; thus, you walk through closed doors or walls as if you were a ghost!

The *Navigation Wheel* is activated by clicking the upper icon on the *Navigation Bar*.

Unfortunately, it is way too early in your Revit endeavors to learn to use the *Navigation Wheel*. You can try this in the chapter on creating photorealistic renderings and camera views. You would typically use this tool in a camera view.

**FIGURE 1-5.6** Navigation Wheel

13. **Close** the *Church Building* project **without** saving.

## Using the Scroll Wheel on the Mouse:

The scroll wheel on the mouse is a must for those using BIM software. In Revit you can *Pan* and *Zoom* without even clicking a zoom icon. You simply **scroll the wheel to zoom** and **hold the wheel button down to pan**. This can be done while in another command (e.g., while drawing walls). Another nice feature is that the drawing zooms into the area near your cursor, rather than zooming only at the center of the drawing window. Give this a try before moving on. Once you get the hang of it, you will not want to use the icons. Also, double-clicking the wheel button does a *Zoom to Fit* so everything is visible on the screen.

*TIP:* Avoid a mouse with a wheel that tilts left and right as this makes using the wheel-button harder to use, making it not ideal for CAD/BIM users.

## Exercise 1-6:
## Using Revit's Help System

This section of your introductory chapter will provide a quick overview of Revit's *Help System*. This will allow you to study topics in more detail if you want to know how something works beyond the introductory scope of this textbook.

1. Click the **round question mark** icon in the upper-right corner of the screen.

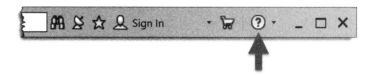

You are now in Revit's Help site (Figure 1-6.1). This is a website which opened in your web browser. The window can be positioned side by side with Revit, which is especially nice if you have a dual-screen computer system. This interface requires a connection to the internet. As a website, Autodesk has the ability to add and revise information at any time, unlike files stored on your hard drive. This also means that the site can change quite a bit, potentially making the following overview out of date. If the site has changed, just follow along as best you can for the next three pages.

**FIGURE 1-6.1** Autodesk Help site

In the upper left you can click the magnifying glass and search the *Help System* for a word or phrase. You may also click any one of the links to learn more about the topic listed. The next few steps will show you how to access the *Help System's* content on the Revit user interface, a topic you have just studied.

2.   On the left, click the **plus symbol** next to **Get Started**.

3.   Now, click the **plus symbol** next to **User Interface** (Figure 1-6.2).

Notice the tree structure on the left. You can use this to quickly navigate the help site.

4.   Finally, click directly on **Ribbon**.

You now see information about the *Ribbon* as shown in the image below. Notice additional links are provided below on the current topic. You can use the browser's *Back* and *Forward* buttons to move around in the *Help System*.

**FIGURE 1-6.2** Help window; Ribbon overview

Next, you will try searching the Revit *Help System* for a specific Revit feature. This is a quick way to find information if you have an idea of what it is you are looking for.

5.   In the upper right corner of the current *Help System* web page, click in the search text box and then type **gutter**.

6.   Press **Enter** on the keyboard.

The search results are shown in Figure 1-6.3. Each item in the list is a link which will take you to information on that topic.

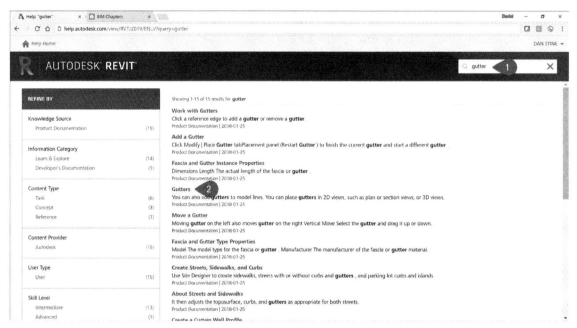

**FIGURE 1-6.3** Help search results

The *Help System* can be used to complement this textbook. It is a reference resource, not a tutorial. As you are working through the tutorials in this book, you may want to use the *Help System* to fill in the blanks if you are having trouble or want more information on a topic.

## Exercise 1-7:
## Introduction to Autodesk 360

We will finish this chapter with a look at Autodesk A360, which is "ground zero" for all of Autodesk's **Cloud Services**. It is important that the student read this information in order to follow along in the book when specific steps related to using these cloud services are covered. The reader does not necessarily need to use Autodesk's cloud services to successfully complete this book.

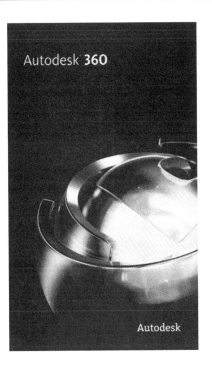

The main features employed in the book are:

- Saving your work to *Autodesk A360* so you can access the data anywhere and know that the files are in a secure, backed up location. This feature is free to anyone, with some limitations to be discussed later.
- Sending your photorealistic rendering project to the *Cloud* to dramatically reduce the overall processing time. This feature is free to students and a free trial is available to everyone else.

Here is how Autodesk describes *Autodesk A360* on their website:

> The Autodesk® A360 cloud-based framework provides tools and services to extend design beyond the desktop. Streamline your workflows, effectively collaborate, and quickly access and share your work anytime, from anywhere. With virtually infinite computing power in the cloud, Autodesk 360 scales up or down to meet business needs without the infrastructure or upfront investment required for traditional desktop software.

Before we discuss *Autodesk A360* with more specificity, let's define what the *Cloud* is. **The Cloud is a service, or collection of services, which exists partially or completely online.** This is different from the *Internet*, which mostly involves downloading static information, in that you are creating and manipulating data. Most of this happens outside of your laptop or desktop computer. This gives the average user access to massive amounts of storage space, computing power and software they could not otherwise afford if they had to actually own, install and maintain these resources in their office, school or home. In one sense, this is similar to a *Tool Rental Center*, in that the average person could not afford, nor would it be cost-effective to own, a jackhammer. However, for a fraction of the cost of ownership and maintenance, we can rent it for a few hours. In this case, everyone wins!

## Creating a Free Autodesk A360 Account

The first thing an individual needs to do in order to gain access to *Autodesk A360* is create a free account at https://a360.autodesk.com/ (students: see tip below); the specific steps will be covered later in this section, so you don't need to do this now. This account is for an individual person, not a computer, not an installation of Revit or AutoCAD, nor does it come from your employer or school. Each person who wishes to access *Autodesk A360* services must create an account, which will give them a unique username and password.

> *TIP:* Students should first create an account at http://www.autodesk.com/education/home. This is the same place you go to download free Autodesk software. Be sure to use your school email address as this is what identifies you as a qualifying student. Once you create an account there, you can use this same user name and password to access *Autodesk A360*. Following these steps will give you access to more storage space and unlimited cloud rendering!

Generally speaking, there are three ways you can access *Autodesk A360* cloud services:
- Autodesk A360 website
- Within Revit or AutoCAD; local computer
- Mobile device, smart phone or tablet

## Autodesk A360 Website

When you have documents stored in the *Cloud* you can access them via your web browser. Here you can manage your files, view them without the full application (some file formats not supported) and share them. These features use some advanced browser technology, so you need to make sure your browser is up to date; Chrome works well.

Using the website, you can upload files from your computer to store in the *Cloud*. To do this, you create or open a project (Fig, 1-7.1) and click the **Upload** option (Fig. 1-7.2).

**FIGURE 1-7.1** Viewing files stored in the cloud

**Tip:** If using Firefox or Chrome, you can drag and drop documents into the *Upload Documents* window. This is a great way to create a secure backup of your documents.

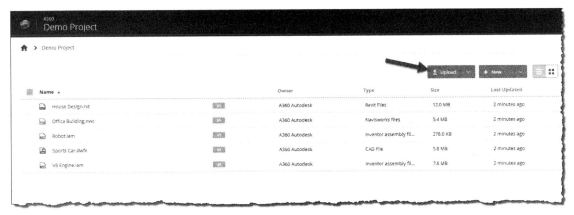

**FIGURE 1-7.2** Upload files to the cloud

You can share files stored in the *Cloud* with others. Private sharing with others who have an *Autodesk A360* account is very easy. Another option is public sharing, which allows you to send someone a link and they can access the file, even if they don't have an A360 account. Simply hover over a file within *Autodesk A360* and click the **Share** icon to see the Share dialog (Figure 1-7.3).

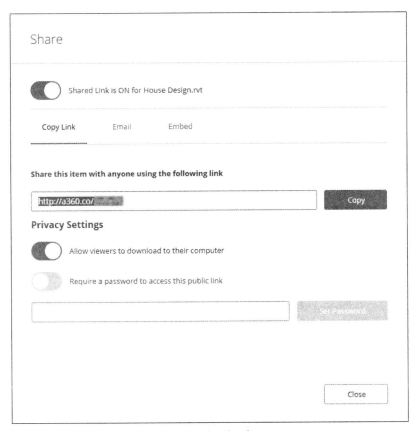

**FIGURE 1-7.3** Sharing files stored in the cloud

## Autodesk A360 within Revit or AutoCAD; local computer

Another way in which you can access your data, stored in the cloud, is from within your Autodesk application; for example, Revit or AutoCAD. This is typically the most convenient as you can open, view and modify your drawings. Once logged in, you will also have access to any *Cloud Services* available to you from within the application, such as rendering or *Green Building Studio*.

To sign in to *Autodesk A360* within your application, simply click the **Sign In** option in the notification area in the upper right corner of the window. You will need to enter your student email address and password (or personal email if you are not a student) as discussed in the previous section. When properly logged in, you will see your username or email address listed as shown in Figure 1-7.4 below. You will try this later in this section.

FIGURE 1-7.4 Example of user logged into Autodesk A360

## Autodesk A360 Mobile

Once you have your files stored in the *Cloud* via Autodesk A360, you will also be able to access them on your tablet or smart phone if you have one. Autodesk has a free app called *A360 – View & Markup CAD files* for both the Apple or Android phones and tablets (Figure 1-7.5).

Some of the mobile features include:
- Open and view files stored in your Autodesk 360 account
- 2D and 3D DWG™ and DWF™ files
- Revit® and Navisworks® files
- Use multi-touch to zoom, pan, and rotate drawings
- View meta data and other details about elements within your drawing
- Find tools that help you communicate changes with your collaborators

The **Android** app is installed via *Google Play* and the **iPhone** app comes from the *Apple App Store*.

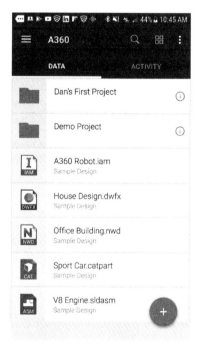

FIGURE 1-7.5
Viewing files on a smart phone

## Setting up your Autodesk A360 account

The next few steps will walk you through the process of setting up your free online account at *Autodesk A360*. These steps are not absolutely critical to completing this book, so if you have any reservations about creating an *Autodesk A360* account – don't do it.

1. To create a free Autodesk 360 account, do one of the following:

    a. If you are a **student**, create an account at
       https://www.autodesk.com/education/home

    b. If you work for a company who has their Autodesk software on
       **subscription**, ask your *Contract Administrator* (this is a person in your office)
       to create an account for you and send you an invitation via
       https://manage.autodesk.com.

    c. **Everyone else**, create an account at https://a360.autodesk.com.

    *FYI:* The "s" at the end of "http" in the *Autodesk A360* URL means this is a secure website.

2. Open your application: AutoCAD or Revit.

3. Click the **Sign In** option in the upper-right corner of the application window (Figure 1-7.6).

**FIGURE 1-7.6** Signing in to Autodesk A360

It is recommended, as you work through this book, that you save all of your work in the *Cloud*, via Autodesk A360, so you will have a safe and secure location for your files. These files can then be accessed from several locations via the two methods discussed here. It is still important to maintain a separate copy of your files on a flash drive, portable hard drive or in another *Cloud*-type location such as *Dropbox*. This will be important if your main files ever become corrupt. You should manually back up your files to your backup location so a corrupt file does not automatically corrupt your backup files.

*TIP:* If you have a file that will not open try one of the following:

- **In Revit:** Open Revit and then, from the *File tab*, select Open, browse to your file, and select it. Click the **Audit** check box, and then click Open. Revit will attempt to repair any problems with the project database. Some elements may need to be deleted, but this is better than losing the entire file.

- **In AutoCAD:** Open AutoCAD and then, from the *Application Menu*, select Drawing Utilities → Recover → **Recover**. Then browse to your file and open it. AutoCAD will try and recover the drawing file. This may require some things to be deleted but is better than losing the entire file.

Be sure to check out the Autodesk website to learn more about Autodesk A360 Mobile and the growing number of cloud services Autodesk is offering.

## Self-Exam:

The following questions can be used as a way to check your knowledge of this lesson. The answers can be found at the bottom of this page.

1. The *View* tab allows you to save your project file. (T/F)

2. You can zoom in and out using the wheel on a wheel mouse. (T/F)

3. Revit is a parametric architectural design program. (T/F)

4. A _____ file allows you to start your project with specific content and certain settings preset the way you like or need them.

5. Autodesk 360 allows you to save your files safely in the _____ .

## Review Questions:

The following questions may be assigned by your instructor as a way to assess your knowledge of this section. Your instructor has the answers to the review questions.

1. The *Options Bar* dynamically changes to show options that complement the current operation. (T/F)

2. Revit is strictly a 2D drafting program. (T/F)

3. The Projects/Views listed in the *Open Documents* list allow you to see which Projects/Views are currently open. (T/F)

4. When you use the *Pan* tool you are actually moving the drawing, not just changing what part of the drawing you can see on the screen. (T/F)

5. Revit was not originally created for architecture. (T/F)

6. The icon with the floppy disk picture ( ) allows you to _____ a project file.

7. Clicking on the _____ next to the *Zoom* icon will list additional zoom tools not currently shown in the *View* toolbar.

8. You do not see the *ViewCube* unless you are in a _____ view.

9. Creating an *Autodesk 360* account is free. (T/F)

10. The *Autodesk A360* App, for mobile devices, is expensive. (T/F)

**Notes:**

## Lesson 2
# Lake Cabin: FLOOR PLAN (The Basics):

In this lesson you will get a down and dirty overview of the functionality of Autodesk® Revit® for architectural design. We will cover the very basics of creating the primary components of a floor plan: Walls, Doors, Windows, Roof, Annotation and Dimensioning. This lesson will show you the amazing "out-of-the-box" powerful, yet easy to use, features in Autodesk Revit. It should get you very excited about learning this software program. Future lessons will cover these features in more detail while learning other editing tools and such along the way.

## Exercise 2-1:
## Walls

In this exercise we will draw the walls, starting with the exterior. Read the directions carefully; everything you need to do is clearly listed.

## Rough Sketch of Lake Cabin Plan:

This sketch is just to give you an idea of what you will be creating in this chapter (Figure 2-1.1).

**FIGURE 2-1.1** Lake Cabin Sketch

## Exterior Walls:

1. Start a new project named **Lake Cabin**. *See Lesson 1 on creating a new project – Architectural Template.*

2. Click **Architecture → Build → Wall** (i.e., the upper part of the icon, not the down-arrow part). See Figure 2-1.2.

**FIGURE 2-1.2** Wall tool

Notice that the *Ribbon, Options Bar* and *Properties Palette* have changed to show options related to drawing walls. Next you will modify those settings.

3. Modify the *Ribbon* and *Options Bar* to the following (Figure 2-1.3):
   a. *Change Element Type (via the Type Selector):* Click the down-arrow and select **Generic – 12″**.
   b. *Height:* Change the height from 20′-0″ to **9′-0″**.
   c. *Location Line:* Set this to **Finish Face: Exterior**.

**FIGURE 2-1.3** Ribbon, Options Bar and Type Selector

You are now ready to draw the exterior walls in the *Level 1* view.

4. In the drawing window, **click** in the upper left corner.

   *TIP: Remember to draw within the four elevation marks (see the image to right).*

5. Start moving the mouse to the right. **Click** when the wall is **48′-0″** long and horizontal.

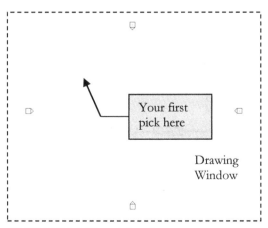

**FIGURE 2-1.4** First pick point

Notice as you move the mouse Revit dynamically displays a length and an angle. If you want a horizontal line you move the mouse straight across the screen. A dashed line and a tooltip will appear when the line is snapped to the horizontal (Figure 2-1.4).

**FIGURE 2-1.5** Horizontal tooltip displayed

> *TIP: If your mouse moved a little when you clicked and the wall is not exactly 48'-0", simply click on the dimension and type 48 and press Enter. You do not need to type the foot symbol.*

You are now ready for your second wall.

6. Start moving your mouse straight down, or South, until the dashed line and tooltip appear (indicating a vertical line); type **26** and press **Enter**.

> *TIP: Once the wall is drawn the temporary dimension will say 25'-6" as it is to the wall centerline on the north corner.*

Typing the length allows you to accurately input a length without having to spend a lot of time setting the mouse in just the right position. However, you can still adjust the dimension after the wall is drawn.

7. Draw the other two exterior walls.

## Interior Walls:

The same tool is used to draw both interior and exterior walls.

8. Select the *Wall* tool and modify the ***Ribbon***, ***Options Bar*** and ***Properties Palette*** to the following:
   a. *Type Selector:* Click the down-arrow and select **Generic – 5"**.
   b. *Location Line:* Set this to **Wall Centerline**.

9. Drawing a wall between bedrooms: *Snap* (you will see a triangle symbol appear before clicking) to the midpoint of the east wall (Figure 2-1.6). Do not click the second point yet; see the next step to finish the wall.

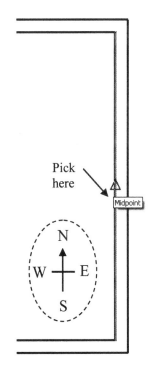

**FIGURE 2-1.6** Interior wall start point

10. While moving the mouse to the West (left) and snapped to the horizontal plane, type **20  2  1/2**.

> *TIP: Type the length as shown; you don't need a dash, the foot or the inch symbol as they are assumed here. You do need two spaces – after the feet and before the fraction.*

11. Draw the vertical wall to close off the bedrooms. Revit allows you to do this with one wall segment by selecting your points in a particular way. See **Figure 2-1.7** for a graphical description of this process; press **Esc** twice to unselect the new wall (first Esc pressed) and cancel the *Wall* command (second Esc pressed).

**FIGURE 2-1.7** Draw wall with object tracking

12. **One More Step:** Draw the two interior walls for the bathroom to complete the interior walls; dimensions are to center of walls (Figure 2-1.1).

13. **Save** your project (*Lake Cabin.rvt*) via the *QAT*.

## Exercise 2-2:
## Doors

In this exercise you will add doors to your cabin floor plan.

1.  Open **Lake Cabin.rvt** created in Exercise 2-1.

## Placing Doors:

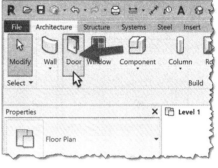

**FIGURE 2-2.1** Door tool

2.  Click **Architecture → Build → Door** (Figure 2-2.1).

Notice that the *Ribbon*, *Options Bar* and *Properties Palette* has changed to show options related to doors. Next you will modify those settings.

The *Type Selector* indicates the door style, width and height. Clicking it lists all the doors loaded into the current project.

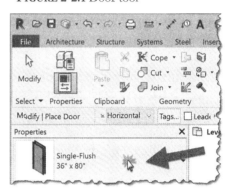

**FIGURE 2-2.2** Door type selected

The default project template that you started from has several sizes for a single flush door. Notice that there are two standard heights in the list. The 80″ (6′-8″) doors are the standard residential height and the 84″ (7′-0″) doors are the standard commercial door height.

3.  On the *Ribbon*, click **Tag on Placement** so it is highlighted (meaning on) and then change the *Type Selector* to **36″ x 80″**; see Figure 2-2.2.

4.  Move your cursor over a wall and position the door as shown in **Figure 2-2.4**. Notice that the swing of the door changes depending on what side of the wall your cursor is favoring (Figure 2-2.4).

5.  Click to place the door and Revit will automatically trim the wall.

6.  While the door is still selected, click on the *change swing (control arrows)* symbol to make the door swing against the wall (Figure 2-2.3).

Click here

**FIGURE 2-2.3** Changing door swing

**FIGURE 2-2.4** Dynamic graphical info during door insertion

Revit allows you to continue inserting doors until you select a different tool from the *Ribbon* or press *Esc*.

7.  Insert the doors into the bedrooms as shown in **Figure 2-1.1**. The exact position is not important in this exercise.

8.  Change the *Type Selector* to **30″ x 80″**.

9.  Insert a door into the bathroom.

Notice that door types recently used are listed at the bottom of the list (Figure 2-2.5). Also, notice the **Search** box near the top—this allows the list to be shortened on large projects with several doors and door types from which to choose.

**FIGURE 2-2.5**
Door Element Types

## Deleting Doors:

Next you will learn how to delete a door. This process will work for most objects (i.e., walls, windows, text, etc.) in Revit.

10. Insert a door between the two bedrooms, any size.

11. Press the **Esc** key twice.

*TIP: You can also click the Modify icon located on the left of every tab on the Ribbon.*

12. Click on the door you just inserted, between bedrooms, and press the **Delete** key on your keyboard.

13. **Save** your project (*Lake Cabin.rvt*).

## Exercise 2-3:
## Windows

In this exercise you will add windows to your cabin floor plan.

1. Open **Lake Cabin.rvt** created in Exercise 2-2.

Placing *Windows*:

2. Click **Architecture → Build → Window** (Figure 2-3.1).

**FIGURE 2-3.1** Window tool

Again, notice that the *Ribbon*, *Options Bar* and *Properties Palette* have changed to show options related to windows. Next you will modify those settings.

The *Type Selector* indicates the window style, width and height. Clicking the *Type Selector* lists all the windows loaded in the current project.

3. On the *Ribbon*, click **Tag on Placement** so it is highlighted and then change the *Type Selector* to **36″ x 72″** (Figure 2-3.2).

**FIGURE 2-3.2** Window types

4. Move your cursor over a wall and place two windows as shown in **Figure 2-3.3**. Notice, as you move your cursor near a wall, that the position of the window changes depending on what side of the wall your cursor is favoring.

5. With the Window tool still active, change the *Type Selector* to **24″ x 72″**.

6. Place the other four windows in the living room area as shown in **Figure 2-1.1**. Again, in this exercise we are not concerned with the exact placement of the windows.

7. Change the *Type Selector* to **24″ x 48″**.

8. Place the remaining five windows: two in each bedroom and one in the bathroom, as shown in **Figure 2-1.1**.

9. **Save** your project (*Lake Cabin.rvt*).

**FIGURE 2-3.3** Two large windows

## Object Snap Symbols:

By now you should be well aware of the snaps that Revit suggests as you move your cursor about the drawing window.

If you hold your cursor still for a moment while a snap symbol is displayed, a tooltip will appear on the screen. However, when you become familiar with the snap symbols you can pick sooner (Figure 2-3.4).

The TAB key cycles through the available snaps near your cursor.

The keyboard shortcut turns off the other snaps for one pick. For example, if you type SE (snap endpoint) on the keyboard while in the Wall command, Revit will only look for an endpoint for the next pick.

Finally, typing SO (snaps off) turns all snaps off for one pick.

See Exercise 3-2 for more information.

| Symbol | Position | Keyboard Shortcut |
|--------|----------|-------------------|
| ✕ | Intersection | SI |
| ☐ | Endpoint | SE |
| △ | Midpoint | SM |
| ○ | Center | SC |
| ✕ | Nearest | SN |
| └ | Perpendicular | SP |
| ⍉ | Tangent | ST |

**FIGURE 2-3.4** Snap Reference Chart

# Exercise 2-4:
# Roof

You will now add a simple roof to your lake cabin.

1.  Open **Lake Cabin.rvt** created in Exercise 2-3 (if necessary).

## Sketching a Roof:

2.  Click **Architecture → Build → Roof** (click the bottom part of the button); a fly-out menu will appear (Figure 2-4.1).

**FIGURE 2-4.1** Roof tool

The fly-out prompts you for the method you want to use to create the roof.

3.  Click **Roof by footprint**.

When Revit detects an issue that might not be appropriate, a warning is displayed. In this case you see *Roof is on the Lowest Level* warning.

Revit notices that you are on Level 1 and asks you if you want to move the roof to another level. In our case we want to move it to Level 2 (Figure 2-4.2).

**FIGURE 2-4.2** Roof is on the Lowest Level prompt

4.  Make sure **Level 2** is selected and click **Yes** (Figure 2-4.2).

You are still on Level 1, but Revit will move the roof to Level 2 once you are finished drawing it. The entire model is grayed out at the moment because you are in "Sketch Mode"; when finished sketching, the roof and everything will return to normal. You will not see the roof as it will be above the current view (i.e., Level 1); you will learn more about this on the next page.

Also notice the *contextual tab* **Create Roof Footprint** has temporarily been added to the *Ribbon*, which has design options relative to the roof (Figure 2-4.3) as with the *Options Bar* directly below the *Ribbon*.

**FIGURE 2-4.3** Roof sketch options on the *Ribbon* and *Options Bar*

5. Pick each of the exterior walls to specify the roof footprint.
   *Be sure to pick the exterior side of the wall.*

6. Click **Finish Edit Mode** via the green checkmark on the *Ribbon*.

You should be on Level 1. You can see this in the *Project Browser*, as Level 1 is bold.

7. To see the roof click the **Default 3D View** icon on the *QAT* (Figure 2-4.4).

The roof has no overhang and is hovering above the exterior walls about 1'-0". We will save these types of modifications for future lessons.

**FIGURE 2-4.4**
Default 3D View

8. Click the **X** on the {3D} drawing tab to close that view. This will close the 3D view but not the project or the Level 1 view. **NOTE:** *Clicking the X on the Titlebar closes Revit.*

## Exercise 2-5:
## Annotation and Dimensions

Adding text is very simple in Revit. In this exercise we will add labels to each room in our lake cabin floor plan. We will also place two dimensions.

## Placing Text:

1. Open **Lake Cabin.rvt** created in Exercise 2-4, if not already open.

2. Make sure your current view is **Level 1**. The word "Level 1" will be bold under the heading *Floor Plans* in your *Project Browser*. If Level 1 is not current, simply double-click on the "Level 1" text in the *Project Browser* (Figure 2-5.1).

3. Select **Annotate → Text → Text**; do not select *Model Text* from the *Architecture* tab of the *Ribbon*.

Text

   *TIP: You can also select the* Text *tool from the Quick Access Toolbar (QAT).*

**FIGURE 2-5.1** Project Browser

Once again, notice the *Ribbon* has changed to display some text options; all of this falls under a *contextual tab* named *Modify | Place Text* (Figure 2-5.2).

**FIGURE 2-5.2** Ribbon: contextual tab for Text tool

The *Type Selector* indicates the text size. From this *Contextual Ribbon* you can also place text with arrow lines, or leaders, and set the text alignment, Left justified, Centered or Right justified. We will not adjust these settings at this time.

4.  You will now place the words "Living Room." **Click** within the living room area to place the text (Figure 2-5.3).

5.  Type **Living Room**, then click somewhere in the plan view to finish the text.

You may notice that the text seems too large. This is a good time to explain what the text height is referring to in the *Type Selector (i.e., ¼″ Arial)*. The text height, in the *Properties Palette*, refers to the size of the text on a printed piece of paper. For example, if you print your plan you should be able to place a ruler on the text and measure ¼″ in height when the text is set to ¼″ in the *Type Selector*.

This can be a complicated process in other CAD programs; Revit makes it very simple. All you need to do is change the *View Scale* for **Level 1** and Revit automatically adjusts the text and annotation to match that scale. Currently our *View Scale* is set to ⅛″ = 1′-0″; we want the *View Scale* to be ¼″ = 1′-0″. With the *View Scale* set to ⅛″ = 1′-0″ our text is twice as big as it should be. Next you will change the *View Scale* for Level 1.

**FIGURE 2-5.3** Placing text

In the lower-left corner of the drawing window, on the *View Control Bar*, click on the text of the listed scale (i.e., ⅛″ = 1′-0″).

6. In the pop-up menu, which lists several standard scales, select **¼″ = 1′-0″** (Figure 2-5.4).

You should now notice that your text and even your door and window tags are half the size they used to be (Figure 2-5.5).

You should understand that this scale adjustment only affected the current view (i.e., Level 1). If you switched to Level 2 you would notice it is still set to ⅛″ = 1′-0″. This is nice because you may, on occasion, want one plan at a larger scale to show more detail.

7. Finally, using the **Text** tool, place a room name label in each room as shown in **Figure 2-1.1** and **Figure 2-5.5** below.

8. **Save** your project.

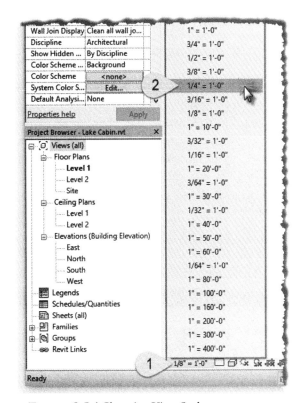

FIGURE 2-5.4 Changing View Scale

FIGURE 2-5.5 Floor Plan with text at ¼″ = 1′-0″

## Place Dimensions:

To finish this exercise you will place two overall plan dimensions.

Aligned

9. Select **Annotate → Dimension → Aligned** (see icon to right).

10. On the *Options Bar*, change the drop-down list that says *Wall centerlines* to **Wall faces**. This option will allow you to dimension to the outside face of your building, as you would normally do when dimensioning the overall footprint of your building.

11. Place a dimension by selecting two walls and then clicking a third point to specify where the dimension line should be located relative to the walls (Figure 2-5.6).

**FIGURE 2-5.6** Placing Dimensions

12. Place one more dimension indicating the depth of the building.

The *Dimension* tool, as just used, places permanent dimensions; they can be deleted, however. Revit also provides a tool to list a distance but not actually place a permanent dimension; this is called the **Measure** tool. The *Measure* tool is convenient when you simply want to know what a dimension is but do not need to document it for the construction drawings.

13. **Save** your project.

## Exercise 2-6:
## Printing

The last thing you need to know to round off your basic knowledge of Revit is how to print the current view. Printing will be covered in more detail later in the text; this section will just brush over the surface of the process.

### Printing the Current View:

1. Select **File Tab → Print** (hover) **→ Print**.

2. Adjust your settings to match those shown in **Figure 2-6.1**.

   - Select a printer from the list that you have access to.
   - Set *Print Range* to **Visible portion of current window**.

**FIGURE 2-6.1** Print dialog

3. Click on the **Setup** button to adjust additional print settings.

4. Adjust your settings to match those shown in **Figure 2-6.2**.

   - Set Zoom to **Fit to page**.

**FIGURE 2-6.2** Print Settings dialog

5. Click **OK** to close the *Print Setup* dialog and return to *Print*.

6. Click **No** if you get the following prompt (Figure 2-6.3).

**FIGURE 2-6.3** Save Print Settings prompt

7. Click the **Preview** button in the lower left corner. This will save paper and time by verifying the drawing will be correctly positioned on the page (Figure 2-6.4).

8. Click the **Print** button at the top of the preview window.

9. Click **OK** to print to the selected printer.

**FYI:**

Notice you do not have the option to set the scale (i.e., $\frac{1}{8}'' = 1'-0''$). If you recall from our previous exercise the scale is set in the properties for each view.

If you want a quick half-scale print you can change the zoom factor to 50%. You could also select **Fit to Page** to get the largest image possible but not to scale – which is selected above as this plan will not fit on $8\frac{1}{2}''$ x 11″ (letter) sized paper at $\frac{1}{4}'' = 1'-0''$.

## Printer versus Plotter?

Revit can print to any printer or plotter installed on your computer.

A **Printer** is an output device that uses smaller paper (e.g., $8\frac{1}{2}''$x11″ or 11″x17″). A **Plotter** is an output device that uses larger paper; plotters typically have one or more rolls of paper ranging in size from 18″ wide to 42″ wide. A roll feed plotter has a built-in cutter that can, for example, cut paper from a 36″ wide roll to make a 24″x36″ sheet.

**FIGURE 2-6.4** Print Preview

**Plotter** with three paper rolls

Color **printer**/copier

## Self-Exam:

The following questions can be used as a way to check your knowledge of this lesson. The answers can be found at the bottom of the page.

1.    The *Measure* tool is used to dimension drawings. (T/F)

2.    Revit will automatically trim the wall lines when you place a door. (T/F)

3.    Snap will help you draw faster and more accurately. (T/F)

4.    A 6'-8" door is a standard door height in _____ construction.

5.    While using the *Wall* tool, the height can be quickly adjusted on the

      _____ bar.

## Review Questions:

The following questions may be assigned by your instructor as a way to assess your knowledge of this section. Your instructor has the answers to the review questions.

1.    The *View Scale* for a drawing/view is set by clicking the scale listed on the *View Control Bar*. (T/F)

2.    Dimensions are placed with only two clicks of the mouse. (T/F)

3.    The relative size of text in a drawing is controlled by the *View Scale*. (T/F)

4.    You can quickly switch to a different view by double-clicking on that view's label in the *Project Browser*. (T/F)

5.    You cannot select which side of the wall a window is offset to. (T/F)

6.    The _____ key cycles through the available snaps near your cursor.

7.    Which specific *Roof* tool did you use in this chapter?  _____

8.    While in the *Door* tool you can change the door style and size via the

      _____ within the *Properties Palette*.

9.    When plotting, you must tell Revit the desired scale (i.e., ⅛" = 1'-0", ¼" = 1'-0", etc.) while in the *Plot* dialog box. (T/F)

10.   The *Quick Access Toolbar* has a tool which gives you quick access to a 3D view of your model. (T/F)

# Lesson 3
# Overview of Linework and Modify Tools:

It may seem odd to you that, in a revolutionary 3D design program, you will begin by learning to draw and edit 2D lines and shapes. However, any 3D object requires, at a minimum, detailed information in at least two of the three dimensions. Once two dimensions are defined, Autodesk® Revit® can begin to automate much of the third dimension for you. Many building components and features will require you to draw the perimeter using 2D lines.

Many of the edit tools that are covered in this lesson are the same tools that are used to edit the 3D building components.

## Exercise 3-1:
## Lines and Shapes

## Drawing Lines:

You will draw many 2D lines in Autodesk Revit, typically in what is called *Sketch* mode. Two dimensional lines in Autodesk Revit are extremely precise drawing elements. This means you can create very accurate drawings. Lines, or any drawn object, can be as precise as 8 decimal places (i.e., 24.999999999) or 1/256.

Autodesk Revit is a vector based program. That means each drawn object is stored in a numerical database. When geometry needs to be displayed on the screen, Autodesk Revit reads from the project database to determine what to display on the screen. This ensures that the line will be very accurate at any scale or zoom magnification.

A raster based program, in contrast to vector based, is comprised of dots that infill a grid. The grid can vary in density and is typically referred to as resolution (e.g., 600x800, 1600x1200, etc.). This file type is used by graphics programs that typically deal with photographs, such as Adobe Photoshop. There are two reasons this type of file is not appropriate for Computer Aided Design (CAD) programs:

- A raster based line, for example, is composed of many dots on a grid, representing the line's width. When you zoom in, magnifying the line, it starts to become pixilated, meaning you actually start to see each dot on the grid. In a vector file you can "infinitely" zoom in on a line and it will never become pixilated because the program recalculates the line each time you zoom in.

- A CAD program, such as Revit, only needs to store the starting point and end point coordinates for each wall. For example, the dots needed to draw the wall are calculated on-the-fly for the current screen resolution, whereas a raster file has to store each dot that represents the full length and width of the line, or lines in the wall, for example. This can vary from a few hundred dots to several thousand dots, depending on the resolution, for the same line.

The following graphic illustrates this point:

# Vector vs. Raster Lines:

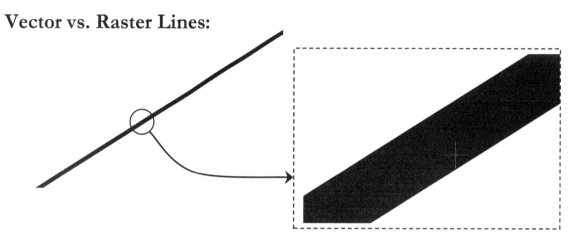

FIGURE 3-1.1 Vector Line Example
*File Size: approx. 33kb*

FIGURE 3-1.1A Vector Line Enlarged 1600%

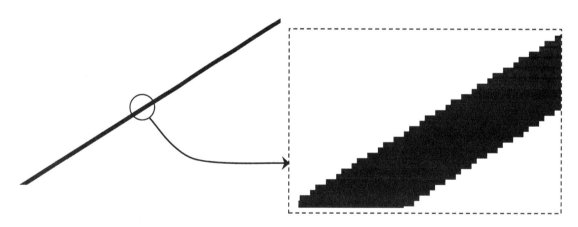

FIGURE 3-1.2 Raster Line Example
*File Size: approx. 4.4MB*

FIGURE 3-1.2A Raster Line Enlarged 1600%

# The Detail Lines Tool:

You will now study the *Detail Lines* tool.

1. **Open** Revit.

Each time you start Revit, you are in the *Recent Files* view. This view is closed automatically when a new or existing project is opened.

2. Start a new project: select **File Tab → New → Project** and then select **Architectural Template** from the drop-down list, and then click **OK**.

The drawing window is set to the *Level 1 Floor Plan* view. The 2D drafting will be done in a drafting view. Next you will learn how to create one of these views.

3. Select **View → Create → Drafting View**.
   (Remember: this means *Tab → Panel → Icon* on the *Ribbon*.)

Drafting
View

4. In the *New Drafting View* dialog box, type **Ex 3-1** for the *Name* and set the *Scale* to **3/4″ = 1′-0″** by clicking the down-arrow at the right (Figure 3-1.3).

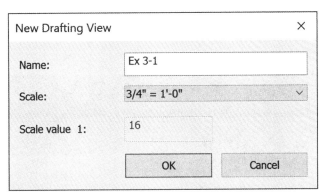

**FIGURE 3-1.3** New Drafting View dialog

You are now in the new view and the *Project Browser* will contain a category labeled *Drafting Views (Detail)*. Here, each *Drafting View* created will be listed.

5. In the *Project Browser*, click the plus symbol next to the label **Drafting Views (Detail)**; this will display the *Drafting Views* that exist in the current project (Figure 3-1.4).

You are now ready to start looking at the *Detail Lines* tool:

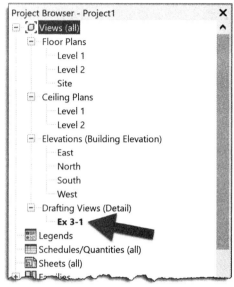

**FIGURE 3-1.4** Project Browser: Drafting Views

6. Select the **_Annotate_** tab on the *Ribbon*.

7. On the *Detail* panel, select **Detail Line** (Figure 3-1.5).

   **Detail Line**

   *TIP: Do not use the "Model Line" tool on the Architecture tab.*

8. **Draw a line** from the lower left corner of the screen to the upper right corner of the screen, by simply clicking two points on the screen within the drawing window (Figure 3-1.6).

   **NOTE:** *Do not drag or hold your mouse button down; just click.*

After clicking your second point, you should notice the length and the angle of the line are graphically displayed; this information is temporary and will disappear when you move your cursor.

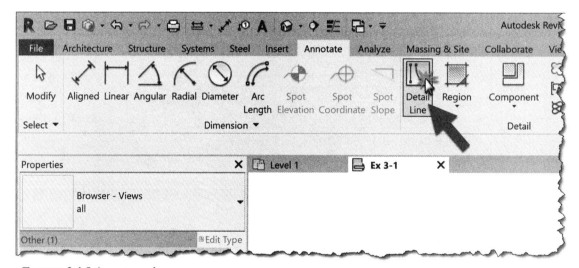

**FIGURE 3-1.5** Annotate tab

You should also notice that the *Detail Line* tool is still active, which means you could continue to draw additional lines on the screen.

9.  After clicking your second point, select the ***Modify*** tool from the left side of the *Ribbon*.

Modify

Selecting *Modify* cancels the current tool and allows you to select portions of your drawing for information or editing. Revit conveniently places the *Modify* tool in the same location on each tab so it is always available no matter which tab on the *Ribbon* is active.

*TIP: Pressing the Esc key twice reverts Revit back to Modify mode.*

---

## Did You Make a Mistake?

Whenever you make a mistake in Revit you can use the **UNDO** command, via the *QAT*, to revert to a previous drawing state. You can perform multiple UNDOs all the way to your previous *Save*.

Similarly, if you press Undo a few too many times, you can use **REDO**.

---

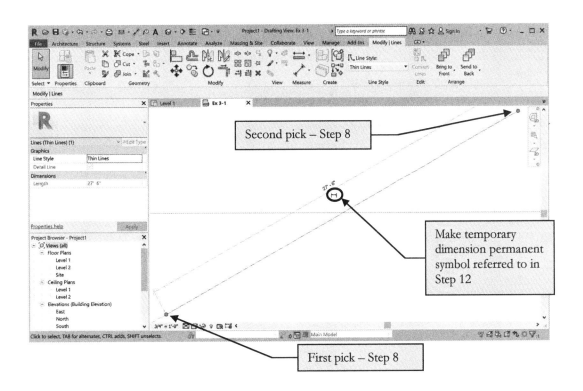

**FIGURE 3-1.6** Your first detail line; exact dimensions are not important at this point.

Notice in the image above, that while the *Detail Line* tool is active, the *Modify | Place Detail Line* contextual tab is shown. As soon as you click the *Modify* button or press Esc, the tab reverts back to the basic *Modify* tab.

This constitutes your first line! However, as you are probably aware, it is not a very accurate line as far as length and angle are concerned. Your line will likely be a different length due to where you picked your points and the size and resolution of your monitor.

Typically, you need to provide information such as length and angle when drawing a line; you rarely pick arbitrary points on the screen as you did in the previous steps. Revit allows you to get close with the on-screen dimension and angle information. Most of the time you also need to accurately pick your starting point. For example, how far one line is from another or picking the exact middle point on another line.

Having said that, however, the line you just drew still has precise numbers associated with its length and angle; this information is displayed after the line is drawn. The dimension and angle information is displayed until you begin to draw another line or select another tool. You can also select the line. While the dimensions are still visible, they can be used to modify the length and angle of the line; you will try that later.

10. If not already selected, click the **Modify** tool from the *Ribbon*.

Notice that the temporary dimensions have disappeared.

While you are in *Modify* mode, you can select lines and objects in the current view.

11. Now **select the line** by clicking the mouse button with the cursor directly over the line.

***FYI:*** *Always use the left button unless the right button is specifically mentioned.*

Notice that the temporary dimensions have returned.

The following step shows how to make a temporary dimension permanent:

If, at any point, you want to make a temporary dimension permanent, you simply click the "make this temporary dimension permanent" symbol near the dimension. You will try this now.

12. With the diagonal line still selected, click the "make this temporary dimension permanent" symbol near the dimension (Figure 3-1.6).

13. Select **Modify** to unselect the line.

The dimension indicating the length of the line is now permanent (Figure 3-1.7). The value of your dimension will not be the same as the one in this book as the size of your monitor and the exact points picked can vary greatly.

**FIGURE 3-1.7** Temp dimension converted to permanent dimension

The following shows how to change the length of the line:

Currently, the line is approximately 20 - 30' long (27'-6" in Figure 3-1.7). If you want to change the length of the line to 22'-6", you select the line and then change the dimension text, which in turn changes the line length. This can also be done with the temporary dimensions; the key is that the line has to be selected. You will try this next.

*FYI: Your detail line length will vary slightly depending on the size and resolution of your computer monitor, as you will be seeing more or less of the drawing area. This also assumes you have not performed any zooming, including spinning the wheel button on your mouse. If your line is way off you should Undo or start over so the next several steps work out as intended.*

    14. In *Modify* mode, select the diagonal line.

    15. With the line currently selected, click on the dimension-text.

A dimension-text edit box appears directly over the dimension, within the drawing window. Whatever you type as a dimension changes the line to match.

    16. Type **22 6** (i.e., 22 *space* 6) and press **Enter** (Figure 3-1.8).

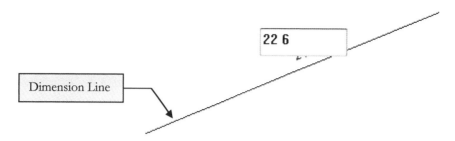

**FIGURE 3-1.8** Editing dimension to change line length

You should have noticed the line changed length. Revit assumes that you want the line to change length equally at each end, so the midpoint does not move. Try changing the dimension to 100′ and then Undo.

## Locking Dimensions:

Revit allows you to *Lock* a dimension, which prevents the dimension and line length from changing. You will investigate this now to help avoid problems later.

17.  Make sure the line is *not* selected; to do this press Esc or click *Modify*.

18.  Select the dimension, not the line, and note the following about the selected dimension (Figure 3-1.9).

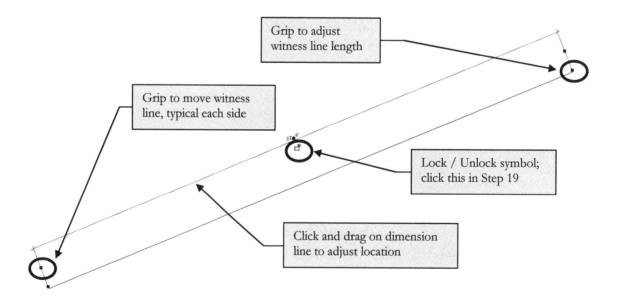

Grip to adjust witness line length

Grip to move witness line, typical each side

Lock / Unlock symbol; click this in Step 19

Click and drag on dimension line to adjust location

**FIGURE 3-1.9** Selected dimension

19. Click on the **Lock/Unlock** padlock symbol to lock the dimension (Figure 3-1.9).

The dimension is now locked. Again, this means that you cannot change the dimension OR the line, though you can move it. The dimension is attached to the line in such a way that changing one affects the other. Next you will see what happens when you try to modify the dimension while it is locked.

Any time the line or dimension is selected you will see the lock or unlock symbol in the locked position.

*FYI: Clicking the dimension's padlock icon anytime it is visible will toggle the setting between locked and unlocked.*

20. Select **Modify** to unselect the *Dimension*.

21. Select the line (not the dimension).

22. Click on the dimension text and attempt to modify the line length to **21′**.

As you can see, Revit will not let you edit the text.

Even though your current view is showing a relatively small area, i.e., your *Drafting View*, it is actually an infinite drawing board.

In architectural CAD drafting, everything is drawn true to life size, or full-scale, ALWAYS! If you are drawing a building, you might draw an exterior wall that is 600′-0″ long. If you are drawing a window detail, you might draw a line that is 8″ long. In either case you are entering that line's actual length.

You could, of course, have an 8″ line and a 600′-0″ line in the same *Drafting View*. Either line would be difficult to see at the current drawing magnification (i.e., approximately 22′ x 16′ area; also recall that your diagonal line is 22′-6″ long). So, you would have to zoom in to see the 8″ line and zoom out to see the 600′-0″ line. Next you will get to try this.

When the diagonal line is selected, notice the *Properties Palette* lists the type of entity selected (i.e., Lines), the *Style* (i.e., Thin Lines) and the *Length* (i.e., 22′-6″). See Chapter 1 for more information on the *Properties Palette* and how to open it if you accidentally closed it.

**FIGURE 3-1.10** Properties Palette with diagonal line selected

# Draw an 8″ Line:

The next steps will walk you through drawing an 8″ horizontal line. Revit provides more than one way to do this. You will try one of them now.

23. Select **Annotate → Detail → Detail Line**.

24. Pick a point somewhere in the upper left corner of the drawing window.

25. Start moving the mouse towards the right and generally horizontal until you see a dashed reference line extending in each direction of your line appear on the screen, as in Figure 3-1.11.

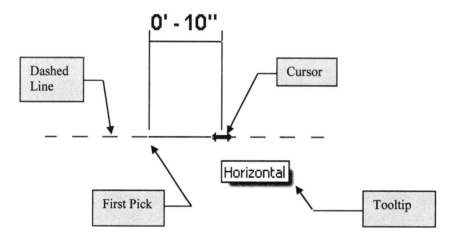

**FIGURE 3-1.11** Drawing a line with the help of Revit

*TIP: You will see a dashed horizontal line and a tooltip when the line is horizontal.*

As you move the mouse left and right, you will notice Revit displays various dimensions that allow you to quickly draw your line at these often used increments. See the next exercise to learn more about how to control the increments shown.

26. With the dashed line and *tooltip* visible on the screen, take your hand off the mouse, so you do not accidentally move it, and type **8″** and then press **Enter**.

    *TIP: Remember, you have to type the inch symbol; Revit always assumes you mean feet unless you specify otherwise. A future lesson will review the input options in more detail.*

You have just drawn a line with a precise length and angle!

27. Use the *Measure* tool to verify it was drawn correctly. Click *Modify* →
    *Measure* → *Measure (down arrow)* → *Measure Between Two References*

28. Use the *Zoom In Region* tool to enlarge the view of the 8″ line via the
    *Navigation Bar* (image to right).

29. Now use the *Zoom to Fit* or *Previous Pan/Zoom* tools so that both lines are
    visible again.

# Draw a 600′ Line:

30. Select the *Detail Line* tool and pick a point in the
    lower right corner of the drawing window.

31. Move the cursor straight up from your first point
    so that the line snaps to the vertical and the dashed
    line appears (Figure 3-1.12).

32. With the dashed line and *tooltip* visible on the
    screen, take your hand off the mouse so you do
    not accidentally move it; type **600** and then press
    **Enter**.

    *TIP #1: Notice this time you did not have to type the foot
    symbol ( ′).*

    *TIP #2: You do not need to get the temporary dimension close to reading 600′; the temporary dimension
    is ignored when you type in a value.*

**FIGURE 3-1.12** Drawing another
Detail Line; 600′-0″ vertical line
– lower right

33. Press the **Esc** key twice to exit the *Detail Line* tool and return to the *Modify* mode.

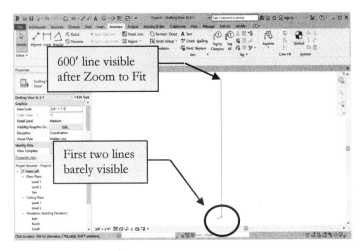

Because the visible portion of
the drawing area is only about
16′ tall, you obviously would
not expect to see a 600′ line.
You need to change the
drawing's magnification by
zooming out to see it.

34. Use *Zoom to Fit* to see
    the entire drawing (Fig. 3-
    1.13).

    *TIP: Double-click your wheel
    button to Zoom Extents.*

**FIGURE 3-1.13** Detail view with three lines

# Drawing Shapes:

Revit provides several tools to draw common shapes like squares, rectangles, circles and ellipses. These tools can be found on the *Ribbon* while the *Detail Line* tool is active. You will take a look at *Rectangle* and *Circle* now.

## Creating a Rectangle:

35. Use **Previous Pan/Zoom**, or *Zoom Region*, to get back to the original view where the diagonal line spans the screen.

36. Select the **Detail Line** tool.

Notice the *Ribbon*, *Options Bar* and *Properties Palette* have changed to show various options related to *Detail Lines* (Figure 3-1.14).

**FIGURE 3-1.14** Place Detail Lines contextual Tab on Ribbon

37. Select the **Rectangle** tool from the *Ribbon*.

> *TIP: Hover your cursor over the icon to see tooltip until you learn what tools the icons represent.*

38. Pick the "**first corner point**" somewhere near the lower center of the drawing window (Figure 3-1.15).

Notice the temporary dimensions are displaying a dimension for both the width and height. At this point you can pick a point on the screen, trying to get the dimensions correct before clicking the mouse button. If you do not get the rectangle drawn correctly, you can click on each dimension-text and change the dimension while the temporary dimensions are displayed; see the next two steps for the rectangle dimensions.

39. Draw a 2'-8" x 4'-4" rectangle using the temporary dimensions displayed on the screen; if you do not draw it correctly do the following:

   a. Click the dimension-text for the horizontal line, then type **2'-8"** and then press **Enter**.

   b. Type **4'-4"** and then press **Enter** for the vertical dimension.

**FIGURE 3-1.15** Drawing with Rectangle and Circle to be added (shown dashed for clarity)

## Creating a Circle:

40. With the *Detail Line* tool active, select **Circle** from the *Ribbon* (Figure 3-1.16).

41. You are now prompted to pick the center point for the circle; pick a point approximately as shown in Figure 3-1.15.

**FIGURE 3-1.16** Detail Line shapes

You should now see a dynamic circle and a temporary dimension attached to your cursor, which allows you to visually specify the circle's size. Move your mouse around to see that you could arbitrarily pick a point on the screen to create a quick circle if needed, then proceed to Step 42 where you will draw a circle with a radius of 1'-6⅝".

42. Type **1 6 5/8** and then press **Enter** (Figure 3-1.17).

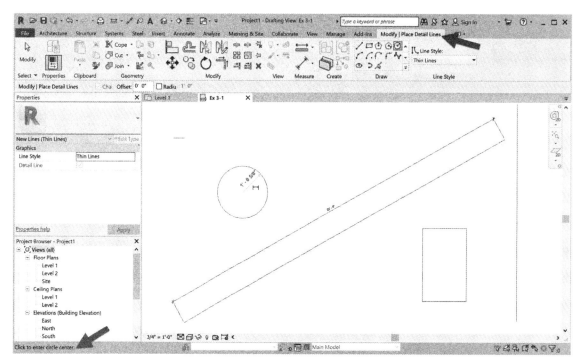

**FIGURE 3-1.17** Drawing with Rectangle and Circle added

Notice in the image above, the *Detail Line* is still active because the *contextual tab*, **Modify | Place Detail Lines**, is visible and the *Status Bar* is prompting to "Click to enter circle center." You need to press **Esc** or click *Modify* to cancel the command; clicking another command will also cancel the current command.

43. **Select the circle** and notice a temporary dimension appears indicating the circle's radius. Press **Esc** to unselect it (Figure 3-1.18).

    *TIP: This temporary dimension can be used to change the radius of the circle while the circle is selected.*

44. **Save** your project as "**ex3-1.rvt**".

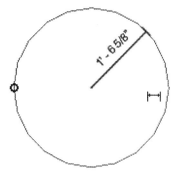

**FIGURE 3-1.18**
Circle selected

## Exercise 3-2:
## Snaps

*Snaps* are tools that allow you to accurately pick a point on an element. For example, when drawing a line you can use *Object Snap* to select, as the start-point, the endpoint or midpoint of another line or wall.

This feature is absolutely critical to drawing accurate technical drawings. Using this feature allows you to be confident you are creating perfect intersections, corners, etc. (Figure 3-2.1).

## Object Snaps Options:

You can use *Object Snaps* in one of two ways.

- o   "Normal" mode
- o   "Temporary Override" mode

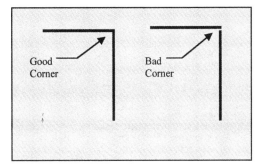

**FIGURE 3-2.1** Typical problem when *Snaps* are not used

"Normal" *SNAP* mode is a feature that constantly scans the area near your cursor when Revit is looking for user input. You can configure which types of points to look for.

*NOTE: The term "normal" is not a Revit term, rather it is simply a description used in this book to differentiate this portion of the Snaps feature from the Temporary Override portion discussed next.*

Using a "Temporary Override" *Object Snap* for individual pick-points allows you to quickly select a particular point on an element. This option will temporarily disable the other *Object Snap* settings, which means you tell Revit to just look for the endpoint on an object, for the next pick-point only, rather than the three or four types being scanned for by the "normal" *Object Snaps* feature.

## Overview of the Snaps Dialog Box:

Revit provides a *Snaps* dialog box where you specify which *Object Snaps* you want enabled. Next you will take a look at it.

1.   Open project **Ex3-1** and select **Manage → Settings → Snaps**.

Snaps

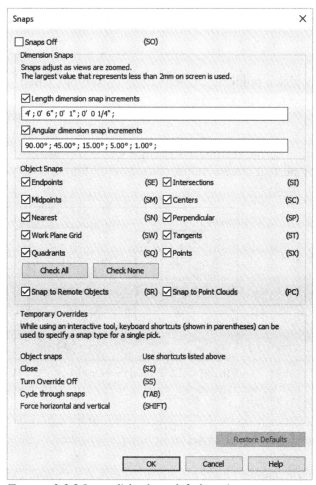

**FIGURE 3-2.2** Snaps dialog box; default settings

You should now see the *Snaps* dialog box (Figure 3-2.2). Take a minute to study the various settings that you can control with this dialog box. Notice the check box at the top that allows you to turn this feature off completely.

*Dimension Snaps*
This controls the automatic dimensions that Revit suggests when you are drawing. Following the given format you could add or remove increments. If you are zoomed in close, only the smaller increments are used.

*Object Snaps*
This controls the "normal" *Object Snaps* that Revit scans for while you are drawing. Unchecking an item tells Revit not to scan for it anymore. Currently, all *Object Snaps* are enabled (Figure 3-2.2).

*Temporary Overrides*
This area is really just information on how to use Temporary Overrides.

While drawing you will occasionally want to tell Revit you only want to *Snap* to an Endpoint for the next pick. Instead of opening the *Snaps* dialog and un-checking every *Object Snap* except for Endpoint, you can specify a *Temporary Override* for the next pick. You do this by typing the two letters, in parentheses, in the *Object Snaps* area of the *Snaps* dialog (Figure 3-2.2).

2.  Make sure the *Snaps Off* option is unchecked in the upper-left corner of the dialog box; this turns Snaps completely off.

3.  Click on the **Check All** button to make sure all *Snaps* are checked.

4.  Click **OK** to close the *Snaps* dialog box.

## Understanding Snap Symbols:

Again, you should be well aware of the *Object Snap* symbols that Revit displays as you move your cursor about the drawing window while you are in a tool like *Wall* and Revit is awaiting your input or pick-point.

If you hold your cursor still for a moment, while a snap symbol is displayed, a tooltip will appear on the screen. However, when you become familiar with the snap symbols you can pick sooner, rather than waiting for the tooltip to display (Figure 3-2.3).

The TAB key cycles through the available snaps near your cursor.

| Symbol | Position | Keyboard Shortcut |
|--------|----------|-------------------|
| ✗ | Intersection | SI |
| ☐ | Endpoint | SE |
| △ | Midpoint | SM |
| ○ | Center | SC |
| ✗ | Nearest | SN |
| ∟ | Perpendicular | SP |
| ◯ | Tangent | ST |

FIGURE 3-2.3 Snap symbols

Finally, typing **SO** turns all snaps off for one pick.

*FYI: The Snaps shown in Figure 3-2.2 are for Revit in general, not just the current project. This is convenient; you don't have to adjust to your favorite settings for each Project or View, existing or new.*

## Setting Object Snaps:

You can set Revit to have just one or all Snaps running at the same time. Let us say you have Endpoint and Midpoint set to be running. While using the *Wall* tool, you move your cursor near an existing wall. When the cursor is near the end of the wall you will see the Endpoint symbol show up; when you move the cursor towards the middle of the line you will see the Midpoint symbol show up.

The next step shows you how to tell Revit which Object Snaps you want it to look for. First you will save a new copy of your project.

5. Select **File Tab → Save-As → Project**.

6. Name the project **ex3-2.rvt**.

7. As discussed previously, open the ***Snaps*** dialog box.

8. Make sure only the following *Snaps* are checked:
   a. Endpoints
   b. Midpoints
   c. Centers
   d. Intersections
   e. Perpendicular

9. Click **OK** to close the dialog box.

---

**For More Information:**

For more on using Snaps, search Revit's *Help System* for **Snaps**. Then double-click **Snap Points** or any other items found by the search.

---

Now that you have the *Snaps* adjusted, you will give this feature a try.

10. Using the ***Detail Line*** tool, move your cursor to the lower-left portion of the diagonal line (Figure 3-2.4).

11. Hover the cursor over the line's endpoint (without picking); when you see the *Endpoint* symbol you can click to select that point.

**Just So You Know**

It is important that you see the *SNAP* symbol before clicking. Also, once you see the symbol you should be careful not to move the mouse too much.

These steps will help to ensure accurate selections.

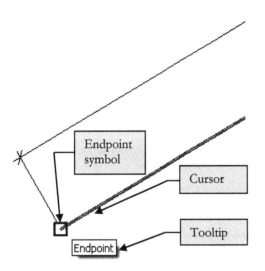

**FIGURE 3-2.4** Endpoint SNAP symbol visible

**While still in the Detail Line tool** you will draw lines using *Snaps* to sketch accurately.

12. Draw the additional lines shown in **Figure 3-2.5** using the appropriate *Object Snap*, changing the selected Snaps as required to select the required points.

> ***TIP #1:*** *At any point while the Line tool is active, you can open the SNAP dialog box and adjust its settings. This will not cancel the Line command.*

> ***TIP #2:*** *Also, remember you can press Tab to cycle through the various snap options below or near your cursor.*

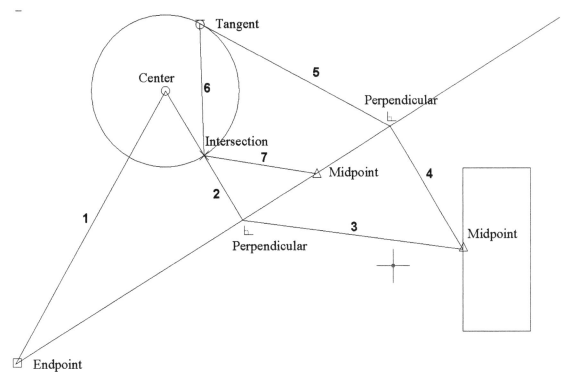

**FIGURE 3-2.5** Lines to draw and Snap to use

13. **Save** your project.

Your drawing might look slightly different depending on where you drew the rectangle and circle in the previous steps.

---

**This is a Residential Example?**

OK, this is not really an architectural example yet. However, the point here is to focus on the fundamental concepts and not architecture just yet.

---

## Save Reminders:

Revit is configured to remind you to save every 30 minutes so you do not lose any work (Figure 3-2.6).

It is recommended that you do not simply click *Cancel*, but do click the **Save the project** option.

**FIGURE 3-2.6** Save reminder

## Exercise 3-3:
## Edit Tools

The *edit tools* are used often in Revit. A lot of time is spent tweaking designs and making code and client related revisions.

**FIGURE 3-3.1** Modify panel

Example: you use the *design tools* (e.g., Walls, Doors, Windows) to initially draw the project. Then you use the *edit tools* to *Move* a wall so a room becomes larger, *Mirror* a cabinet so it faces in a different direction, or *Rotate* the furniture per the owner's instructions.

You will usually access the various edit tools from the Modify tab on the *Ribbon*. You can probably visualize what most of the commands do by the graphics on the icons; see Figure 3-3.1. When you hover over an icon, the tool name will appear. The two letters shown to the right is its keyboard shortcut; pressing those two keys, one at a time, activates that tool.

In this exercise you will get a brief overview of a few of the edit tools by manipulating the tangled web of lines you have previously drawn.

1. **Open** project **ex3-2.rvt** from the previous lesson.

2. **Save-As "ex3-3.rvt"**.

*FYI: You will notice that instructions or tools that have already been covered in this book will have less "step-by-step" instruction.*

## Delete Tool:

It is no surprise that the *Delete* tool is a necessity; things change and mistakes are made. You can *Delete* one element at a time or several. Deleting elements is very easy: you select the elements, and then pick the *Delete* icon. You will try this on two lines in your drawing.

3. While holding the **Ctrl** key, select the lines identified in **Figure 3-3.2**.

   *TIP: See the section below Figure 3-3.2 on Selecting Entities.*

4. Select **Delete** from the *Ribbon* (or press the **Delete** key on the keyboard).

The lines are now deleted from the project.

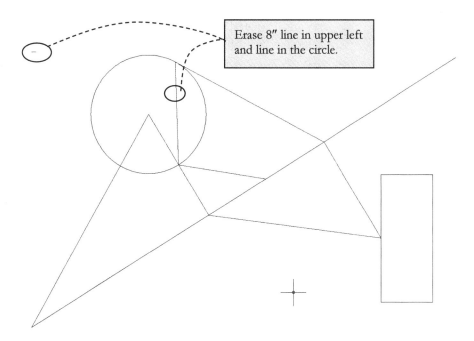

**FIGURE 3-3.2** Lines to be erased

## Selecting Objects:

At this time we will digress and take a quick look at the various techniques for selecting entities in Revit. Most tools work the same when it comes to selecting elements.

When selecting entities, you have two primary ways to select them:
o   Individually select entities one at a time
o   Select several entities at a time with a window

You can use one or a combination of both methods to select elements when using the *Copy* tool.

Individual Selections:
When prompted to select entities to copy or delete, for example, you simple move the cursor over the element and click; holding the **Ctrl** key you can select multiple objects. Then you typically click the tool you wish to use on the selected items. Press **Shift** and click on an item to subtract it from the current selection set.

*Continued on next page*

<u>Window Selections:</u>
Similarly, you can pick a *window* around several elements to select them all at once. To select a *window*, rather than selecting an object as previously described, you select one corner of the *window* you wish to define. That is, you pick a point in "space" and hold the mouse button down. Now, as you move the mouse you will see a rectangle on the screen that represents the windowed area you are selecting; when the *window* encompasses the elements you wish to select, release the mouse.

You actually have two types of windows you can select. One is called a **window** and the other is called a **crossing window**.

**Window:**
This option allows you to select only the objects that are completely within the *window*. Any lines that extend out of the *window* are not selected.

**Crossing Window:**
This option allows you to select all the entities that are completely within the *window* and any that extend outside the *window*.

**Using Window versus Crossing Window:**
To select a *window* you simply pick and drag from left to right to form a rectangle (Figure 3-3.3a).

Conversely, to select a *crossing window*, you pick and drag from right to left to define the two diagonal points of the window (Figure 3-3.3b).

**Selecting a chain of lines (hover, tab, click):**
Revit provides a quick and easy way to select a chain of lines, that is, a series of lines (or walls) whose endpoints are perfectly connected. You simply hover your cursor over one line so it highlights, then press the Tab key once, and then click the mouse button. This trick can be used to quickly select all the exterior walls on a building, for example.

Turning off **Drag Element on Selection** on the *Status Bar* helps to avoid accidentally clicking directly on an element and moving it rather than starting the intended first corner of a selection window.

Remember, all these draw, modify and select tools have direct application to working with Revit's 3D building components, not just the 2D geometry being covered in this chapter.

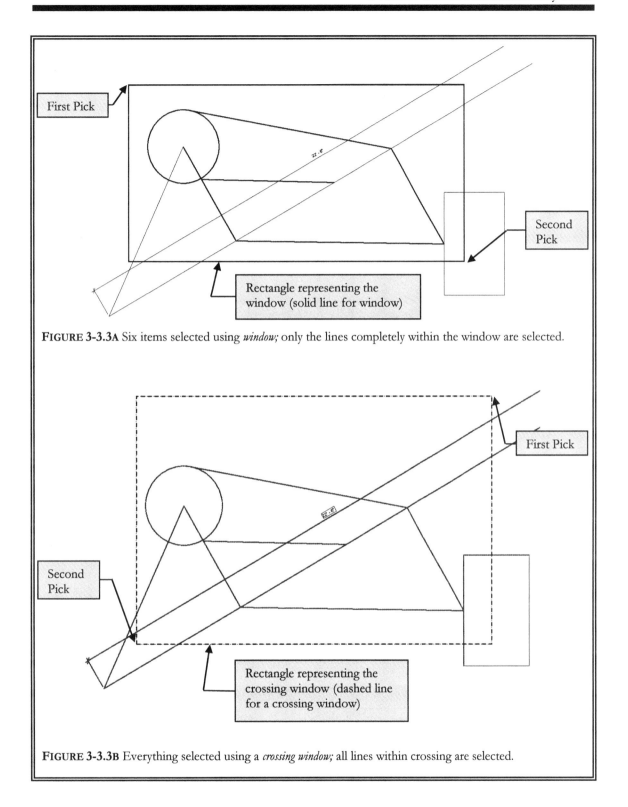

First Pick

Second
Pick

Rectangle representing the
window (solid line for window)

**FIGURE 3-3.3A** Six items selected using *window;* only the lines completely within the window are selected.

First Pick

Second
Pick

Rectangle representing the
crossing window (dashed line
for a crossing window)

**FIGURE 3-3.3B** Everything selected using a *crossing window;* all lines within crossing are selected.

## Copy Tool:

The *Copy* tool allows you to accurately duplicate an element(s). You select the items you want to copy and then pick two points that represent an imaginary vector, which provides both length and angle, defining the path used to copy the object. You can also type in the length if there are no convenient points to pick in the drawing. You will try both methods next.

5. **Select the circle.**

6. Select **Copy** from the *Ribbon.*

*Notice the prompt on the Status Bar:* Click to enter move start point.

7. Pick the **center** of the **circle** (Figure 3-3.4).

> ***FYI:*** *You actually have three different Snaps you can use here: Center, Endpoint and Intersection. All occur at the exact same point.*

*Notice the prompt on the Status Bar:* Click to enter move end point.

8. Pick the **endpoint** of the angled line in the lower left corner (Figure 3-3.4).

> ***FYI:*** *If you want to make several copies of the circle, select* Multiple *on the* Options Bar.

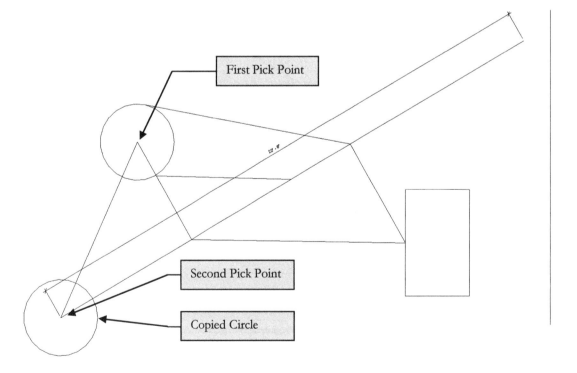

**FIGURE 3-3.4** Copied circle; also indicates points selected

9. **Select the rectangle** *(all four lines).*

   *TIP: Try the "hover, tab, click" method discussed on page 3-22.*

10. Select **Copy**.

11. Pick an arbitrary point on the screen. In this scenario it makes no difference where you pick; you will see why in a moment.

At this point you will move the mouse in the direction you want to copy the rectangle, until the correct angle is displayed, and then type in the distance rather than picking a second point on the screen.

12. Move the mouse towards the upper right until 45 degrees displays, then type **6′** and then press **Enter** (Figure 3-3.5).

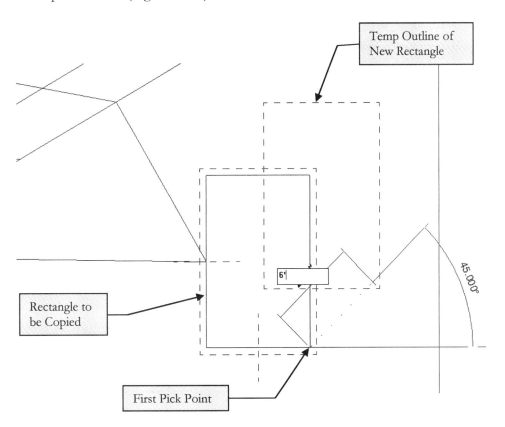

Temp Outline of New Rectangle

Rectangle to be Copied

6′

First Pick Point

45.000°

**FIGURE 3-3.5** Copying rectangle; angle set visually and distance typed in

*NOTE: Your drawing may look a little different than this one because your drawing is not completely to scale.*

## Move Tool:

The *Move* tool works exactly like the *Copy* tool except, of course, you move the element(s) rather than copy it. Given the similarity to the previous tool covered, the *Move* tool will not be covered now. You are encouraged to try it yourself; just Undo your experiments before proceeding.

## Rotate Tool:

With the *Rotate* tool, you can arbitrarily or accurately rotate one or more objects in your drawing. When you need to rotate accurately, you can pick points that define the angle, assuming points exist in the drawing to pick, or you can type a specific angle.

Rotate involves the following steps:
- Select element(s) to be rotated
- Select *Rotate*
- Determine if the Center of Rotation symbol is where you want it.
  - If you want to move it:
    - Simply drag it, or
    - Click *Place* on the *Options Bar*
- Select a point to define a reference line and begin rotation.
- Pick a second point using one of the following methods:
  - By selecting other objects or using the graphic angle display *or*
  - You can type an angle and press **Enter**.

13. **Select the new rectangle** you just copied *(all four lines)*.

14. Select **Rotate** on the *Ribbon*.

Notice that the "Center of Rotation" grip, by default, is located in the center of the selected elements. This is the point about which the rotation will occur. See Figure 3-3.6.

You will not change the "Center of Rotation" at this time.

15. Pick a point directly to the right of the "Center of Rotation" grip; this tells Revit you want to rotate the rectangle relative to the horizontal plane (Figure 3-3.6).

Now, as you move your mouse up or down, you will see the temporary angle dimension displayed. You can move the mouse until the desired angle is displayed and then click to complete the rotation, or you can type the desired angle and then press **Enter**. If you recall, the *Snaps* dialog box controls the increments of the angles that Revit displays; they are all whole numbers. So if you need to rotate something 22.45 degrees, you must type it as Revit will never display that number as an option.

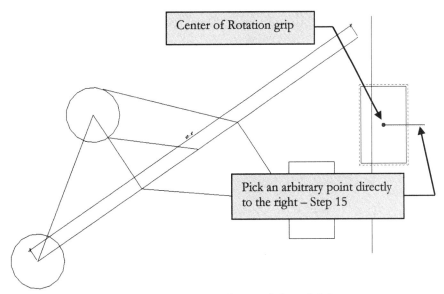

FIGURE 3-3.6 Rotate tool; first step – select lines and then click Rotate

16. Move the mouse up and to the left until 90 degrees is displayed and then click to complete the rotation (Figure 3-3.7).

FIGURE 3-3.7 Rotate tool; last step – select angle visually or type angle

The previous steps just rotated the rectangle 90 degrees counter-clockwise about its center point (Figure 3-3.8).

17. Select the **Undo** icon.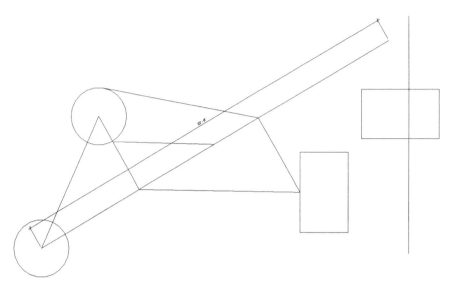

FIGURE 3-3.8 Rotate tool; rectangle rotated about its center point

Now you will do the same thing, except with a different angle and "Center of Rotation."

18. **Select the rectangle** and then pick **Rotate**.

19. Click and drag the "Center of Rotation" grip to the left and *Snap* to the midpoint of the vertical line (Figure 3-3.9).

    *TIP: You can also click the* **Place** *button on the Options Bar.*

20. Pick a point to the right, creating a horizontal reference line.

21. Start moving your mouse downward, then type **22.5** and then press **Enter** (Figure 3-3.10).

The rectangle is now rotated 22.5 degrees in the clockwise direction (Figure 3-3.11).

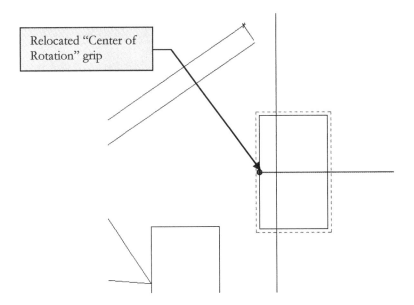

Relocated "Center of Rotation" grip

FIGURE 3-3.9 Rotate tool; relocated Center of Rotation grip

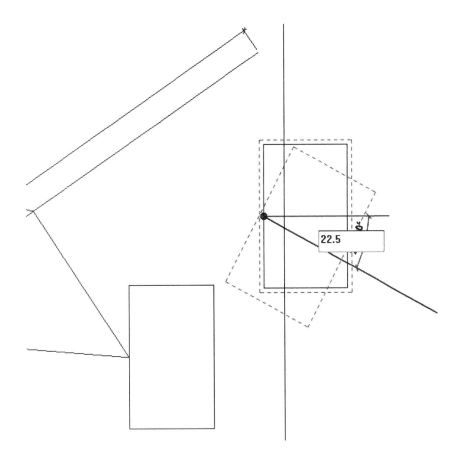

22.5

FIGURE 3-3.10 Rotate tool; typing in exact angle

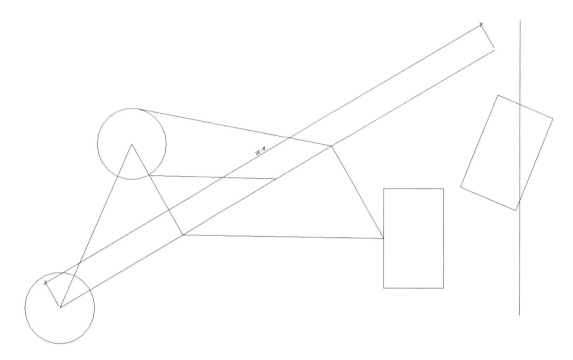

**FIGURE 3-3.11** Rotate tool; rectangle rotated 22.5 degrees

# Scale Tool:

The *Scale* tool has steps similar to the *Rotate* tool. First you select what you want to scale or resize, specify a scale factor and then you pick the base point. The scale factor can be provided by picks on the screen or entering a numerical scale factor (e.g., 2 or .5, where 2 would be twice the original size and .5 would be half the original size).

Next you will use the *Scale* tool to adjust the size of the circle near the bottom.

Before you resize the circle, you should use the *Modify* tool/mode to note the **diameter** of the circle. Select the circle and view its temporary dimensions. After resizing the circle, you will refer back to the temporary dimensions to note the change. This step is meant to teach you how to verify the accuracy and dimensions of entities in Revit.

22. Select the bottom circle.

23. Select the **Scale** icon from the *Ribbon*.

On the *Options Bar* you will specify a numeric scale factor of .5 to resize the circle to half its original size.

24. Click **Numerical** and then type **.5** in the textbox *(see the Options Bar above)*.

You are now prompted **Click to enter origin** on the *Status Bar*. This is the base point about which the circle will be scaled; see examples in Figure 3-3.13 on the next page.

25. Click the center of the circle.

You just used the *Scale* tool to change the size of the circle from 1'-6 5/8″ to 9 5/16″ radius. A scale factor of .5 reduces the entities to half their original scale (Figure 3-3.12).

---

**Selecting the Correct Center of Rotation *(Base Point)*:**

You need to select the appropriate *Center of Rotation*, or Base Point, for both the *Scale* and *Rotate* commands to get the results desired. A few examples are shown in Figure 3-3.13. The dashed line indicates the original position of the entity being modified. The black dot indicates the base point selected.

---

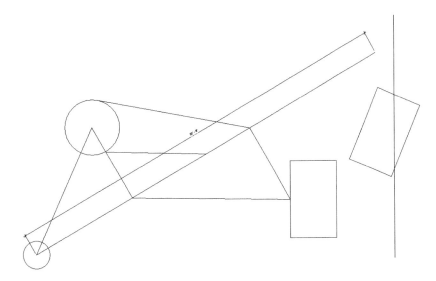

**FIGURE 3-3.12** Resize circle; notice it is half the size of the other circle

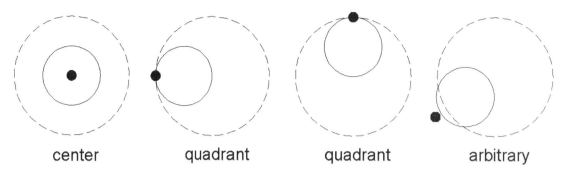

**center**     **quadrant**     **quadrant**     **arbitrary**

**Center of Rotation Options: Scale Command**

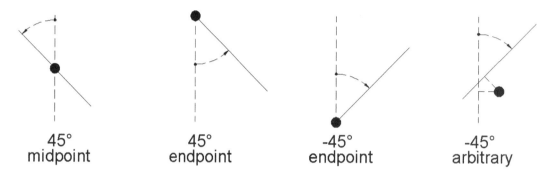

**45°**
**midpoint**

**45°**
**endpoint**

**-45°**
**endpoint**

**-45°**
**arbitrary**

**Center of Rotation Options: Rotate Command**

**FIGURE 3-3.13** Center of Rotation Options and the various results

This will conclude the brief tour of the *Edit* tools. Do not forget, even though you are editing 2D lines, the edit tools work the same way on 3D elements such as walls, floors, roofs, etc. Exception: you cannot *Scale* walls, doors, etc.; these objects have to be modified by other methods. You would not typically change the door thickness when changing its width and height as would happen if you could use the *Scale* tool on it.

As you surely noticed, the *Modify* panel on the *Ribbon* has a few other tools that have not been investigated yet. Many of these will be covered later in this book.

26. **Save** the project. Your project should already be named "ex3-3.rvt" per Step 2 above.

Carter Residence

## Exercise 3-4:
## Annotations

Annotations, or text and notes, allow the designer and technician to accurately describe the drawing. Here you will take a quick look at this feature set. There is a chapter, later in the book, dedicated to annotation which covers these tools in greater detail.

## Annotations:

Adding annotations to a drawing can be as essential as the drawing itself. Often the notes describe a part of the drawing that would be difficult to discern from the drawing alone.

For example, a wall framing drawing showing a bolt may not indicate, graphically, how many bolts are needed or at what spacing. The note might say *"5/8″ anchor bolt at 24″ O.C."*

Next you will add text to your drawing.

1. **Open** project **ex3-3.rvt** from the previous lesson.

2. **Save-As** "ex3-4.rvt".

3. Use **Zoom** if required to see the entire drawing, except for the 600' line which can run off the screen.

4. Select **Annotate → Text → Text**.

   Note that the *Model Text* tool on the *Architecture* tab is only for drawing 3D text; *Drafting Views* are only 2D so that command is not even an option currently.

Text

From the *Text* icon tooltip (see image to the right) you can see that the keyboard shortcut for the *Text* tool is **TX**. Thus, at any time you can type T and then X to activate the *Text* tool; if you have another command active, Revit will cancel it.

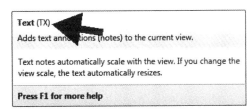

Text (TX)
Adds text annotations (notes) to the current view.

Text notes automatically scale with the view. If you change the view scale, the text automatically resizes.

**Press F1 for more help**

Text icon's tooltip (hover cursor over icon)

Experienced and efficient designers use a combination of keyboard shortcuts and mouse clicks to save time. For example, while your left hand is typing TX, your right hand can be moving toward the location where you want to insert the text. This process is generally more efficient than switching between tabs on the *Ribbon* and clicking icons, or fly-out icons which require yet another click of the mouse.

Notice the current *prompt* on the *Status Bar* at the bottom of the screen; you are asked to "Click to start text or click and drag rectangle to create wrapping text." By clicking on the screen you create one line of text, starting at the point picked, and press **Enter** to create additional lines. By clicking and dragging a rectangle you specify a window, primarily for the width, which causes Revit to automatically move text to the next line. When the text no longer fits within the window it is pushed below, or what is called "text wrapping" (Figure 3-4.1).

**FIGURE 3-4.1** Status Bar while Text tool is active

You should also notice the various text options available on the *Ribbon* while the *Text* tool is active (Figure 3-4.2). You have two text heights loaded from the template file you started with, text justification icons (Left, Center, Right) and the option to attach leaders, or pointing arrows, to your drawings. The *Text* tool will be covered in more detail later in this book.

*FYI: The text heights shown (i.e., ¼", 3/32" via Type Selector) are heights the text will be when printed on paper, regardless of the view scale.*

**FIGURE 3-4.2** Ribbon and Properties Palette with the Text tool active

5.  Pick a point in the upper left portion of the view as shown in Figure 3-4.3.

6.  Type "**Learning Revit is fun!**"

7.  Click anywhere in the view, except on the active text, to finish the *Text* command; pressing **Enter** will only add new lines.

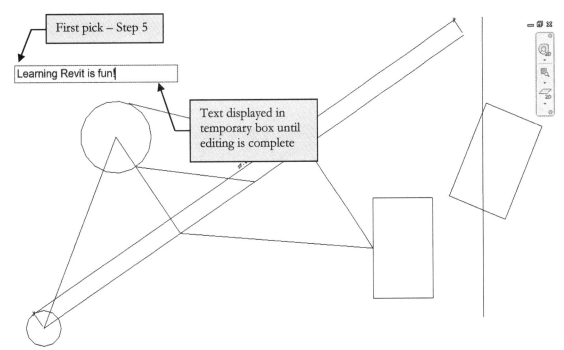

**FIGURE 3-4.3** Text tool; picking first point and typing text.

As soon as you complete the text edit, the text will still be selected and the *Move* and *Rotate* symbols will be displayed near the text; this allows you to more quickly *Move* or *Rotate* the text after it is typed (Figure 3-4.4).

**FIGURE 3-4.4** Text tool; text typed with Move and Rotate symbols showing.

8. Finish the *Text* tool completely by pressing *Modify* or clicking in the drawing.

*TIP: Notice that the text is no longer selected and the symbols are gone; the contextual tab also disappears on the Ribbon.*

Your text should generally look similar to Figure 3-4.5.

9. Print your drawing; refer back to page 2-15 for basic printing information. Your print should fit the page and look similar to Figure 3-4.5.

10. **Save** your project.

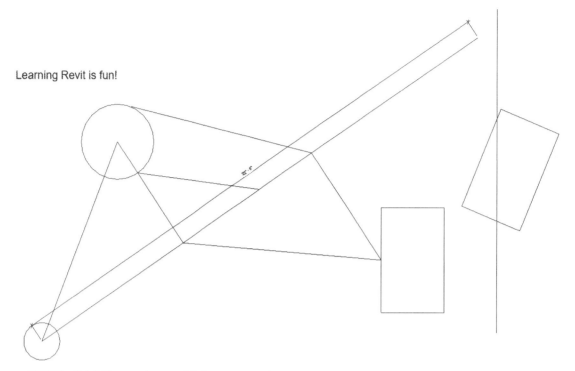

Learning Revit is fun!

**FIGURE 3-4.5** Text tool; text added to current view

Carter Residence

Images courtesy of LHB
www.LHBcorp.com

## Self-Exam:

The following questions can be used as a way to check your knowledge of this lesson. The answers can be found at the bottom of the page.

1.  Revit is only accurate to three decimal places. (T/F)

2.  The triangular shaped Snap symbol represents the Midpoint snap. (T/F)

3.  You can move or rotate text via its modify symbols when text is selected. (T/F)

4.  Use the _____ tool to duplicate objects.

5.  When selecting objects, use the _____ to select all the objects in the selection window and all objects that extend through it.

## Review Questions:

The following questions may be assigned by your instructor as a way to assess your knowledge of this section. Your instructor has the answers to the review questions.

1.  Revit is a raster based program. (T/F)

2.  The "Center of Rotation" you select for the *Rotate* and *Scale* commands is not important. (T/F)

3.  Entering 16 for a distance actually means 16'-0" to Revit. (T/F)

4.  Use the *Detail Line* tool, with _____ selected on the *Ribbon*, to create squares.

5.  You can change the height of the text from the *Type Selector*. (T/F)

6.  Pressing the _____ key cycles you through the snap options.

7.  Where do the two predefined text heights come from? _____

8.  Specifying degrees with the *Rotate* tool, you must type the number when Revit does not display the number you want; the increments shown on-screen are set in the

    _____ dialog box.

9.  List all the Snap points available on a circle (ex. Line: endpoint, midpoint,

    nearest) _____.

10. The Snaps Off option must not be checked in the Snaps dialog box to automatically and accurately select snap points while drawing. (T/F)

**Notes:**

## Lesson 4
# Drawing 2D Architectural Objects:

This lesson is intended to give you practice drawing in Autodesk® Revit®; while doing so you will become familiar with the various shapes and sizes of the more common symbols used in a residential design.

Do not forget that learning to draw 2D is important in Autodesk Revit. You often define 3D items, like walls, in 2D floor plans, while Autodesk Revit takes care of the third dimension automatically. Additionally, you will often want to embellish a view with 2D lines; for example, the exterior elevation, which is a 2D projection of a 3D model.

If you have used other design programs, like AutoCAD or AutoCAD Architecture, these lessons will help you understand the different ways to draw using Autodesk Revit, a more visual or graphic based input system.

Each drawing will be created in its own *Drafting View*.

For some of the symbols to be drawn, you will have step-by-step instruction and a study on a particular tool that would be useful in the creation of that object. Other symbols to be drawn are for practice by way of repetition and do not provide step by step instruction.

**Do NOT draw the dimensions provided; they are for reference only.**

## Exercise 4-1:
## Sketching Rectilinear Objects

## Overview:

All the objects you will draw in this exercise consist entirely of straight lines, either orthogonal or angular.

As previously mentioned, all the objects MUST BE drawn in SEPARATE *Drafting Views*. Each object will have a specific name provided, which is to be used to name the *Drafting View*. All views will be created in one Revit project file which should be saved in your personal folder created for this course.

## *view name:* **Bookcase**

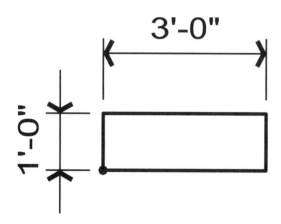

This is a simple rectangle that represents the size of a bookcase.

1. **Open** a new project; **Save** the project as **Ex4-1.rvt**.

2. Create a new *Drafting View* named **Bookcase** (Figure 4-1.1) *(from the View tab)*.

3. Select **Detail Line** from the *Annotate* tab.

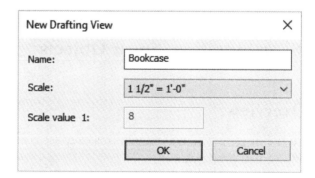

By default, the current line thickness is set to *Thin Lines*. You can see this on the *Ribbon* when the *Detail Line* tool is active. You will change this to *Medium* next.

4. Set the line thickness to **Medium Lines** (Figure 4-1.2; also see image to the right).

> *NOTE: Use this setting for all the drawings in this chapter.*

5. Click the **Rectangle** button on the *Ribbon* (Figure 4-1.2).

6. **Draw a rectangle**, per the dimensions shown above, generally in the center of the drawing window.

> *TIP: You should be able to accurately draw the rectangle using the temporary dimensions; if not, click on the dimension text to change it.*

**FIGURE 4-1.1** New Drafting View dialog

**FIGURE 4-1.2** Ribbon; Medium Lines and Rectangle selected

## *view name:* **Coffee Table**

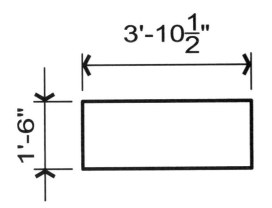

7. Create a new *Drafting View.*

   **NOTE:** *This step will be assumed for the rest of the drawings in this exercise.*

8. Similar to the steps listed above, plus the suggestions mentioned below, create the coffee table shown to the left.

Draw the rectangle as closely as possible using the visual aids; you should be able to get the 1'-6" dimension correct. Then click on the text for the temporary horizontal dimension and type in 3'-10 1/2".

Entering fractions: the 3'-10½" can be entered in one of four ways.

| | | |
|---|---|---|
| o | 3 10.5 | *Notice there is a space between the feet and inches.* |
| o | 3 10 1/2 | *Two spaces separate the feet, inches and fractions.* |
| o | 0 46.5 | *This is all in inches; that is 3'-10½" = 46.5".* |
| o | 46.5" | *Omit the feet and use the inches symbol.* |

## *view name:* **Desk-1**

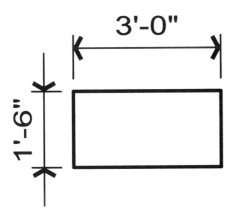

9. Draw the *Desk* in its own view, similar to the steps outlined above.

*TIP: You should double-check your drawing's dimensions using the* Measure *tool. Pick the icon from the* Modify *tab and then pick two points. A temporary dimension will display.*

*view name:* **Night Table**

Obviously, you could draw this quickly per the previous examples. However, you will take a look at copying a *Drafting View* and then modifying an existing drawing.

You will use the *Move* tool to stretch the 3'-0" wide desk down to a 1'-6" wide night table.

First you will look at *Drafting Views* and how they are organized in the *Project Browser*, and then you will copy the *Desk-1 Drafting View* to start the *Night Table* drawing/view.

10. Locate the **Drafting Views** section in the *Project Browser* and expand it by clicking on the "plus" symbol.

Notice that the three views you previously created are listed (Figure 4-1.3). The *Desk-1* view is shown with bold text because it is the current view. All *Drafting Views* are listed here and can be renamed, copied or deleted at any time by right-clicking on the item in the list. You will copy the *Desk-1* view next.

**FIGURE 4-1.3** Project Browser: Drafting Views section expanded

11. Right-click on the *Desk-1* view (Figure 4-1.4).

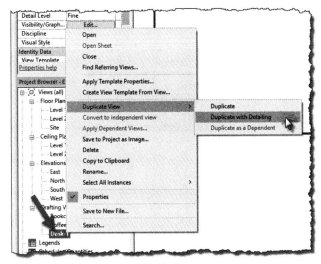

**Figure 4-1.4** Drafting Views list –
Right click on Desk-1 view for menu

Next you will select *Duplicate with Detailing* which will copy the *View* and the *View's* contents, whereas the *Duplicate* option will only copy the *View* and its settings but without any line work.

12. Select **Duplicate View →  Duplicate with Detailing** from the pop-up menu (Figure 4-1.4).

You now have a new View named *Copy of Desk-1* in the *Drafting Views* list. This *View* is open and current.

13. **Right-click** on the new view name, *Copy of Desk-1*, and select **Rename** from the pop-up menu.

14. Type **Night Table** and then click **OK** (Figure 4-1.5).

You are now ready to modify the copy of the *Desk-1* linework. You will use the *Move* tool to change the location of one of the vertical lines, which will cause the two horizontal lines to stretch with it. Autodesk Revit *Detail Lines* automatically have a parametric relationship to adjacent lines when their endpoints touch them.

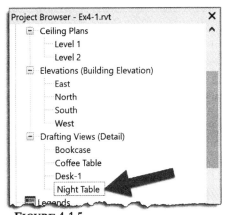

**FIGURE 4-1.5**
Rename View dialog – Night Table entered

15. Select the vertical line on the right and then click the **Move** icon on the *Ribbon*.

16. Pick the midpoint of the vertical line, then move the mouse 1′-6″ to the left and click again (Figure 4-1.6).

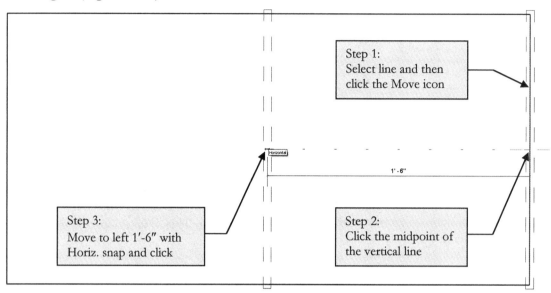

**FIGURE 4-1.6** Move tool used to stretch a rectangle

The rectangle is now resized, or stretched, to be half its original width.

You will notice that the horizontal lines automatically adjusted.

Revit assumes a special relationship between a line being edited and any line whose endpoint is directly touching it.

*TIP: You can select "Disjoin" on the Options Bar while in the Move command if you don't want other lines to move or stretch with it. You will not do that here though.*

**FIGURE 4-1.7** Stretched rectangle (using Move tool)

17. **Save** your project.

*view name:* **Dresser-1**

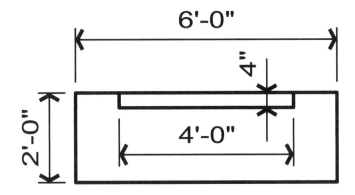

18. Draw the dresser using the following tip:

    *TIP: Simply draw two rectangles. Move the smaller rectangle into place using the Move tool and Snaps.*

*view name:* **Dresser-2**

19. Draw this smaller dresser.

*view name:* **Desk-2**

20. Draw this desk in the same way you drew *Dresser-1*.

*view name:* **File Cabinet**

21. Draw this file cabinet.

*view name:* **Chair-1**

22. Draw this chair per the following tips:

Draw the 2′x2′ square first, and then draw three separate rectangles as shown to the right. Move them into place with *Move* and *Snaps*. Next, delete the extra lines so your drawing looks like the one shown on the left. Pay close attention to the dimensions!

*view name:* **Sofa**

23. *Duplicate* and *Rename* the *Chair-1* view to start this drawing.

*TIP: See the next page for more information on creating this drawing.*

You can create the *Sofa* in a similar way that you created the *Night Table*; that is, you will use the *Move* tool. Rather than selecting one vertical line, however, you will select all the lines on one side of the chair.

You can select all the lines on one side in a single step, rather than clicking each one individually while holding the Ctrl key. You will select using a *window* selection, not a *crossing window* selection.

24. **Select** all the lines on the right side (Figure 4-1.8).

   *TIP: Pick from left to right for a* window *selection.*

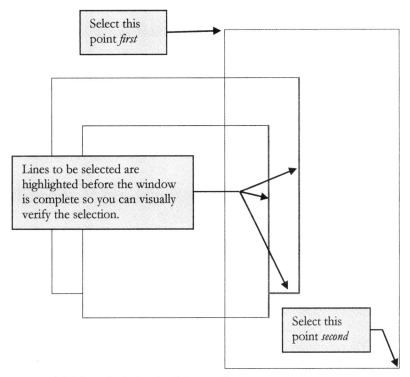

Select this
point *first*

Lines to be selected are
highlighted before the window
is complete so you can visually
verify the selection.

Select this
point *second*

**FIGURE 4-1.8** Stretch chair using Move tool

25. Use the ***Move*** tool to extend the chair into a sofa.

   *TIP: The difference between the chair width and the sofa width is the distance the lines are to be moved.*

You have just successfully transformed the chair into a sofa! Do not forget to *Save* often to avoid losing work. Also, use the *Measure* tool to verify your drawing's accuracy.

*view name:* **Bed-Double**

26. Draw this bed using lines and rectangles; the exact sizes of items not dimensioned are not important.

**FIGURE 4-1.9** Floor Plan example using similar furniture to that drawn in this exercise.

*Image courtesy of Stanius Johnson Architects*
*www.staniusjohnson.com*

## Exercise 4-2:
## Sketching Objects with Curves

Similar to the previous exercise, you will draw several shapes; this time the shapes will have curves in them.

You will look at the various commands that allow you to create curves, like *Arc*, *Circle* and *Fillet*.

Again, you will not draw the dimensions as they are for reference only; each drawing should be drawn in its own *Drafting View*. Name the view with the label provided.

Finally, you can ignore the black dot on each of the drawings below. This dot simply represents the location from which the symbol would typically be inserted or placed.

*view name:* **Laundry-Sink**

This is a simple rectangle that represents the size of a laundry sink, with a circle that represents the drain.

1. **Open** a new Revit project and name it **Ex4-2.rvt**.

2. Draw the rectangle shown; refer to Exercise 4-1 for more information.

3. Use the **Measure** tool to verify the size of your rectangle.

Next you will draw a circle for the drain. The drain needs to be centered left and right and 5" from the back edge. The following steps will show you one way in which to do this.

4. Select the **Detail Line** tool from the *Annotate* tab.

5. Select the **Circle** icon from the *Ribbon* (Figure 4-2.1).

**FIGURE 4-2.1** Sketch Options for detail lines

6. Pick the midpoint of the top line (Figure 4-2.2).

   *FYI: This is the center of the circle.*

7. Type **0 1** for the radius and press **Enter** (0 1 = $0' - 1''$).

   *FYI: This creates a 2″ diameter circle.*

**FIGURE 4-2.2** Creating a circle and moving it into place.

At this point you may get an error indicating the "Line is too short" or "Element is too small on screen" (Figure 4-2.3). This is supposed to prevent a user, like yourself, from accidentally drawing a very small line when you click the mouse twice right next to each other or trying to change the dimension to a previously drawn line to something less than 1/32″. If you get this error, you simply zoom in on your drawing more so the circle is more prominently visible on the screen.

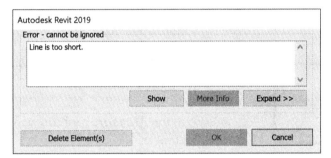

**FIGURE 4-2.3** Possible Revit error message when creating the circle

8. If you did get the error message just described, click *Cancel, Zoom In* and then draw the circle again.

9. Select the circle and then the ***Move*** tool.

10. **Move** the circle straight down 5″ (Figure 4-2.2).

That's it! Do not forget to save your *Ex4-2* project often.

*view name:* Dryer

Here you will draw a dryer with rounded front corners. This, like all the other symbols in this lesson, is a plan view symbol, as in "viewed from the top."

11. Draw a 30"x26" Rectangle.

12. Use the *Measure* tool to verify your dimensions.

Next, you will draw the line that is 2½" from the back of the dryer. You will draw the line in approximately the correct position and then use the temporary dimensions to correct the location.

13. Select the **Detail Line** tool and then pick a point approximately 3"down from the upper-left corner; a temporary dimension will be displayed before you click your mouse button (Figure 4-2.4).

14. Complete the horizontal line by picking a point perpendicular to the vertical line on the right (Figure 4-2.4).

15. With the temporary dimensions still displayed, click the text for the 0'-3" dimension, type **0 2.5** and then press **Enter** (Figure 4-2.5).

16. Click *Modify* to clear the selection and make the *Temporary Dimensions* go away.

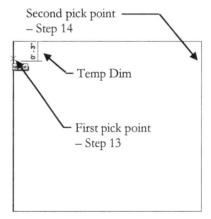

**FIGURE 4-2.4** Drawing a line

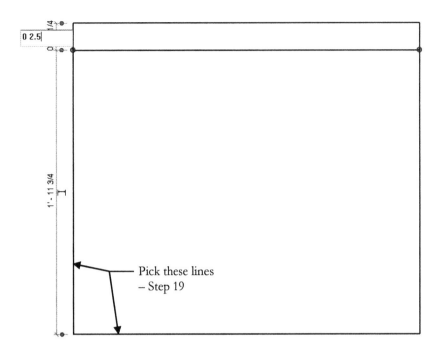

**FIGURE 4-2.5** Adjusting new lines position via temporary dimensions

Next you will round the corners. You still use the *Detail Line* tool, but use a *Draw* option called *Fillet Arc*, pronounced "Fill it." You will try this next.

17. With the ***Detail Lines*** tool active, select the **Fillet Arc** *Draw* option on the *Ribbon* (Figure 4-2.6).

18. Check **Radius** and enter **0′ 2″** in the text box on the *Options Bar* (Figure 4-2.6).

**FIGURE 4-2.6** Ribbon and Options Bar; options for Detail Lines in Fillet mode

19. Pick the two lines identified in Figure 4-2.5.

The intersection of the two lines is where the arc is placed; notice the two lines you picked have been trimmed back to the new *Fillet Arc*.

20. Repeat the previous step to **Fillet** the other corner.

*view name:* **Washer**

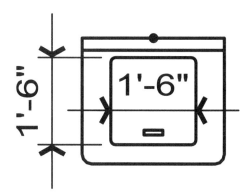

This drawing is identical to the *Dryer* except for the door added to the top. You can duplicate the *Dryer Drafting View* to get a jump start on this drawing.

To draw the door you will use the **Offset** option, which is part of the *Detail Line* tool.

The *Offset* tool is easy to use; to use it you:
o   Select the *Detail Line* tool
o   Select the *Pick Lines* icon on the *Ribbon*
o   Enter the *Offset* distance on the *Options Bar*
o   Select near a line, and on the side to offset

21. Select the ***Detail Line*** tool.

22. Select the **Pick Lines** icon on the *Ribbon* (Figure 4-2.7).

**FIGURE 4-2.7** Ribbon and Options Bar: options for Detail Lines in Pick Lines mode

Note that the *Pick Lines* icon toggles you from *Draw* mode to *Pick Lines* mode. The *Pick Lines* mode allows you to use existing linework to quickly create new linework. You should notice the available options on the *Options Bar* have changed after selecting *Pick Lines*; you can switch back by selecting the *Draw* icons on the *Ribbon* (Figure 4-2.7).

23. Enter **0′ 6″** for the *Offset* distance (Figure 4-2.7).

Next you will need to select a line to offset. Which side of the line you click on will indicate the direction the line is offset. Revit provides a visual reference line indicating which side the line will be offset to and its location based on the offset distance entered.

Without clicking the mouse button, move your cursor around the drawing and notice the visual reference line. Move your mouse from side-to-side over a line to see the reference line move to correspond to the cursor location.

24. **Offset** the left vertical line towards the right.

> *TIP: Make sure you entered the correct offset distance in the previous step (Figure 4-2.8).*

You will need to look at the washer drawing and the dryer drawing dimensions to figure out the door size.

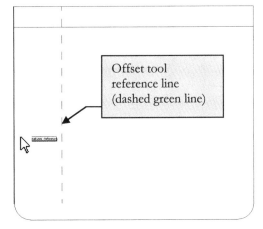

Offset tool reference line (dashed green line)

25. **Offset** the other three sides; your sketch should look like Figure 4-2.9.

26. Use the *Fillet Arc* sketch mode, in the *Detail Line* tool, to create a 1″ radius on the four corners.

27. Click *Modify* to finish the current command.

**Figure 4-2.8** Offset left vertical line towards the right 6″

All four corners should now be rounded off.

28. Draw a small 4″x1″ rectangle to represent the door handle. Draw it anywhere. Then using *Snaps*, move it to the midpoint of the bottom door edge, and then move the handle 2″ up.

29. **Save** your project. Make sure the view name is *Washer*.

FIGURE 4-2.9 All four lines offset inward to create outline for washer door

> *TIP: Revit also provides an Offset tool on the Modify tab of the Ribbon. The steps required are very similar to those just described.*

*view name:* **Range**

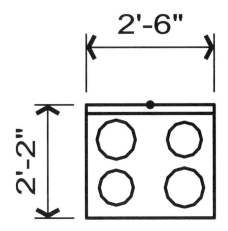

2'-6"

2'-2"

Now you will draw a kitchen *Range* with four circles that represent the burners.

In this exercise you will have to draw temporary lines, called *construction lines*, to create reference points needed to accurately locate the circles. Once the circles have been drawn, the construction lines can be erased.

30. Draw the range with a 2″ deep control panel at the back; refer to the steps described to draw the dryer if necessary.

31. Draw the four construction lines shown in Figure 4-2.10. Use the ***Ref Plane*** tool on the *Architecture* tab.

32. Draw two 9½″ Dia. circles and two 7½″ Dia. circles using the intersection of the construction lines to locate the centers of the circles (Figure 4-2.10).

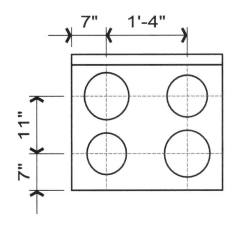

7"    1'-4"

11"

7"

**FIGURE 4-2.10** Range with four temporary construction lines (shown dashed for clarity)

*TIP: Refer back to the Laundry-Sink for sketching circles.*

33. **Erase** the four **Ref Plane** lines (construction lines).

34. **Save** your project.

*TIP: When using the* Measure *tool, you can select* Chain *on the* Options Bar *to have Revit calculate the total length of several picks. For example, you can quickly get the perimeter of a rectangle by picking each corner. Notice, as you pick points, the* Total Length *is listed on the* Options Bar.

## *view name:* **Chair-2**

Now you will sketch another chair. You will use *Detail Line* with *Offset* and the *Arc* settings.

First you will draw the arc at the perimeter.

35. Select *Detail Line* and then **Center – Ends Arc** from the *Ribbon* (Figure 4-2.1).

Notice on the *Status Bar* you are prompted to "**Click to enter arc center**."

36. *First Pick:* Pick a point somewhere in the middle of a new *Drafting View* named *Chair-2* (Figure 4-2.11).

You are now prompted, on the *Status Bar*, "**Drag arc radius to desired location**."

37. *Second Pick:* Move the cursor towards the left, while snapped to the horizontal, until the temporary dimension reads **1'-3"** (Figure 4-2.11).

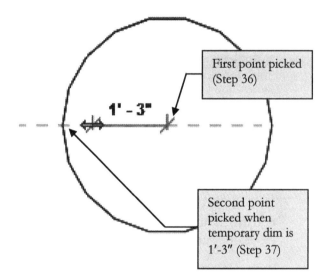

**FIGURE 4-2.11** Sketching an arc; picking second point

*NOTE: As you can see, Revit temporarily displays a full circle until you pick the second point. This is because Revit does not know which direction the arc will go or what the arc length will be. The full circle allows you to visualize where your arc will be (Figure 4-2.11).*

38. *Third Pick:* Move the cursor to the right until the arc is 180 degrees and snapped to the horizontal again (Figure 4-2.12).

*TIP: Notice that your cursor location determines on which direction or side the arc is created; move the cursor around before picking the third endpoint to see how the preview arc changes on screen.*

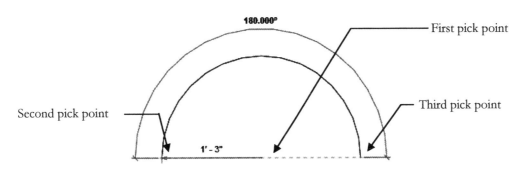

**FIGURE 4-2.12** Pick points for arc command

Next you will draw the three *Detail Lines* to complete the perimeter of the chair.

39. Draw two vertical lines **1'-3"** long, attached to the arc endpoints.

   **TIP:** *Do not forget to use* Medium Lines *when sketching detail lines; if you forgot you can select the lines, while in* Modify *mode, and select* Medium Lines *from the* Element Type Selector *on the* Ribbon.

40. Draw the **2'-6"** line across the bottom.

Notice the radius is 1'-3". You did not have to enter that number because the three points you picked were enough information for Revit to determine it automatically.

If you had drawn the three lines in Steps 39 and 40 before the arc, you would not have had the required center point to pick while creating the arc. However, you could have drawn a temporary horizontal line across the top to set up a center pick that would allow you to draw the circle in its final location; or even better, use the **Start-End-Radius** *Detail Line* option.

You have now completed the perimeter of the chair.

41. Use the *Offset* tool to offset the arc and two vertical lines the required distance to complete the sketch.

42. **Save** your project.

## *view name:* **Love-Seat**

You should be able to draw this *Love-Seat* without any further instruction. Use the same radius as *Chair-2*.

You can create the drawing using a combination of the following tools:
- *Detail Line*
- *Fillet Arc*
- *Offset*
- *Move*

## *view name:* **Tub**

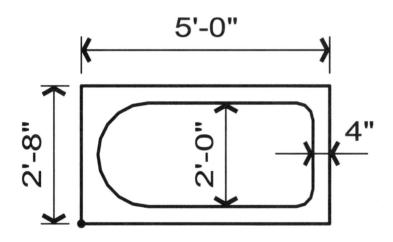

Now you will draw a bathtub. You will use several commands previously covered.

You will use the following tools:
- *Detail Line*
- *Fillet Arc*
- *Offset*
- *Move*

You may also wish to draw one or more construction lines to help locate things like the large radius, although it can be drawn without them.

*view name:* **Lav-1**

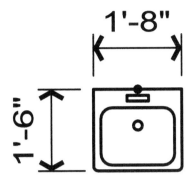

Draw this lavatory per the following specifications:

- o Larger arcs shown shall have a 2½″ radius
- o Smaller arcs shown shall have a 1″ radius, outside corners
- o Sides and Front of sink to have 1½″ space, offset
- o Back to have 4″ space, offset
- o Small rectangle to be 4½″x1″ and 1½″ away from the back
- o 2″ Dia. drain, 8″ from back

*view name:* **Lav-2**

Next you will draw another lavatory. This time you will use the *Ellipse* tool.

43. Create a new *Drafting View.*

44. Select *Detail Lines* and then **Ellipse** from the *Options Bar* (Figure 4-2.1).

Notice the *Status Bar* prompt: "**Click to enter ellipse center.**"

45. Pick near the middle of the screen.

46. With the cursor snapped to the vertical, point the cursor straight down and then type **0 9.5**; press **Enter**.

*NOTE: 9½″ is half the HEIGHT, which is 1′-7″.*

Now you need to specify the horizontal axis of the ellipse.

47. Again, snapping to the horizontal plane, position the cursor towards the right then type **0 11** and then press the **Enter** key.

*NOTE: 11″ is half the width: 1′-10″.*

That's all it takes to draw an ellipse!

48. *Copy* the ellipse vertically downward **3½"** (Figure 4-2.13).

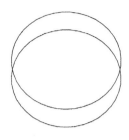

Next you will use the *Scale* tool to reduce the size of the second ellipse. To summarize the steps involved:
- Select the ellipse to be resized
- Select the *Scale* icon
- Pick the origin
- Pick the opposite side of the ellipse
- Enter a new value for the ellipse.

**FIGURE 4-2.13** Ellipse copied downward 3½"

49. Select the lower ellipse.

50. Select the **Scale** icon on the *Ribbon,* on the *Modify* tab.

Notice the *Status Bar* prompt: "**Pick to enter origin.**" The origin, or base point, is a point on, or relative to, the object that does not move.

51. *First Pick:* Pick the top edge, midpoint, of the selected ellipse (Figure 4-2.14).

52. *Second Pick:* Pick the bottom edge, midpoint, of the same ellipse (Figure 4-2.14).

53. Type **1 2** (i.e., 1'-2") and press **Enter;** this will be the new distance between the two points picked.

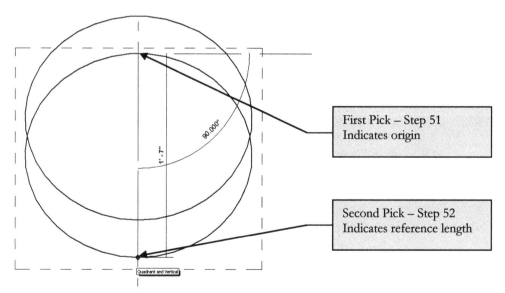

First Pick – Step 51
Indicates origin

Second Pick – Step 52
Indicates reference length

**FIGURE 4-2.14** Scaling the ellipse

Next you need to draw the faucet and drain. As it turns out, the faucet and drain for *Lav-1* are in the same position relative to the middle and back (black dot). So to save time, you will *Copy/Paste* these items from the *Lav-1* drafting view into the *Lav-2* view.

54. Open **Lav-1** *Drafting View*.

55. Select the entire *Lav-1* sketch.

56. Pick **Modify | Lines → Clipboard → Copy** while the *Lav-1* linework is selected.

57. Switch back to the *Lav-2* view and press **Ctrl + V** on the keyboard. Press both keys at the same time.

58. Pick a point to the side of the *Lav-2* sketch (Figure 4-2.15).

59. Select the faucet, the small rectangle, and the drain (i.e., the circle).

   *TIP: Use a* window *selection, picking from left to right.*

60. Select the ***Move*** tool; pick the middle/back of the *Lav-1* sketch and then pick the middle/back of the *Lav-2* sketch.

   *NOTE: These two points represent the angle and distance to move the selected items.*

61. **Erase** the extra *Lav-1* linework from the *Lav-2* view.

You should now have the faucet and drain correctly positioned in your *Lav-2* view.

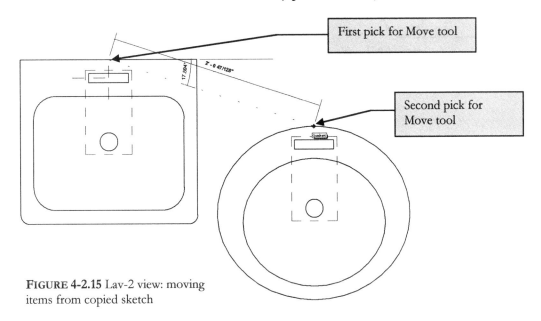

**FIGURE 4-2.15** Lav-2 view: moving items from copied sketch

*view name:* **Sink-1**

Draw this lavatory per the following specifications:

- o 2″ space, offset at sides and front
- o 3″ Dia. Circles centered in sinks
- o 2″ rad. for Fillets
- o 1½″ Dia. at faucet spaces; 3½″ apart

*view name:* **Water-Closet**

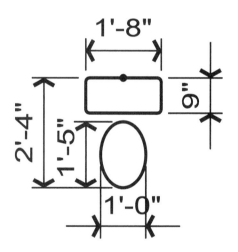

You should be able to draw this symbol without any help.

***TIP:*** *Draw a construction line from the Origin (i.e., black dot) straight down 11″ (2′-4″ – 1′-5″ = 11″). This will give you a point to pick when drawing the ellipse.*

*view name:* **Tree**

62. Draw one large circle and then copy it similar to this drawing.

63. Draw one small 1″ diameter circle at the approximate center.

64. **Save** your project.

*view name:* **Door-36**

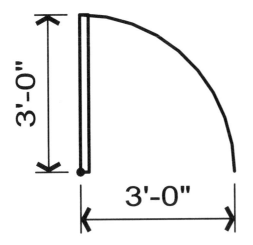

This symbol is used to show a door in a floor plan. The arc represents the path of the door as it opens and shuts.

A symbol like this, 90 degrees open, helps to avoid the door conflicting with something in the house like cabinets or a toilet. Existing doors are typically shown open 45 degrees so it is easier to visually discern new from existing.

Revit has an advanced door tool, so you would not actually draw this symbol very often. However, you may decide to draw one in plan that represents a gate in a reception counter or one in elevation to show a floor hatch. Refer back to Figure 4-1.9 for a floor plan example with door symbols.

65. Draw a **2″x3′-0″ rectangle**.

66. Draw an arc using **Center – Ends Arc**; select the three points in the order shown in Figure 4-2.16.

   *TIP: Be sure your third pick shows the cursor snapped to the horizontal plane.*

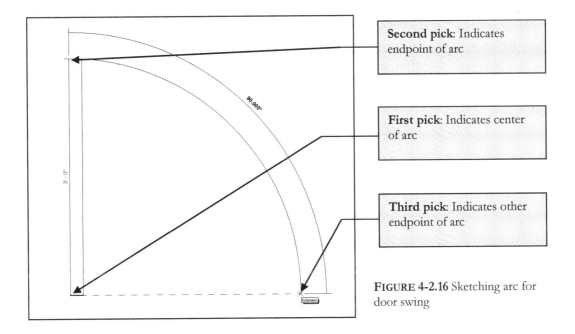

**Second pick**: Indicates endpoint of arc

**First pick**: Indicates center of arc

**Third pick**: Indicates other endpoint of arc

**FIGURE 4-2.16** Sketching arc for door swing

*view name:* **Door2-36**

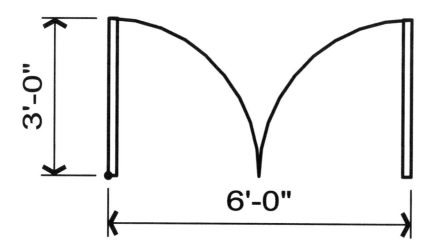

Here you will use a previous drawing and the *Mirror* tool to quickly create this drawing showing a pair of doors in a single opening.

67. Right-click on **Door-36** view label in the *Project Browser*, select "**Duplicate with detailing**" from the pop-up menu.

68. **Rename** the new *Detail View* **Door2-36**.

Next you will mirror both the rectangle and the arc. By default, Revit wants you to select a previously drawn line to be used as the "axis of reflection," but you do not have a line that would allow you to mirror the door properly to the left, so you have to pick the *"Draw Mirror Axis"* option on the *Ribbon*.

69. Select the rectangle and the arc, use a *crossing window* by picking from right to left, and then pick the **Modify | Lines → Modify → Mirror - Draw Axis** tool from the *Ribbon*.

70. Make sure **Copy** is checked on the *Options Bar*. See image to the right; this is the default.

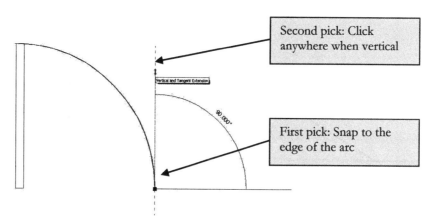

**FIGURE 4-2.17** Creating axis of reflection

Notice the *Status Bar* is prompting you to "**Pick Start Point for Axis of Reflection.**"

71. Pick the two points shown in **Figure 4-2.17**.

At this point the door symbol, the rectangle and arc, is mirrored and the *Mirror* tool is done.

72. Select *Modify* to end the command and unselect everything.

73. **Save** your project as "Ex4-2.rvt".


*view name:* **Clg-Fan-1**

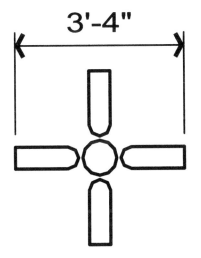

You will use the *Array* command while drawing this ceiling fan.

The *Array* command can be used to array entities in a rectangular pattern (e.g., columns on a grid) or in a polar pattern (i.e., in a circular pattern).

You will use the polar array to rotate and copy the fan blade all in one step!

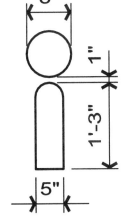

74. Start a new drawing and create the portion of drawing shown in the figure to the right.

75. Select the fan blade and then select **Array** from the *Ribbon*.

Similar to the *Rotate* tool, you will relocate the *Center of Rotation Symbol* to the center of the 8″ circle. This will cause the fan blade to array around the circle rather than the center of the first fan blade.

76. Click *Radial* on the *Options Bar* and then click and *drag* the **Rotation grip** to the center of the 8″ circle (or click the *Place* button on the *Options Bar*); make sure Revit snaps to the center point before clicking (see Figure 4-2.19).

77. Make the following changes to the *Options Bar* (Figure 4-2.18).

**FIGURE 4-2.18** Array options on the Options Bar

78. After typing the angle in the *Options Bar*, press **Enter**.

You should now see the three additional fan blades and a temporary array number. This gives you the option to change the array number if desired.

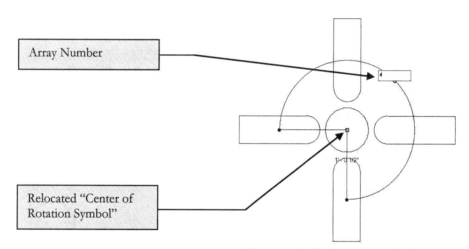

**FIGURE 4-2.19** Arraying fan blades

79. Click **Modify** to complete the *Array* and finish the ceiling fan.

Because you left *Group and Associate* checked on the *Options Bar* when you created the array, you can select any part of a fan blade and the array number will appear, like a temporary dimension, and allow you to change the number. You can select *Ungroup* from the *Ribbon* to make each item individually editable as if you had drawn everything from scratch.

80. **Save** your project.

*FYI: You can export each Drafting View to a file and import it back into any project file. It can then be placed as a symbol into floor plans. This would make for smaller files on large projects, such as a large hospital complex. The major downside is that you would not see anything in your 3D views for furniture. Thus, you will not likely use these for your Revit plans, but you will be able to utilize every skill learned in this section!*

## Self-Exam:

The following questions can be used as a way to check your knowledge of this lesson. The answers can be found at the bottom of the page.

1. Revit does not allow you to copy *Detail Views*. (T/F)

2. Entering 4 3.25 in Revit means 4'-3¼". (T/F)

3. Reference Planes (aka, construction lines) are useful drawing aids. (T/F)

4. Use the _____ tool to sketch an oval shape.

5. When you want to make a previously drawn rectangle wider you would use

   the _____ tool.

## Review Questions:

The following questions may be assigned by your instructor as a way to assess your knowledge of this section. Your instructor has the answers to the review questions.

1. Use the *Offset* option to quickly create a parallel line(s). (T/F)

2. If Revit displays an error message indicating a line is too small to be drawn, you simply zoom in more and try again. (T/F)

3. Use the _____ command to create a reverse image.

4. With the *Move* tool, lines completely within the selection window are actually only moved, not stretched. (T/F)

5. You can relocate the "center of rotation" when using *Radial Array*. (T/F)

6. Occasionally you need to draw an object and then move it into place to accurately locate it. (T/F)

7. The _____ is an option within the *Detail Line* tool which allows you to create a rounded corner where two lines intersect.

8. When using the *Mirror* tool, you occasionally need to draw a temporary line that represents the *Axis of Reflection*. (T/F)

9. Which line style was required to be selected in the *Type Selector*, in the *Properties Palette*, for all the linework in this Lesson? _____

10. In the *Detail Line* tool, how many options allow you to draw arcs? _____

SELF-EXAM ANSWERS:
**1** – F, **2** – T, **3** – T, **4** – Ellipse, **5** – Move

**Notes:**

## Lesson 5
# FLOOR PLAN (First Floor):

In this lesson you will draw the first floor plan of a single family residence. The project will be further developed in subsequent chapters. It is recommended that you spend adequate time on this lesson as later lessons build upon this one.

## Exercise 5-1:
## Project Setup

## The Project:

You will model a two-story residence located in a suburban setting. Just to the North of the building site is a medium sized lake. For the sake of simplicity, the property is virtually flat.

The main entry is from the South side of the building. You enter the building into a large foyer. The second floor has a railing that looks down onto the foyer.

This building is not meant to meet any particular building code. It is strictly a tool to learn how to use Autodesk Revit 2019. Having said that, however, there are several general comments as to how codes may impact a particular part of the design; each must be verified with your local rules and regulations.

## Creating the Project File:

A Building Information Model (BIM), as previously mentioned, consists of a single file. This file can be quite large. For example, the prestigious architectural design firm SOM used Autodesk Revit to design the Freedom Tower in New York. As you can imagine, a skyscraper would be a large BIM file, whereas a single-family residence would be much smaller.

Large databases are just starting to enter the architectural design realm. However, banks, hospitals, etc. have been using them for years, even with multiple users!

When Autodesk Revit is launched, the *Recent Files* view is loaded. Template files have several items set up and ready to use (e.g., some wall, door and window types). Starting with the correct template can save you a significant amount of time.

Autodesk Revit provides a handful of templates with particular project types in mind. They are *Commercial, Construction* and *Residential.*

In this exercise you will use the *Residential* template. It has several aspects of the project file pre-setup and ready for use. A few of these items will be discussed momentarily.

As your knowledge in Revit increases, you will be able to start refining a custom template, which probably originated from a standard template. The custom template will have things like a firm's title block and a cover sheet with abbreviations, symbols etc. all set up and ready to go.

Next you will create a new project file.

1. Select *File Tab* → *New* → *Project*.

   You are now in the *New Project* dialog box. Rather than clicking *OK*, which would use a stripped-down default architectural template, you will select *Browse* so you can select a specialized template (Figure 5-1.1).

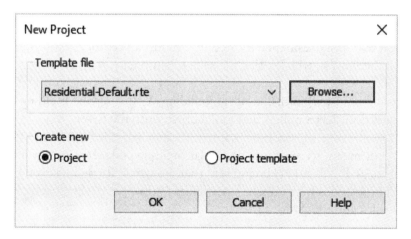

**FIGURE 5-1.1** New Project dialog

2. Click the **Browse...** button.

3. Select the template named **Residential-Default.rte** from the list of available templates (Figure 5-1.2).

4. Click **Open** to select the highlighted template file.

5. Click **OK** to complete the *New Project* dialog.

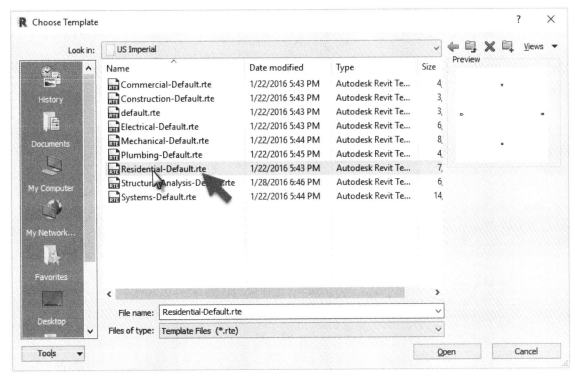

**FIGURE 5-1.2** Choose Template dialog

You have just set up a project file that you will use for the **remainder of this book**, so be sure you selected the correct template file!

Next, you will take a look at the predefined wall types that have been loaded with the template file.

6. Select **Architecture → Build → Wall**.

7. Click the *Type Selector* down-arrow on the *Properties Palette* (Figure 5-1.3). When done looking at the wall types, press the **Esc** key three times to close the *Type Selector* and cancel the command.

## Wall Types:

Notice the wall types that have been preloaded as part of the *Residential* template. These wall types are many of the types of walls one would expect to find on a typical residential construction project.

**FIGURE 5-1.3** Preloaded wall types

The walls are mostly wood stud walls, both interior and exterior. If you look at the *Default* or *Commercial* templates, you will see mostly metal stud and concrete block (CMU) wall types.

Additionally, the thicknesses of materials can vary between commercial and residential; this is also accounted for in the templates. For example, gypsum board is typically ⅝″ thick on commercial projects, whereas it is usually only ½″ on residential work.

To reiterate the concept, consider the following comparisons between a typical commercial interior wall and a typical residential interior wall.

- Typical Commercial Wall
  - ⅝″ Gypsum Board
  - 3⅝″ Metal Stud
  - ⅝″ Gypsum Board
    - Total thickness: **4⅞″**

- Typical Residential Wall
  - ½″ Gypsum Board
  - 2x4 Wood Stud (3½″ actual)
  - ½″ Gypsum Board
    - Total Thickness: **4½″**

# Project Browser:

Take a few minutes to look at the *Project Browser* and notice the views and sheets that have been set up via the template file you selected (Figure 5-1.4).

Many of the views that you need to get started with the design of a residence are set up and ready to go.

Practically all the sheets typically found on a residential project have been created; see Figure 5-1.4 under the *Sheets (all)* heading of the *Project Browser*. Also, notice the sheets with a plus symbol next to them. These are sheets that already have views placed on them. You will study this more later, but a view, such as your *East Elevation* view, is placed on a sheet at a scale you select. This means your title block sheets will have printable information as soon as you start sketching walls in one of your plan views.

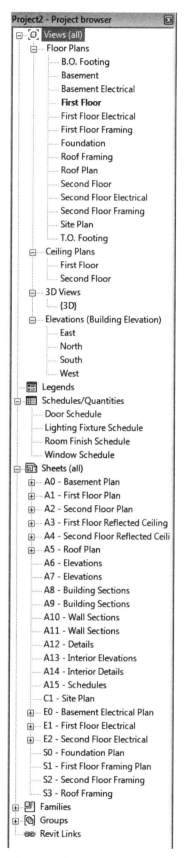

**FIGURE 5-1.4** Project Browser: various items preloaded

## Project Information:

Revit provides a dialog to enter the basic project information, such as client name, project address, etc. Next you will enter this information.

8. Select **Manage → Settings → Project Information**.

Project
Information

9. Enter the *Project Information* shown in Figure 5-1.5.

> *FYI: For now you will enter three question marks for the date.*

| | |
|---|---|
| *Project Issue Date:* | **???** |
| *Project Status:* | **Preliminary** |
| *Client Name:* | **John Brown** |
| *Project Name:* | **New Residence** |
| *Project Number:* | **2016-048** |

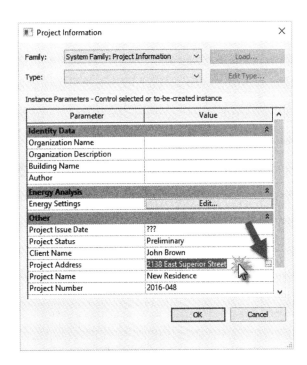

**FIGURE 5-1.5** Project Information dialog

10. Click in the field next to the *Project Address* parameter and then click the small icon that appears to the right (Figure 5-1.5).

11. Enter the project address shown in Figure 5-1.6.

> *FYI: This is the address where the house is going to be built, not the client's current address.*

*Enter:*
**2138 East Superior Street
Duluth, MN 55812**

*NOTE: You can enter any address you want to at this point; the address suggested is made up.*

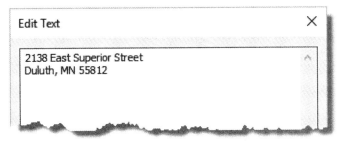

**FIGURE 5-1.6** Adding Project Address (partial view)

12. Click **OK.**

13. Click the **Edit** button next to the *Energy Settings* parameter (Figure 5-1.7).
    a. Enter/select the information shown.
    b. Notice that the address must be entered a second time here.

14. Click **OK.**

15. Click **OK** to close the *Project Information* dialog box.

**FIGURE 5-1.7** Adding Energy Data (partial view)

The project information is now saved in your Revit project database. Revit has already used some of this information to infill in a portion of your title block on each of your sheets. You will verify this next.

Note that the *Energy Data* information is mainly used by external applications or *Revit's MEP* tools to perform energy analyses like heating and cooling loads. Using Revit in conjunction with programs like *Autodesk Insight 360, Autodesk Green Building Studio, Sefaira* or *IES Virtual Environment* can help create more energy efficient buildings because you can study the design impacts on energy consumption earlier in the project when changes are still possible.

16. Under the **Sheets** heading, in the *Project Browser*, double-click on the sheet **A1 – First Floor Plan**.

17. **Zoom** in to the lower right area of the title block (Figure 5-1.8).

Notice that much of the information is automatically filled in, and this is true for every sheet!

Your project database is now set up.

18. **Save** your project as **Ex5-1.rvt.**

**FIGURE 5-1.8** Sheet A1 – First Floor Plan: Title block with Project Information added automatically

## Exercise 5-2:
## Exterior Walls

You will begin the first floor plan by drawing the exterior walls. Like many projects, early on you might not be certain what the exterior walls are going to be. So, you will start out using the generic wall styles. Then you will change them to a custom wall style, which you will create once you have decided what the wall construction is.

Often a residence is designed with a specific site in mind. However, to keep in line with most drafting and design classes, where floor plans are studied before site plans, you will develop the plans now.

## Completed Plans – For Reference:

The following two images show the floor plans as they will look when you are done with this book. You should not need to use any information from these images; they are simply meant to introduce you to the project.

First Floor:
Living Room, Kitchen, Formal Dining, Coat Closet, ½ Bath, Mud Room, Garage

Second Floor:
Master Bath & Bedroom, Two Bedrooms,
Bathroom, Linen Closet, Office

## Adjust Wall Settings:

1. Switch to *First Floor* view; select **Wall** from the *Architecture* tab.

2. Make the following changes to the wall options within the *Ribbon*, *Options Bar* and *Properties Palette* (Figure 5-2.1):
   - *Wall style:*     Basic Wall: **Generic – 8″**
   - *Height:*          **Unconnected**
   - *Height:*          **19′ 0″**
   - *Location Line:* **Finish Face; Exterior**
   - *Chain:*         **checked**

**FIGURE 5-2.1** Ribbon and Option bar – Wall command active

## Draw the Exterior Walls:

3. **Draw** the walls shown in Figure 5-2.2. Make sure your dimensions are correct. Use the *Measure* tool, on the *QAT,* to double check your dimensions. Center the building between the elevation tags (see Figure 1-2.1). Move the elevation tags as needed by selecting the square part of the tag and using the *Move* tool (do not delete them).

   *NOTE: If you draw in a clockwise fashion, your walls will have the exterior side of the wall correctly positioned. You can also use the spacebar to toggle which side the exterior face is on.*

   *TIP: In the Options Bar, while you are in the Wall tool, you can click Chain to continuously draw walls. When Chain is not selected you have to pick the same point twice: once where the wall ends and again where the next wall begins.*

**FIGURE 5-2.2** Exterior walls

# Modifying Wall Dimensions:

Now that you have the exterior walls drawn, you might decide to adjust the building size for masonry coursing if you have a concrete block foundation, or subtract square footage to reduce cost.

Editing walls in Revit is very easy. You can select a wall and edit the temporary dimensions that appear, or you can use the *Move* tool to change the position of a wall. Any walls whose endpoints touch the modified wall are also adjusted (i.e., they grow or shrink) automatically.

Next, you will adjust the dimensions of the walls just drawn. You will assume the house will have a concrete block (CMU) foundation.

4. Click the **Modify** button (not the tab) and then select the far left wall (Figure 5-2.3).

Clicking *Modify* cancels the current command and de-selects everything. Sometimes you have to press it twice to completely clear everything.

5. Select the temporary dimensions text (35′-0″) and then type **34 8** (Figure 5-2.3).

> *FYI: Remember you do not need to type the foot or inch symbol; the space distinguishes between them.*

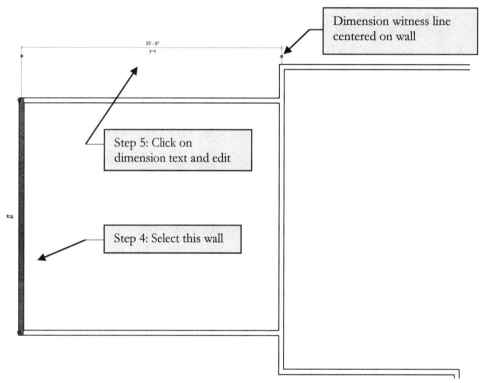

**FIGURE 5-2.3** Editing wall dimensions

> *TIP: Whenever you want to adjust the model via temporary/permanent dimensions, you need to select the object you want to move first and then select the text, or number, of the temporary or permanent dimension.*

6. In the lower right corner of the floor plan, select the wall shown in Figure 5-2.4.

7. Edit the 4′-4″ dimension to **4′-0″**.

> *TIP: Just type 4 and press Enter; Revit will assume feet when a single number is entered.*

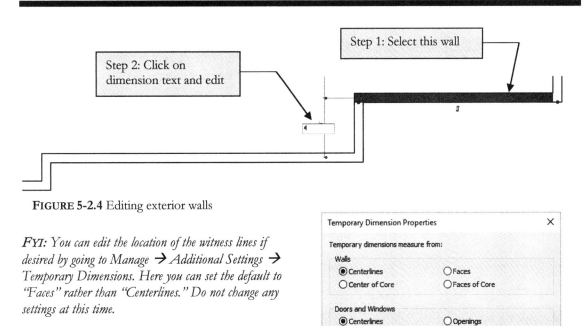

**FIGURE 5-2.4** Editing exterior walls

*FYI: You can edit the location of the witness lines if desired by going to Manage → Additional Settings → Temporary Dimensions. Here you can set the default to "Faces" rather than "Centerlines." Do not change any settings at this time.*

---

**TIP:**

Concrete blocks (or CMU) come in various widths, and most are 16″ long and 8″ high. When drawing plans, there is a simple rule to keep in mind to make sure you are designing walls to coursing. This applies to wall lengths and openings within CMU walls.

Dimension rules for CMU coursing in floor plans:
- $e'$-0″ or $e'$-8″      where $e$ is any even number (e.g., 6′-0″ or 24′-8″)
- $o'$-4″      where $o$ is any odd number (e.g., 5′-4″)

---

## Using the Align Tool with Walls:

Revit has a tool called *Align* that allows you to quickly make one element align with another. You will make the South wall of the garage align with the wall you just modified. After they are aligned, you will *Lock* the relationship so the two walls will always move together, which is great when you know you want two walls to remain aligned but might accidentally move one, maybe while zoomed in and you cannot see the other wall.

8.  Select the **Modify** (tab) → **Modify** (panel) → **Align** icon.

   *TIP:* Or just type **AL** to start the Align tool

Notice the *Status Bar* is asking you to select a reference line or point. This is the wall, or linework, that is in the correct location; the other wall(s) will be adjusted to match the reference plane.

9.  Select the exterior face of the horizontal wall you just modified: Set *Prefer* to **Wall Faces** on the *Options Bar* (Figure 5-2.5). You should notice a temporary dashed line appear on screen. This will help you to visualize the reference plane.

**FIGURE 5-2.5** Align tool: wall selected

Notice the *Status Bar* is prompting you to select an entity to align with the temporary reference plane.

10. Now, select the exterior face of the South garage wall (Figure 5-2.6).

**FIGURE 5-2.6** Align tool: select wall(s) to be aligned

Note that if you would have selected the interior face of the wall that side of the wall would have aligned with the reference plane rather than the exterior as it did. If you made a mistake, click *Undo* and try it again.

Also, notice that you have a padlock symbol showing. Clicking the padlock symbol will cause the alignment relationship to be maintained, a parametric relationship. Next you will lock the alignment relationship and experiment with a few edits to see how modifying one wall affects the other.

11. Click on the **padlock** symbol (Figure 5-2.6).

The padlock symbol is now in the locked position.

12. Click the **Modify** button to unselect the walls (or just press the **Esc** key).

13. Select the garage wall identified in Figure 5-2.6.

Next you will make a dramatic change so you can clearly see the results of that change on both locked walls.

14. Change the 4'-0" dimension to **20'-0"** (Figure 5-2.7).

Notice that both walls moved together (Figure 5-2.7). Also notice that when either wall is selected, the padlock is displayed, which helps in identifying "locked" relationships while you are editing the project. Whenever the padlock symbol is visible, you can click on it to unlock it or remove the aligned relationship.

Grip mentioned in tip below

**FIGURE 5-2.7** Wall edit: Both walls move together

Next you will make a few more wall modifications, on your own, to get the perimeter of the building to masonry coursing.

15. Modify wall locations by selecting a wall and modifying the temporary dimensions; the selected wall will move to match Figure 5-2.8; do not draw the dimensions at this time.

*TIP: Make sure you use the* Measure *tool to verify all dimensions before moving on!*

*TIP: Clicking the grip on the witness line of a Temporary Dimension causes the witness line to toggle locations on the wall (i.e., exterior face, interior face and center). You can also drag the grip to a different wall. See page 5-27 for more information on this.*

**FIGURE 5-2.8** Exterior walls with final dimensions

## Changing a Wall Type:

In the next several steps, you will learn how to change the generic walls into a more refined wall type. Basically, you select the wall(s) you want to change and then you pick a different wall type from the *Type Selector* on the *Properties Palette*. Remember, the *Ribbon*, *Options Bar* and *Properties Palette* are context sensitive, which means the wall types are only listed in the *Type Selector* when you are using the *Wall* tool or you have a wall selected.

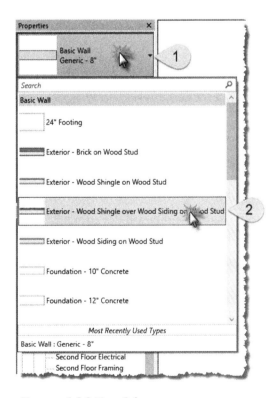

16. Select all the walls in your *First Floor* plan view.

    *TIP: You can select all the walls at once: click and drag the cursor to select a window. Later in the book you will learn about "Filter Selection" which also aids in the selection process.*

**FIGURE 5-2.9** Type Selector

17. From the *Type Selector* on the *Properties Palette*, select **Exterior – Wood Shingle over Wood Siding on Wood Stud** (Figure 5-2.9).

18. Click **Modify** to unselect the walls.

If you zoom in on the walls, you can see their graphic representation has changed a little. It would have changed a lot, of course, if you had selected a brick and CMU cavity wall. But you typically try to start with a wall closest to the one you think you will end up with, though you may never even have to change the wall type.

Even though the wall did not change much graphically in this plan view, it did change quite a bit. In a 3D view, which you will look at in a moment, the wall now has siding and trim! The image to the right is a snapshot of the 19'-0" tall wall you now have in your model.

Next, you will create a custom wall type for the walls around the garage. You will need a wall type similar to the one you just selected, but with 2x4 studs rather than 2x6s. You will start by making a copy of the existing wall type and then modify the copy.

## Create a Custom Wall Type:

As previously mentioned, Revit provides several predefined wall styles, from wood studs with gypsum board to concrete block and brick cavity walls. However, you will occasionally need a wall style that has not yet been predefined by Revit. You will study this process next.

First, you will take a close look at the predefined wall type you are using for the exterior walls.

19. Select the *Wall* tool, pick the wall type **Exterior – Wood Shingle over Wood Siding on Wood Stud** from the *Type Selector* drop-down list (Figure 5-2.9).

20. Click the **Edit Type** button on the *Properties Palette*.

21. You should be in the *Type Properties* dialog box (Figure 5-2.11).

**FIGURE 5-2.10** Edit Type button

22. Click the **Edit** button next to the *Structure* parameter (Figure 5-2.11).

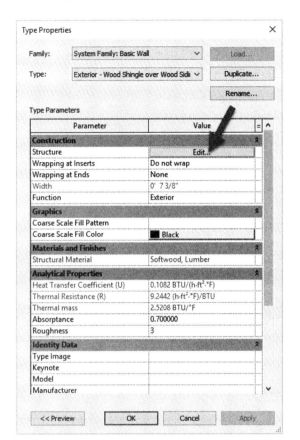

**FYI:**
Here is the difference between the two Element Properties dialogs:

Properties Palette (Instance Properties): This is information that can vary by instance (i.e., individual walls, doors, windows, etc.). For example, the height to the bottom of a window or the fire rating of a wall or door; these values can vary from instance to instance.

Type Properties: This is information that is the same for every instance of a specific type. For example, the width and height of window type "W1" should be the same for all, and the width of wall type "S6" should be the same for all. Any changes to these values changes all previously drawn, and to be drawn, objects in the model.

**FIGURE 5-2.11** Type Properties

23. Finally, you are in the *Edit Assembly* dialog box. This is where you can modify existing wall types. Click **<<Preview** to display a preview of the selected wall type (Figure 5-2.12).

Here, the *Edit Assembly* dialog box allows you to change the composition of an existing wall or to create a new wall.

Things to notice (Figure 5-2.12):

- The exterior side is labeled at the top and interior side at the bottom.

- You will see horizontal lines (i.e., *Layers*) identifying the core material. The core material can be used to place walls and dimension walls. For example, the *Wall* tool will let you draw a wall with the interior or exterior core face as the reference line. On an interior wall you might dimension to the face of stud rather than to the finished face of gypsum board; this would give the contractor the information needed for the part of the wall he will build first.

- Each row is called a *Layer*. By clicking on a *Layer* and picking the **Up** or **Down** buttons, you can reposition materials within the wall assembly.

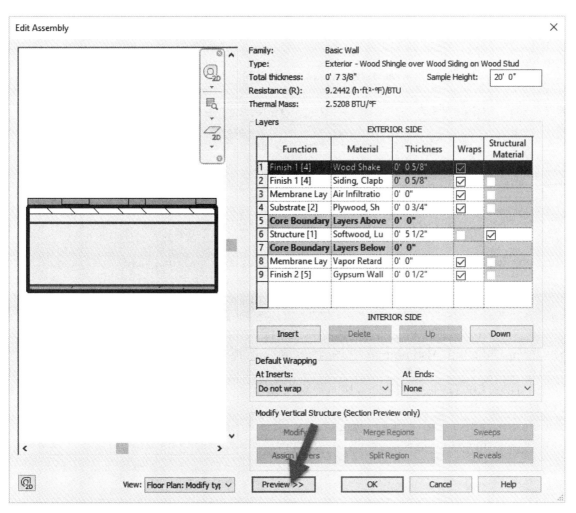

**FIGURE 5-2.12** Edit Assembly

24. Click **Cancel** to close the open dialog box.

Next, you will instruct Revit to create a new wall type which will be based on a copy of the currently selected wall type.

25. Click the **Duplicate** button (Figure 5-2.11).

26. Enter **Exterior – Wood Shingle over Wood Siding on 2x4 Wood Stud** for the new wall type name, and then click **OK** (Figure 5-2.13).

   *FYI: Notice that you have simply added "2x4" as a descriptor, making the name distinguishable from the others. Be sure to remove the "2" at the end, which was automatically added by Revit in case you did not change the name.*

**FIGURE 5-2.13** New wall type name

27. Click the **Edit** button next to the *Structure* parameter.

Next you will simply change the size of the wood stud layer and then save your changes.

28. Change the *Thickness* of the **Softwood, Lumber** *Layer* (Row 6) to **0′ 3 ½″**.

29. Your dialog should look like **Figure 5-2.14**. Notice the total wall thickness is listed near the top. Also note the *Total Thickness* and *R-Value* updated.

30. Click **OK** to close all dialog boxes.

You now have access to your newly defined wall. You can sketch new walls using the *Wall* tool or you can change existing walls to your new wall type using the *Modify* tool.

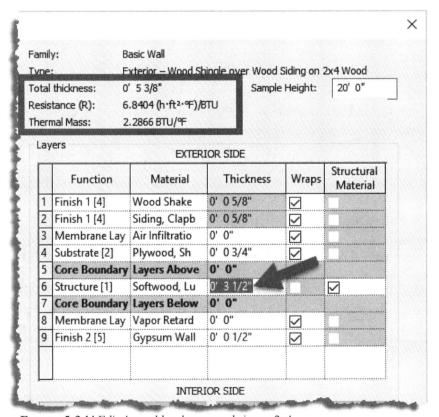

**FIGURE 5-2.14** Edit Assembly; change stud size to 2x4

The next step is to change the wall type for the three walls around the garage.

31. Select the **Modify** button from the *Ribbon*; this cancels any active commands and allows you to select elements in your model.

32. **Zoom out** so you can see the entire plan. Dragging your mouse from upper-right to lower-left, make a *crossing window* to select the three garage walls, **or** hold down **Ctrl** and click each wall.

33. With the walls selected, pick **Basic Wall: Exterior – Wood Shingle over Wood Siding on 2x4 Wood Stud** from the *Type Selector* drop-down; see tip below.

You should notice the wall thickness change; the reference line (face, center, etc.) does not move. You had *Finish Face: Exterior* selected when you drew the walls, so the exterior side of the wall does not move, which is good.

*TIP: If, after selecting all the walls, the* Type Selector *is grayed out and the contextual tab says* Multi-Select, *you have some other type of element selected, such as text or dimensions (although you have not been instructed to draw anything but walls yet) or one of the four elevation tags. Try to find those objects and delete them, but DO NOT delete the elevation tags. You can also click on the* Filter *button, located on the Ribbon when objects are selected, and uncheck the types of elements to exclude from the current selection.*

For many of the walls, Revit can display more refined linework and hatching within the wall. This is controlled by the *Detail Level* option for each view. At the moment, making this change will only reveal the exterior sheathing, but this is helpful information. You will change the *Detail Level* for the *First Floor Plan* view now.

34. Click on the **Detail Level** icon in the lower-left corner of the drawing window (Figure 5-2.15).

35. Select **Medium**.

*FYI: This view adjustment is only for the current view, as are all changes made via the* View Control Bar.

**FIGURE 5-2.15** Detail Level; set to medium

You may need to zoom in, but you should now see a line added for the exterior sheathing. If you did not pay close enough attention when drawing the walls originally, some of your walls may show the sheathing to the inside of the building.

*TIP: On the View tab you can select* Thin Lines *to temporarily turn off the line weights; this has no effect on plotting.*

36. Select **Modify** (or press **Esc**); select a wall. You will see a symbol appear that allows you to flip the wall orientation by clicking on that symbol (Figure 5-2.16).

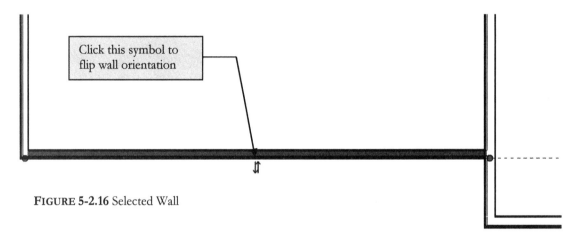

Click this symbol to flip wall orientation

**FIGURE 5-2.16** Selected Wall

37. Whether you need to adjust walls or not, click on the flip symbol to experiment with its operation.

*TIP: The flip symbol is always on the exterior side, or what Revit thinks is the exterior side, of the wall.*

38. If some walls do need to be adjusted so the sheathing and flip symbol are to the exterior, do it now. You may have to select the wall(s) and use the *Move* tool to reposition the walls to match the required dimensions.

*TIP: Walls are flipped about the Location Line, which can be changed via the Properties Palette. So changing the Location Line to Wall Centerline before flipping the wall will keep the wall in the same position. Be sure to change the Location Line back to Exterior Face.*

*TIP: You can use the MOVE tool on the Ribbon to accurately move walls. The steps are the same as in the previous chapters!*

*Follow these steps to move an element:*
- *Select the wall*
- *Click the Move icon*
- *Pick any point on the wall*
- *Start the mouse in the correct direction; do not click!*
- *Start typing the distance you want to move the wall and press Enter.*

39. You can see your progress nicely with a 3D view. Click the **Default 3D View** icon on the *QAT*. In the enlargement image, walls are shaded to make the image more clear (Figure 5-2.17).

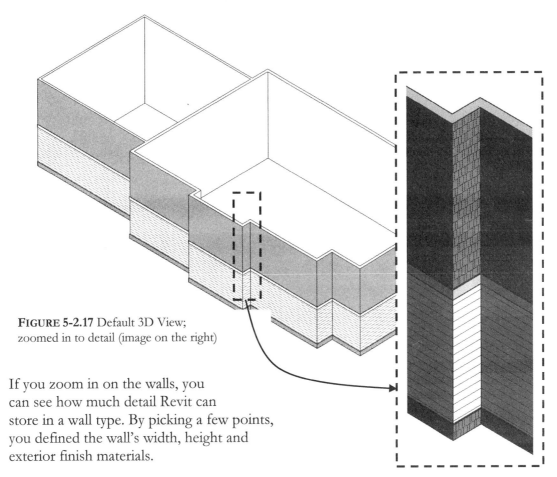

**FIGURE 5-2.17** Default 3D View; zoomed in to detail (image on the right)

If you zoom in on the walls, you can see how much detail Revit can store in a wall type. By picking a few points, you defined the wall's width, height and exterior finish materials.

The last thing you will do in this exercise is to adjust the height of the walls at the garage and a portion of the living room; refer to image on the book's cover. Revit allows you to modify the building model in any view. You will make the wall height adjustments in the current 3D View, per the following steps.

40. In the *3D View*, click to select the three exterior garage walls.

> ***TIP:*** *Holding down the Ctrl key allows you to select multiple elements, while holding down the Shift key allows for subtraction from the current selection set. The total number of selected items is listed in the lower right, on the Status Bar; make sure it says "3."*

You will notice, similar to other views, when an element is selected in a 3D view the entire object temporarily turns blue and becomes transparent. This helps to see which objects are in the current selection set when several items are selected.

You should also see the *Ribbon* has been populated with options for the selected walls, just like the plan views. You will adjust the height setting in the *Properties Palette* next.

41. In the *Properties Palette*, change the *Unconnected Height* parameter to **12'-0"** and then press **Enter**.

42. Make the same height adjustment to the three exterior walls at the Eastern most portion of the living room (Figure 5-2.18).

43. Close the *3D View* and switch back to the *First Floor Plan* view.

44. Using the **Save As** command, save your project as **ex5-2.rvt**.

**Figure 5-2.18** Completed exercise

*TIP: Holding down the Shift key while pressing the wheel button on the mouse allows you to orbit around the building. You will have to experiment with how the mouse movements relate to the building orbit. Selecting an item first causes that item to remain centered on the screen during orbit.*

## Exercise 5-3:
## Interior Walls

In this lesson you will draw the interior walls for the first floor. Using the line sketching and editing techniques you have studied in previous lessons, you should be able to draw the interior walls with minimal information.

# Overview on How Plans are Typically Dimensioned:

The following is an overview of how walls are typically dimensioned in a floor plan. This information is intended to help you understand the dimensions you will see in the exercises, as well as prepare you for the point when you dimension your plans, in a later lesson.

Wood or metal stud walls are typically dimensioned to the centers of the walls. This is one of the reasons the walls do not need to be the exact thickness. Here are a few reasons why you should dimension to the center of the stud rather than to the face of the gypsum board:

**Dimension Example**
– Two Stud Walls

o   The contractor is laying out the walls in a large "empty" area. The most useful dimension is to the center of the stud; that is where they will make a mark on the floor. If the dimension was to the face of the gypsum board, the contractor would have to stop and calculate the center of the stud, which is not always the center of the wall thickness; for example, a stud wall with one layer of gypsum board on one side and two layers of gypsum board over resilient channels on the other side of the stud.

o   When creating a continuous string of dimensions, the extra dimensions indicating the thickness of the walls would take up an excessive amount of room on the floor plans, space that would be better used by notes.

Occasionally, you should dimension to the face of a wall rather than the center; here's one example:

o   When indicating design intent or building code requirements, you should reference the exact points/surfaces. For example, if you have uncommonly large trim around a door opening, you may want a dimension from the edge of the door to the face of the adjacent wall. Another example would be the width of a hallway; if you want a particular width you would dimension between the two faces of the wall and add the text "clear" below the dimension to make it known without question that the dimension is not to the center of the wall.

Dimensions for masonry and foundation walls:

**Dimension Example**
– Two masonry Walls

o   Foundation and masonry walls are dimensioned to the nominal
     face and not the center. These types of walls are modular (e.g.,
     8″x8″x16″) so it is helpful, for both designer and builder, to
     have dimensions that relate to the masonry wall's "coursing."

Dimensions from a stud wall to a masonry wall:

o   The rules above apply for each side of the dimension line.
     For example, a dimension for the exterior foundation wall to
     an interior stud wall would be from the exterior face of the
     foundation wall to the center of the stud on the interior wall.

**Dimension Example**
– Stud to masonry

Again, you will not be dimensioning your drawings right away, but Revit
makes it easy to comply with the conventions above.

## Adjust Wall Settings:

1.   Select **Wall** from the *Architecture* tab on the *Ribbon*.

2.   Make the following changes to the wall options in the *Properties Palette* and *Options Bar*
      (similar to Figure 5-2.1):
      • Wall style: **Interior – 4 ½″ partition**
      • Height: **Second Floor** (rather than unconnected)
      • Location Line: **Wall Centerline**

Contos Residence

*Image courtesy of Anderson Architects*
*Alan H. Anderson, Architect, Duluth, MN*

## Drawing the Interior Walls:

Now that you have the perimeter drawn, you will draw a few interior walls. When drawing floor plans it is good practice to sketch out the various wall systems you think you will be using; this will help you determine what thickness to draw the walls. Drawing the walls at the correct thickness helps later when you are fine-tuning things.

Although Revit provides most of the wall types required, it is a good idea for the student to understand exactly what is being drawn.

Take a moment to think about the basic interior wall in a residential project. It typically consists of the following:

- o 2x4 wood studs
  (actual size is 1½″ x 3½″)
- o ½″ gypsum board

**FIGURE 5-3.1**
Sketch – Plan view of interior wall system

The wall system described above is shown in Figure 5-3.1.

Note: All your interior walls should be drawn **4½″** <u>for each floor</u>.

3. Draw a wall approximately as shown in Figure 5-3.2. You will adjust its exact position in the next step. *TIP: Click near the center of each exterior wall and make sure the wall is snapped to the vertical reference plane (vertical relative to the computer screen).*

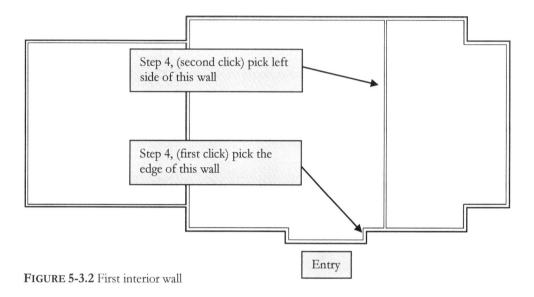

Step 4, (second click) pick left side of this wall

Step 4, (first click) pick the edge of this wall

Entry

**FIGURE 5-3.2** First interior wall

4. Use the ***Align*** tool to align the interior wall you just drew with the edge of the exterior wall (Figure 5-3.2). Set *Prefer* to *Wall Faces* on the *Options Bar*. When you are done, the wall should look like Figure 5-3.3.

*FYI: You do not need to lock this alignment.*

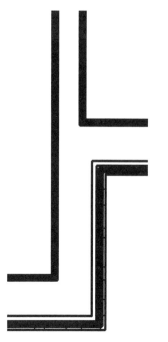

5. Create the same wall for the West side of the entry, repeating the steps above.

Next, you will draw a handful of walls per the given dimensions. You will use the same partition type (4½″ partition).

6. Draw the interior walls shown in Figure 5-3.4; see the tips below which should help you sketch the walls more accurately.

   a. All dimensions are from exterior face of exterior walls and centerline of interior walls.

**FIGURE 5-3.3** Aligned wall

**FIGURE 5-3.4** Layout dimensions for first floor interior walls

**TIP - DIMENSION WITNESS LINE CONTROL:**

When sketching walls, you can adjust the exact position of the wall after its initial placement. However, the temporary dimensions do not always reference the desired wall location (left face, right face, or center). You will see how easy it is to adjust a dimension's witness line location so you can place the wall exactly where you want it.

First, you will be introduced to some dimension terminology. The two "boxed" notes below are only for permanent dimensions, the others are for both permanent and temporary.

Next you will adjust the witness lines so you can modify the inside clear dimension, between the walls, in the above illustration.

When you select a wall you will see temporary dimensions, similar to the image on the next page.

**TIP - DIMENSION WITNESS LINE CONTROL: (CONTINUED FROM PREVIOUS PAGE)**

*NOTE: Some elements do not display temporary dimensions; in that case you can usually click the "Activate Dimensions" button on the Options Bar to see them.*

Clicking, not dragging, on the witness line grip causes the witness line to toggle between the location options (left face, right face, center). In the example below, the grip for each witness line has been clicked until both witness lines refer to the "inside" of the room.

Click the witness line grip until the witness line references the element location you prefer; repeat for the other side.

Selected Wall

In the above example, the temporary dimension could now be modified, which would adjust the location of the wall to a specific inside or clear dimension.

Not only can you adjust the witness line about a given element, you can also move the witness line to another element. This is useful because Revit's temporary dimensions, for a selected element, do not always refer to the desired element. You can relocate a witness line (temporary or permanent) by clicking and dragging the grip; see example below.

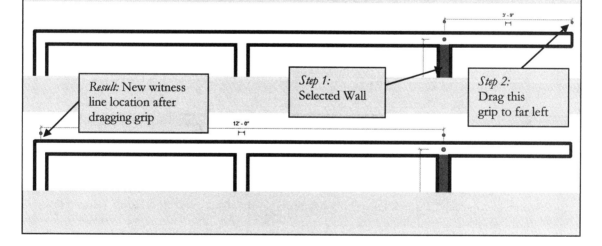

*Result:* New witness line location after dragging grip

*Step 1:*
Selected Wall

*Step 2:*
Drag this grip to far left

Next you will use the *Trim* tool to remove a portion of wall that is not needed.

7. Select **Trim** from the *Modify* tab.

8. Select the two walls identified in Figure 5-3.5.

   *FYI: The walls can be selected in either order.*

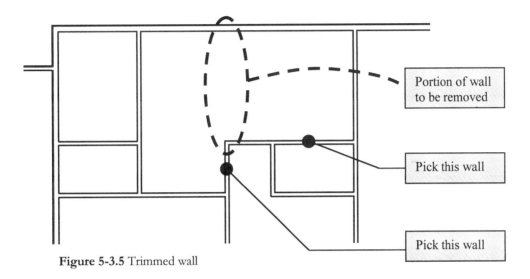

**Figure 5-3.5** Trimmed wall

## Modify an Existing Wall:

Next you want to change the portion of wall between the house and the garage. Currently, the wall is your typical exterior wall which includes siding on the garage side. The entire vertical wall is one element, so to only change the interior portion you will need to split the current wall, trim the corners and then draw a new interior wall.

9. **Zoom** in on the interior garage wall and select the **Modify → Modify → Split Element** tool.

   *FYI: This will break a wall into two; when used in plan it splits the wall vertically and when used in a section a horizontal split results.*

10. Pick somewhere in the middle of the wall (Figure 5-3.6a).

11. Use the **Trim** tool to trim the corners so the exterior wall only occurs at exterior conditions. Select **Unjoin Elements** (see "Warning Prompt" section on the next page).

   *TIP: Select the portion of wall you wish to retain (Figure 5-3.6b).*

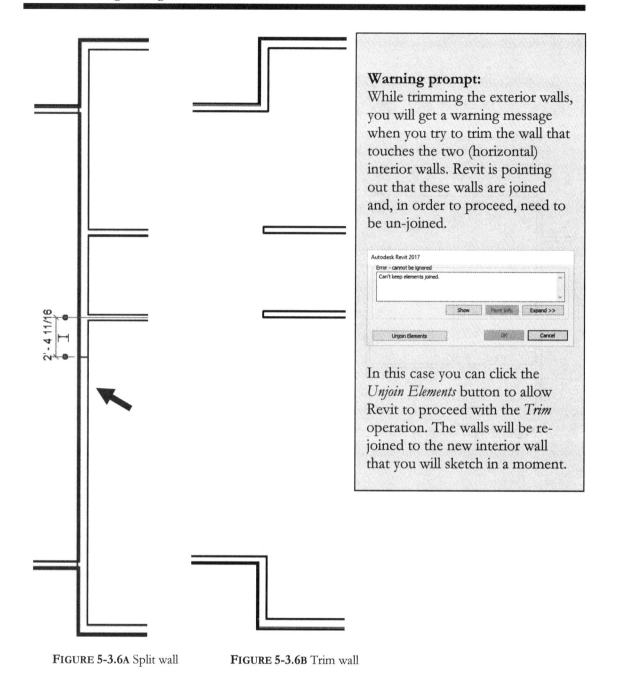

**Warning prompt:**
While trimming the exterior walls, you will get a warning message when you try to trim the wall that touches the two (horizontal) interior walls. Revit is pointing out that these walls are joined and, in order to proceed, need to be un-joined.

In this case you can click the *Unjoin Elements* button to allow Revit to proceed with the *Trim* operation. The walls will be re-joined to the new interior wall that you will sketch in a moment.

**FIGURE 5-3.6A** Split wall          **FIGURE 5-3.6B** Trim wall

## Additional Custom Wall Types:

Next, you will create a new interior partition type using a copy of the original exterior wall type as a starting point. It is easier to start with a wall that is similar to the one you wish to create.

Structurally, this wall could probably only require 2x4 studs. However, directly above this wall will be an exterior wall (the portion above the garage roof) that wants to have 2x6 studs to allow for adequate insulation. Additionally, you will want to insulate the interior garage wall; this helps with noise and heat loss when the large garage door is opened in -20 degree weather!

Truthfully, in this case it may be easier to start with a new wall, given the complexity of the exterior wall you are about to modify. However, this will give you a little more insight on how the exterior wall is constructed and the interworking of Revit's wall assembly.

12. Using wall type **Exterior – Wood Shingle over Wood Siding on Wood Stud** as a starting point, create a new wall type named **Exterior – Garage Wall (Interior)**. *(Remember to click Edit Type and then Duplicate; see page 5-15.)*

13. Click the **Edit** button next to the *Structure* parameter.

Typically you will want to give walls more generic names so they can be used elsewhere in the project. Because you know this wall will only be used once, it is easier to give it a more descriptive name so it is not confused with other wall types later.

**FIGURE 5-3.7** Edit Assembly dialog

The *Edit Assembly* dialog shown in Figure 5-3.7 will be modified in the following way. This is just an overview; the detailed instructions will follow:

- First, you will delete the horizontal sweeps.
  - A sweep is a closed 2D shape that is extruded along the length of a wall at a given height; a unique material can be specified.
  - This wall type currently has two sweeps (refer back to Figure 5-2.17): one at the base of the wall and another near the second floor line.

- Second, you will merge the two "vertically stacked" exterior finish layers so you can delete the exterior finish layers.
  - A layer can be split vertically into multiple regions; the exterior layer of this wall style is split into two regions. One has the material "Wood-Shakes" assigned to it and the other has "Finishes – Exterior – Siding / Clapboard" assigned to it.
  - Looking at Figure 5-3.7, you can visually see which layers are spilt vertically by looking at the Thickness column; the shaded "Thickness" cells are "vertically stacked" layers.
  - Vertically stacked layers must be *Merged* back into one region before they can be deleted from the layers list.

- Finally, you will change the plywood sheathing to gypsum board and move the air barrier between the gypsum board and the studs.

14. In the *Edit Assembly* dialog make sure the *Preview* pane is visible (*click on the <<Preview button*) and then select **Section: modify type attributes** from the *View* list (Figure 5-3.7).

15. Click the **Sweeps** button to load the *Wall Sweeps* dialog.

16. Delete both *Wall Sweeps*: click on the row number to select the row, and then click the **Delete** button (Figure 5-3.8). Click **OK** to close the dialog box when done.

**FIGURE 5-3.8** Wall Sweeps to be deleted

The two rectangular shaped sweeps, which represented the horizontal trim, are now removed from the preview section.

Also, notice in Figure 5-3.8, this is where the material is assigned to the sweep.

Next you will merge the two "vertically stacked" layers into one region. The tricky part here is that Revit will let you merge any two regions, so you need to keep an eye on the cursor and the pop-up tooltip.

17. Select the **Merge Regions** button.

18. Using the *scroll wheel* on the mouse, zoom in on the region split line at the top edge of the vertical dimension; you need to click in the *Preview* window to activate that area first (Figure 5-3.7).

19. Move your cursor over the short horizontal line and then tap the **Tab** key until the cursor changes to a horizontal line with an arrow pointing downward and the tooltip states that **Layer 1 and Layer 2 will be merged** (see Figure 5-3.7), and then click.

    *FYI: You can also* Pan *in the Preview pane using your scroll wheel button.*

20. Individually select the *Layer* numbers 1 and 2 to select the row, and **Delete** them. This will delete the two exterior finish layers: shakes and siding.

    *FYI: Watch the Preview pane while you do this.*

21. Click the *Air Infiltration Barrier* **Membrane Layer** (row 1) and then click the **Down** button to move the location of the air barrier within the wall.

22. Do not change the wood stud layer; leave it at 5½".

23. Change the ¾" sheathing layer by clicking in each cell in that row and then clicking the down-arrow that appears to the right; change the *Function* to **Finish 1** [4], *Material* to **Gypsum Wall Board**, *Thickness* to ½" (Figure 5-3.9).

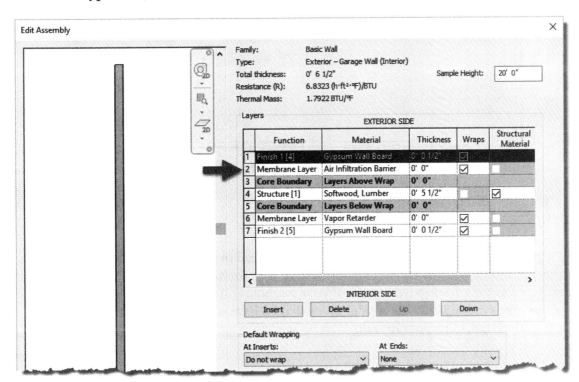

**FIGURE 5-3.9** Modified edit assembly dialog

Now that you have created a new wall type, you can sketch the wall in the first floor plan view.

24. With your new wall type selected in the *Type Selector*, use the **Wall** tool to sketch a wall between the garage and the house.

   a. Set the wall *Height* to **Second Floor**.

   b. Set the *Location Line* to **Finish Face**: **Interior** and then select the interior corner of the exterior wall.

**FIGURE 5-3.10** New interior garage wall added

It is important to remember that the "flip control" symbol is displayed on the exterior side of the wall when the wall is selected; this corresponds to the *Exterior Side* and *Interior Side* designations with the wall type editor. If your symbol is on the wrong side, click it to flip the wall and the symbol to the other side. You will then have to *Move* or *Align* the wall so it is flush with the adjacent exterior wall.

25. Save your project as **Ex5-3.rvt**.

## Exercise 5-4:
## Doors, Openings and Windows

This lesson will take a closer look at inserting doors and windows.

Now that you have sketched the walls, you will add some doors. A door symbol indicates which side the hinges are on and the direction the door opens.

New doors are typically shown open 90 degrees in floor plans, which helps to avoid conflicts such as the door hitting an adjacent base cabinet. Additionally, to make it clear graphically, existing doors are shown open only 45 degrees.

**Door symbol Example** – New Door drawn with 90 degree swing

**Door symbol Example** – Existing Door shown with 45 degree swing

One of the most powerful features of any CAD program is its ability to reuse previously drawn content. With Revit you can insert entire door systems (door, frame, trim, etc). You drew a 2D door symbol in Lesson 4; however, you will now use Revit's powerful *Door* tool which is fully 3D.

For those new to drafting, you may find this comparison between CAD and hand drafting interesting: when hand drafting, one uses straight edges or a plastic template that has doors and additional often used symbols to trace.

**Hand Drafting Template** – Plastic template with holes representing common residential shapes, at ¼″ = 1′-0″

*Image used by permission, Timely Templates*
www.timelytemplates.com

Doors in stud walls are dimensioned to the center of the door opening. On the other hand and similar to dimensioning masonry walls, doors in masonry walls are dimensioned to the face (see example below).

**Door Dimension Example** – Dimension to the center of the door opening

**Door Dimension Example** – Dimension the opening size and location

# Loading Additional Door Families:

Revit has done an excellent job providing several different door families. This makes sense seeing as doors are an important part of an architectural project. Some of the provided families include bi-fold, double, pocket, sectional (garage), and vertical rolling to name a few.

The default template you started with *(Residential-Default.rte)* only provides four door *families*; each family contains multiple door sizes. If you want to insert other styles, you will need to load additional *families* from the library. The reason for this step is that, when you load a family, Revit actually copies the data into your project file. If every possible family was loaded into your project at the beginning, not only would it be hard to find what you want in a large list of doors, but also the project file would be several megabytes in size before you even drew the first wall.

You will begin this section by loading a few additional families into your project.

1.  Open project ex5-3.rvt and **Save-As ex5-4.rvt**.

2.  With the *Door* tool selected, select **Load Family** on the *Ribbon* (Figure 5-4.1).

Load Family

3.  Browse through the ***Doors\Residential*** folder for a moment. The *Doors* folder is a sub-folder of the *US Imperial* library; Revit should have taken you there by default; if not, you can browse to C:\ProgramData\Autodesk\RVT 2019\Libraries\US Imperial\Doors.

**FIGURE 5-4.1** Load content from Library

Each file represents a *family*, each having one or more *Types* of varying sizes (Figure 5-4.2).

**FIGURE 5-4.2** Door families on hard drive

4.  Click **Cancel** to close the *Load Family* dialog.

# Load Content Provided with this Book:

Next you will load some content provided with this book. See the inside front cover of this book for instructions on how to access this content.

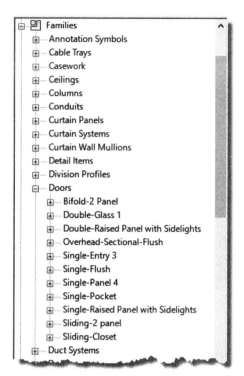

5.  Load the following families provided with this book:
    a. **Bifold-2 Panel**
    b. **Single-Panel 4**
    c. **Sliding-2 panel**
    d. **Double-Raised Panel with Sidelights**
    e. **Single-Entry 3**
    f. **Single-Pocket**
    g. **Opening-Elliptical Arch**
    h. **Overhead-Sectional-Flush**

6.  In the *Project Browser*, expand the *Families* category and then *Doors* to see the loaded door families (Figure 5-4.3).

**FIGURE 5-4.3** Loaded door families

If you expand the *Doors* families in the *Project Browser* you see the predefined door sizes (i.e., Family Types) associated with that family. Right-clicking on a door size allows you to rename, delete or duplicate it. To add a door size, you duplicate and then modify properties for the new item, similar to how you created a new wall. Note that the *Opening-Elliptical Arch* does not display here; it actually shows up under *Generic Model*.

You may want to create a folder where you save all the families you download. This would make future access more convenient, especially if you did not have internet access at that time. This folder should probably not be in Revit's standard folder location as it may be difficult to migrate the data after an upgrade (i.e., sorting the custom files from the default files).

Revit content can be found at various locations on the internet. You can try an internet search with text that reads something like *"autodesk revit families."* As Revit's popularity grows, more and more product manufacturers are starting to make families available that represent their products, thus making it easier for designers to incorporate those products into a project. For example, one can also download an extensive wall and ceiling library from United States Gypsum (USG) at www.usgdesignstudio.com. Additionally, you can visit www.augi.com (Autodesk Users Group International), or www.revitcity.com for Revit related resources and content.

Next you will start inserting the doors into the first floor plan.

7.  With the *Door* tool selected, pick **Single-Entry 3: 36″ x 80″** from the *Type Selector* on the *Properties Palette*.

8. Select **Tag on Placement** on the *Ribbon* to toggle it on if needed (it is on when highlighted with blue as shown in Fig. 5-4.1), and then place one door in the North wall of the garage as shown in Figure 5-4.4.

Immediately after the door is inserted, or when the door is selected, you can click on the horizontal or vertical flip-controls to position the door as desired.

Since "Tag on placement" was selected on the *Ribbon*, Revit automatically adds a *Door Tag* near the newly inserted door. The door itself stores information about the door that can then be compiled in a door schedule. The doors are automatically numbered in the order they are placed. The number can be changed at any time to suit the designer's needs; you will do this later in the door schedule section. Most architects and designers use 1x or 1xx (i.e., 12 or 120) numbers for the first floor and 2x or 2xx numbers for the second floor door numbers.

The *Door Tag* can be moved simply by clicking on it to select it, and then clicking and dragging it to its new location. You may need to press the *Tab* key to pre-highlight the tag before you can select it.

Also, with the *Door Tag* selected you can set the vertical/horizontal orientation and whether a leader should be displayed when the tag is moved; it is done via the settings on the *Options Bar*. The tag must be selected.

**FIGURE 5-4.4** First door placed at rear of garage

9. Click *Modify* and then select the newly placed door; take a moment to review the information displayed in the *Properties Palette*.

   ***TIP:*** *If the Properties Palette is not visible, simply type "pp" on the keyboard; do not press Enter.*

Notice, in Figure 5-4.5, you see the *Instance Parameters* which are options that vary with each door, e.g., *Sill Height* and *Door Number (Mark)*. These parameters control selected or to-be-created items.

The *Type Parameters* are not visible in this dialog. To be sure you want to make changes that affect all doors of that type, Revit forces you to click the *Edit Type* button and make changes in the *Type Properties* dialog. Also, in the *Type Properties* dialog, you can add additional pre-defined door sizes to the *"Single-Entry 3"* door family by clicking the *Duplicate* button, providing a new name and changing the "size" dimensions for that new *Type*.

**FIGURE 5-4.5**
Properties for door

10. Finish inserting doors for the first floor (Figure 5-4.6). Use the following guidelines:

    a.  Use the door styles shown in Figure 5-4.6.

    b.  Doors across from each other in the *Mud Room* should align with each other.

    c.  Place doors approximately as shown; exact location is not important.

    d.  See the next page for information on sliding pocket doors.

    e.  While inserting doors, you can control the door swing by moving the cursor to one side of the wall or the other and by using the spacebar on the keyboard.

    f.  The order in which the doors are placed does not matter; this means your doors may have different numbers than the ones shown below.

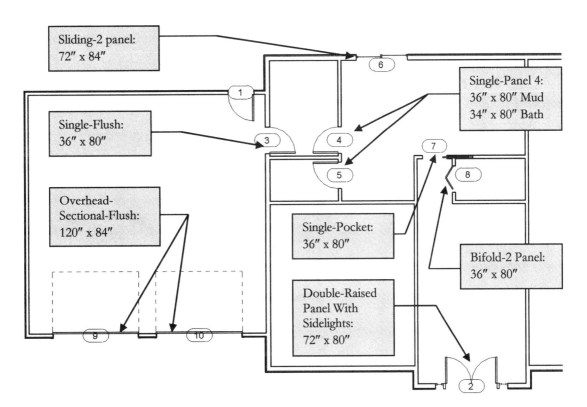

**FIGURE 5-4.6** Doors to be inserted

## Sliding Pocket Doors:

Sliding pocket doors are doors that slide into the wall rather than swinging open into a room. This type of door is convenient when the door will be open most of the time and you do not want, or have room for, an open door. On the other hand, if the door will be used often, like the door from the hallway into the bathroom, you should use a swinging door for ease of use and long-term durability.

One important thing to keep in mind when designing a room with a sliding door: the entire width of the door is in the wall when the door is fully open. That means you need space in the wall next to the door that equals the width of the door plus a few inches depending on the manufacturer. This includes plumbing and electrical that might be in the wall.

ROUGH OPENING
IN WIDTH IS 2 TIMES
THE DOOR SIZE
PLUS 2" (50.8mm).
R.O. IN HEIGHT IS
4" (101.6 mm) MORE
THAN DOOR HEIGHT.

ROUGH OPENING     FRAME INSTALLED IN ROUGH OPENING.     FRAME AND DOOR INSTALLED. READY FOR DRYWALL.

**POCKET DOOR EXAMPLES –** Double door and Single door photos (top); Installation illustration (bottom)

*Images used by permission, KrisTrack* www.kristrack.com

# Insert Openings:

With the first floor doors in place, you will add three openings. An opening is similar to a door in that, when placed, it removes a portion of wall automatically creating a circulation route. Also, like doors, openings come in different predefined shapes and sizes.

One common mistake is to break a wall so the floor plan appears to have an opening. However, when a section is cut through the opening there is no wall above the opening. This is also problematic for the room tagging feature and the *Ceiling Placement* tool.

One of the keys to working successfully in Revit is to model the building project just like you would build it because that is the way Revit is designed to work.

Next, you will place two larger openings in the walls between the *Foyer* and the *Living Room* and the *Dining Room*. A smaller opening will be placed in the wall between the *Dining Room* and the *Kitchen*. All three openings are from a family you previously loaded: *Opening-Elliptical Arch*.

The *Type Properties* dialog is shown below (Figure 5-4.7). Notice the various fields that can be filled in. For example, you could enter how much it would cost to construct an opening with an arched top in the *Cost* field.

**FIGURE 5-4.7** Type Properties for *Passage-Elliptical Arch* family.
*Note:* If downloaded from the web, this family is named *Opening-Elliptical Arch*

11. Select **Architecture → Build → Component**; just click the upper part of the icon which defaults to the *Place a Component* option, seen via down-arrow selection.

Component

12. Place the three **openings** as shown in Figure 5-4.8.

> *TIP: Select the appropriate opening (family/type) from the Type Selector on the Properties Palette.*

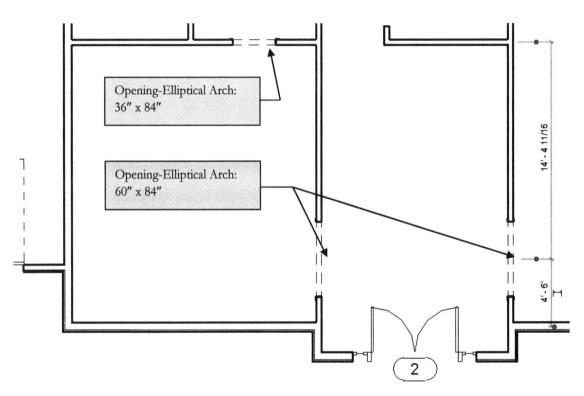

**FIGURE 5-4.8** Openings placed in first floor plan

# Insert Windows:

Adding windows to your project is very similar to adding doors. The template file you started from has three families preloaded into your project: <u>Window-Casement-Double</u>, <u>Window-Double-Hung</u> and <u>Fixed with Trim</u>. Looking at the *Type Selector* drop-down you will see the various sizes available for insertion. Additional families can be loaded, similar to how you loaded the doors. In this book, you will use the <u>Fixed with Trim</u> window and one provided with this book called <u>Double Hung with Trim</u>.

13. Similar to the steps just completed for the doors, download the window family **Double Hung with Trim** and load it into your project.

14. Click the ***Window*** button on the *Architecture* tab, select **Double Hung with Trim: 36″ x 72″** in the *Type Selector* and make sure **Tag on Placement** is on, via the *Ribbon*.

15. Insert 9 windows as shown in **Figure 5-4.9**; be sure to adjust the window locations to match the dimensions shown, but do not add the dimensions. Be sure to click towards the exterior side of the wall, so the window has the proper orientation.

   *TIP: To edit location: Modify → select window → adjust temporary dimension witness lines → edit temporary dimension text.*

**FIGURE 5-4.9** (9) windows added: Double Hung with Trim: 36″ x 72″

With a window *Type*, within a family, not only is the window size pre-defined, but the vertical distance off the ground is as well. Next you will see where this setting is stored.

16. Select one of the windows that you just placed in the walls and then notice the information presented in the *Properties Palette.*

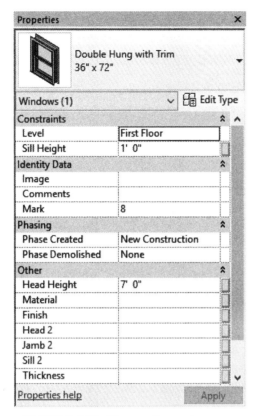

**FIGURE 5-4.10a** Element Properties

As previously discussed, this palette shows the various settings for the selected item: a window in this case (Figure 5-4.10).

As you might guess, the same size window could have more than one sill height (i.e., distance from the floor to the bottom of the window). So Revit lets you adjust this setting on a window-by-window basis; this is called an *Instance Parameter*.

Another setting you might have noticed by now is *Phase Created*. This is part of what makes Revit a 4D program; the fourth dimension is time. Again, you might have several windows that are existing and several new ones in an addition, all the same size window. Revit lets you do that!

**FIGURE 5-4.10b** Window selected

Notice a Flip Control icon is shown when the window is selected, similar to doors. This icon should be on the exterior side of the wall. If not, simply click on the icon to flip the window's orientation within the wall.

17. Make sure the *Sill Height* is **1′-0″** and the **Flip Control** icon is on the exterior side of the wall; if not, change all nine windows.

Next, you will insert several double hung windows that are not as tall in the less prominent rooms, also in the *Kitchen* so cabinets will fit below the window. However, if you did place the tall windows in the *Kitchen*, you would realize it as soon as you tried to place the base cabinets and generate interior elevations or sections in the *Kitchen*. This is because the entire Revit project is one 3D database.

Compare the above mentioned conflict with traditional CAD, where the 2D elevations have nothing to do with the floor plans, sections, or interior elevations. With traditional CAD, you could draw the exterior elevations with the tall windows and place cabinets under it in plan view and then draw an interior elevation showing the cabinets and a shorter window. The windows are usually ordered and rough openings framed based on the exterior elevations. Revit helps to avoid these types of costly mistakes.

18. Insert window **Double Hung with Trim: 36″ x 48″** as shown in **Figure 5-4.11**; use *Instance Properties* to make sure the *Sill Height* is set to **3′-0″**; place 9 windows total.

**FIGURE 5-4.11** (9) windows added: Double Hung with Trim: 36″ x 48″

# Creating a New Window Type:

You will add four more windows to the East wall. These will be high windows, two on either side of a fireplace. Rather than using one of the predefined window sizes, you will create a new size within an existing family.

These windows will be fixed, non-operable, so you will be adding a new type to the *Fixed with Trim* family.

19. Select the **Window** tool and then select the **Edit Type** button on the *Properties Palette*.

20. Set the *Family* drop-down to **Fixed with Trim** and then set the *Type* drop-down to **36″ x 24″** (Figure 5-4.12). **Do not select the Double Hung window!**

   *FYI: You could have selected this in the* Type Selector *before clicking the* Edit Type *button.*

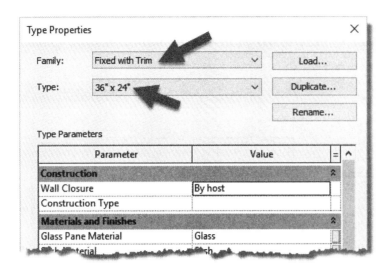

**FIGURE 5-4.12** Type Properties – *Family*: Fixed with Trim; *Type*: 36" x 24"

21. Click the **Duplicate** button.

22. Enter **36" x 20"** for the name and then click **OK**.

You are now viewing the *Type Properties* for the new 36" x 20" type you just created. However, the name has nothing to do with actually changing the window size. You will do this next.

23. Change the *Height* parameter to **1'-8"** (Figure 5-4.13).

24. Change the *Default Sill Height* to **5'-4"**. *(This makes the top of all your windows align at 7'-0".)*

25. Click **OK** to close the *Type Properties* dialog.

26. Add the windows as dimensioned in Figure 5-4.14.

   a. Before placing the first window, make sure the *Sill Height* is set to **5'-4"** in the *Properties Palette*.

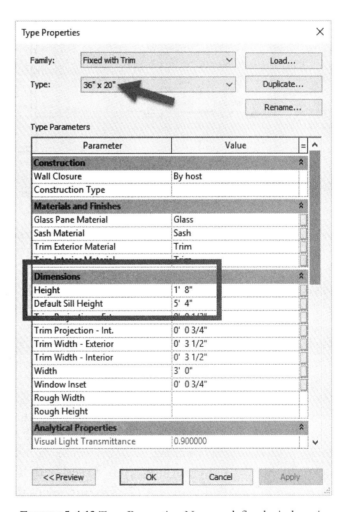

**FIGURE 5-4.13** Type Properties: New predefined window size

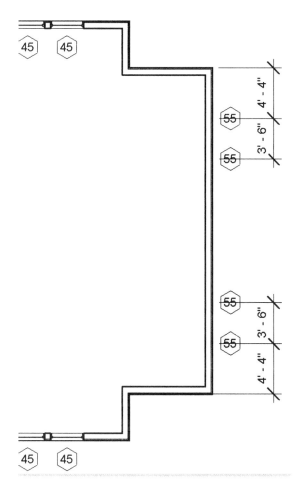

You are probably wondering where the windows are? They are tagged and you can select them. However, they are not visible.

With your project being a 3D model, Revit has to cut through the model at a certain elevation when generating the plan view. The default *Cut Plane* is 4'-0" above the floor line.

As you should recall, the sill of the new window type you just created is 5'-4" (Figure 5-4.13). If it is not, you should select the 36"x20" windows and adjust the sill height in the *Properties Palette*, so the window occurs above the cut line.

The windows will show up just fine in elevation and section views. Next you will see where the *Cut Plane* is set for each plan view.

***POWER TIP:*** *If you want the windows to be visible, or a high stair landing to show, you can create a* Plan Region*, which allows you to override the cut plane within the selected area. See Help for more on this.*

**FIGURE 5-4.14**
First floor plan: last four windows added

27. Click the ***Modify*** tool on the *Ribbon* to unselect elements and cancel any active commands. This will cause the *Properties Palette* to show information about the current view.

28. Scroll down, in the *Properties Palette*, and select **Edit** next to *View Range*.

Notice the *Cut Plane* is set to 4'-0" (Figure 5-4.15). Try changing it and closing the dialog to see the various effects it has on your *Floor Plan* view; also look at the high windows.

**Be sure to set the *Cut Plane* back to 4'-0" before proceeding.**

29. Click **OK** to close the *View Range* dialog box.

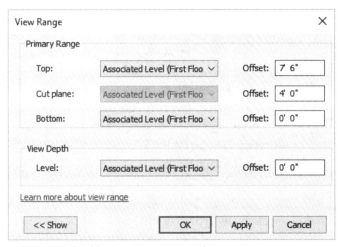

**FIGURE 5-4.15** View Range properties

## Cleaning House:

As previously mentioned, you can view the various *Families* and *Types* loaded into your project via the *Project Browser*. The more families and types you have loaded the larger your file is, whether or not you are using them in your project. Therefore, it is a good idea to get rid of any door, window, etc., that you know you will not need in the current project. You do not have to delete any at this time, but this is how you do it:

**Figure:** Project Browser

- In the *Project Browser*, navigate to Families → Windows → Fixed with Trim. Right-click on **36″ x 48″** and select **Delete**.

Another reason to delete types is to avoid mistakes. As you have seen, loading a door family brings in 6′-8″ and 7′-0″ tall doors. On a residential project you would rarely use 7′-0″ tall doors, so it would be a good idea to delete them from the project so you don't accidentally pick them.

That concludes the exercise on adding doors, openings and windows to the first floor plan.

## Exercise 5-5:
## Adding a Fireplace

The last thing you will do in this lesson is to add a fireplace to the *Living Room*. Creating a fireplace family is beyond the scope of this introductory book, so you will use one provided with this book.

1. Using techniques previously described to download doors from SDC Publications, download the following items (Figure 5-5.1):
   a. **Mantel 1**
   b. **Masonry Chimney-Wall**

Mantel 1          Masonry Chimney-Wall

**FIGURE 5-5.1** Mantel and Chimney to be used

2. **Load** the downloaded families into your project (see page 5-41).

You are now ready to place the fireplace in the first floor plan.

3. With the *First Floor Plan* view current, select **Architecture → Build → Component** from the *Ribbon*.

4. From the *Type Selector*, pick **Masonry Chimney-Wall : Chimney**.

The chimney will be looking for a wall to be inserted into; this is a *wall hosted family*. When your cursor is near a wall, you will see a "ghost" chimney to help you visually place the element; when the cursor is not near a wall, Revit does not display the "ghost" image because it is not a valid location to place the selected element.

Try moving the cursor around the plan for a minute. Notice, again, that when the cursor is near a wall you see the "ghost" image and the image orients itself with the wall (e.g., vert., horiz., angled). When the element encounters another element placed within a wall, you will see a small circle with a diagonal line through it indicating the two elements cannot overlap. Furthermore, the element flips to the side of the wall the cursor is on. Try moving the cursor from one side of the wall to the other and observe the image flip back and forth.

5. Move your cursor to the middle portion of the easternmost wall, between the high windows; with your cursor on the exterior side of the wall, click to place the fireplace.

6. Adjust the temporary dimensions so the chimney is centered on the wall (Figure 5-5.2).

Next you will place the mantel in the plan view. This is less automatic as it does not attach to the wall, so you will insert the mantel in the middle of the living room, rotate it and then move it into place.

**FIGURE 5-5.2** Chimney added

7. Use the **Component** tool to insert **Mantel 1:80″ x 58¾″** into the middle of the *Living Room*.

8. Select the *Mantel* and use the ***Rotate*** tool to rotate the mantel 90 degrees in the clockwise direction.

*TIP: You could have also pressed the spacebar during placement in step 7 and then skipped step 8.*

**FIGURE 5-5.3** 3D view of mantel

9. With the *Mantel* still selected, use the **arrow keys** on your keyboard to "nudge" the element into place, or try using the *Align* tool (Figure 5-5.4).

10. Take a minute to look at the *3D View* of all that you have completed so far (Figure 5-5.5).

11. **Save** your project as **Ex5-5.rvt**.

**FIGURE 5-5.4** Mantel added in plan view

**FIGURE 5-5.5** 3D View of completed chapter

## Self-Exam:

The following questions can be used as a way to check your knowledge of this lesson. The answers can be found at the bottom of the page.

1.  The *Options Bar* allows you to select the height at which your wall will be drawn. (T/F)

2.  It is not possible to draw a wall with the interior or exterior face of the core as the reference point. (T/F)

3.  Objects cannot be moved accurately with the *Move* tool. (T/F)

4.  The _____ tool, on the *Ribbon*, has to be selected in order to select an object in your project.

5.  A wall has to be _____ to see its flip icon.

## Review Questions:

The following questions may be assigned by your instructor as a way to assess your knowledge of this section. Your instructor has the answers to the review questions.

1.  Revit comes with many predefined doors and windows. (T/F)

2.  The *Project Information* dialog allows you to enter data about the project, some of which is automatically added to sheet borders. (T/F)

3.  You can delete *families* and *types* in the *Project Browser*. (T/F)

4.  It is not possible to add a new window *type* to a window *family*. (T/F)

5.  It is not possible to select which side of the wall a window should be on while you are inserting the window. (T/F)

6.  What tool will break a wall into two smaller pieces? _____

7.  The _____ tool allows you to match the surface of two adjacent walls.

8.  Use the _____ key, on the keyboard, to flip the door swing while placing doors using the *Door* tool.

9.  You adjust the location of a dimension's witness line by clicking on, or dragging, its _____.

10. The _____ file has a few doors, windows and walls preloaded in it.

## Lesson 6
# FLOOR PLANS (Second Floor and Basement Plans):

In this lesson you will develop the second floor plan as well as the basement. This will involve copying objects from the first floor with some modifications along the way. You will also add stairs and dimensions to your plans.

## View Setup and Enclosing the Shell

## Discussion: Second Floor View Current Conditions

1. Open **Ex5-5.rvt** and switch to the **Second Floor** view under *Floor Plans* in the *Project Browser*; double-click on the view name.

You should see a plan view similar to Figure 6-1.1. The geometry you are seeing is a result of two things:

- First, the height of walls drawn on the first floor:
    - i. Some of the exterior walls that you sketched in the first floor plan are 19'-0" tall.
    - ii. From the elevation views, you can see that the second floor is 9'-0" above the first.
    - iii. As you may recall from the last chapter, the default *View Range* – Cut Line is 4'-0" above the floor.
    - iv. So, relative to the first floor, the second floor Cut Plane is 13'-0" above it (9'-0" + 4'-0").
    - v. Therefore, the 19'-0" tall walls extend past the second floor Cut Plane; that is why they are bold (elements in section automatically have a heavier line weight).
    - vi. The exterior walls of the garage and east living room walls are only 12'-0", which is below the Cut Plane. It is still within the *View Range* so it shows up in "elevation" or projection. Elements in *projection* (i.e., beyond the Cut Plane) have lighter lines than those in section (i.e., at the Cut Plane).

- Second, the *Underlay* feature:
    - i. In the *Properties Palette* (View Properties) for the *Second Floor Plan* view, you will see a parameter labeled *Underlay* (Figure 6-1.2).
    - ii. This feature is currently set to *First Floor*.
    - iii. The *Underlay* feature causes the selected view's walls to be displayed as light gray lines for reference.

iv. The walls shown as part of an underlay cannot be selected using a *window* selection but can be selected, and even deleted, by picking directly on a wall or anything else.

**FIGURE 6-1.1** Second Floor: initial view

You do not need to see the first floor walls at the moment, so you will turn them off.

2. In the *Properties Palette* dialog set (Underlay) **Range: Base Level** to **none**. *(Click Modify first if the View Properties are not currently shown.)*

Now you should only see the exterior walls (Figure 6-1.3).

Next, you will sketch two more exterior walls to enclose the second floor. These walls only occur above the second floor line so they will only have wood shakes for siding.

**FIGURE 6-1.2** View Properties: Second Floor view

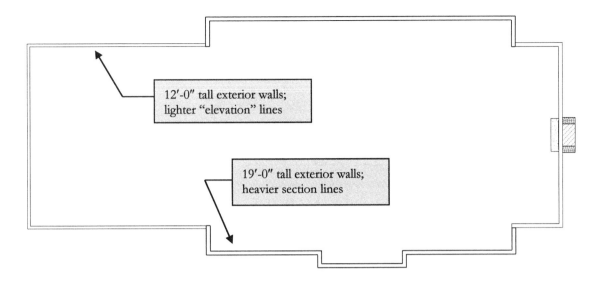

**FIGURE 6-1.3** Second Floor: underlay turned off

3. Using the *Wall* tool, select **Exterior – Wood Shingle on Wood Stud** from the *Type Selector.*

If you look at the properties for this wall you will see that it is very similar to your primary exterior wall assembly. The main difference is that the vertical elements are stripped away: horizontal siding and two sweeps. You will see another wall type with just horizontal siding as well. These two walls are loaded in the template for the reason you are about to use one: as infill between the main, more complex, wall type. The image to the right shows, from left to right, horizontal siding only, shakes only and then the main wall you have previously used.

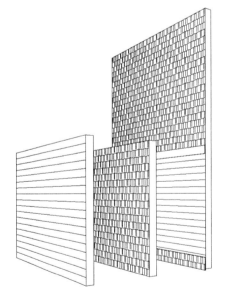

If you tried to use the wall type "Basic Wall: Exterior – Wood Shingle over Wood Siding on Wood Stud," the horizontal wood siding would start at the second floor line for any wall placed on the second floor. This is why you need a wall that just has wood shingles and no sweeps (i.e., horizontal trim boards).

4. Draw the two walls as shown in Figure 6-1.4, using the following information:
   - Set the *Height* to **Roof** (*Options Bar*).
   - Set the *Location Line* to **Finished Face: Interior** (*Options Bar*).
   - Pick the interior side of the existing wall; press the *spacebar* if you need to flip the wall before picking the wall end point.

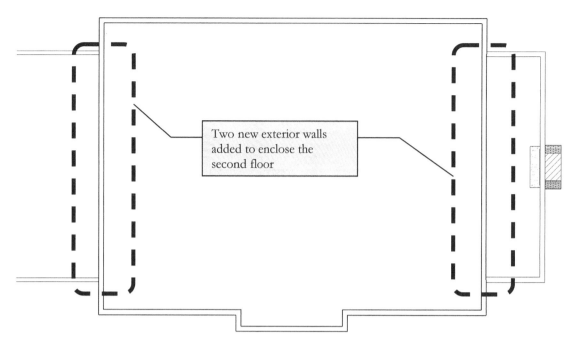

**FIGURE 6-1.4** Second Floor: two exterior walls added

The height of the walls will change later when the roof is drawn. In fact, the height will vary as it extends up to the underside of the gable end roof; see image on the book cover.

The two walls just drawn will be supported by the second floor, which has not been drawn yet. The bottom of the walls is aligned with *Level 2* because of the view you are in.

You may have noticed that the exterior face of the wall does not appear to align perfectly with the adjacent walls. You will explore this problem and correct it in the next steps.

5.  Select one of the walls just placed.

6.  Click the **Edit Type** button on the *Properties Palette*.

7.  In the *Type Properties* dialog, click **Edit** next to the ***Structure*** parameter.

8.  Take note of the overall wall thickness and the thickness of the various layers (Figure 6-1.5A).

9.  Close the dialog boxes, *Edit Assembly* and *Type Properties*, by clicking **OK**.

10. Follow the previous steps to look at the structure properties for the **Exterior – Wood Shingle over Wood Siding on Wood Stud**.

    *NOTE: The sheathing thickness is not the same (Figures 6-1.5a and b). You will change one so they both match.*

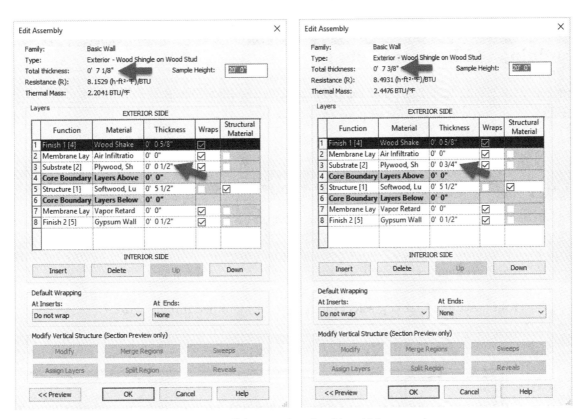

**FIGURE 6-1.5A & B** Comparing two walls' properties; sheathing thickness varies

11. Modify the *Sheathing* from ½″ to ¾″ for *Exterior – Wood Shingle on Wood Stud*.

12. **Save** your project as **Ex6-1.rvt**.

---

**FYI:**
Just as a reminder: the four elevation tags should not be deleted. You will study these more thoroughly later. This is what they represent:

The default template has four elevation tags shown in plan view. These symbols represent what the four preset views listed in the *Project Browser* will see. Therefore, you should always start drawing your plan in the approximate center of the four symbols. The symbols can be moved by dragging them with your mouse.

Again, do not delete these elevation tags as that will delete the actual views from the *Project Browser*.

Any view (e.g., plan, elevation or section) can be recreated, but all the notes and dimensions, which are view specific, would have to be manually recreated.

## Exercise 6-2:
## Adding the Interior Walls

This short exercise will help reinforce the commands you have already learned. You will add walls, doors and windows to your project.

## Copying Walls From the First Floor:

Often, you will have walls occur in the same location on each floor. The easiest thing to do is copy/paste between floors. You will try this now.

1. Switch to the *First Floor Plan* view.

2. Hold down the **Ctrl** key; select the four walls identified in Figure 6-2.1.

**FIGURE 6-2.1** First Floor: Selected walls, (4) total, to be copied/pasted to the Second Floor

3. With the four walls selected, select **Modify | Walls → Clipboard → Copy**; this command is different than *Copy* in the *Modify* panel which only works in the current view.

4. Click **Modify** to unselect the first floor walls and then switch back to the ***Second Floor Plan*** view.

   *TIP: Press Ctrl + Tab to switch between open views.*

5. Select **Modify → Clipboard → Paste → Aligned to Current View** (Figure 6-2.2).

You should now see the four walls in your *Second Floor Plan* view (Figure 6-2.3).

**FIGURE 6-2.2**
Modify tab: Paste Aligned fly-out

**Why did we not just draw these four first floor walls 19′-0″ high like the exterior walls?**

Simulating real-world construction is ideal for several reasons. Mostly, you can be sure exterior walls align from floor to floor. Although the four walls align, they do not necessarily have to because they are separated by floor construction; this allows one floor to later be modified easily. However, if an exterior wall is moved in any plan view, you want to make sure it moves everywhere, so these walls are drawn full height.

6. Select **Modify** to deselect the walls via the *Ribbon*.

Any time a wall is copied, or copy/pasted, any hosted elements attached to the wall(s) are copied with the wall. Next, you will delete the openings that were copied with the walls from the first floor.

7. Individually select each of the four openings and delete them.

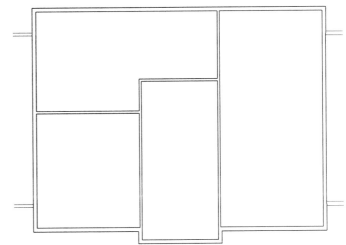

**FIGURE 6-2.3** Second Floor: walls copied, doors deleted

Your first floor walls have their *top constraint* set to the second floor, so when you copied the walls from the first floor to the second floor Autodesk® Revit® Architecture automatically sets the *top constraint* to the next level above the first floor: the *Roof* level. This is fine for now.

Next you will add a few more interior walls.

8. Using the **Wall** tool, draw the walls shown in Figure 6-2.4 using the following information:
   a. Wall type: **Interior – 4½″ Partition**
   b. Location Line: *use whatever is appropriate*
   c. Height: **Roof**
   d. Do not draw the dimensions at this time.
   e. Notice that one of the interior walls from Figure 6-2.3 gets extended and another gets trimmed; the walls previously created have a heavy dashed line over them (Figure 6-2.4).

FIGURE 6-2.4 Second Floor: additional walls added

## Joining Geometry:

Occasionally the intersection of two walls will not clean up, so you can use the *Join Geometry* icon on the *Tools* toolbar. The steps are as follows:

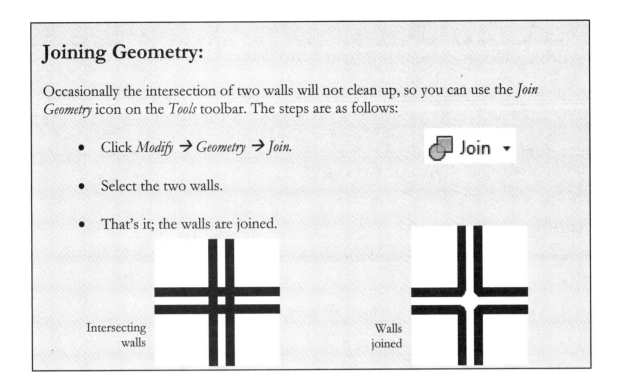

- Click *Modify* → *Geometry* → *Join*.

- Select the two walls.

- That's it; the walls are joined.

Intersecting walls

Walls joined

## Controlling the View Scale

The size of the dimensions and door and window tags is controlled by the *View Scale*. Each *View* has its own scale setting. To facilitate the creation of this book, the *View Scale* has been set to 3/32" = 1'-0" typical. At that scale, Revit makes the text and symbols larger so it is legible at the smaller scale. However, the images in this book are not to scale.

The default *View Scale* is ¼" = 1'-0" for the plan views, floor, ceiling and framing plans. This is good and should not be changed for this tutorial. In addition to controlling the text and symbols, it also controls the size, or scale, of that drawing on the plot sheet (i.e., one of the sheets in a set of drawings). This only makes sense seeing as *View Scale* has everything to do with what scale that view is intended to be printed at.

The *View Scale* can be controlled via the *View Properties* dialog or more conveniently on the *View Control Bar* at the bottom of the drawing window (Figure 6-2.5).

9. Save your project as **ex6-2.rvt**.

**FIGURE 6-2.5**
View Scale

## Exercise 6-3:
## Adding Doors, Openings and Windows

Do not forget to keep a backup of your files on a separate disk (i.e., flash drive, CD or DVD) or in the Cloud via Autodesk A360 or Dropbox. Your project file should be about 8-10 MB when starting this exercise. Remember, your Revit project is one large file and not many small files. You do not want anything to happen to it. Make sure you have a copy of this file in two places at all times – do this daily!

## Adding More Doors

Now you will add the second floor doors and openings, but first you must load one more *door family* into your project.

1.  Open project ex6-2.rvt and **Save-As ex6-3.rvt**.

2.  Load the door Family **Bifold–4 Panel.rfa** into your project.

    ***Reminder:*** *Insert → Load Family, and then browse to folder containing the doors you downloaded.*

3.  Add the doors as shown in Figure 6-3.1:
    a.  Center the closet doors in the closet.

    ***TIP:*** *With the inserted door selected, you can "nudge" the door using the arrow keys.*

    ***FYI:*** *The more zoomed in you are, the more accurate the "nudge" increments are.*

---

## Residential Door Sizes!
Doors come in many shapes and sizes.

**Thickness:** $1\frac{3}{8}''$, $1\frac{3}{4}''$ and $2\frac{1}{4}''$
*The $1\frac{3}{8}''$ door is most often used in residential construction and the $2\frac{1}{4}''$ door is typically only used on exterior doors for high-end projects, i.e., big budget.*

**Size:** ranges from $1'-0'' \times 6'-8''$ to $4'-0'' \times 9'-0''$
*The height of a residential door is usually $6'-8''$. This writer recently worked on a project where $7'-0''$ high doors were specified. The contractor was so used to the standard $6'-8''$ dimension he framed all the exterior openings at $6'-8''$. To top it off, the exterior walls were concrete (ICF system), so the openings could not be modified. Thus, $6'-8''$ doors were used.*

You can find more information on the internet; two examples are
   masonite.com/architectural/home  and  madawaska-doors.com
   *(wood veneer door mfr.)*                    *(custom solid wood door mfr.)*

---

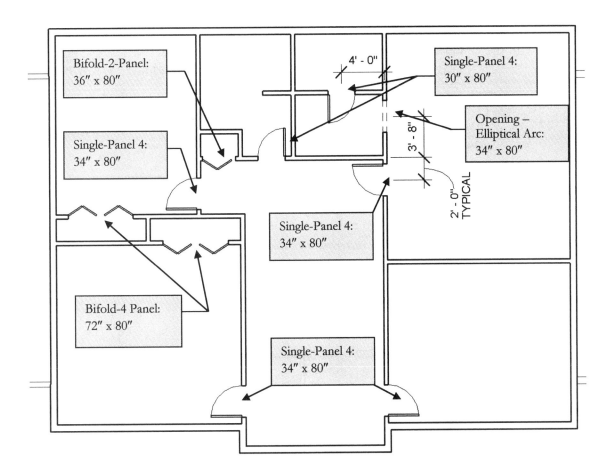

**FIGURE 6-3.1** Second Floor; doors added

The door numbers were temporarily hidden from view for clarity. On your plans you notice that the new doors have different numbers while the windows have the same number. Why is this? It relates to industry standards for architectural drafting. Each window that is the same size and configuration has the same type number throughout the project. Each door has a unique number because doors have so many variables (i.e., locks, hinges, closer, panics, material, and fire rating). To make doors easier to find, many architectural firms will make the door number the same as the room number the door opens into. You can change the door number by selecting the tag and then clicking on the text. The door schedule will be updated automatically.

## Adding More Windows:

4. Add the windows as shown in Figure 6-3.2.

   a. Verify via the *Properties Palette* that each window's *Head Height* is set to 7'-0".

      *TIP: Type* PP *if you accidentally closed the* Properties Palette.

   b. All windows are **Double Hung with Trim: 36" x 48"** unless otherwise noted in Figure 6-3.2.

   c. Similar to the previous image, the door and window tags have been temporarily hidden from view; you will learn how to do this next.

   d. All dimensions are from the center of the window to the exterior face of wall.

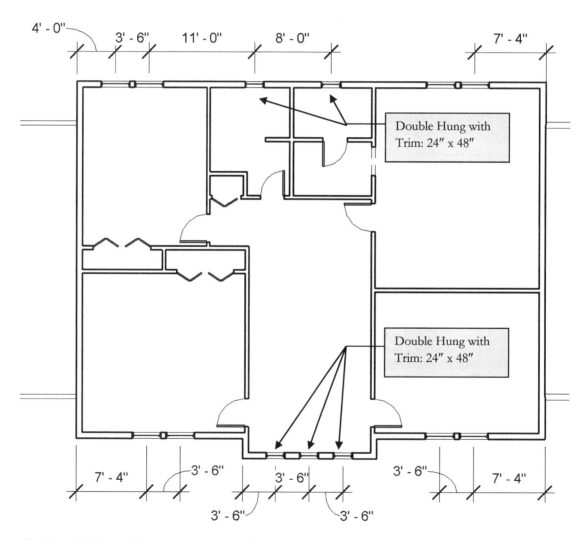

**FIGURE 6-3.2** Second floor plan: windows added

# Using Hide/Isolate to Control Visibility:

Now you will shift gears for a moment and look at the *Hide/Isolate* feature. This allows you to temporarily hide or isolate the selected elements or all the elements in the same category as those selected.

This feature is accessed via the *View Control Bar*, similar to the *View Scale* feature previously discussed.

5.  Holding the **Ctrl** key, select one door tag and one window tag.

6.  On the *View Control* bar click the **Temporary Hide/Isolate** icon (looks like sunglasses).

7.  From the pop-up menu, select **Hide Category** (Figure 6-3.3).

**FIGURE 6-3.3** View Control bar: Hide/Isolate selected

You should notice two things. First, all the door and window tags are gone. Second, the *Hide/Isolate* icon has a cyan background and the drawing window has a heavy cyan border around it, with text in the upper left stating "Temporary Hide/Isolate," which reminds you that some thing(s) is temporarily removed from the current view.

As implied by the feature name, the tags are temporarily hidden from view; they have not been deleted.

If you would have selected *Hide Element*, only the selected elements would have been hidden from view rather than the entire category.

To restore this temporary setting, do the following:

8.  Click the **Temporary Hide/Isolate** icon again (nothing has to be selected).

9.  Select **Reset Temporary Hide/Isolate** from the pop-up menu.

> *FYI: Hiding items does affect printing. If you close the project and reopen it the temporary override will be gone.*

All is now back to normal. Try a few other variations on this feature and observe the results. Select *Reset Temporary Hide/Isolate* before proceeding.

## Apply Hide/Isolate to View:

If you temporarily hide a few elements or categories and you want those items to be permanently hidden, you can select **Apply Hide/Isolate to View** from the *Hide/Isolate* icon menu shown in Figure 6-3.3.

This feature allows you to hide (or isolate) individual items; for example, you could select a single window tag and hide it. The only way to see it again in that view is to select the **Reveal Hidden Elements** icon on the *View Control Bar* (Figure 6-3.4a).

You should notice two things. First, all the hidden window tags are magenta and everything else is light gray. Second, the *Reveal Hidden Elements* icon has a magenta background and the drawing window has a heavy magenta border around it with a label in the upper left which reminds you that the current view settings are currently being modified.

**FIGURE 6-3.4A** Reveal Hidden Elements mode active

## Restoring Hidden Elements:

To restore a hidden item you first click the *Reveal Hidden Elements* (Figure 6-3.4a) icon and then select the element(s) to be restored to view. Once the item(s) is selected, you click **Unhide Element** or **Unhide Category** from the *Ribbon (Figure 6-3.4b)*. Finally, you select the *Reveal Hidden Elements* icon again to return to the normal "current view" settings.

**FIGURE 6-3.4B**
*Ribbon:* Reveal Hidden Elements panel

## Exercise 6-4:
## Basement Floor Plan

## Basement Floor Plan:

Now you will sketch the basement floor plan. Not all residences have basements; they mostly occur in cold climates where the foundation walls are deep to avoid frost heave. Once you have dug out for the deep foundation walls along the entire perimeter of the building, it does not take much more effort or resources to create a basement. Drawing a basement is the same as the other floors; you draw the exterior walls, concrete foundation walls in this case, the interior walls, etc. Once again, with the residential template that you started with being set up for the typical residential project, it should not surprise you that a typical foundation wall type is already set up and ready to be sketched; both 10″ and 12″ walls have been predefined.

1. Open your project file ex6-3.rvt and **Save As ex6-4.rvt**.

2. Switch to the *Foundation* floor plan view, <u>not</u> the *Basement* plan.

You should see a grayed out representation of the first floor.

3. In *View Properties* do the following two steps:

    a. Note the **Underlay** parameter is set to **First Floor**; if not set properly, you should change it now so *First Floor* is the current *Underlay*.

    b. Set the **Discipline** to **Architectural**.

This underlay setting gives you an outline of your building that can be used to sketch the foundation walls.

4. Using the *Wall* tool, draw the foundation walls using the following information (see *Type Selector* and *Options Bar* image below):
    a. *Wall type:*      **Foundation – 12″ Concrete**
    b. *Location Line:*  **Finish Face: Exterior**
    c. *Depth:*          **T.O. Footing** (i.e., Top of Footing).

    *FYI: Notice this setting on the Options Bar changes from "Height" to "Depth" when a "foundation" wall is selected!*

    d. Check **Chain** on the *Options Bar*.
    e. Start anywhere by snapping to one of the exterior corners of the *Underlay*; work in a clockwise direction.

When finished, your plan should look like Figure 6-4.1. The garage area will be slab-on-grade (i.e., no basement under it), so make sure you sketch a foundation wall between the garage and basement as shown.

**FIGURE 6-4.1** Foundation Floor Plan; with First Floor Underlay turned on

5.  Set the *Underlay* parameter for "Foundation" floor plan to **None** in the *Properties Palette*.

## So What Exactly Did You Just Draw?

You just drew a foundation where the **top** is based on the current level, a level named Foundation in this example, and the "Depth" parameter on the *Options Bar* controls the **bottom** of the wall (T.O. Footing in this example).

The image to the right should make this concept perfectly clear (Figure 6-4.2).

*FYI: Each level datum has a corresponding floor plan view when the target is blue (as seen in the image to the right). You may not need all of these views in a set of construction documents, but they are useful for creating the Building Information Model (BIM).*

**FIGURE 6-4.2**
Foundation wall in section

# Creating a New Foundation Wall Type:

Because the garage area is slab-on-grade, both sides of the foundation wall will have earth against them. The main basement walls act like a retaining wall because they only have earth on one side of the wall. Therefore, you will change the three exterior foundation walls, at the garage area, to 8″ concrete. You will have to create a new wall type to accommodate this need.

*NOTE: When the "Wall Function" is set to Retaining in the "Type Parameters" for a wall, the wall cannot be room bounding, so Room/Room Tags cannot be added.*

---

**Disclaimer:**
All dimensions and sizes shown in this book are solely for the purpose of learning to use the software. Under no circumstances should any information be assumed to be appropriate for a real-world project. A structural engineer should be consulted if you do not have adequate expertise in that area.

---

6. Select the *Wall* tool and then select **Foundation – 12″ Concrete** from the *Type Selector*.

7. Create a new wall type based on the current selection; name it **Foundation – 8″ Concrete**.

    *REMEMBER: Properties Palette → Edit Type → Duplicate.*

8. Adjust the *Type Parameters* of the new wall so the Width is **8″**.

    *FYI: This is through Properties Palette → Edit Type → Edit Structure.*

9. Select the three exterior garage foundation walls while holding down the Ctrl key, and then select your new wall in the *Type Selector*.

    *REMEMBER: Click Modify first to cancel the Wall tool.*

    *TIP: Hover your cursor over one wall, press Tab to highlight all three walls (a chain of walls), and then click to select all three walls at once!*

Your basement plan should look like Figure 6-4.3.

Because the *Location Line* was set to Finish Face: Exterior, the exterior side of the foundation wall is stationary when walls of a different width are selected; this is the desired result in this situation.

*FYI: You will add footings below the foundation walls in Exercise 10-2.*

**FIGURE 6-4.3** Basement Floor Plan; with 8″ foundation walls at the garage

## Adding Interior Walls in the Basement:

To make things simple, for this tutorial and structurally, you will copy all the walls from the first floor to the basement. In the process of accomplishing this task you will also study the selection **Filter** function.

First you will switch to the first floor and select a large area using a *crossing window* (i.e., picking from right to left), and then use the *Filter* function to strip the selection down to just the walls.

    10. Switch to the ***First Floor*** view and select all the interior walls using a *crossing window* (Figure 6-4.4).

Everything within or passing through the *crossing window* is now selected. Next you will filter out everything except for the walls.

**FIGURE 6-4.4** First Floor Plan; selecting all walls with a crossing window

11. With everything from the previous step still selected, click the **Filter** icon on the *Status Bar* (Figure 6-4.5).

**FIGURE 6-4.5** Filter Selection icon

You are now in the *Filter* dialog (Figure 6-4.6). This lists all the element types or categories that are in the current selection set. When you click OK, only the items checked will be part of the current selection set.

**FIGURE 6-4.6** Filter dialog

12. Uncheck everything except the **Walls** item in the *Filter* dialog (Figure 6-4.6).

13. Click **OK** to update the current select set.

*TIP: Notice the number of selected items is listed in the lower right corner of the program window (image to the right). If you know you want to delete 3 doors and the count shows 4 items, you would not want to click Delete before you unselect the fourth item!*

Now only the walls are selected. Next you will copy them to the *Clipboard* and then *Paste* them into the basement floor plan.

This selection technique can be used in many ways. For example, you could select all the walls and change their *Top Constraint* via the *Properties* dialog.

14. From the *Ribbon* select **Modify | Walls → Clipboard → Copy**.

15. Switch to the **Basement** view, not the Foundation view.

16. Select **Modify** on the *Ribbon*, and then **Modify → Clipboard → Paste → Aligned to Current View**.

You should get the following warning (Figure 6-4.7):

This error is indicating that the wall(s) you just placed overlaps another wall (vertically or horizontally). In this case it may be that the *Top*

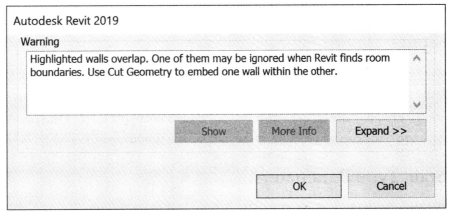

**FIGURE 6-4.7** Wall placement warning

*Offset* is not set to 0″, but to 6″, which causes the wall to extend 6″ above the *Top Constraint* (which is the first floor line). So, if the first floor walls start at the first floor line, the basement walls extend up into the first floor walls by 6″, and the two walls would be overlapping vertically.

17. If you get this warning, click **OK** to close it. Then select all the interior walls in the basement and make sure the *Top Offset* is set to 0″ via the *Properties Palette*.

When finished, your plan should look like Figure 6-4.8.

**FIGURE 6-4.8** Walls added to the basement floor, copied from the first floor

Even though the doors were not selected, they were still copied with the walls just as before. This is fine; to save time you will leave the doors as they are.

18. **Save** your project as **ex6-4.rvt**.

## Exercise 6-5:
## Stairs

Next you will add stairs to your floor plans. Revit provides a powerful stair tool that allows you to design stairs quickly with various constraints specified in the *family* which was loaded with the template you started from (e.g., 7″ maximum riser).

## Stair Type Parameters:

Before you draw the stair, it will be helpful to review the options available in the stair family.

1.  Open ex6-4.rvt and *Save As* **ex6-5.rvt**. Open the **First Floor** plan.

2.  From the *Project Browser*, expand the *Families* → *Stairs* → Assembled *Stair* (i.e., click the plus sign next to these labels).

3.  Right-click on the stair type **Residential – Closed 2 Sides**, and select the **Type Properties…** option from the pop-up menu.

You should now see the options shown in Figure 6-5.1.

Take a couple minutes to see what options are available. We will quickly review a few below.

- Tread Depth: Treads are typically 12″ deep (usually code min.) and 1″ of that depth overlaps the next tread; so only 11″ is visible in plan view. This overlap is called the *nosing*.
- Riser: This provides Revit with the maximum dimension allowed (by code, or if you want it, less). The actual dimension will depend on the floor-to-floor height.
- Stringer dimensions: These dimensions usually vary per stair depending on the stair width, run and materials, to name a few.
- Cost: Estimating placeholder.

*FYI: Closed 2 Sides (part of the name of the stair family) means there will be a wall on each side of the stair; thus a stringer will be visible above the stair.*

**FIGURE 6-5.1** Stair type properties

# Calculate Tread and Riser Size:

Although Revit automatically calculates the rise and tread dimensions for you, it is still a good idea to understand what is happening.

The *riser* is typically calculated to be as large as building codes will allow. Occasionally a grand stair will have a smaller riser to create a more elegant stair.

Similarly, the *tread* is usually designed to be as small as allowable by building codes.

The largest riser and shortest tread create the steepest stair allowed. This takes up less floor space (Figure 6-5.2). A stairway that is too steep is uncomfortable and unsafe.

Building codes vary by location; for this exercise you will use 7″ (max.) for the risers and 9″ (min.) for the treads.

Codes usually require that each tread be the same size, likewise with risers.

Calculate the number and size of the risers:

>  Given:
>  Risers: **7″** max.          Floor to floor height: **9′-0″**.

>  Calculate the number of risers:
>  9′-0″ divided by 7″ (or 108″ divided by 7″) = 15.429

Seeing as each riser has to be the same size we will have to round off to a whole number. You cannot round down because that will make the riser larger than the allowed maximum (9′-0″ / 15 = 7.2″). Therefore you have to round up to 16. Thus: 9′-0″ divided by 16 = 6.75.

So you need **16** risers that are **6¾″** each.

**FIGURE 6-5.2** Stair rise/run comparison

# Drawing the Stairs in Plan:

You will be drawing a U-shaped stair from the first floor to the second and an L-shaped stair from the basement to the first floor. At first, when using Revit to draw stairs, it may be helpful to manually figure out the number of risers and landings. That information will be helpful when drawing the stair. As you become more familiar with the *Stair* tool, you will not need to do those calculations to draw a stair.

To get an idea about what you are going to draw next, take a moment to look at Figure 6-5.3. The image below is at the first floor, and the "UP" label indicates where you would access the stair on the first floor. (Everything else rises from there, of course, to the second floor.)

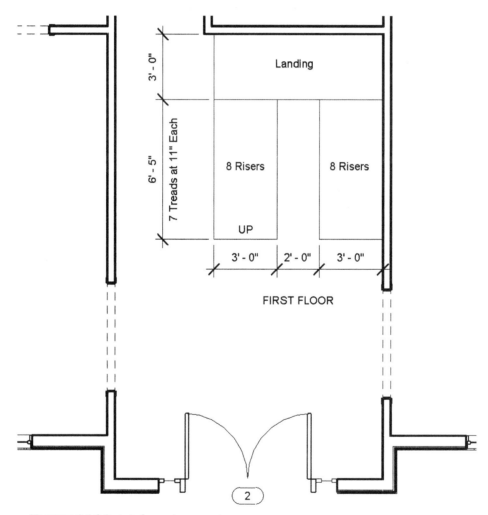

**FIGURE 6-5.3** Stair information overview

The first thing you will do, to prepare to draw the stair from the first floor to the second floor, is to draw a temporary reference line. This line will be used to accurately pick a starting point while using the *Stair* command (you will be picking a starting point near the middle of the room – next to the "UP" label in Figure 6-5.3). After the stair is drawn, you will erase the line.

You have had plenty of practice drawing lines in previous chapters, so you will be given minimal instruction on how to draw the line.

4.  Make sure you are in the ***First Floor Plan*** view.

5.  **Zoom in** to the front *Entry Foyer*.

6.  Using the ***Detail Line*** tool from the *Annotate* tab, draw the temporary line in the ***First Floor Plan*** view, as shown in Figure 6-5.4.

**FIGURE 6-5.4** Draw a temporary detail line

7.  Click on the *Architecture* tab on the *Ribbon*.

8.  Select **Architecture → Circulation → Stair**

9.  Click the *Edit Type* button in the *Properties Palette*.
    Notice the *Minimum Run Width* is 3'-0". Click **OK**.
    Also notice the **Actual Run Width** is set to **3'-0"** on the *Options Bar*.

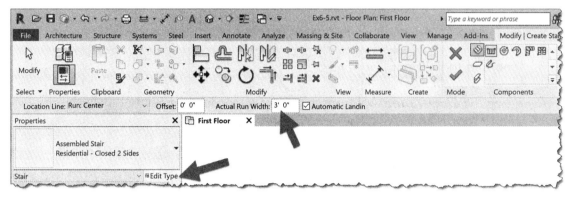

**FIGURE 6-5.5** Stair tool active; Select Edit Type from the Properties Palette

10. Notice the *Top Level* is set to **Second Floor** (Figure 6-5.6).

11. Click the endpoint of your temporary detail line as shown in **Figure 6-5.7**; you are selecting the start point for the first step. Make sure you are snapping to the line for accuracy; a tooltip will appear stating "endpoint" before you click.

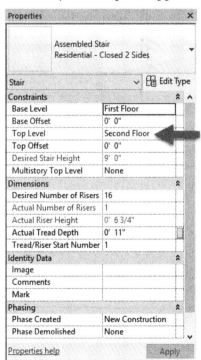

12. Pick the remaining points as shown in Figures 6-5.7, 6-5.8 and 6-5.9.

    *FYI: For the second run, set the Location Line to **Left** on the Options Bar.*

    > *TIP:*
    > *Notice the palette to the left is the* Instance Properties *which controls selected or to-be-created instances. In this case, of course, we are talking about a to-be-created instance.*
    >
    > *Clicking the* Edit Type *button here would make changes to this stair and any others previously created. Your project does not have any previously created stairs at this time.*

**FIGURE 6-5.6** Stair instance properties

Notice as you draw the stairs, Revit will display the number of risers drawn and the number of risers remaining to be drawn to reach the next level, or whatever level is selected as *Top Level* in *Properties*.

If you click *Finish Stairs*, the green check mark on the *Ribbon*, before drawing all the required risers, Revit will display a warning message. You can leave the problem to be resolved later.

**Pick #2**: After picking the first point below, begin moving the cursor straight up; click when the label below the stairs reads "8 Risers Created, 8 Remaining."

**Pick #1**: Pick the endpoint of your temporary line as the starting point for the stair.

8 RISERS CREATED, 8 REMAINING

**FIGURE 6-5.7** Beginning to sketch the stair

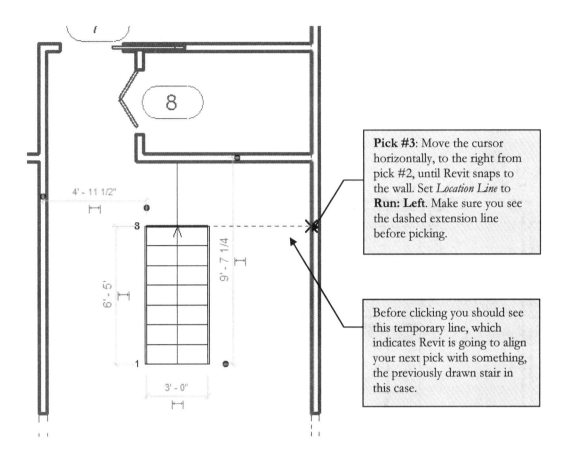

**Pick #3**: Move the cursor horizontally, to the right from pick #2, until Revit snaps to the wall. Set *Location Line* to **Run: Left**. Make sure you see the dashed extension line before picking.

Before clicking you should see this temporary line, which indicates Revit is going to align your next pick with something, the previously drawn stair in this case.

**FIGURE 6-5.8** Continuing to sketch the stair

**Pick #4**: Move the cursor straight down until Revit indicates "8 Risers Created, 0 Remaining."

*TIP: You can move the mouse past that point; you do not need to click directly on it.*

**FIGURE 6-5.9** Last step in sketching the stair

13. Click the **green check mark** to *Finish* the stair on the *Ribbon* (Figure 6-5.5).

14. **Erase** the temporary detail line; you may need to tap the Tab key (i.e., tap, not hold down) to select it rather than the stair.

Your stair should now look like Figure 6-5.10! Notice that Revit adds a break-line at the *Cut Plane* and everything above that is dashed in.

As soon as you click *Finish Stair*, Revit will automatically add the landing, creating it between the two stair runs sketched. The width of the landing will match the stair width, which is 3'-0". This is true for any stair configuration using the above method. You will see this momentarily when you sketch an L-shaped stair in the basement.

**FIGURE 6-5.10** Finished stair

The second floor plan also shows this stair but with a down arrow and no break lines because it does not pass through that view's *Cut Plane*!

## Modeling the Basement Stairs:

Now you will draw the L-shaped stairs from the basement to the first floor.

To get an idea about what you are going to draw next, take a moment to look at Figure 6-5.11. The image below is at the basement level, and the "UP" label indicates where you would access the stair on the basement level. Everything else rises from there, of course, to the first floor.

15. Save your project as **ex6-5.rvt**; remember to save often.

16. Switch to the **Basement** floor plan view.

17. Select the **Stair** tool.

FIGURE 6-5.11 Stair information overview

18. In the *Properties Palette* make the following changes:

    a.   Change the *Type Selector* to **Residential – Open 2 Sides**.

    b.   Make sure the *Top Level* is set to **First Floor**; the *Stair* tool defaults to the next *Level* up – which is "foundation" level and not "first floor" in your case.

19. Select the **Railing** button on the *Ribbon*.

20. Select **None** and **OK** (see image to right).

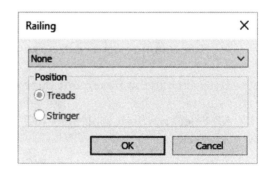

21. Using the same techniques you employed to sketch the first floor stair, draw the basement stair per the information given in Figure 6-5.11.

*TIP: While sketching the stairs, you can select a window (picking from left to right) around a run of stairs and move it. Also, do not forget to draw a temporary line(s) if you think it will help.*

Your stair should look like Figure 6-5.12. If not, select one of the riser/tread lines and press the *Delete* key on the keyboard to erase the stair and try again. It can get a little frustrating when you are not familiar with the ins-and-outs of what Revit is doing or what information it needs to proceed. Take your time; take a break if necessary.

Next you will draw three walls next to the stair. This will close off the two open sides and the bottom of the stair.

*TIP: If a stair needs to be modified at any time in the future, you do not actually have to delete the stair and start over; it is recommended above for practice. If you select a stair, you can click the Edit Sketch icon on the Ribbon to re-enter Sketch mode for that stair.*

**FIGURE 6-5.12** Finished basement stair

22. Using the **Wall** tool, draw the three interior walls as shown in **Figure 6-5.13**.

- Use the standard interior wall you used for the other floors.

  **TIP #1:** *You can select one and see what type it is in the Type Selector.*

  **TIP #2:** *You can also select a wall and right-click, and then select "Create Similar" from the pop-up menu to add another wall of the type selected.*

- Click the *Chain* option if not already checked.

- Set *Location Line* to one of the finished wall faces.

- *Top Constraint* set to **First Floor**.

- Click the inside points of the stair. Press the *spacebar* if needed to flip the wall so it is created outside of the stair footprint.

- Draw the third wall under the stair, at the fifth riser line.

**FIGURE 6-5.13** Three walls added at stairs

**FIGURE 6-5.14** 3D view of stair

A cutaway 3D view of your model looks something like this; you will learn to do cutaway views later in the book.

You should notice two things about this 3D view:

*First:* The basement wall you just added extends through the basement stair. You will fix that in the building sections lesson.

*Second:* No floors have been drawn yet. You will draw floor systems in a future chapter.

23. **Save** your project.

*FYI: Normally you would not rename your project file. You do it here in the book for grading and restore options, should things get really corrupted.*

## Modify the Building's Floor-to-Floor Height:

You will not need to do this for this tutorial, but you can modify the building's floor-to-floor height (or Level). The reasons for doing this vary. Some examples might be to make the building shorter or taller, to accommodate ductwork in the ceilings or the depth of the floor structure; the longer the span, the deeper the structure. The default floor-to-floor height in the template file you started from is 9'-0", which is fine for this project. However, should you want to change this for another project, here is how to do it:

- Open any exterior elevation from the *Project Browser*.

- Change the floor-to-floor height to be 12'-0" for each level; in this example, to the right.

- Select the floor elevation symbol, and then select the text displaying the elevation. You should now be able to type in a new number. Press Enter to see the changes. Notice the windows move because the sill height has not been changed (Figure A).

**FIGURE A** Exterior elevation: modifying Level 3 elevation

- The floor-to-floor height is a good thing to figure out, when possible, before drawing the stairs, as it affects the number of risers and treads required, not to mention floor area.

## Self-Exam:

The following questions can be used as a way to check your knowledge of this lesson. The answers can be found at the bottom of the page.

1.  The default settings for the floor plan view shows the walls for the floor below. (T/F)

2.  Click the green check mark to finish the stair command. (T/F)

3.  You should start drawing your floor plan generally centered on the default elevation marks in a new project. (T/F)

4.  You can use the *Align* tool to align one wall with another. (T/F)

5.  Where do you change the maximum riser height? _____

## Review Questions:

The following questions may be assigned by your instructor as a way to assess your knowledge of this section. Your instructor has the answers to the review questions.

1.  It is not possible to copy/paste elements from one floor to another and have them line up (with the original objects). (T/F)

2.  Changing an instance parameter affects the selected or to-be-created elements. (T/F)

3.  Each Revit view is saved as a separate file on your hard drive. (T/F)

4.  You select the part of the wall to be deleted when using the *Trim* tool. (T/F)

5.  You cannot "finish stair" if you have not drawn all the treads or risers that are required between the two specified levels. (T/F)

6.  What parameter should be set to none, in the *View Properties* dialog, if you

    do not want to see the walls from the floor below? _____

7.  Use the Temporary Hide/Isolate tool to get a better look at your model. (T/F)

8.  You can use the _____ tool to quickly select a certain type of element from a large group of selected objects.

9.  The number of _____ remaining is displayed while sketching a stair.

**Notes:**

## Lesson 7
# Annotation:

This chapter covers annotation in Revit: text, dimensions, tags, shared parameters and keynotes. In printed form, the drawings are often not enough to convey the design intent. These tools provide for effective communication to those using the final printed drawings to both bid and build the building. Several of the chapters following this one will utilize many of these concepts.

All of the tools covered in this chapter are found on the Annotate tab. Three of the tools on this tab are also on the Quick Access Toolbar because they are used often; they are **Dimension**, **Tag by Category** and **Text**.

**TIP:** It is interesting to note that every tool on the Annotate tab is 2D and view specific.

## Exercise 7-1:
## Text

This section covers the application of notes using the **Text** command in Revit. We will also look at Revit's **Spell Check** and **Find/Replace** tools, including their limitations.

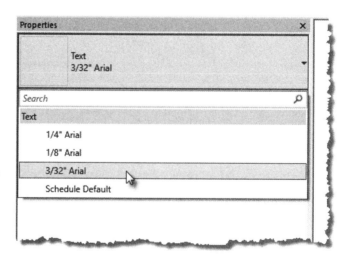

The first thing to know about the text tool is that it should be used as little as possible! Rather, live tags, keynotes and dimensions are preferred over static text to ensure the information is correct. Text will not update or move when something in the model changes—especially if the text is not visible or in the view where the model is being changed.

With that said, the text command is still necessary and used often within Revit.

> Steps to add new Text to a view:
> - Start the **Text** command
> - Verify the **Text Style**
> - Define the starting point; **click** *or* **click and drag**
> - **Type** the desired text, typically without pressing *Enter*
> - **Click away** from the text to finish the command
>
> Steps to edit existing text:
> - Select the text
> - Click again to enter edit mode

## Text

The Text tool can be started from the **Quick Access Toolbar**, the **Annotate** tab or by typing **TX** on the keyboard.

The first thing to do is consider the current text type in the Type Selector (Figure 7-1.1). The name of a text type should, at a minimum, contain the size and font. The size is the **actual size on the printed page** regardless of the drawing scale.

**FIGURE 7-1.1** Type selector with text command active

There are additional steps that are optional, but at this point you could click, or click and drag, within the drawing window and start typing.

Here is the difference between **click** and **click and drag** options when starting text:

- **Click**; Defines the starting point for new text. No automatic return to next line while typing. An Enter must be pressed to start a new line; this is called a "hard return" in the word processing world.

- **Click and Drag**; This defines a windowed area where text will be entered. The height is not really important. The width determines when a line automatically returns to the next line while typing. Using this method allows paragraphs to be easily adjusted by dragging one of the corners of the selected textbox.

As long as "hard returns" are not used, the textbox width and number of rows can be adjusted at any time in the future. To do this, the text must be selected and then the round grip on the right (See Figure 7-1.1) can be repositioned via click and drag with left mouse button.

**FIGURE 7-1.2** Selecting text and adjusting width of the textbox

The image to the right, Figure 7-1.3, shows the result of adjusting the width of the textbox—the text element went from two lines to four.

If an Enter is pressed at the end of each line of text, when originally typed, the text will not automatically adjust as just described. An example of this can be seen in the following two images, Figure 7-1.4 & 5. Note that in some cases this is desirable to ensure the formatting of text is not changed.

**FIGURE 7-1.3** Text width adjusted

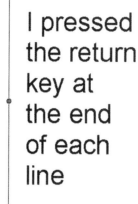

**FIGURE 7-1.4**
Text with hard returns

**FIGURE 7-1.5**
Text does not adjust when textbox width is modified

Keep in mind that this text tool is strictly 2D and view specific. If the same text is required in multiple views, the text either needs to be retyped or Copy/Pasted. However, for general notes that might appear on all floor plans sheets, for example, a Legend View can be utilized. Revit has a separate tool, on the Architecture tab, called **Model Text** for instances when 3D text is needed within the model.

## Formatting Text

In addition to the basic topics just covered, there are a number of formatting options which can be applied to text. These adjustments can be applied while initially creating the text or at any time later.

The formatting options are mainly found on the Ribbon while in the Text command or when text is selected.

**FIGURE 7-1.6** Formatting options on the Ribbon while creating text

The formatting options identified in the image are:
1. Leader options
2. Leader position options
3. Text Justification/Alignment

**Leader Options**

A leader is a line which extends from the text, with an arrow on the end, used to point at something in the drawing.

The default option, when using the text command, is no leader. This can be seen as the highlighted option in the upper left.

The remaining three options determine the graphical appearance of the leader; one segment, two segment or curved as seen in Figure 7-1.7. Often, a design firm will standardize on one of these three options for a consistent look.

ONE SEGMENT LEADER

TWO SEGMENT LEADER

CURVED LEADER

**FIGURE 7-1.7** Leader formatting options

Here are the steps to include a leader with text:
- Start the **Text** command
- Select text type via **Type Selector**
- Select **Leader** option
- Specify **leader location**
- **Type** text
- Click **Close,** or click away from text, to finish

*Leader Options*

Once the text with leader is created, it can be selected and modified later if needed. In the next image, Figure 7-1.8, notice the two **circle grips** associated with the leader; at the arrow and the change in direction of the line (the other two circle grips are for the text box as previously described in this section). These two grips can be repositioned by clicking and dragging the left mouse button.

FIGURE 7-1.8 Text with leader selected; notice leader grips and Ribbon options

When text is selected the Ribbon displays slightly different options for leaders as seen in the image above. It is possible to have multiple leaders (i.e. arrows) coming off the text—denoted by the green "plus" symbol. In the next image, Figure 7-1.9, an additional leader was added to the left and one was also added to the right. It is not possible to have both curved and straight leader lines for the same text element. In this example, the curved leader options are grayed out as seen in Figure 7-1.8.

FIGURE 7-1.9 Multiple leaders added

Back in Figure 7-1.8, also notice that leaders can also be removed—even to the point where the text does not have any leaders. The one catch with the **remove leader** option is that they can only be removed in the order added.

The **Leader Arrowhead** can be changed graphically (i.e. solid dot, loop leader, etc.). This will be covered in the section on Managing Text Types as this setting is in the Type Properties for the text itself.

*Good to know...*
Text can be placed in **any view** and on **sheets**. The only exception is the Text command does not work in schedule views.

Text can also be in a **Group**. When the group only has elements from the Annotate tab, it is a Detail Group. When the group also has model elements, the text is in something called Attached Detail Group. When a Model Group is placed, selecting it gives the option adding the Attached Detail Group.

## Leader Position Options

These six toggles control the position of the leader relative to the text as seen in the two images below (Figures 7-1.10 and 11). These options also appear in the Properties Palette when text is selected, called **Left Attachment** and **Right Attachment**.

**FIGURE 7-1.10** Leader position toggles – example A

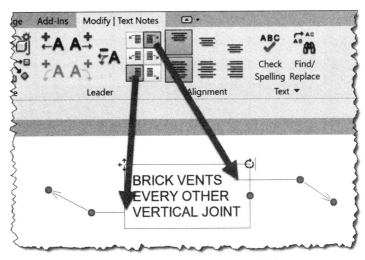

**FIGURE 7-1.11** Leader position toggles – example B

Similar to leader type, a design firm will often select a standard that everyone is expected to follow so construction documents look consistent.

## Text Justification

When text is selected there are three options for horizontal justification on the Ribbon when text is selected: Left, Center and Right. The results can be seen in the three images for Figure 7-1.12.

This option also appears in the Properties Palette when text is selected, called **Horizontal Align**. Keep in mind that all options in the Property Palette are instance parameters—meaning they only apply to the instance(s) selected. Thus, each text entity in Revit can have different settings.

## Text Formatting

The next section to cover is the options to make text Bold, Italic or be Underlined.

These options do not appear in the Properties Palette because they can be applied to individual words (or even individual fonts). In the example below, the word "Brick" is bold, "other" is italicized and "vertical" is underlined.

If all the text is selected and set to one of these three options, an edit made in the future will also have these settings.

*FYI:* Notice the formatting options are different when editing the text, compared to when the text element is just selected.

**FIGURE 7-1.12** Text justification options

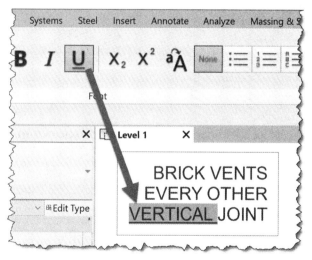

**FIGURE 7-1.13** Text formatting

## Text Formatting

The next section to cover is the **List** options on Paragraph panel. This feature is only available while editing the contents of the text element; to do this, select the text and then click on the text to enter edit mode.

| | |
|---|---|
| • 4" FACE BRICK | 1. 4" FACE BRICK |
| • 1" AIR SPACE | 2. 1" AIR SPACE |
| • 3" RIGID INSULATION | 3. 3" RIGID INSULATION |
| • 8" CONCRETE MASONRY UNIT (CMU) | 4. 8" CONCRETE MASONRY UNIT (CMU) |
| • 3 5/8" MTL STUDS AT 16" O.C. | 5. 3 5/8" MTL STUDS AT 16" O.C. |
| • 5/8" GYP BD | 6. 5/8" GYP BD |
| a. 4" FACE BRICK | A. 4" FACE BRICK |
| b. 1" AIR SPACE | B. 1" AIR SPACE |
| c. 3" RIGID INSULATION | C. 3" RIGID INSULATION |
| d. 8" CONCRETE MASONRY UNIT (CMU) | D. 8" CONCRETE MASONRY UNIT (CMU) |
| e. 3 5/8" MTL STUDS AT 16" O.C. | E. 3 5/8" MTL STUDS AT 16" O.C. |
| f. 5/8" GYP BD | F. 5/8" GYP BD |

**FIGURE 7-1.14** Four options to define a line within text

This is one case where you must press Enter to force the following text to a new line and automatically generate a list (i.e. bullet, letter or number).

Clicking the **Increase Indent** tool will indent the list as shown below (Figure 7-1.15). To undo this later, click in that row and select **Decrease Indent**. There does not appear to be a way to change what the indented listed value is. Using the backspace key and then indenting again allows an indent without a number/letter.

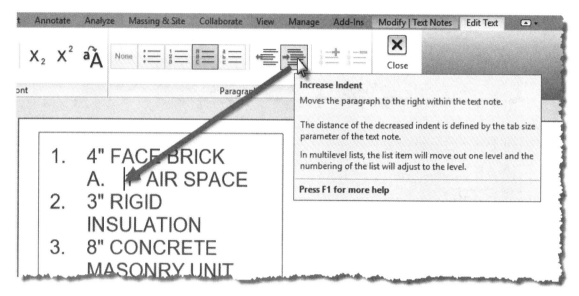

**FIGURE 7-1.15** Indenting within a list

Clicking within the first row, clicking on the **plus** or **minus** icons will let you change the starting number/letter of the list.

The text formatting options also allow for **subscript** and **superscript** as shown in the example below (Figure 7-1.16).

**FIGURE 7-1.16** Superscript example

Also, notice the **All Caps** icon; clicking this icon will change selected text to all upper case. When this feature is used, Revit remembers the original formatting—thus, toggling off the App Caps feature later will restore the original formatting.

## Managing Text Types

When using the text tool, the options listed in the Type Selector are the result of **Text Types** defined in the current project. Most design firms will have all the Text Types they need defined within their template.

There are two ways to access the text type properties. One is to start the Text command and then click **Edit Type** in the Properties Palette. The other is to click the arrow within the Text panel on the Annotate tab as pointed out in the image below.

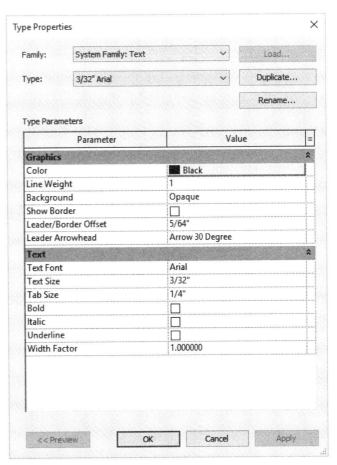

The **Type Properties**, as shown in the example to the right (Figure 7-1.17) are fairly self-explanatory. Below is a brief description of each.

**FIGURE 7-1.17** Text type properties

| Command | What it does... |
|---|---|
| Color | This can affect printing, so it is often set to black. |
| Line Weight | This is only for the leader. |
| Background | *Toggle:* Opaque or Transparent |
| Show Border | *Check box:* Show or Hide |
| Leader/Border Offset | Space between text and board and leader – helpful when Background is set to Opaque. |
| Leader Arrowhead | Select from a list of predefined arrow types |
| Text Font | Select from a list of installed fonts on your computer |
| Text Size | Size of text on the printed page |
| Tab Size | Size of space when Tab is pressed (size on printed paper) |
| Bold | Default setting – can be changed while in edit mode |
| Italic | Default setting – can be changed while in edit mode |
| Underline | Default setting – can be changed while in edit mode |
| Width Factor | Adjusts the overall width of a line of text |

### Colors

The color applies to the text and the leader. The color is often set to black. If any other color is used, this can affect printing. For example, any color becomes a shade of gray when printed to a black and white printer—similar to printing a document from Microsoft Word where green text is a darker shade of gray than yellow text. In the Print dialog there is an option to print all color as Black Lines which can make colored text black. However, this also overrides gray lines and fill patterns.

### Custom Fonts

Be careful using custom fonts installed on your computer as others who do not have those fonts will likely not see the formatting the same as intended. Custom fonts can come from installing other software such as Adobe InDesign. In fact, Autodesk also installs several custom fonts which are supposed to match some of the special SHX fonts which come with AutoCAD.

### Custom Fonts

It is not possible to create custom arrowheads. However, the list of arrowheads is based on styles defined here: **Manage → Additional Settings → Arrowheads**. This provides many options for how these items look.

### Width Factor

Some firms will use a Width Factor like 0.75, 0.85 or something similar to squish the text to fit more information on a sheet. Getting any narrower than this makes the text hard to read. This option actually changes the proportions of each letter, not just the space between them.

### Misc.

Note that Text does not have a phase setting. Thus the phase filters and overrides do not apply to text. It is sometimes desired to have text noting existing elements, such as ductwork, to be a shade of gray rather than solid—black being reserved for things that are new.

# Check Spelling

Revit has a tool which allows the spelling to be checked. Keep in mind this only works on text created with the Text command and only for the current view. Revit cannot check the spelling of text in keynotes, tags or families. Neither can it check the entire project.

The Spell Check tool can be found on the Annotate tab or on the Ribbon when text is selected. When Spell Check is selected, the dialog to the right appears if there are any misspellings found (Figure 7-1.18).

When Revit finds a word not in the dictionary it will provide a list of possible correct words. Often the first suggestion is the right one. If not, select from the list.

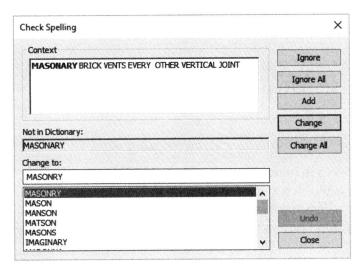

**FIGURE 7-1.18** Check Spelling dialog

Clicking the **Change** button will correct the highlighted word.
Clicking **Change All** will change all of the words with this same misspelling in the current view.

Sometimes Revit will flag a word that is not misspelled. This might be a company name, your name, a product name or an industry abbreviation. In this case one might select the Add option to add the word to the custom dictionary so you don't have to deal with this every time you run spell check.

The image to the right shows the settings related to the Spell Check engine. The options are self-explanatory. In an office, consider placing the custom dictionary on the server and point all users to it.

**FIGURE 7-1.19** Check Spelling in Options dialog

Don't totally rely on Spell Check. A word may be spelled correctly but still be the wrong word. For example:

- Fill the **whole** with concrete and trowel level and smooth.
- File the **hole** with concrete and trowel level and smooth.

In this example the word "whole" is wrong but spelled correctly. Also keep in mind that Revit does not have a grammar check system like the popular word processing systems.

# Find/Replace

Revit has a tool which allows words to be found or replaced within a view. Keep in mind this only works on text created with the Text command. Revit cannot find or replace text in keynotes, tags or families. Unlike the spelling tool, this tool can search the entire project.

When this tool is selected the dialog to the right appears (Figure 7-1.20).

In this example, the current view is being searched for a brand name, **Sheetrock**, so it can be replaced with the generic industry standard term, **Gypsum Board**.

**FIGURE 7-1.20** Find/Replace dialog

Selecting **Entire project** and then clicking **Find All** tells Revit to list all matches in the middle section of the dialog. For each row, you can click to select and see the context the found word(s) is used in.

When items are found, the **Replace** or **Replace All** buttons can be used to swap out the text in one location or all. When clicking Replace, only the selected row is replaced.

This tool can be used to just find something and not replace it. For example, on a large project with hundreds of views in the Project Browser, using the Find/Replace to search for the details with the word "roof drain" can significantly speed up the process of locating the desired drawing.

### Replacing a Text Type

In addition to replacing content within a text element, there is a way to replace the text type as well. For example, some imported details use a different font and you want everything to match and be consistent. This is not really associated with the Find/Replace tool, but it is important to know how to accomplish this task.

Replacing a Text Type within a view or project:
- **Select** one text element within the project
- **Right-click** (Fig. 7-1.19)
- Pick **Select All Instances** →
  o Visible in View
  o In Entire Project
- Select a different type from the **Type Selector**

This procedure will replace all the text in either the current view or the entire project. Even text which has been hidden with the "Hide in View" right-click option will be changed.

When a specific text type is selected, the selection count, in the lower right corner of the Revit window, will indicate the total number of elements selected (Figure 7-1.22). This can be used as a quick double check before replacing the text type. For example, if the intent was to just replace a few rouge text instances but the count was several hundred, this would be a clue that some other view uses this text type and perhaps should not be changed as it was created by someone else on the project. This can be especially true if multiple disciplines are working in the same project.

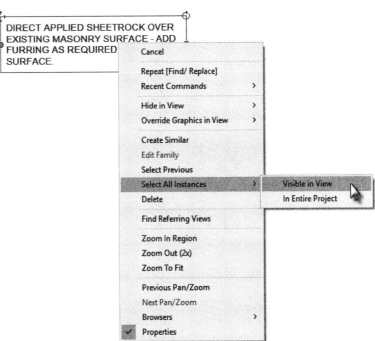

**FIGURE 7-1.21** Select all instances via right-click

**FIGURE 7-1.22** Total element selected count

## Exercise 7-2:
## Dimensions

This exercise will cover the ins and outs of dimensioning in Revit.

The first thing to understand about dimensions is that they are 2D and view specific—like all commands on the Annotate tab.

Dimension elements have an association with the thing(s) being dimensioned. If that thing(s) is deleted the dimension will also be deleted, even if the dimension is not visible in the current view. For example, if a wall is deleted from a 3D view, then any dimensions associated with that wall, in a floor plan view, which may not even be open, will be deleted.

Because dimensions have an association with specific elements in the model it is important to make sure the correct elements are selected while placing the dimension. In a floor plan, for example, the place to click to add a dimension may have several elements stacked on top of each other: grid line, wall edge, floor edge, window edge, wall sweep. It may be necessary to tap the Tab key to cycle through the options to select the correct item (while tabbing, the highlighted element will be listed on the status bar across the bottom of the screen).

Each dimension command will be covered in the order they appear on the Annotate as seen in the image below.

| Command | *What it does…* |
|---|---|
| 1. *Aligned* | Most used dimension tool; dimension between parallel references (e.g. walls or ducts) or multiple points |
| 2. *Linear* | Dimensions between points and always horizontal or vertical |
| 3. *Angular* | Measures angle between two references |
| 4. *Radial* | Indicates the radius of a curved line or element |
| 5. *Diameter* | Indicates the diameter of an arc or circle |
| 6. *Arc Length* | Measures the length of a line/element along a curve |
| 7. *Spot Elevation* | Lists the elevation at a selected point, on an element (e.g. floor, ceiling, toposurface) |
| 8. *Spot Coordinate* | Indicates the N/S and E/W position of a selected point |
| 9. *Spot Slop* | Used to indicate the slope of a ramp in plan or the pitch of a roof in elevation |

The following example floor plan below shows each of the dimension types used. This is a middle school choir room with various conditions to dimension, such as angled walls, curved lines and multiple floor elevations.

**FIGURE 7-2.1** Example floor plan used for dimensioning study

**Aligned - Dimension**

This dimension tool is the most used of the dimension tools, and for this reason it is also located on the Quick Access Toolbar (QAT).

Steps to add Aligned dimensions:
- Review **Type Selector** and **Options Bar** selections
- **Select first reference**
  - Click on element *or*
  - Press tab to select specific reference or intersection
- **Select second reference**
- Optional: Select additional references (creates a dimension string)
- **Click away** from anything dimensionable to finish command

The **Align** dimension tool is able to create angled, horizontal and vertical dimensions. When the tool is first started, the default option is to select a **Wall Centerline**, per the selection on the Options Bar, just by clicking on a wall. This in turn starts a dimension line perpendicular to that wall. The second point could then be another wall at the same angle or the endpoint or intersection of lines.

In the example to the right, if the vertical wall is rotated the dimension will also rotate. If the dimension needs to remain horizontal, then the Linear dimension should be used.

The image below shows the User Interface while the Aligned dimension tool is active.

**FIGURE 7-2.2** Using the Aligned dimension tool

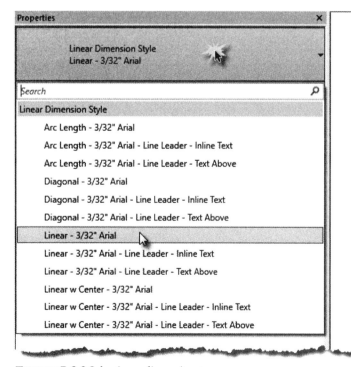

**FIGURE 7-2.3** Selecting a dimension type

Here is a description of the numbered items in the image above:
1. Type Selector
2. Selection Preference
3. Individual or Automatic Dimension
4. Switch to another dimension tool

Type Selector:
Once the dimension tool is active, select the desired **Type** from the *Type Selector* (Figure 7-2.3). This list will vary depending on the template the project was started with and any modifications made.

Selection Preference:

The default is **Wall Centerlines** which means just clicking on a wall, even when zoomed way out, the dimension will reference the centerline of the wall. The other options listed (Figure 7-2.4) are self-explanatory. Another option, rather than changing this drop-down list, is to hover the cursor over the desired face, e.g. **Wall faces**, and then tap the Tab key until that face is highlighted and then click. This can save the time it takes to keep moving the cursor all the way up to the Options Bar and changing the formal setting.

**FIGURE 7-2.4** Specify the selection preference for dimensions

Individual versus Automatic Dimensions:

Revit defaults to **Individual References** option so the designer can deliberately select each reference to dimension to (Figure 7-2.5).

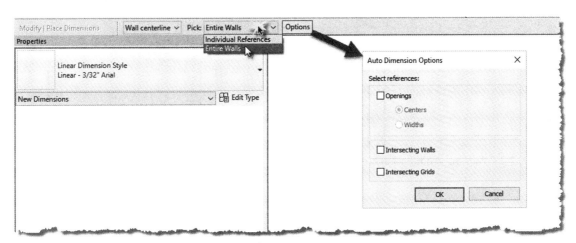

**FIGURE 7-2.5** Specify individual or automatic dimensioning

Switching this option to **Entire Wall**, by default, will just add a dimension for the entire length of a selected wall. If **Wall Faces** is selected as well, the overall dimension is created as shown in the next image (Figure 7-2.6). Again, this dimension was created by simply clicking on the wall (with the door and windows); one click to specify the reference and another to position the line.

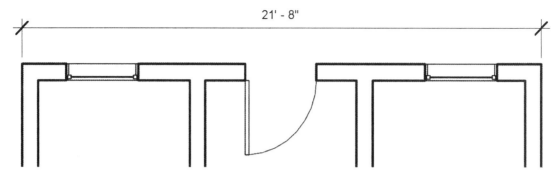

**FIGURE 7-2.6** Automatic dimension created – example 1

When the Entire Wall options is selected, the Options button becomes active. Clicking this presents several options as shown in Figure 7-2.5. With the <u>Options Bar</u> set to **Wall Centerlines** and the <u>Options</u> dialog box set to **Openings\Centerlines** and **Intersecting Walls**, the string of dimensions shown below is automatically created (Figure 7-2.7).

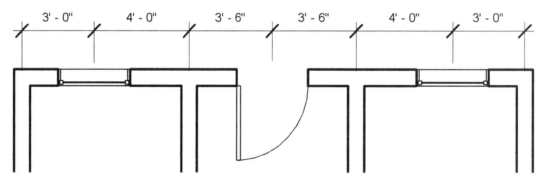

**FIGURE 7-2.7** Automatic dimension created – example 2

In this next example, Figure 7-2.8, with the <u>Options Bar</u> set to **Wall Faces** and the <u>Options</u> dialog box set to **Openings\Width** and **Intersecting Walls**, the string of dimensions shown below is automatically created

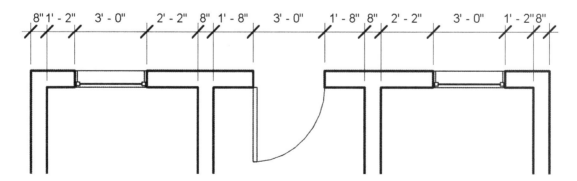

**FIGURE 7-2.8** Automatic dimension created – example 3

**Linear - Dimension**

Use this tool to force Revit to maintain horizontal and vertical dimension segments or strings.

> Steps to add Linear dimensions:
> - Review **Type Selector** selection
> - **Select first reference**
>   - Intersection of walls and/or grids *or*
>   - Press tab to select specific reference or intersection
> - **Select second reference**
> - Optional: Select additional reference
> - **Click away** from anything dimensionable to finish command

This tool will automatically pick points rather than the face of an element. In the example shown to the right, after picking the two points to be dimensioned, the direction the mouse is moved (in this case, up or to the left) will determine if the dimension is horizontal or vertical—pressing the Space Bar will also toggle between the two orientations.

If the model is adjusted, these dimensions will automatically update regardless of which view they are in. Similarly, if one of these elements is deleted, these dimensions will also be deleted.

**Angular - Dimension**

Use this tool to indicate the angle between two references.

> Steps to add Angular dimensions:
> - Review **Type Selector** and **Options Bar** selections
> - **Select first reference**
> - **Select second reference**
> - **Click** to place the location of the dimension line and text

Using the angular tool provides a way to measure the angle between two elements. In the example to the right, the dimension could be in three different positions: one where it is, one in the lower right and the larger obtuse angle on the left.

If the two references are modified the angular dimension will update no matter which view it is in.

### Radius - Dimension

Use this tool to indicate the radius of an arc or circular reference. This can be the edge of a floor, wall, duct or detail lines.

> Steps to add a Radius dimension:
> - Review **Type Selector** and **Options Bar** selections
> - **Select the reference**
> - **Click** to place the location of the dimension line and text

By default, the Radius dimension extends to the center point of the arc or circle. If a plan view is cropped, and Annotation Crop is active for the view, the center point must be visible within the cropped area.

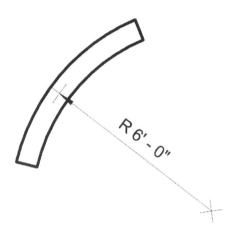

Once the Radius is placed, the radius dimension can be selected and the grip at the center point can be repositioned closer to the arc. Additionally, it is possible to turn off the **Center Mark** symbol via the Type properties. However, in some cases the location of the center mark itself should be dimensioned so the contractor can accurately position the element within the building.

### Diameter - Dimension

Use this tool to indicate the diameter of an arc or circular reference. This can be the edge of a floor, wall, duct or detail lines.

> Steps to add a Diameter dimension:
> - Review **Type Selector** and **Options Bar** selections
> - **Select the reference**
> - **Click** to place the location of the dimension line and text

### Arc Length - Dimension

Use this tool to measure the length of a line along a curved reference. This can be the edge of a floor, wall, duct or detail lines.

> Steps to add an Arc Length dimension:
> - Review **Type Selector** and **Options Bar** selections
> - **Select the reference**
> - **Click** to place the location of the dimension line and text

**Spot Elevation - Dimension**
Use this tool to indicate the elevation of a surface.

> Steps to add a Spot Elevation dimension:
> - Review **Type Selector** and **Options Bar** selections
> - **Select the reference**
> - **Click** to place the location of the text and leader

The elevation listed is based on one of three options as listed below. This is a Type Property called Elevation Origin. Thus, it is possible to use all three options, even right next to each other.

Elevation Origin options for a Spot Elevation type:
- Project Base Point
- Survey Point
- Relative

Project Base Point:
This option is related to the **level datum** numbers in the project. For example, the default templates which come with Revit have Level 1 at elevation 0'-0". In this example, all Spot Elevations set to Project Base Point will be relative to 0'-0" within a project.

16' - 6"

Survey Point:
The Survey Base point is an **alternate coordinate system** used to align with the actual position on earth and elevation above sea level. Thus, any Spot Elevation set to Survey Point will display a value relative to the Survey Point settings. For example, where the Level 1 floor's Project Base Point is set to 0'-0" (or 100'-0") the Survey value for Level 1 might be 650'-0" to match the elevation numbers shown for the contours on the Civil Engineer's grading plan. Revit has the ability to track both coordinate systems within the context of the Spot Elevation tool.

116' - 6"

Relative:
When a Spot Elevation has the Elevation Origin set to Relative, the values listed are related to the plan view in which they are placed.

6"

## Spot Coordinate

Use this tool to indicate the North/South, East/West position of a point within the model.

> Steps to add a Spot Coordinate dimension:
> - Review **Type Selector** and **Options Bar** selections
> - **Select the reference point**
> - **Click** to place the location of the text and leader

This feature can be used to indicate the position of one, or more, corners of the building on the site. This is usually relative to a predefined Survey Point which is relative to a bench mark or municipal coordinate system. On a typical commercial project this information is only provided on the civil drawings and therefore not required in the Revit model or documents.

N 65' - 4 1/4"
E -279' - 9 3/4"

Similar to the Spot Elevation tool, the Spot Coordinate can also be set to Relative or Project Base Point. This could be used to position items within the project, but is not practiced in many cases as the contractor or installer would need to have a direct line of sight between the two points.

**Spot Slope**
Use this tool to indicate the **Slope** in a <u>floor plan view</u> or the roof **Pitch** in an <u>elevation view</u>.

> Steps to add a Spot Elevation dimension:
> * Review **Type Selector** and **Options Bar** selections
> * **Click** to both select a reference and place the location of the dimension element

<u>Plan views:</u>
In a plan view the Spot Slope can be used to indicate the slope of a floor, such as a ramp. However, as it currently works, the Ramp element cannot have a Spot Slope annotation applied to it. Thus, ramps should be modeled as a sloped floor, which can have a Spot Slope applied.

<u>Elevation View:</u>
In an elevation view the Spot Slope can be used to indicate the pitch of a roof as shown in the example to the right.

**TIP:** When placing the Spot Elevation on a hip roof, in elevation, use the Tab key to select the correct surface. By default the hip line will be selected, which is not the same slope as the roof face itself.

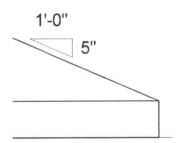

The Spot Slope element has an Instance Parameter, in the Properties Palette, which toggles between Arrow and Triangle, the two options shown above.

# Modifying a Dimension

When dimensions need to be modified, there are a few things to know.

> Ways to Modify a Dimension:
> * Edit Witness Lines
> * Modify text
> * Reposition text
> * Lock a Dimension
> * Drive the location of geometry
> * Change type

Edit Witness Lines:
After a dimension is placed, a wall or opening may be added, and rather than deleting a dimension string and adding a new one, Revit provides the **Edit Witness Line** tool. Simply select a dimension and click the Edit Witness Line button, shown to the right, from the Ribbon. Once active, click new references to **add witness lines** and click existing references to **remove witness lines**.

Modify text:
When a dimension is selected, clicking on the text, the dimension value, the Dimension Text dialog appears (Figure 7-2.9).

**FIGURE 7-2.9** Dimension Text dialog

Figure 7-2.10 shows the relative position of each of the "text fields."

When **Replace With Text** is selected, the dimension value can be replaced with text. For example, "PAINT WALL" or "EXISTING CORRIDOR WIDTH – VERIFY IN FIELD."

Revit will not allow a dimension value in the text replacement box.

Above
Prefix 21' - 8" Suffix

Below

**FIGURE 7-2.10** Dimension text field positions

Reposition text:
When a dimension is selected, clicking and
dragging on the text grip allows the text to be
repositioned.

When the text is moved past one of the witness
lines, Revit will add a leader by default as
shown to the right (Figure 7-2.11). Right-
clicking on a dimension reveals related
commands on the pop-up menu (Figure 7-
2.12); selecting **Reset Dimension Text
Position** will move the text back to the original
location.

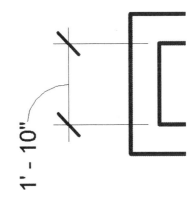

**FIGURE 7-2.11** Dimension Text leader

Lock a Dimension:
When a dimension is selected, clicking the lock icon
(Figure 7-2.13), will prevent that dimension value from
changing. This will not prevent model elements from
moving, but to maintain the dimension value, both
reference elements will move. For example, if a
dimension is locked between two walls which define a
corridor, moving one wall will move the other wall to
ensure the corridor width does not change.

**FIGURE 7-2.12** Right-click options

When elements are selected which are in some way
constrained, Revit will show the lock symbol. This is
true even if the locked dimension is not visible in the
current view (Figure 7-2.14). Clicking this icon will
unlock the constraint.

When a locked dimension is deleted, Revit asks if the constraint should also be
removed. Thus, it is possible to delete the dimension but leave the constraint in
place.

**FIGURE 7-2.13** Dimension selected

**FIGURE 7-2.14** Locked element

Drive the location of geometry:
Like temporary dimensions, permanent dimensions can also be used to reposition geometry, such as walls, ducts and more. The key is to select the element to be repositioned first and then click on the dimension text. A common mistake is to select the dimension directly and then click the text. This only opens the Dimension Text dialog. Also, consider that Revit would not know which referenced element to move if just selecting the dimension and not the element; move the left one, move the right element or both equally?

*TIP:* A temporary dimension can be turned into a permanent dimension by clicking the "dimension icon" below the temporary dimension text.

**FIGURE 7-2.15**
Temporary dimension selected

Change Dimension Type:
When a dimension is selected, click the Type Selector and click from the available options. Changing the type can affect the graphic appearance, the rounding and when alternate units appear (e.g. metric).

# Create and Modify Dimension Types

Sometimes it is necessary to modify a dimension type to match a graphically firm standard or a client requirement. Revit allows dimension types to be created and modified. Use caution changing dimension type as all dimensions of that type will be updated in the current project. These changes will not have any effect on any other projects or templates.

To modify existing types, either start the dimension command and click Edit Type or select one of the "Types" options in the extended panel area of the dimension panel on the Annotate tab (Figure 7-2.16).

**FIGURE 7-2.16** Editing Dimension types

To create new Types, click the **Duplicate** option in the Type Properties dialog.

Figure 7-2.17 shows the various options which can be changed.

One option is **Units Format**. Selecting this option opens the Format dialog shown in Figure 7-2.18. Notice a dimension style can be tied to the Project Units as set on the Manage tab. Un-checking this option allows this dimension style to round in a specific way and do a few other things like "Suppress 0 feet:" and control the symbol (e.g. monetary symbol).

Setting up all dimension styles typically needed in a template file will save a lot of time and help to enforce a firm's standard.

*TIP*: To see how many instances use a specific dimension style in a project, select one and then right-click and pick Select All Instances → In Entire Project. The total number selected will be listed in the lower right corner of the screen by the filter icon on the status bar.

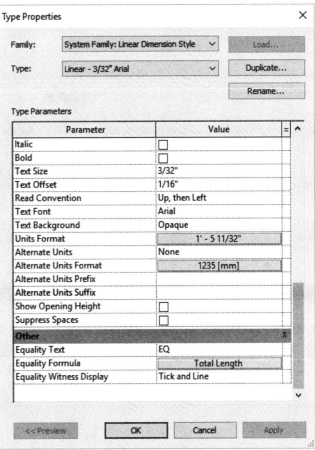

**FIGURE 7-2.17** Dimension type properties

**FIGURE 7-2.18** Dimension unit format

## Dimension Equality

When a dimension string is selected, an **EQ** symbol appears with a red slash through it as seen in Figure 7-2.19. Clicking this toggle will make all dimension segments, in that string, equally spaced between the two ends.

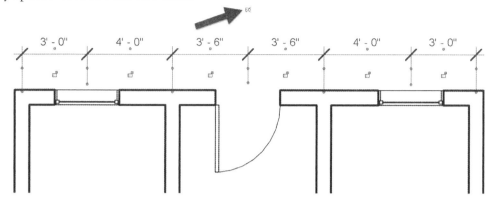

**FIGURE 7-2.19** Dimension string selected and EQ symbol pointed

The image below (Figure 7-2.20) shows the result of clicking the EQ icon; the walls, windows and door all moved with the now equally spaced witness lines. Notice the EQ icon no longer has a slash through it. If one of the end walls are moved, all elements are moved to remain equally spaced. Setting the Dimension's **Equality Display** property to Value shows the dimension value rather than the "EQ" abbreviation.

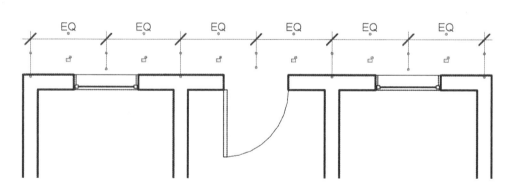

**FIGURE 7-2.20** Dimension string with equality activated

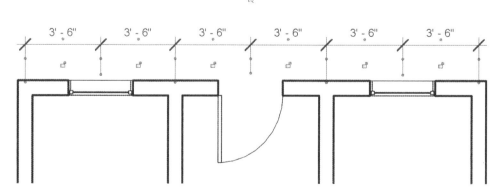

**FIGURE 7-2.21** Dimension string with equality activated and dimension value shown

## Exercise 7-3:
## Tagging

This section will study how **tags** work in Revit. This is an important feature in Revit, one used extensively by designers. This feature is often used on casework and ductwork as well as many other elements within the Revit model.

The basic premise of a *tag* is to be able to textually represent, in a drawing view, information found within an element, that is, an *Instance* or *Type Parameter*. One example found in nearly every set of construction documents is the door tag. This tag in Revit has been set up to list the contents of a specific door's **Mark** parameter, which is an *Instance Parameter*.

> The process to tag an element is simple:
> - Select the **Tag by Category** tool from the *Quick Access Toolbar.*
> - Adjust the settings on the *Options Bar* if needed.
> - Click the element(s) to be tagged.
>
>     *FYI: Different tags are placed based on the category of the element selected.*
>
> - Click the *Modify* button or press the Esc key when done.

A *tag* is view specific, meaning if you add the tag to the **Level 1 Finish Plan**, it will not automatically show up in the **Level 1 Furniture Plan**. If you want the tag to appear in two Level 1 plan views, you need to add it twice. *(TIP: Use Copy/Paste.)* The advantage is you can adjust the tag location independently in each view. One view may have furniture showing and the other floor finishes. Each view might require the tag to be in a different location to keep it readable.

Tags are dependent on the element selected during placement. You cannot simply move a tag near another similar element and expect Revit to recognize this change. Similarly, if an element is deleted, the tag will also be removed from the model, even if the tag is in another view in the project.

The image below has several tags added to a floor plan view. All the listed information is coming from the properties of the elements which have been tagged. For example, the "M1" tag within the diamond shape is listing the wall type (i.e., *Type Mark*). Because the wall tag(s) is/are listing a *Type Parameter*, all wall instances of that type will report the same value, i.e., "M1." The door number "1" is reporting the element's **Mark** value, which is an *Instance Parameter*. Therefore, each door instance may have a different number. Notice some tags have the *Leader* option turned on. This is especially helpful if the tag is outside the room. Any 3D element visible in a view may be tagged, even the floor. In this case the *Floor Tag* is actually reporting the *Type Name* listed in the *Type Selector*. The leader can be modified to have an arrow or a dot.

**FIGURE 7-3.1** Floor plan with tags added

All of these tags were placed using the same tool: *Tag by Category*. Later you will learn how to specify which tag gets used for each category (e.g., walls, furniture, floors, windows, etc.).

The section / interior elevation below (Figure 7-3.2) shows many of the same elements tagged, as were tagged in the floor plan view on the previous page. If the wall's *Type Mark* is changed, the wall *Tag* will be instantly updated in all views: plans, elevations, sections, and schedules.

The tags had to be manually added to this view. They are not added here automatically just because you added one in the floor plan view, unlike when you add a section mark. If the view is deleted from the project, all these tags will automatically be deleted.

Some tags can actually report multiple parameter values found within an element. For example, the *Ceiling Tag* used in this example lists the *Type Name*, the ceiling height, and has fixed text which reads "A.F.F." Many tags can be selected and directly edited, which actually changes the values within the element. Changing the 8'-0" ceiling height will actually cause the ceiling position to change vertically.

It is possible to tag an element multiple times. You could add the same tag more than once. In the example below, you could place a *Wall Tag* on each side of the door. You can also add different tags which report different information from the same element. The *Wall Tag* "M1" and the *Material Tag* "PT-1" are two different tags extracting information from the same wall.

**FIGURE 7-3.2** Section / interior elevation with tags added

Most design firms spend a little time adjusting the provided tags to make the text a little smaller and modify or delete the line work. This can easily be done by selecting a tag and then clicking *Edit Family* on the *Ribbon*. Revised tags can then be loaded back into the project and saved to a company template for future use.

With the more recent versions of Revit it is now possible to add tags in 3D views (Figure 7-3.3b). Before tagging a 3D view, you must *Lock* it (Figure 7-3.3a) to prevent changing the view and interfering with the position of the tags relative to the elements being tagged.

**FIGURE 7-3.3A** Locking a 3D view

When the *Leader* option is off, the tag is placed centered on the elected element. This initial position is not always desirable (e.g., note the D1 and C1 tags below) and you must move each tag so it is readable.

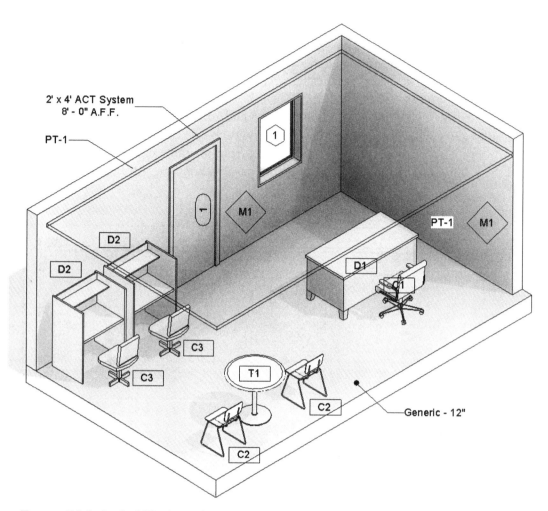

**FIGURE 7-3.3B** Locked 3D view with tags added

It is not possible to add *Room Tags* to 3D views yet.

It is helpful to understand where the information displayed in tags is stored. It is often necessary to change these values. In Figure 7-3.4 you can see that "PT-1" is the *Description* for the *Material* assigned to the wall type.

> **TIP:** *To find the* Material *assigned to a specific wall type: Select the wall → Edit Type → Edit Structure → observe the Material column.*

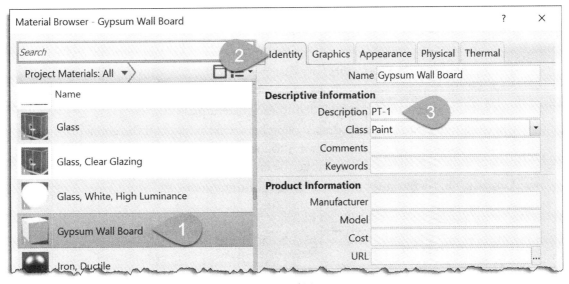

FIGURE 7-3.4 Material description value used in Material Tag

**FYI:** In the image above, the preview icons on the left with a gold triangle in the lower left corner are legacy materials, which are superseded by newer physically accurate materials.

A wall's *Type Mark* is found in the *Type Properties* dialog; select a wall → *Edit Type* from the *Properties Palette*. Notice in Figure 7-3.5 that the *Type Mark* is set to "M1." If you were to edit this value, all the tags for this wall will be updated instantly.

Seeing as all the information displayed in a tag is actually stored in the element being tagged, you will never lose any information by deleting a tag.

> *FYI: A tag will move with the element even if the element is moved in another view where the tag is not visible.*

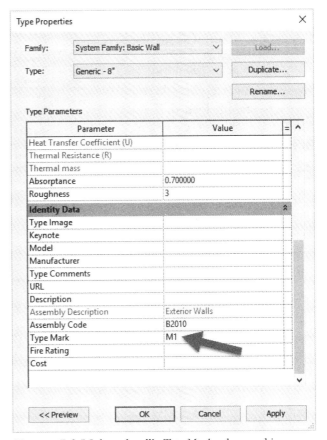

FIGURE 7-3.5 Selected wall's *Type Mark* value used in wall tag

The image below (Figure 7-3.6) shows the settings available on the *Options Bar* when the *Tag* tool is active.

- The tag can only be ***Horizontal*** or ***Vertical.***
- Clicking the **Tags…** button allows you to specify which tags are used when multiple tags for the same category are loaded in the current project.
- Checking the ***Leader*** option draws a line between the tag and the element.
  - *Attached End:* the leader always touches the tagged element.
  - *Free End:* allows you to move the end of the leader.
- **Length**: This determines the initial length of the leader.

**FIGURE 7-3.6** Tag options during placement

When clicking the ***Tags…*** button you get the ***Loaded Tags*** dialog as shown in Figure 7-3.7.

Notice some categories do not have a tag family loaded. If you tried to tag a *Casework* element, Revit would prompt you to load a tag.

Clicking on a tag name in the right-hand column will allow you to select from multiple tag types/families, if available in the current project.

If you use one tag type in plan views and another in elevation views, you would visit this dialog just before tagging in plan views and then again adjust before tagging in elevation views.

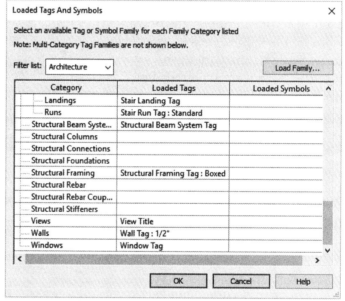

**FIGURE 7-3.7** Loaded tags dialog

*FYI: It is possible to just let Revit place the default tag and then select the placed tag and swap it out via the* Type Selector.

*TIP: If you want to swap several tags with another type: Select one of the tags* → *right-click* → **Select All Instances** *and then pick either* **Visible in View** *or* **In Entire Project**. *You now have all the tags selected and can pick something else via the* Type Selector.

The reader should be aware that some tags may be placed automatically when content is being added to the model. For example, when placing a window, the *Ribbon* has a toggle called **Tag on Placement** (Figure 7-3.8). When this is selected, which it is NOT by default, a door tag is placed next to every door. Note that the tag is only added to the current view, which could be an elevation, plan, etc.

You typically want to turn this off in the early design stages as the tags will just get in the way. Also, existing elements are not usually tagged, thus you would toggle this option off so you do not have to come back and delete the tag later.

FIGURE 7-3.8 Tag on Placement option; **off** (shown on left) and **on** (on right)

If you did not add tags, or some were deleted along the way, you will need to add them at some point. The easiest way to do this is by using the **Tag All** tool; this tool used to be called *Tag All Not Tagged*. When you use this tool, you can add a door tag to every door in the current view that does not already have a door tag. This is great on large projects with hundreds of doors and you want to make sure you do not miss any. You may still have to go around and rotate and reposition a few tags, but overall this is much faster!

Before concluding this introduction to tags we will take a brief look at how tags are created. If you select a tag and then click *Edit Family* on the *Ribbon*, you will have opened the tag for editing in the *Family Editor*. Keep in mind that your project is still open in addition to the tag family.

If you select a furniture tag and edit it you will see text (sample value shown) and four lines (Figure 7-3.9). Here the lines can be selected and deleted if desired. Also, the text can be selected and then you can click *Edit Type* to change the text properties (e.g., height, font, width factor, etc.).

If you select the text and then click the **Edit Label** option on the *Ribbon*, you can change the parameter being reported, or report multiple parameters (Figure 7-3.9).

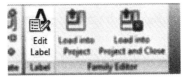

*TIP: Open a tag family, edit it and then do a* Save-As *to make a new tag type.*

**FIGURE 7-3.9** Editing a tag label in the family editor

In the *Edit Label* dialog above you can click the **New** icon in the lower left to load a *Shared Parameter* which allows you to create a tag which reports custom information. See the next section for more on this topic. Also, the last icon all the way to the right of the "New" icon allows you to override the formatting for numeric parameters (Figure 7-3.10).

This concludes the introduction to using tags in Revit. The next section continues this discussion with a more advanced concept called *Shared Parameters*.

**FIGURE 7-3.10** Editing a label's format

## Exercise 7-4:
## Shared Parameters

*FYI: You will not be using Shared Parameters in the tutorial but this information is essential for a designer to be proficient and properly leverage Revit's power.*

## Introduction

Revit has many features which are unique when compared to other building design programs; one of these is *Shared Parameters*. The main idea with *Shared Parameters* is to be able to manage parameters across multiple projects, families and template files. This feature allows Revit to know that you are talking about the same piece of information in the context of multiple unconnected files. Here we will cover the basics of setting up *Shared Parameters*, some of the problems often encountered, and a few tricks.

The main reason for using **Shared Parameters** is to make custom information show up in tags; however, there are a few other uses which will be mentioned later. In contrast, a **Project Parameter** is slightly easier to make in a project but cannot appear in a tag; Revit has no way of knowing the parameter created in the family, info to be tagged, and the parameter created in the tag are the same bit of information. Both *Project* and *Shared Parameters* may appear in schedules.

The image below depicts the notion of a common storage container (i.e., the **Shared Parameter** file) from which uniquely coded parameters can be loaded into content, annotation and projects. This creates a connected common thread between several otherwise disconnected files.

Content            Tags                        Projects

## Shared Parameter File

Creating a *Shared Parameter* is fairly straightforward, but afterwards, managing them can be troublesome. Select **Manage → Shared Parameters** from the *Ribbon* to open the *Shared Parameters* dialog box (Figure 7-4.1). This dialog basically modifies a simple **text file** which should not be edited manually. If a text file has not yet been created, you will need to select the **Create** button and provide a file name and location for your *Shared Parameter* file.

It is important to keep in mind that this file will be the main record of all your *Shared Parameters*. From this file you create *Shared Parameters* within Projects, Templates and Families. Therefore, it is ideal to only maintain one file for the entire firm, even if you have multiple locations. Of course, there is

**FIGURE 7-4.1** Edit Shared Parameters dialog

always an exception to the rule. This single file should be stored on the server and the software deployment should be set up to automatically point user computers to the *Shared Parameters* file. This can also be done manually by clicking the *Browse* button in the *Shared Parameters* dialog.

Once a *Shared Parameter* is loaded into a project, template or family, the text file is no longer referenced. So you technically do not need to send this file with your project file when transmitting to a consultant or contractor.

The name of the file should be simple and easy to find. You should create a new text file for each version of Revit you are using; include this in the file name. Some newer parameter types will cause older versions of the software to reject the text file.

## Creating a Shared Parameter

Open the *Shared Parameters* dialog box. Here you can easily create *Groups* and *Parameters*. *Groups* are simply containers, or folders, used to organize the multitude of parameters you will likely create over time. When starting from scratch, you must first create one *Group* before creating your first *Shared Parameter*.

To create a new *Group*, click the **New** button under the *Groups* heading. In a multi-discipline firm you should have at least one group for each discipline. Parameters can be moved around later so do not worry too much about that at first.

Click the **New** button under the *Parameters* heading to create a new parameter in the current *Group.* You only need to provide three bits of information:

- Name
- Discipline
- Type of Parameter
- Tooltip

**FIGURE 7-4.2** Setting Parameter Properties

In this example, see image to the right (Figure 7-4.2); we will create a parameter called "Clear Width" which will be used in our door families (but can be used with other categories as this is not specified at this level). The other standard options, such as *Instance* versus *Type*, are assigned when the parameter is set up in the project or family.

The **Discipline** option simply changes the options available in the *Type of Parameter* drop-down. The **Type of Parameter** drop-down lets Revit know what type of information will be stored in the parameter you are creating. Many programming languages require parameters to be declared before they are used and cannot later be altered. Revit is basically a graphical programming language in this sense.

The **Edit Tooltip** button allows a description of the parameter to be entered. Anyone working in the project will see the description when they hover their cursor over the parameter in the Properties Palette or Edit Type dialog.

When a new *Shared Parameter* is created, a unique code is assigned to it. The image below (Figure 7-4.3) shows the code created for the "Clear Width" parameter just created. For this reason, it is not possible to simply create another *Shared Parameters* file a few months from now and have it work the same.

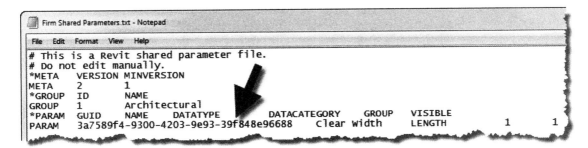

**FIGURE 7-4.3** Shared Parameters text file

## Creating a Shared Parameter in a Family

Now that you have created the framework for your *Shared Parameters*, i.e., the text file, you can now begin to create parameters within content; the next section covers creating *Shared Parameters* in project files.

Open a family file – in this example we will open the **Door - Single – Panel.rfa** file (C:\ProgramData\Autodesk\RVT 2019\Libraries\US Imperial\Doors). Select the *Family Types* icon. Click the *New Parameter* icon on the lower-left (Figure 7-4.5). Now select *Shared parameter* and then the *Select* button (Figure 7-4.4). This will open the shared parameter text file previously created. Select "Clear Width" and then **OK**.

Now you only have two bits of information left to provide. Is the parameter *Type* or *Instance* and what is the "Group parameter under" option? This controls which section the parameter shows up under in the *Properties Palette*.

Notice how the bits of information specified in the *Shared Parameters* file are grayed out here.

**FIGURE 7-4.4** Parameter properties

They cannot be changed as this would cause discrepancies between families and project files. This information is hard-wired.

**FIGURE 7-4.5** Family Types in family editor environment

Once the parameter has been created in the family it can be used just like a *Family Parameter*. In this example we created a formula to subtract the frame stops and the hinge/door imposition on the opening (Figure 7-4.5). Keep in mind that this value could now appear in a custom tag if desired, thus listing the clear width for each door in a floor plan. Maybe the code official has required this. Using *Shared Parameters* is the only way to achieve this short of using dumb text, that is, text manually typed which does not change automatically.

Next we will look at creating a door tag that lists the clear width. This is similar to the steps just covered for the door family as a tag is also a family. The only difference is this parameter will be associated to a *Label*.

Open the default **Door Tag.rfa** family (location: C:\ProgramData\Autodesk\RVT 2019\Libraries\US Imperial\Annotations\Architectural). Do a *Save As* and rename the file to **Door Tag – Clear Width.rfa**. Delete the linework, if desired. Select the text and click the *Edit Label* button on the *Ribbon*. In the *Edit Label* dialog you need to create a new parameter, by clicking the icon in the lower left; see image below. Your only option here is to select a *Shared Parameter*, as previously mentioned, only *Shared Parameters* can be tagged. Once the new parameter is created, click to move it to the right side of the dialog, in the *Label Parameters* column. Next, select the original *Mark* parameter and remove it. Finally, edit the *Sample Value* to something like 2′-10″; this is what appears in the family to give you an idea of what the tag will look like in the project.

*FYI: The* Mark *parameter could be left in the tag if you wanted both the* Mark *and* Clear Width *to appear together. The other option is to have two separate tags which can be moved independently. Keep in mind it is possible to tag the same element multiple times. In this case you would have two door tags on the same door, each tag being a different type.*

Load your new door and door tag families into a new project file. In the next section you will see how these work in the project environment.

## Using Shared Parameters in a Project

Now that you have your content and tags set up you can use them in the project. First, draw a wall and then place an instance of the *Single – Flush* door (turn off *Tag on Placement*). Select the door and notice the *Clear Width* parameter is showing up in the *Properties Palette*; it is an <u>Instance Parameter</u>. Add another door to the right of this one and change the width to 30″ via the *Type Selector*. Notice the *Clear Width* value has changed.

Next you will tag the two doors. Select the **Tag by Category** icon from the *Quick Access Toolbar*. Uncheck the *Leader* option and select each door. In the image below, the tag was also set to be *Vertical* via the *Options Bar*. If the tag placed is the door number, select the door tag and change it to the *Clear Width* option via the *Type Selector*.

*TIP: If the text does not fit on one line you have to go back into the family and increase the width of the text box and reload the family into the project.*

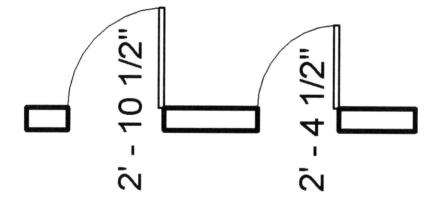

## Things to Know

Only content which contains the *Shared Parameters* will display the parameter placeholder in a project. Try loading another door family (e.g., *Double – Flush*) into your test project without changing it in any way. Place an instance and then notice the *Clear Width* option does not appear in the *Properties Palette*. This means all content must have the *Shared Parameter* added to it. It is possible to create a *Project Parameter*, in the project/template file, but you have to specify *Instance* or *Type*. If this varies you cannot use a *Project Parameter*. The *Project Parameter* takes precedence and will change loaded content.

Selectively associating parameters with content is a great trick when it comes to certain categories having a variety of items, such as *Furniture* or *Mechanical Equipment*. Only loading

*Shared Parameters* into file cabinets or Air Handling Units (AHU) will make it so those parameters do not appear in your lounge chairs or VAV boxes.

> *FYI: This also works with* Family Parameters *but this information cannot be tagged or scheduled.*

# Dealing with Problems

A number of problems can be created when *Shared Parameters* are not managed properly. The most common is when two separate *Shared Parameters* are created with the same name. This often happens when new users delete or otherwise lose a *Shared Parameter* file. They then try to recreate it manually, not knowing that the unique code, mentioned previously, is different and Revit will see this as a different *Shared Parameter*. The first place this problem typically shows up is when a schedule in the project has blank spaces even though the placed content has information in it. In this case, the schedule is using one specific version of the *Shared Parameter* and only the content using that same version of the *Shared Parameter* will appear in that schedule.

The fix for this problem is to open the bad content and re-associate the parameters with the correct *Shared Parameter*. It is not necessary to delete the bad parameter, which is good as this could cause problems with existing formulas.

If you get content from another firm you are working with and they have used *Shared Parameters* it is possible to export those parameters from the *Family Editor* into your *Shared Parameter* file. They will initially be located in the *Exported Parameters* group, but can then be moved to a more appropriate location. This allows that unique code to be recreated in your file.

If you have a *Shared Parameter* with the same name as another firm's *Shared Parameter,* and you are working on the same model, that is a problem. You will have to decide whose version to use. There are some tools one can use to add and modify *Shared Parameters* in batch groups of families. One is found in the new *Extensions for Revit 2019*, which is available via the subscription website.

# Conclusion

Using *Shared Parameters* is a must in order to take full advantage of Revit's powerful features. Like any sophisticated tool, it takes a little effort to fully understand the feature and its nuances. Once you have harnessed the power of the feature and implemented it within your firm's content and templates you can be much more productive and have less potential for errors and omissions on your projects.

## Exercise 7-5:
## Keynoting

This exercise will present an overview of the keynoting system in Revit. There are no steps to be applied to the project in this section. At the end of the next chapter, Chapter 10 - Elevations, Sections and Details, you will apply some of these concepts.

## Hybrid Method

A simple way to manage keyed notes is to use a custom Symbol family with the symbol and descriptive text, where the text visibility can be toggled off per family instance. Thus, the keyed notes are placed in plan with the text hidden and the same keyed notes are also placed in a legend (or drafting view) with the text visible.

Notice in the plan view below, the keyed note is selected and the custom instance parameter **Description Visible** is toggled off (Figure 7-5.1).

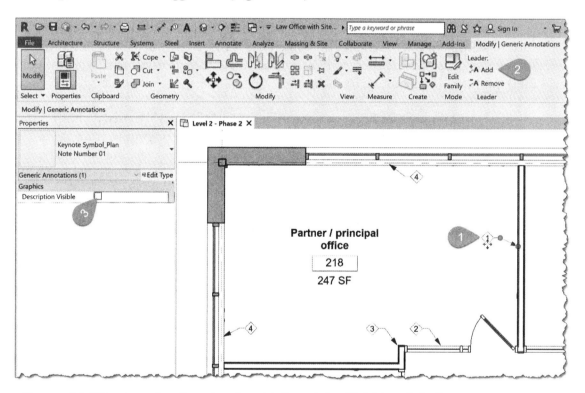

FIGURE 7-5.1 Keyed note in a floor plan view with 'Description Visible' toggled off

The next image shows the same family placed and then selected in a Legend view. In this view the **Description Visible** is checked (Figure 7-5.2).

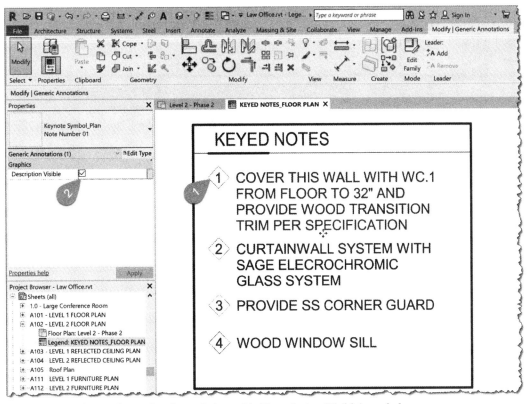

**FIGURE 7-5.2** Keyed note in a legend view with 'Description Visible' toggled on

The image to the right shows the type properties for keyed note number 1. Notice the Keynote and Description are type parameters. This helps prevent someone from using the same number multiple times with a different description.

This method requires a different family for each plan type: e.g. Plan, Finish, Demo, Code, etc. Each family having one type for each note.

**FYI:** This example uses the **Multiline** parameter introduced in Revit 2016.

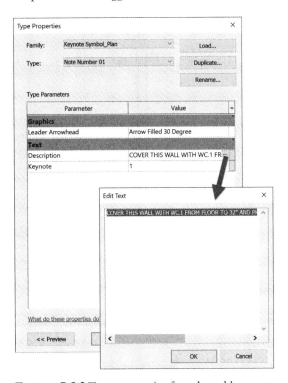

**FIGURE 7-5.3** Type properties for selected key note

## Material Keynotes

We often want to identify a material in the model with "smart" text. In this case, we are talking about a Revit material defined within a **System Family** (e.g. Wall, Ceiling, Floor), a **Loadable Family** (e.g. Furniture, Casework, Doors, etc.) or **Painted** on a surface (which overrides the material defined in the Family).

There are two ways to identify materials within a Revit model (Figure 7-5.4):

- **Material Keynote**

- **Material Tag**

FIGURE 7-5.4 Material keynote and tag tools on the Annotate tab

**FYI:** It should be pointed out, that even though we can define multiple materials for some elements, e.g. several layers within a wall (Brick, Insulation, Studs, Gypsum Board, etc.), we can only keynote/tag a material exposed in a view—i.e. we can click on it. Materials hidden within a wall or equipment family cannot be tagged.

The two examples, Material Keynote and Material Tag, are shown in the image below—referencing the wall and the wall/base cabinets (Figure 7-5.5). The boxed text is a Keynote and the adjacent text is a Material Tag.

FIGURE 7-5.5 Material keynote applied to two elements (wall and cabinets)

Both values represented in the previous image are defined within the Material Browser as seen in the image below (Figure 7-5.6).

- Material Keynote → **Keynote**
  - o *The value must be selected from the Keynote file (more on this later)*
- Material Tag → **Mark**
  - o *The user can enter any value here*

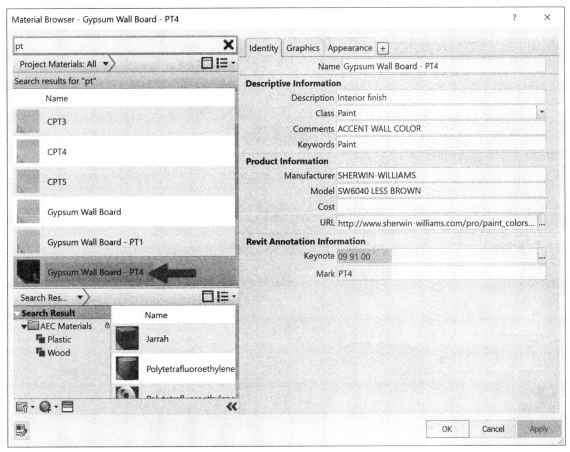

**FIGURE 7-5.6** Annotation information within a Revit material

When either of these methods are used, the tags will update automatically if the family/type is changed (which also changes the material) or if a different material is painted on the elements being tagged.

**When a Material is copied** the Keynote value is also copied (i.e. same keynote value is listed for the new material); however, the Mark value is not. The latter is preferred if you want to ensure the same value is not used for multiple materials.

## Element Keynotes

Keynotes can be used to nearly eliminate "dumb" text in Revit. Here we will quickly cover the basics of how keynotes work and then advance from there.

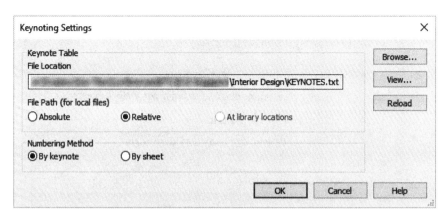

FIGURE 7-5.7 Keynoting settings dialog

First, the keynote information is stored in a simple text file (more on this in a minute). A Revit project can only reference one keynote file. The location to this file is defined in the **Keynoting Settings** file (Figure 7-5.7) via **Annotate → Keynotes**.

FIGURE 7-5.8 Keynote type parameter

Secondly, every model-based element in Revit has a **Keynote** type parameter (Figure 7-5.8). Editing this field opens the **Keynotes** dialog (Figure 7-5.9), which is a list based on the aforementioned external text file.

Third, use the **Element Keynote** tool to "tag" an element based on the predefined keynote value.

Fourth, create a **Keynote Legend** and place it on any sheets with keynoted views.

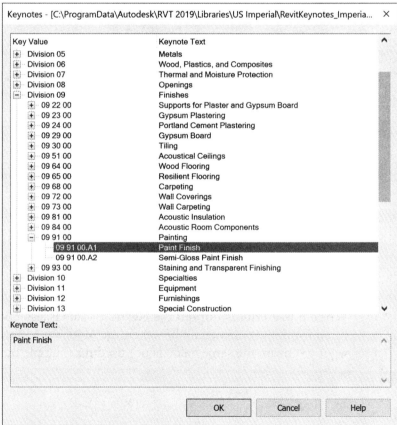

FIGURE 7-5.9 Keynotes dialog as viewed from within Revit

The result can be seen in the sheet view below (Figure 7-5.10). The default keynote tag shows the keynote number which corresponds to the same number and description in the legend. The result is "clean" looking drawings without excessive text.

**FIGURE 7-5.10** Example of a keynote legend and a view with keynotes

The keynote legend will only list keynotes that actually appear on a given sheet. Opening the keynote legend view directly will show all keynotes in the project. Keep in mind, the keynote legend only lists items which have been keynoted using the Keynote tool. It will not list a keynote just because an element's type property has a keynote value applied.

**TIP:** Use a Filter, in Schedule Properties, to limit the list if needed.

This represents a basic overview of how keynotes work in Revit – with an emphasis on the way it works out-of-the-box (OOTB). Next we will look at a variation on this system, using "normal" notes rather than MasterFormat section numbers (https://www.csiresources.org/practice/standards/masterformat).

For this alternate method we will start by creating a custom keynote file. Simply create an empty file using Microsoft Notepad and save it somewhere in your project folder (Figure 7-5.11).

To better understand the format of this file, note the following:

1. **Group definition**
   - unique number
   - descriptive text
2. **Keynote number**
3. **Keynote text**
4. **Group identifier**

The keynote text file must be stored on the server where all users have access to it (not necessarily edit rights).

Results below explained on the next page…

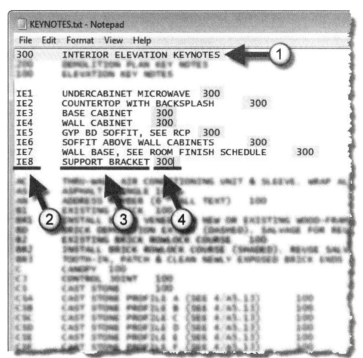

FIGURE 7-5.11 Anatomy of a keynote file

FIGURE 7-5.12 Keynotes added to elements in elevation - no "dumb" text

The elevation shown on the previous page has Element Keynotes added. The default Keynote tag has type properties to hide the keynote number & box and show the keynote number.

All the elements in the model have firm-approved standard notes applied to the Keynote type property. This information can be prepopulated within the content library to streamline production and produce consistency across the firm.

## Keynote Manager + Add-in for Revit

One challenge with maintaining the keynoting system in Revit is the text file can only be edited by one person at a time. Also, after changes are made, the changes must be manually reloaded (note the **Reload** button on the Keynoting Settings dialog) to see the changes in the current session of Revit (Figure 7-5.12).

Using **Keynote Manager +**, a third-party add-in for Revit, can help. This tool has the following features:

- Multiple users
- Auto reload
- Spellcheck
- Indicates keynotes used in project (with house icon)
- Auto sequencing
- Add comments and URL links

**FYI:** To store the additional comments and external links, a same named XML file is created right next to the keynote file.

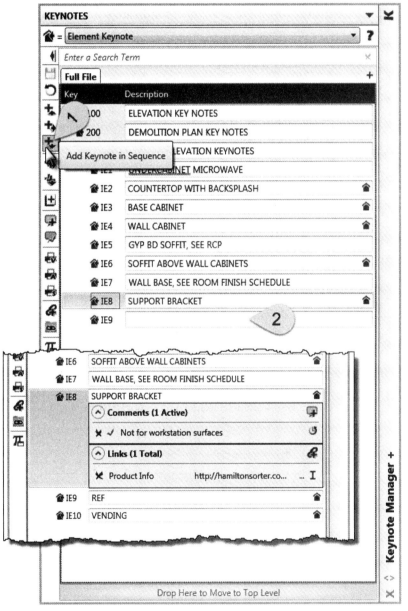

FIGURE 7-5.13 Keynote manager palette in Revit

Be sure to check out **Keynote Manager**, by Revolution Design, Inc., for a powerful add-in tool to help simplify the use of Keynotes in Revit. Multiple users can also work in the keynote file at the same time.
URL: http://revolutiondesign.biz/products/keynote-manager/features/

## User Keynotes

User Keynotes work the same way as Element Keynotes with one exception…

When the **User Keynote** tool is selected, the user is prompted to select an element to keynote. Next, a selection must be made from the keynote list (i.e. the text file).

Although this adds some flexibility to the process, it provides an opportunity for selecting the wrong keynote. In the example below, Figure 7-5.14, the selected base cabinet is tagged with three keynotes (highlighted in yellow). One is an **Element Keynote** and two are **User keynotes**—both user keynotes indicate something completely different.

**FIGURE 7-5.14** Multiple user keynotes applied to a single model element

Used correctly, the User Keynote tool can be helpful. However, those using it must be trained and pick carefully every time they use this tool.

## Exercise 7-6:
## Adding Dimensions

Next you will add dimensions to your floor plans. Revit provides a powerful dimension tool that allows you to quickly dimension drawings. This process is much easier than other CAD programs. Revit has a dimension style all set up and ready to use, which works for most designers. Furthermore, the size of the text and ticks are tied to the *View Scale* feature to make sure the dimensions always print at the correct size. For example, a dimension's text and ticks would get twice as big just by changing the *View Scale* from ¼″ = 1′-0″ to ⅛″ = 1′-0″. You will try this in a moment.

Industry standard dimensioning conventions were covered in the previous lesson. You may want to take a minute and review that information (see page 5-23).

Drawing dimensions in Revit involves the following steps:

- Select the *Aligned* dimension tool from the *Annotate* tab.

- *Ribbon*, *Options Bar* and *Type Selector*:
    - ○ Select one of the predefined styles from the *Type Selector*.
    - ○ Select the kind of dimension you want: Linear, Angular, Radial, Arch Length.
    - ○ Tell Revit what part of the wall you want to dimension to: Wall centerlines, Wall Face, Center of Core, Face of Core; this can change for each side of a dimension's line.

- Select two, or more, walls to dimension between.

- Select a location for the dimension line.


## Adding Dimensions to the First Floor Plan:

1. Open ex6-5.rvt and **Save-As ex7-6.rvt**.

2. Switch to the *First Floor Plan* view.

3. **Zoom in** on the North wall of the garage.

4. Select the **Annotate → Dimension → Aligned** tool.

Notice the *Ribbon, Options Bar* and *Type Selector* changes to give you control over the various options mentioned above (Figure 7-6.1).

**FIGURE 7-6.1** Ribbon, Option Bar and Type Selector: Dimension tool active

5. Set the *Type Selector* to **Linear – 3/32" Arial**.

6. Click the **Edit Type** button on the *Properties Palette*.

Notice the various properties you can adjust for the selected dimension type (Figure 7-6.2).

Creating a new, custom, dimension type is the same as for walls, doors, etc.; just click the *Duplicate* button, provide a name and then adjust the properties.

All the dimensions you see here are multiplied by the *View Scale*. For example, the 3/32" text is multiplied by 48 when the *View Scale* is set to ¼" = 1'-0"; thus, the text is 4½" tall in ¼" drawings. When the ¼" view is placed on a *Sheet*, Revit automatically scales the view down 1/48. At this point the text is 3/32" again. This makes the view actually a ¼" = 1'-0" on the *Sheet*, which is actual sheet size

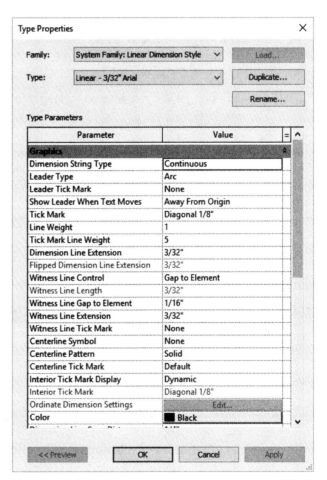

**FIGURE 7-6.2** Properties for selected dimension type

– say 22" x 34". Finally, all this is changed automatically whenever the *View Scale* is changed: dimension and text size as well as the *View* size on sheets! You will learn about *Sheets* later in the book.

7. Click **OK** to close the dialog box.

*The Aligned* dimension tool allows you to place dimensions by picking walls. You will try this now.

8. Next, select **Wall Faces** on the *Options Bar* (Figure 7-6.1).

9. Draw your first dimension by clicking the three points as identified in **Figure 7-6.3**.

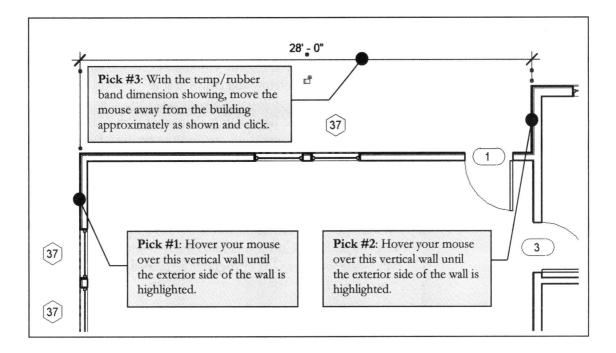

**FIGURE 7-6.3** First Floor plan: first dimension added

*FYI: In the figure above (7-6.3), you can select points 1 and 2 in the opposite order as well.*

10. Dimension the rest of the North exterior wall as shown in Figure 7-6.4. You may not be able to read the dimensions in the image provided, but you can still determine the number of dimensions required and Revit provides the dimension text anyway. See the next page for dimension comments.

Once you have drawn one dimension, as in Step 10, the remaining dimensions in that "string" should align with the first. Revit helps you make the third pick (as in Figure 7-6.3) by automatically snapping to the previous dimension when you move your cursor to it.

**Edit Witness Lines**

**Witness Lines**

You can add a "string" of dimensions by simply clicking on parallel walls. When done, click somewhere away from any Revit elements to position and finish the dimension string. To edit a string of dimensions after it has been placed, simply select it and pick the **Edit Witness Lines** tool on the *Ribbon*. You can also *Tab/Select* a single dimension within a dimension string and delete it without deleting the entire string.

Yet another feature Revit offers that other programs do not is the ability to automatically snap to the center of a door or window opening. In other programs you might have to draw a line from one door jamb to the other; use the dimension command to snap to the midpoint of the line and then delete it. Then you are left with dimensions that just look like they dimension to the center. Remember, Revit's dimensions are able to modify the drawing, kind of a two-way road if you will, whereas other CAD programs are mostly a one-way road.

In addition to snapping to the center of doors and windows, Revit will also snap to the jambs, depending on where your mouse is relative to the element being dimensioned.

You will notice that Revit does not care if a dimension's witness line overlaps a door or window tag. The tags need to be selected and moved manually, individually or in groups.

Next you will dimension the west side of the building.

**FIGURE 7-6.4**
First Floor: rotated 90 degrees
to increase image size in book

11. Dimension the West exterior walls and openings as shown in **Figure 7-6.5**.

**TIP:**
If you click on this dimension, you can drag its grip to the left to shorten the witness line. Revit will still reference the correct wall.

**FIGURE 7-6.5** First Floor: dimensions added to the West wall

The last two images in the exercise give you an idea of what each dimension type which was loaded with the residential template looks like. Similar to other elements in Revit, you can select a dimension and verify what type it is by looking at the *Type Selector* on the *Properties Palette*. Also, you can change the type by selecting the desired type from the *Type Selector*.

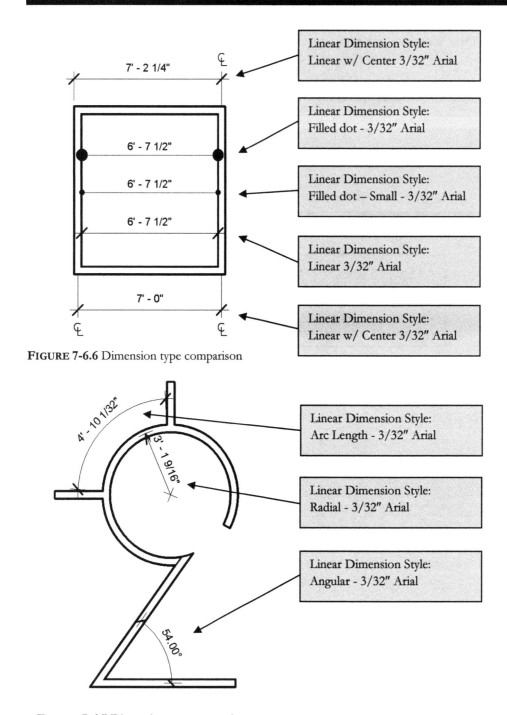

**FIGURE 7-6.6** Dimension type comparison

**FIGURE 7-6.7** Dimension type comparison

This should be enough for you to understand how to dimension your plans. If you want more practice, you can dimension the rest of the *First Floor Plan* and then the other two floors; your instructor may require this. See Revit's *Help System* if you want to dig a little deeper in to Revit's dimensioning options.

12. **Save** your Project as **ex7-6.rvt**.

## Self-Exam:

The following questions can be used as a way to check your knowledge of this lesson. The answers can be found at the bottom of this page.

1. Deleting a dimension with equality toggled on will always also delete the constraint in the model. (T/F)

2. To move an element, simply click on the dimension and edit the text. (T/F)

3. Material Keynote and Material Tag are the two ways to annotate a material. (T/F)

4. Pressing Enter in a text element limits the ability to modify using the text box grips and have the number of rows adjust. (T/F)

5. To measure the length along a curved line, use this dimension tool:

   _____.

## Review Questions:

The following questions may be assigned by your instructor as a way to assess your knowledge of this section. Your instructor has the answers to the review questions.

1. A dimension string set to Equality can only display 'EQ' and not the actual dimension value. (T/F)

2. A single text element can have both curved and straight leaders. (T/F)

3. Spell check only works on text elements, not tags or keynotes. (T/F)

4. The use of basic text should be minimized. (T/F)

5. The same element can be tagged more than once, even in the same view. (T/F)

6. Use a Linear dimension to ensure a dimension remains horizontal. (T/F)

7. Revit's keynoting system requires an external text file. (T/F)

8. Text leaders can only be removed in the reverse order they were added. (T/F)

9. Revit can dimension all the openings in a wall at once. (T/F)

10. A 'user keynote' presents an opportunity for user error by selecting the wrong item from a list each time this tool is used. (T/F)

SELF-EXAM ANSWERS:
1 – F, 2 – F, 3 – T, 4 – T, 5 – Arc Length

**Notes:**

## Lesson 8
# ROOF:

This lesson will look at some of the various options and tools for designing a roof for your building. You will also add skylights.

### Exercise 8-1:
### Roof Design Options (Style, Pitch and Overhang)

In this lesson you will look at the various ways to use the *Roof* tool to draw the more common roof forms used in architecture today.

## Start a New Revit Project:

You will start a new project for this lesson so you can quickly compare the results of using the *Roof* tool.

1.  Start a new project using the **default.rte** template.

2.  Switch to the **North** elevation view and rename the level named *Level 2* to **T.O. Masonry**. This will be the reference point for your roof. Click **Yes** to rename corresponding views automatically.

    *TIP: Just select the* Level *datum and click on the level datum's text to rename.*

3.  Switch to the *Level 1 Floor Plan* view.

## Drawing the Buildings:

4.  Set the Level 1 *"Detail Level"* to **medium**, so the material hatching is visible within the walls.

    *TIP: Use the View Control Bar at the bottom.*

5.  Using the *Wall* tool with the wall *Type* set to **"Exterior - Brick on Mtl. Stud,"** and draw a **40'-0" x 20'-0"** building (Figure 8-1.1).

    *FYI: The default Wall height is OK; it should be 20'-0".*

Be sure to draw the building within the elevation tags.

*TIP: You can draw the building in one step if you use the* Rectangle *option on the Ribbon while using the* Wall *tool.*

Elevations tags – (4) are shown which correspond to the (4) elevation views listed in the *Project Browser*.

**FIGURE 8-1.1** Bldg. and Elev. tags

You will copy the building so that you have a total of four buildings. You will draw a different type of roof on each one.

6. Drag a window around the walls to select them. Then use the **Array** command to set up four buildings **35′-0″ O.C.** (Figure 8-1.2). See the *Array Tip* below.

*TIP: Zoom in and make sure the brick is on the exterior side of the wall. If not, you can select each wall and click its* flip *icon.*

*ARRAY TIP: Select the first building, select* Array, *and then, just like the* Copy *command, define a copy 35′ to the right, then enter the number of copies.*

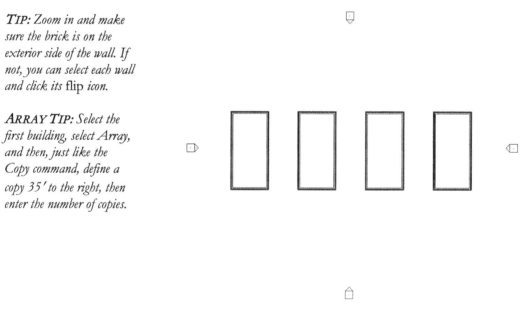

**FIGURE 8-1.2** Four buildings

7. Select all of the buildings and click **Ungroup** from the *Ribbon*.

Ungroup

# Hip Roof:

The various roof forms are largely defined by the *"Defines slope"* setting. This is displayed in the *Options Bar* while the *Roof* tool is active. When a wall is selected and the *"Defines slope"* option is selected, the roof above that portion of wall slopes. You will see this more clearly in the examples below.

8.   Switch to the **T.O. Masonry** *Floor Plan* view.

9.   Select the **Architecture → Build → Roof** *(down-arrow)* → **Roof by Footprint** tool.

10.  Set the overhang to **2'-0"** and make sure **Defines slope** is selected (checked) on the *Options Bar*.

11.  Select the four walls of the West building, clicking each wall one at a time.

> *TIP: Make sure you select towards the exterior side of the wall; notice the review line before clicking.*

12.  Click **Finish Edit Mode** (i.e., the green check mark) on the *Ribbon* to finish the *Roof* tool.

13.  Click **Yes** to attach the roof to the walls.

14.  Switch to the **South** elevation (Figure 8-1.3).

**FIGURE 8-1.3** South elevation – Hip roof

You will notice that the default wall height is much higher than what we ultimately want. However, when the roof is drawn at the correct elevation and you attach the walls to the roof, the walls automatically adjust to stop under the roof object. Additionally, if the roof is raised or lowered later, the walls will follow; you can try this in the South elevation view by simply using the *Move* tool. **REMEMBER:** *You can make revisions in any view.*

15. Switch to the **3D** view using the icon on the *QAT* (Figure 8-1.4).

You can change the "model graphics style" to **Shading** if you would like. Select the *Visual Style* icon on the *View Control Bar* at the bottom.

**FIGURE 8-1.4** 3D view – hip roof

## Gable Roof:

16. Switch back to the **T.O. Masonry** view (not the ceiling plan for this level).

17. Select the **Roof** tool and then **Roof by Footprint**.

18. Set the overhang to **2'-0"** and make sure **Defines slope** is selected (checked) on the *Options Bar*.

19. Only select the two long (40'-0") walls.

20. **Uncheck** the **Defines slope** option.

21. Select the remaining two walls (Figure 8-1.5).

22. Pick the **green check mark** on the *Ribbon* to finish the roof.

23. Select **Yes** to attach the walls to the roof.

24. Switch to the **South** elevation view (Figure 8-1.6).

**FIGURE 8-1.5** Gable – plan view

**FIGURE 8-1.6** South elevation – gable roof

25. Switch to the **3D** view (Figure 8-1.7).

Notice the wall extends up to conform to the underside of the roof on the gable ends.

*FYI: You may be wondering why the roofs look odd in the floor plan view. If you remember, each view has its own cut plane. The cut plane happens to be lower than the highest part of the roof – thus, the roof is shown cut at the cut plane. If you go to Properties Palette → View Range (while nothing is selected) and then adjust the cut plane to be higher than the highest point of the roof, then you will see the ridge line.*

FIGURE 8-1.7 3D view – gable roof

## Shed Roof:

26. Switch back to the **T.O. Masonry** view.

27. Select the **Roof** tool, and then **Roof by Footprint**.

28. Check **Defines slope** on the *Options Bar*.

29. Set the overhang to **2′-0″** on the *Options Bar*.

30. Select the East wall (40′-0″ wall, right-hand side).

31. Uncheck **Defines slope** in the *Options Bar*.

32. Select the remaining three walls (Figure 8-1.8).

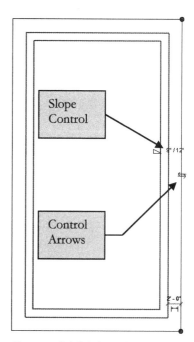

FIGURE 8-1.8 Selected walls

33. Set the **Slope**, or roof pitch, to 3/12 (Figure 8-1.9) on the *Properties Palette*.

34. Click **Apply** on the *Properties Palette*.

35. Pick the **green check mark** on the *Ribbon* to finish the roof.

36. Select **Yes** to attach the walls to the roof.

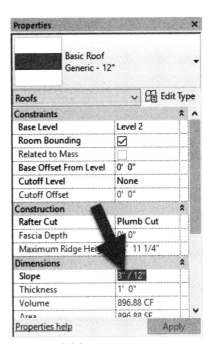

**FIGURE 8-1.9**
Properties for Roof tool

*FYI: You can also change the slope of the roof by changing the Slope Control text (see Figure 8-1.8); just select the text and type a new number.*

*TIP: You can use the Control Arrows, while the roof line is still selected, to flip the orientation of the roof overhang if you accidentally selected the wrong side of the wall and the overhang is on the inside of the building.*

37. Switch to the **South** elevation view (Figure 8-1.10).

**FIGURE 8-1.10** South elevation – shed roof

38. Switch to the *Default 3D* view (Figure 8-1.11).

**FIGURE 8-1.11** Default 3D view – shed roof

Once the roof is drawn, you can easily change the roof's overhang. You will try this on the shed roof. You will also make the roof slope in the opposite direction.

39. In **T.O. Masonry** view, select **Modify** from the *Ribbon*, and then select the shed roof.

40. Click **Edit Footprint** from the *Ribbon*.

Edit
Footprint

41. Click on the East roof sketch-line to select it.

42. Uncheck **Defines slope** from the *Options Bar*.

43. Now select the West roofline and check **Defines slope**.

If you were to select the green check mark now, the shed roof would be sloping in the opposite direction. But, before you do that, you will adjust the roof overhang at the high side.

44. Click on the East roofline again, to select it.

45. Change the overhang to **6'-0"** in the *Options Bar*.

Changing the overhang only affects the selected roofline.

46. Select the **green check mark**.

47. Switch to the South view to see the change (Figure 8-1.12).

**FIGURE 8-1.12** South elevation – shed roof (revised)

Thus you can see it is easier to edit an object than to delete it and start over. Just remember you have to be in sketch mode (i.e., *Edit Sketch*) to make changes to the roof. Also, when a sketch line is selected, its properties are displayed in the *Properties Palette*. That concludes the shed roof example.

## Flat Roof:

48. Switch back to the **T.O. Masonry** *Floor Plan* view.

49. Select **Architecture → Roof → Roof by Footprint**.

50. Set the overhang to **2'-0"** and make sure **Defines slope** is not selected (i.e., unchecked) in the *Options Bar*.

51. Select all four walls.

52. Pick the **green check mark**.

53. Select **Yes** to attach the walls to the roof.

**FIGURE 8-1.13** South elevation – flat roof

54. Switch to the South elevation view (Figure 8-1.13).

55. Also, take a look at the **Default 3D view** (Figure 8-1.14).

**FIGURE 8-1.14** Default 3D view – flat roof

56. Save your project as **ex8-1.rvt**.

---

**Want More?**

Revit has additional tools and techniques available for creating more complex roof forms. However, that is beyond the scope of this book. If you want to learn more about roofs, or anything else, take a look at one of the following resources:

- Revit **Web Site:** www.autodesk.com
- Revit **Newsgroup** (potential answers to specific questions)
  www.augi.com; www.revitcity.com; www.autodesk.com; www.revitforum.org
- Revit **Blogs** information from individuals (some work for Autodesk and some don't)
  www.BIMchapters.blogspot.com, www.revitoped.com, revitclinic.typepad.com

## Reference material: Roof position relative to wall

The remaining pages in this chapter are for reference only and do not need to be done to your model. You are encouraged to study this information so you become more familiar with how the *Roof* tool works.

The following examples use a brick and concrete wall example. The image below shows the *Structure* properties for said wall type. Notice the only item within the *Core Boundary* section is the *Masonry – Concrete Block* (i.e., CMU) which is 7⅝″ thick (nominally 8″). Keep this in mind as you read through the remaining material.

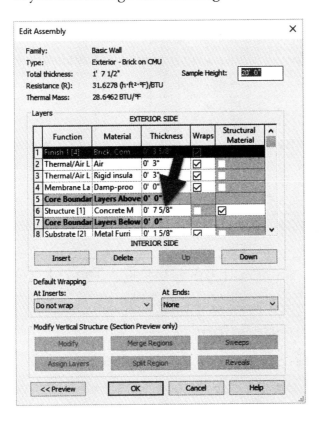

The following examples will show you how to control the position of the roof system relative to the wall below, both vertically and horizontally. The roof properties that dictate its position basically involve relationships between three things: the **Level Datum**, the exterior **Wall System** and the bottom edge of the **Roof System**. There are several other properties (e.g., pitch, construction, fascia, etc.) related to the roof that will not be mentioned at the moment so the reader may focus on a few basic principles.

The examples on this page show a sloped roof sketched with *Extend into wall (to core)* enabled and the *Overhang* set to 2'-0". Because *Extend into wall (to core)* was selected, the bottom edge of the roof is positioned relative to the *Core Boundary* of the exterior wall rather than the finished face of the wall. See the discussion about the wall's *Core Boundary* on the previous page.

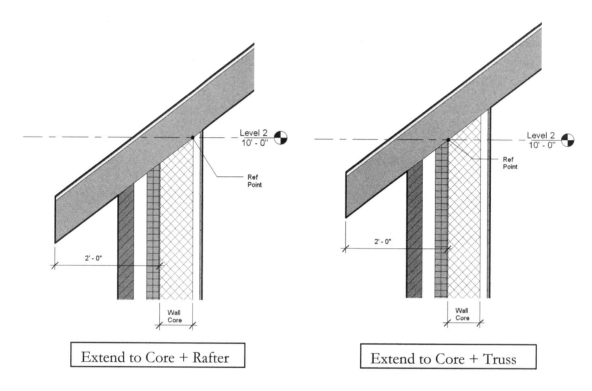

Extend to Core + Rafter          Extend to Core + Truss

## Revit Roof Properties under Consideration:

**Extend Into Wall: (To Core)**    This option was *checked* on the *Options Bar* while sketching the roof.

**Rafter Or Truss:**    This option is an *Instance Parameter* of the roof object; the example on the above left is set to *Rafter* and the other is set to *Truss*.

*NOTE: The* Extend into Wall (to core) *option affects the relative relationship between the wall and the roof, as you will see by comparing this example with the one on the next page.*

**Base Level:**    Set to *Level 2*: By associating various objects to a level, it is possible to adjust the floor elevation (i.e., *Level Datum*) and have doors, windows, floors, furniture, roofs, etc., all move vertically with that level.

**Base Offset: From Level**    Set to *0'-0"*: This can be a positive or negative number which will be maintained even if the level moves.

The examples on this page show a sloped roof sketched with *Extend into wall (to core)* NOT enabled and the *Overhang* set to 2'-0″. Notice that the roof overhang is derived from the exterior face of the wall (compared to the *Core Boundary* face on the previous example when *Extend into wall* was enabled).

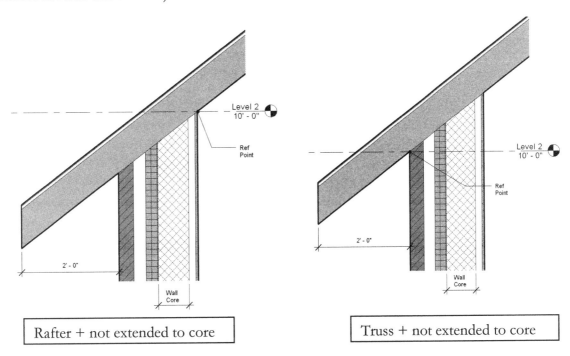

| Rafter + not extended to core | Truss + not extended to core |

## Revit Roof Properties under Consideration:

**Extend Into Wall:**
**(To Core)**    This option was *NOT checked* on the *Options Bar* while sketching the roof.

**Rafter Or Truss:**    This option is an *Instance Parameter* of the roof object; the example on the above left is set to *Rafter* and the other is set to *Truss*.

**NOTE:** *The* Extend into wall (to core) *option affects the relative relationship between the wall and the roof, as you will see by comparing this example with the one on the previous page.*

**Base Level:**    Set to *Level 2*. By associating various objects to a level, it is possible to adjust the floor elevation (i.e., *Level Datum*) and have doors, windows, floors, furniture, roofs, etc., all move vertically with that level.

**Base Offset:**
**From Level**    Set to *0'-0″*. This can be a positive or negative number which will be maintained even if the level moves.

As you can see from the previous examples, you would most often want to have *Extend to wall (to core)* selected while sketching a roof because it would not typically make sense to position the roof based on the outside face of brick or the inside face of gypsum board for commercial construction.

Even though you may prefer to have *Extend to wall (to core)* selected, you might like to have a 2'-0" overhang relative to the face of the brick rather than the exterior face of concrete block. This can be accomplished in one of two ways:

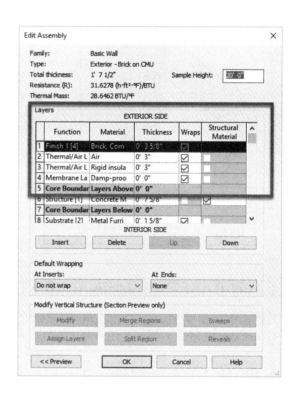

**(A)** You can modify the overhang, while sketching the roof, to include the wall thickness that occurs between the face of wall and face of core: $2'-0'' + 9\frac{5}{8}'' = 2'-9\frac{5}{8}''$. See the image to the right.

**(B)** The second option is to manually edit the sketch lines. You can add dimensions while in *Sketch* mode, select the sketch line to move, and then edit the dimension. The dimension can also be *Locked* to maintain the roof edge position relative to the wall. When you finish the sketch the dimensions are hidden.

## Energy Truss:

In addition to controlling the roof overhang, you might also want to control the roof properties to accommodate an energy truss with what is called an *energy heal*, which allows for more insulation to occur directly above the exterior wall.

To do this you would use the *Extend into wall (to core)* + *Truss* option described above and then set the *Base Offset from Level* to 1'-0" (for a 1'-0" energy heal). See the image and the *Properties Palette* shown on the next page.

Many other properties and techniques exist which one can use to develop the roof for a project, things like the *Rafter Cut* and *Fascia Depth* which control the fascia design. Also, you can apply a sweep to a roof edge to add a 1x fascia board around the building. These are intermediate to advanced concepts and will not be covered here.

This concludes the study of the *Roof* tool!

The template file you started with already has a *Roof Plan* view created. You can think of this as the top plate height for your wall. This *Roof Plan* view creates a working plane for the *Roof* tool. After creating a high roof over the two story areas, you will create a *Low Roof* view and design roofs over the one story areas: the garage and a portion of the family room.

## Create Gable Roof:

1.  Open ex7-6.rvt and **Save As ex8-2.rvt**.

2.  Switch to the ***Roof Plan*** view.

Your image should look something like Figure 8-2.1. The walls you can see in the *Roof Plan* view were created in Lesson 5. The specified height extends into the *Roof Plan's View Range*, whereas the two walls you cannot see were created on the second floor, in Lesson 6, and the specified height does not extend up into the *Roof Plan's View Range*. This does not really matter because, as you will see in a moment, you have enough information visible to create the footprint of the roof; also, you will *Attach* the walls to the roof, just like the previous exercises, which causes them to conform to the underside of the roof.

Because the walls do not connect, neither will the overhang lines you will be sketching. Before you can "finish" a roof sketch, you must have the entire perimeter of the roof drawn with line endpoints connected. Revit allows you to sketch additional lines and use tools like *Trim* to complete the perimeter of the roof sketch.

3.  Select the ***Roof*** tool drop-down from the *Architecture* tab.

4.  Select ***Roof by Footprint*** from the drop-down menu.

5.  Make sure ***Pick Walls*** is selected on the *Ribbon*.

**FIGURE 8-2.1** Roof Plan; initial view

First you will specify the roof overhang for the entire roof.

6. Set the *Overhang* to **1'-6"** on the *Options Bar*.

You only need to select four walls to define the extents of the gable roof you are about to create. However, the perimeter will not be closed after selecting the four walls.

7. With *Defines slope* **checked** on the *Options Bar*, select the two walls as shown in Figure 8-2.2; make sure the overhang lines are on the exterior side of the building.

   ***TIP:*** *Use the flip control icon while the line is still selected if your overhang is on the wrong side (i.e., interior).*

8. With *Defines slope* **NOT checked** on the *Options Bar*, select the two walls as shown in Figure 8-2.2; make sure the overhang lines are on the exterior side of the building.

Step #7 – select this wall with *Defines slope* selected

Step #8 – select this wall with *Defines slope* NOT selected

Step #8 – select this wall with *Defines slope* NOT selected

Step #7 – select this wall with *Defines slope* selected

**FIGURE 8-2.2** Roof Plan; four walls selected for sketching roof footprint

9.  Change the roof pitch, or *Slope*, to **8″** on the *Properties Palette* (Figure 8-2.3).

10. Click **Apply**.

Note that the four walls, just selected, can be selected in any order. Of course it would be easier to select all the sloping edges first and then all the non-sloping edges second. That way you do not have to keep toggling the *Defines slope* option on and off.

Next you will use the *Trim* tool to close the perimeter of the roof footprint. Many of your 2D drafting skills learned early in this book can be applied to this type of *Sketch* mode.

Finally, notice the roof type is set to **Generic – 12″** as seen in the image to the right. This can be modified similar to walls via the *Edit Type* button.

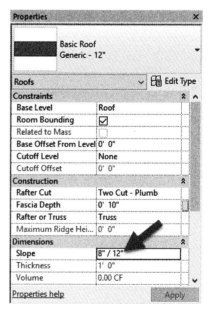

**FIGURE 8-2.3** Roof Properties

11. Select *Modify* from the *Ribbon*.

12. Select the *Trim* icon from the contextual tab on the *Ribbon*, and then select the roof lines that are not yet connected to make them connected (Figure 8-2.4).

**FIGURE 8-2.4** Roof Plan; entire roof perimeter defined

Now that the roof footprint is complete you can finish the roof.

13. Select the **green checkmark** from the *Ribbon*.

14. Click **Yes** to attach the walls (Figure 8-2.5).

**FIGURE 8-2.5** Roof Plan; attachment warning

15. Switch to your *Default 3D* view.

Your project should look like Figure 8-2.6. Notice that the walls that were visible in the *Roof Plan* view are now attached to the roof. The East and West walls that have not been attached can be attached manually.

Select this wall in step 16

**FIGURE 8-2.6** 3D View; gable roof added

16. While in the 3D view, select the East wall that has not been attached to the roof yet. Notice how the wall is transparent when selected.

17. Select the *Attach Top/Base* button from the *Ribbon*, then **select the roof** (Figure 8-2.7).

18. Repeat the previous two steps with the West wall.

    *TIP: Click in the upper left corner of the Front face of the ViewCube to quickly view that side of the building (see image to right).*

FIGURE 8-2.7 3D View; wall attached to roof

# Main Entry Gable:

Next you will draw the gable roof element over the main entry.

You can modify the existing roof to add this design feature.

19. Switch back to the *Roof Plan* view.

20. Select the existing **roof,** and then *Edit Footprint* from the *Ribbon.*

21. Select *Pick Walls* and then make sure the overhang is still **1'-6"** and the pitch is **8"/12".**

22. Edit the roof sketch to look like Figure 8-2.8.

*TIP: Use the* Split *and* Trim *tools to modify the existing sketch.*

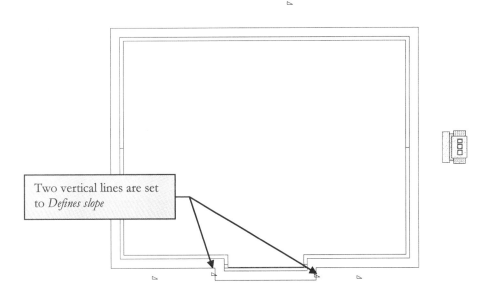

Two vertical lines are set to *Defines slope*

FIGURE 8-2.8 Edit roof sketch

23. Select the **green checkmark** to finish the roof.

*NOTE: If you get any errors, make sure all the "defines slope" sketch lines have the same slope.*

This is where the power of Revit really begins to shine. As you can see in the *Roof Plan* view (Figure 8-2.9 below), Revit was able to interpret the sketch using the *Pitch* and *Defines slope* information to create the proper roof complete with ridgelines and valleys.

Next you will change the *View Range* of the *Roof* view so you can see the low roof, which will be added in the next exercise.

24. Select **Edit** next to *View Range* in the *Properties Palette* (make sure nothing is selected in the model first – this will make sure the *View Properties* are shown).

25. Change both *Bottom* and *View Depth* to **Unlimited**.

26. Click **OK**.

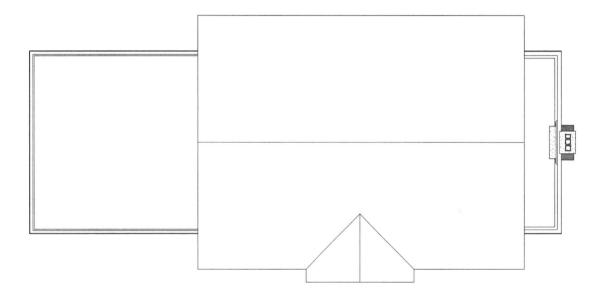

**FIGURE 8-2.9** Site plan view; revised roof created

27. Switch to the ***Default 3D*** view.

When finished, your 3D view should look like Figure 8-2.10.

> **TIP:**
> Custom fascias, gutters and soffits are beyond the scope of this tutorial. However, you can take a look at the *Help* system for more information on this.
>
> After reviewing the *Help* system, try adding these techniques to your Revit project.

This entry roof element could have been drawn as a separate element. This would be useful if the fascia/eaves did not align, for example.

**FIGURE 8-2.10** 3D view; Entry roof element added

28. Save your project as **Ex8-2.rvt**.

> *TIP: You have probably figured this out by now: the last view open when you close will be the current view the next time the project is opened.*

## Exercise 8-3:
## Low Roof Elements

In this exercise you will add the lower roof elements, which will involve adding a new level datum for reference.

## Create a New Level:

1. Open ex8-2.rvt and **Save As ex8-3.rvt**.

2. Open the *South* elevation view.

3. Click **Architecture → Datum → Level** from the *Ribbon*.

4. Draw a *Level* symbol at the top of the low exterior walls, at elevation 12'-0". Draw the symbol so both ends align with the other symbols below and above it (Figure 8-3.1).

   *TIP: Hover your cursor over the top of the garage wall (do not click). Next, move your cursor towards the left and pick two points across from each other horizontally, picking from left to right.*

**FIGURE 8-3.1** South elevation; new level added

Notice that Revit automatically names the level and creates a floor plan and reflected ceiling plan views with the same name (Figure 8-3.2). Next, you will rename the *Level* datum.

5. Press **Esc** or select *Modify* from the *Ribbon*.

6. Now select the *Level* symbol you just created in the drawing window.

**FIGURE 8-3.2** South elevation; new level added (named Level 8 in this example)

7. With the *Level* symbol selected, **drag the small circle grip** near the target symbol (see image below) to the right. This will relocate all the level targets away from the building.

8-25

8. With the *Level* symbol still selected, click on the text to rename the level label. Press *Undo* if you accidentally click an icon and change the level position; you may need to zoom in to click the text.

9. Change the label to **Low Roof** (Figure 8-3.3).

**FIGURE 8-3.3** South elevation; renaming a level datum

10. Click **Yes** when prompted to rename corresponding views (Figure 8-3.4).

Notice the *Low Roof* label is now listed in the *Floor Plans* and *Ceiling Plans* sections of the *Project Browser*.

Add another gable roof:

**FIGURE 8-3.4** Rename prompt

11. Open the newly created **Low Roof Floor Plan** view.

   *TIP: You may want to close the Ceiling Plan views so you don't accidentally click on them.*

12. Select the **Roof** tool (down-arrow) from the *Ribbon*.

13. Select **Roof by footprint** from the drop-down list.

14. Set the overhang to **1'-6"** on the *Options Bar*.

15. You are now prompted to select exterior walls to define the footprint. Select ONLY the three wall segments that define the *Living Room* area per **Figure 8-3.5**. Only the horizontal sketch lines are to be *Defines slope* as shown.

   *REMEMBER: Pick the exterior side of the walls.*

You will notice in Figure 8-3.5 that there is one section that still needs to be sketched to close the footprint or outline.

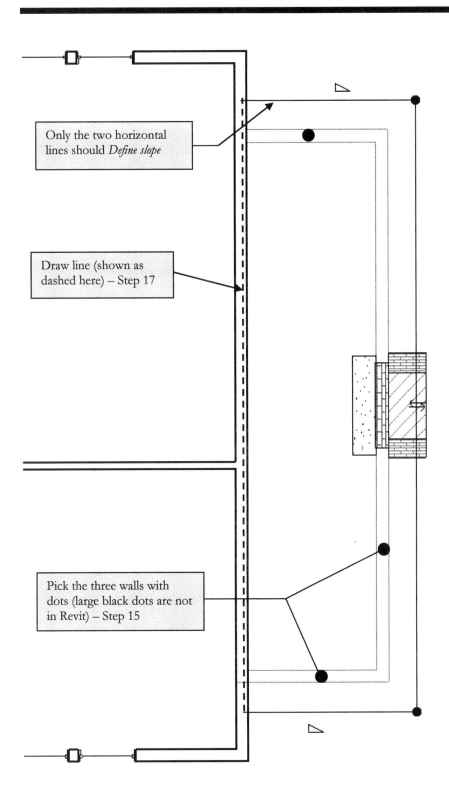

Only the two horizontal lines should *Define slope*

Draw line (shown as dashed here) – Step 17

Pick the three walls with dots (large black dots are not in Revit) – Step 15

**FIGURE 8-3.5** Low Roof plan view; adding roof

16. Select the *Line* tool from the *Ribbon* (Figure 8-3.6).

17. Draw the line to create a complete rectangle (i.e., footprint), making sure you use *Snaps* to accurately snap to the endpoints of the lines already present (Figure 8-3.5). Use *Trim* if needed. *Defines Slope* should be off here.

18. Change the *Slope* to **8" / 12"** in the *Properties Palette*.

19. Click **Apply** in the *Properties Palette*.

**FIGURE 8-3.6** Roof sketch options

Again, this will make the roof pitch 8/12, which means for every 12" of horizontal run, the roof will *rise* 8" vertically.

20. Now click the **green checkmark** from the *Ribbon* to finish the roof.

21. Click **Yes** when prompted to attach the highlighted walls to the roof (Figure 8-3.7).

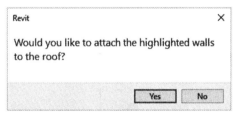

**FIGURE 8-3.7** Prompt

You will now see a portion of the roof in your plan view. The cutting plane is 4'-0" above the floor level, so you are seeing the roof thickness in section at 4'-0" above the *Low Roof* level (Figure 8-3.9 on next page).

- Switch to an elevation view to see the roof, the South elevation, shown in Figure 8-3.8.

- You can also switch to the *Default 3D* view to see the roof in isometric view.

**FIGURE 8-3.8** South elevation

After looking at the roof you have created, switch back to the plan view: *Low Roof.* You will now add a roof over the garage.

22. **Zoom in** on the garage area.

23. Select the *Roof* tool and click *Roof by Footprint*.

24. With *Defines slope* checked in the *Options Bar*, pick the two horizontal walls: North and South (Figure 8-3.10).

25. Uncheck *Defines slope*, select the West wall, and then use the *Line* tool to sketch a line to close the footprint, as shown in Figure 8-3.11. Be sure to use *Snaps* to accurately draw the enclosed area.

26. Make sure the *Slope* is set to **8"/12"** and then select the **green checkmark** from the *Ribbon* (Figure 8-3.6).

27. Click **Yes** when prompted to attach the highlighted walls to the roof (Figure 8-3.7).

**FIGURE 8-3.9** Low Roof plan view

**FIGURE 8-3.10** Low Roof plan view at garage

28. Switch to the *South* elevation view (Figure 8-3.11).

**FIGURE 8-3.11** South elevation view; garage roof added

The 3D model is shown shaded and has *Ambient Shadows* turned on (Figure 8-3.12).

Revit content is set up to make glass in windows and curtain walls transparent.

**FIGURE 8-3.12** Shaded model

# Changing to a Hip Roof:

Now that you have drawn the roof, you will see what is involved to modify the gable roof to a hip roof. In the first exercise in this Lesson, you learned how to create a hip roof from scratch. Here you will modify a previously drawn gable roof into a hip roof.

29. Switch to the **Roof Plan** view.

30. Click on the main roof element to select it.
    *TIP: Select one of the lines at the perimeter of the roof.*

Edit
Footprint

31. Select **Edit Footprint** from the *Ribbon*.

32. Select the vertical line on the left.

33. With the left vertical line selected, check **Defines slope** on the *Options Bar*.

34. Repeat these steps for the right vertical line.

Your screen should look like Figure 8-3.13.

**FIGURE 8-3.13** Roof Plan; vertical lines set to *Defines slope*

35. Select the **green check mark** from the *Ribbon*.

36. Switch to the *South* exterior elevation view.

You now have a hip roof. However, there is a little problem with the lower roofs; they do not properly intersect. This could be a problem when it rains!

**FIGURE 8-3.14** South Elevation; main roof changed to a hip roof

37. Switch to the *Default 3D* view.

38. Select **Modify → Geometry → Join/Unjoin Roof** tool from the *Ribbon*.

39. *Join* the lower roof over the garage to the upper roof.

> *TIP: Select the edge of the low roof and then select the face of the upper roof, which will be the face you wish to extend the roof to. Hover your cursor over the icon on the ribbon to see the extended tooltip for more information.*

40. Now *Join* the low roof over the *Living Room* with the upper roof.

Your model should look similar to Figure 8-3.15.

**FIGURE 8-3.15** 3D view; low roofs joined to upper roof

Here you can see that the bottoms of the roofs, to be joined, do not have to align with each other.

After looking at the two roof options, the client decides they like the gable option so you will change it back. Do not simply click *Undo*; the next steps will show you how to *Unjoin* the roof.

    41. Switch to the ***Roof Plan*** view.

    42. Select **Modify → Geometry → Join/Unjoin Roof**.

This tool, as its name implies, allows you to both *Join* and *Unjoin* roof elements. To *Unjoin*, you simply click on a line that has been created by a *Join* and the entire *Join* will go away.

    43. Select the valley line as shown in **Figure 8-3.16**.

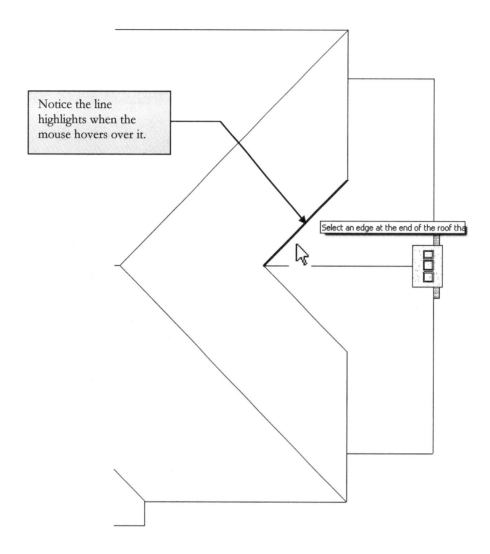

Notice the line highlights when the mouse hovers over it.

Select an edge at the end of the roof tha

**FIGURE 8-3.16** Roof plan; Unjoining the lower roof from the upper roof

As soon as you click the valley line, the roof is unjoined.

44. Repeat this process to *Unjoin* the West lower roof.

45. Change the hip roof back to a gable using the techniques previously covered.

When finished, your 3D view should look like 8-3.12 again.

46. **Save** your project.

## Exercise 8-4:
## Skylights

This short exercise covers inserting skylights in your roof. The process is much like inserting windows. In fact, Revit lists the skylight types with the window types, so you use the *Window* tool to insert skylights into your project.

## Inserting Skylights:

You will place the skylights in an elevation view.

1. Load project file **ex8-3.rvt**.

Load
Family

2. Switch to the **North** elevation view.

3. Select the **Window** tool and use the *Load Family* icon to import the skylight family **skylight.rfa** from the families provided with this book, into the current project. The skylight in Revit's *Windows* folder can also be used, but it will be different dimensions that that shown in this section.

4. Select **Skylight: 24″ x 27″** from the *Type Selector*.

You are now ready to place skylights in the roof. Revit will only look for roof objects when placing skylights; this is what is called a *roof hosted family*, so you do not have to worry about a skylight ending up in a wall.

5. Roughly place two skylights as shown in Figure 8-4.1.

   *FYI: This can be done directly in the elevation view.*

**FIGURE 8-4.1** North elevation, skylights added

6. Press **Esc** or click the *Modify* tool to cancel the *Window* tool.

Next, you will want to align the skylights with each other.

7. Switch to the *East* elevation view.

8. Select one of the visible skylights.

You should now have the skylight selected and see the reference dimensions that allow you to adjust the exact location of the object. Occasionally, the dimension does not go to the point on the drawing that you are interested in referencing from. Revit allows you to adjust where those temporary dimensions reference.

9. Click and drag the grip shown in Figure 8-4.2 to (wait until it snaps) the ridge of the main roof (Figure 8-4.3).

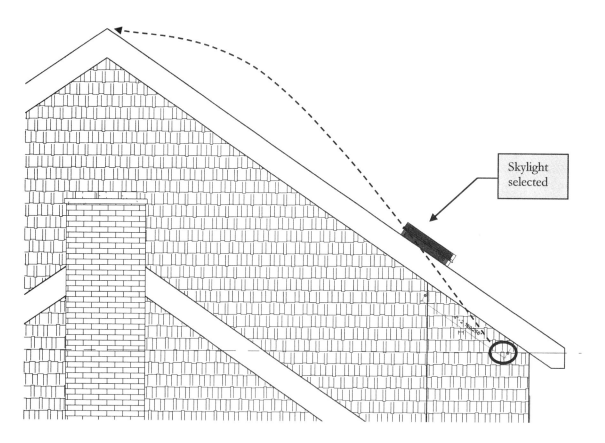

**FIGURE 8-4.2** East elevation; temporary dimension shown after selecting the skylight.

10. Click on the dimension text and change the text to **18′-0″**.

    *NOTE: This will adjust the position of the skylight relative to the ridge.*

11. Select the other skylight and adjust it to match the one you just revised.

**FIGURE 8-4.3** East elevation; temp dimension witness line adjusted.

Your skylights now align vertically on the roof. The same step would allow you to align the skylight horizontally.

12. Use the temporary dimensions to center the skylight over the second floor windows that are below it, on the North elevation.

13. **Zoom in** on one of the skylights.

The number may vary; it is not a problem if it does vary.

14. Select the skylight's tag. You should see a symbol appear near the bottom of the tag; this is the *Move* icon (Figure 8-4.4).

15. Drag on the *Move* icon to position the skylight tag so the tag does not overlap the skylight (Figure 8-4.5).

This can be done with any tag (i.e., Door tag, Room tag, etc.).

**FIGURE 8-4.4** Enlarged view of skylight

16. Adjust the other skylight tag which is a *Window Tag*. As you reposition these tags, you may see a reference line appear indicating the symbol will automatically align with an adjacent symbol.

   **REMEMBER:** *The size of the tag is based on the View Scale setting.*

Take a minute to look at your shaded 3D view and try changing the view so you can see through the skylight glass into the space below (Figure 8-4.6).

17. **Save** as **ex8-4.rvt**.

**FIGURE 8-4.5** Enlarged skylight view – revised

**FIGURE 8-4.6** Shaded skylight view

**FIGURE 8-4.7** Roof plan

## Self-Exam:

The following questions can be used as a way to check your knowledge of this lesson. The answers can be found at the bottom of the page.

1. You do not have to click the *green check mark* to finish a roof. (T/F)

2. The wall below the roof automatically conforms to the underside of the roof when you join the wall to the roof. (T/F)

3. The roof overhang setting is available from the *Options Bar*. (T/F)

4. To create a gable roof on a building with four walls, two of the walls should not have the _____ option checked.

5. Is it possible to change the reference point for a temporary dimension that is displayed while an element is selected? (Y/N)

## Review Questions:

The following questions may be assigned by your instructor as a way to assess your knowledge of this section. Your instructor has the answers to the review questions.

1. When creating a roof using the *"create roof by footprint"* option, you need to create a closed perimeter. (T/F)

2. The *Defines slope* setting can be changed after the roof is finished. (T/F)

3. Skylights need to be rotated to align with the plane, or pitch, of the roof. (T/F)

4. Skylights have the glass transparent in shaded views. (T/F)

5. While using the **Roof** tool, you can use the _____ tool from the *Ribbon* to fill in the missing segments to close the perimeter.

6. You use the _____ parameter to adjust the vertical position of the roof relative to the current working plane (view).

7. While using the *Roof* tool, you need to select the _____ tool from the *Ribbon* before you can select a roofline for modification.

8. You need to use the _____ to flip the roofline when you pick the wrong side of the wall and the overhang is shown on the inside.

9. The _____ from the *Modify* tab (on the *Ribbon*) allows you to extend one roof element over, and into, another.

10. Changing the name of a level tag (in elevation) causes Revit to rename all the corresponding views (plan, ceiling, etc.) if you answer yes to the prompt.

SELF-EXAM ANSWERS:
1 - F, **2** – T, **3** – T, **4** – defines slope, **5** – Y

**Notes:**

## Lesson 9
# FLOOR SYSTEMS AND REFLECTED CEILING PLANS:

In this lesson you will learn to create floor structures and reflected ceiling plans.

Even though you currently have floor levels defined, you do not have an object that represents the mass of the floor systems. You will add floor systems with a hole for the stair.

Ceiling systems allow you to specify the ceiling material by room and the height above the floor. Once the ceiling has been added, it will show up in section views. Sections are created later in this book.

## Exercise 9-1:
## Floor Systems

Similar to other Autodesk® Revit® elements, you can select from a few predefined floor types. You can also create new floor types. In your residence you will use a predefined floor system for the first and second floors and then create a new type for the basement and garage.

## Basement Floor, Slab on Grade:

Sketching floors is a lot like sketching roofs; you can select walls to define the perimeter and draw lines to fill in the blanks, and add holes, or cut-outs, in the floor object.

1. Open ex8-4.rvt and **Save As ex9-1.rvt**.

2. Switch to the **Basement** *Floor Plan* view.

Floor

3. Select **Architecture → Build → Floor** *(just the icon, not the down-arrow)*.

4. Click the **Edit Type** button on the *Properties Palette*.

5. Select **Concrete Slab – 4″** from the *Type* drop-down list near the top.

6. Click **Duplicate**.

7.  Type **4″ Slab on Grade over Vapor Barrier**, then **OK**.

8.  Click the **Edit** button next to the *Structure* parameter.

Here you could change the thickness of the slab, but you will leave it at 4″ for the basement.

Next you will add a vapor barrier and sand bed below the slab.

9.  Insert a new layer:
    a. *Function:* **Membrane Layer**
    b. *Material:* **Vapor Retarder**
    c. *Thickness:* **0″**

*NOTE: Vapor barriers do have a thickness, of course (4mil, 6mil, etc). However, the thickness is typically ignored on drawings. A Membrane is the only layer which can have no thickness; that is, a zero value.*

10. Add another layer:
    a. *Function:* **Substrate [2]**
    b. *Material:* **Sand** *(see TIP below)*
    c. *Thickness:* **4″** (Figure 9-1.1).

*NOTE: The sand is sometimes placed over the vapor barrier. The sand helps to protect the vapor barrier until the rebar and concrete slab are in place. Additionally, the sand allows the concrete to cure more evenly with less chance of cupping. On the other hand, a vapor barrier directly below the slab helps prevent some floor finishes from delaminating due to moisture in the sand.*

*TIP: You can change the position of layers within a system. Simply select the row and then click the Up or Down button until positioned.*

*TIP: To load the Sand material, search for sand in the box at the top of the Material Browser (via Manage tab →  Materials tool), and then double-click the Sand option in the Autodesk Library near the bottom. See Figure 9-1.2.*

11. Click **OK** to close the open dialog boxes.

12. Select the walls in the ***Basement Plan*** as shown in Figure 9-1.3.

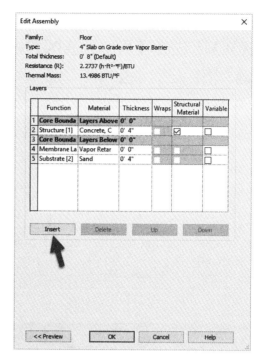

**FIGURE 9-1.1** New floor system

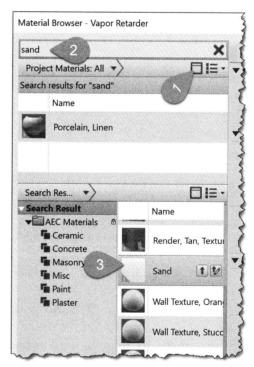

**FIGURE 9-1.2** Materials Dialog

*TIP: Select the interior side of the wall. You can use the control arrows if needed, opposite of what you did for the roof.*

13. Click the **green check mark** on the *Ribbon.*

*TIP: If you get any errors, see the information in the box below.*

## Common Errors Finishing a Floor Sketch:

If you get an error message when trying to finish a floor sketch, it is probably due to a problem with the sketched perimeter lines. Here are two common problems:

### Perimeter not closed:
You cannot finish a floor if there is a gap, large or small, in the perimeter sketch.
*FIX:* Sketch a line to close the loop.

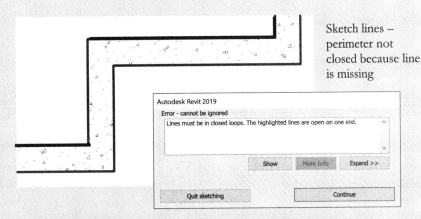

Sketch lines – perimeter not closed because line is missing

Error message after clicking finish sketch

### Perimeter lines intersect:
You cannot finish a floor if any of the sketch lines intersect.
*FIX:* Use *Trim* to make it so all line endpoints touch.

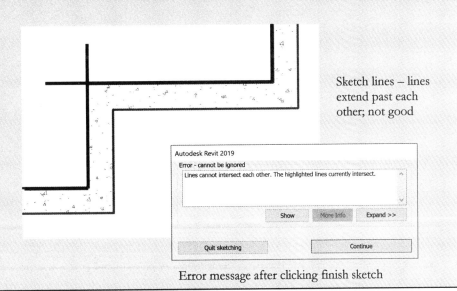

Sketch lines – lines extend past each other; not good

Error message after clicking finish sketch

**FIGURE 9-1.3** Basement floor plan; floor slab sketched

You now have a floor at the basement level. You should see a stipple pattern representing the floor area. You would most likely want to turn that pattern off for a floor plan. You will do that next.

14. In the ***Basement Floor Plan*** view, type **VV**; this is the keyboard shortcut for *Visibility/Graphic Overrides*.

    ***TIP:*** *You may have to click within the drawing window before typing the keyboard shortcut for Revit to recognize it.*

15. In the *Visibility/Graphic Overrides* dialog, on the *Model Categories* tab and in the **Floors** row, click the empty cell in the **Projection/ Surface** → **Patterns** column (Figure 9-1.4).

16. With the word *Override* now showing, click the exact same location again.

FIGURE 9-1.4 Visibility/Graphics Overrides: Editing the floor surface pattern visibility

17. Uncheck both **Visible** options, which will make the floor surface pattern not visible in the current view (Figure 9-1.5).

18. Click **OK** to close the dialogs.

The stipple pattern is no longer visible. The *Visibility/Graphic Overrides* dialog now indicates that the surface pattern is hidden (Figure 9-1.6). Keep in mind, this override is only for the current view. If you create another floor using the same 4″ concrete type you just created in the Level 1 floor plan view, it would have the stipple pattern. It would even show up if in another basement level floor plan, as it is possible to create more than one view which references the same *Level Datum*.

FIGURE 9-1.5 Fill Pattern Graphics

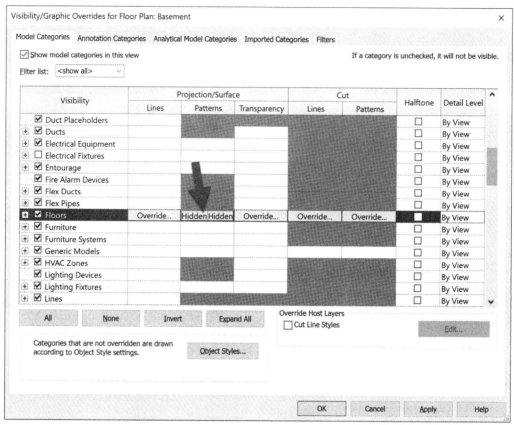

**FIGURE 9-1.6** Visibility/Graphics Overrides

## Garage Floor, Slab on Grade:

Now you will sketch the floor slab for the garage area. Because this floor will have vehicles parking on it, you will create a new slab type that is 6″ thick.

19. Switch to the *First Floor Plan* view.

20. Select the *Floor* tool.

21. Using the floor type you just created as a starting point, create a new floor type named **6″ Slab on Grade over Vapor Barrier**.

    *TIP: Properties Palette → Edit Type → Duplicate*

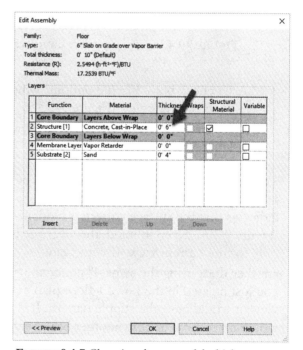

**FIGURE 9-1.7** Changing the conc. slab thickness

22. Click the **Edit** button next to the *Structure* parameter.

23. Change the *Concrete* thickness from **4″** to **6″** (Figure 9-1.7).

24. Click **OK** to close the open dialog boxes.

25. With *Pick Walls* selected on the *Ribbon*, select the interior side of the four walls surrounding the garage (Figure 9-1.8).

26. Click the **green check mark** to finish the floor. Click **No** when prompted to join the wall and the floor.

You now have a floor slab in the garage area. You will notice that the floor element has a stipple pattern, even though you turned that stipple pattern off in the *Basement* view. Remember: the visibility settings are controlled by view, not project-wide, although they can be. You will turn this off later.

Notice the **Span Direction** symbol identified in the image to the right. This can be ignored for this type of floor. It is meant to define the flute direction for a metal floor/roof deck, which your residential floors will not have.

*FYI: The Span Direction button on the Ribbon, visible while in the Floor tool, will allow you to change the span direction by picking a different sketch line.*

**FIGURE 9-1.8** First floor: floor slab sketched

When floors are created, the top of the floor aligns with the level (see image below). Each floor plan view is associated with a level (which cannot be changed), so the view in which you create the floor determines the default level the floor references. The referenced floor level can be changed at any time. The top of the floor will stay aligned with the level even if the floor thickness is changed. However, it is possible to select the floor and change its "Height Offset From Level" parameter to change the default behavior.

Top of floor aligns with level

# First Floor (Wood Joists):

27. Use the floor type *Wood Joist 10" - Wood Finish* as a starting point to create a new floor type named **Wood Joist 14" - Wood Finish**.

28. Change the *Structure* settings per the following image (Figure 9-1.9).

    **FYI:** *This has all been covered previously.*

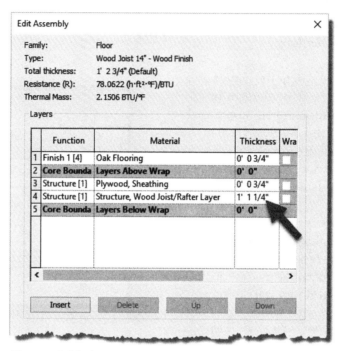

**FIGURE 9-1.9** Floor properties

Creating the first and second floors will be a little more involved than were the basement and garage floors. This is because the upper floors require openings. For example, you need to define the openings for the stair. Revit makes the process very simple.

You should still be in the *Floor* tool.

29. On the *Options Bar*, check **Extend into wall (to core)**.

    **FYI:** *The* Extend into wall (to core) *option will extend the slab under your wall core (wood stud and sheathing are in the core in our example) and go under the gypsum wall board. This is similar to the information presented at the end of the previous chapter.*

30. Select the exterior walls indicated in Figure 9-1.10. Select the exterior side of the wall; use the flip control arrows if needed.

**FIGURE 9-1.10** First Floor – floor system sketched

Next you will define the hole in the floor for the stair that leads down to the basement. You will need to use the *Lines* option from the *Draw* panel to define this area.

31. While the *Floor* tool is still active, **Zoom In** to the stair area.

32. Select the **Rectangle** icon on the *Ribbon*; see image below.

33. Draw a rectangle defining the stair opening; use Revit's snaps to accurately pick the points as shown in **Figure 9-1.11**.

**FIGURE 9-1.11** First Floor – sketching floor opening

*FYI: This floor opening has a big problem. You will see this problem when you get to the building sections exercise later in this book.*

34. Click the **green check mark** to finish the floor.

Next, you will get two prompts: one asks if you want the walls below, whose tops are set to terminate at the first floor, to attach to the new floor. The other prompt asks if you want the floor to attach to the exterior walls. You will answer **Yes** to both.

35. Click **Yes** to the prompt *"Would you like the walls that go up to this floor's level to attach to its bottom?"* (Figure 9-1.12). Also, click **OK** if prompted with a "highlighted walls are attached, but miss…" warning.

> *FYI: This will allow the walls to dynamically change if the floor elevation or thickness is changed.*

36. Click **Yes** for the prompt to join the walls that overlap the floor system (Figure 9-1.13).

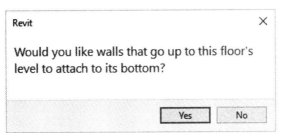

FIGURE **9-1.12** Join walls below to new floor prompt

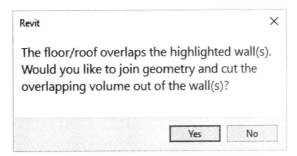

FIGURE **9-1.13** Join walls that overlap the new floor prompt

Now that the floor is placed, you should see a dense horizontal line pattern that represents the finished wood floor. This would be nice for presentation drawings, but like the basement, you will turn the floor hatch off so the floor plan is not too cluttered.

37. Change the first floor's *Visibility* to turn off the floor hatch.

## Copy/Paste the First Floor to the Second:

That completes the first floor system. Next you will copy the floor you just created to the second floor. It would probably be easier to just create a floor from scratch, but you will get more practice editing existing elements.

38. Select the floor you just created, in the first floor plan view, and select **Modify | Floors → Clipboard → Copy to Clipboard** on the *Ribbon*. See *TIP* on next page.

*TIP: Selecting elements that overlap, like the exterior walls and the edge of floor system, may require the use of the Tab key. The only way to select a floor element is by picking its edge. Revit temporarily highlights elements when you move your cursor over them. But, because the floor edge may not have an "exposed" edge to select, you will have to toggle through your selection options for your current cursor location. With the cursor positioned over the edge of the floor, probably with an exterior wall highlighted, press the Tab key to toggle through the available options. A tooltip will display the elements. When you see* floors: floor:floor-name, *click the mouse; also watch the Status Bar.*

39. Pick **Modify → Clipboard → Paste → Aligned to Selected Levels**.

40. Select **Second Floor** and then **OK**.

*TIP: You can press Ctrl and select more than one level.*

41. Switch to the **Second Floor**.

You now have a copy of the first floor's "floor system" in the *Second Floor Plan* view (Figure 9-1.14); keep in mind that all the views are looking at a single 3D model. You will edit the sketch lines of the second floor slab to make the stair hole larger and remove a portion of the floor that extends past the East exterior wall.

**FIGURE 9-1.14** New floor added to level 2 using the paste aligned option

42. Select the floor element in the *Second Floor Plan* view.

   *TIP: The edge of the floor is "exposed" at the stair opening; this would be the easiest place to select the floor.*

43. Click **Edit Boundary** from the *Ribbon*. See icon to right.

**Edit Boundary**

You are now in *Sketch* mode, where you can change the perimeter and holes for the selected floor element. You can select lines and delete them, sketch new lines, and use *Trim* to modify lines.

44. Modify the lines at the far right, using *Delete* and *Trim*, so your sketch looks like Figure 9-1.15.

45. *Stair opening:* Move the West vertical line **4′-10″** farther West; the horizontal sketch lines should automatically extend, as shown in Figure 9-1.15. The overall width of the stair opening should be 8′-0″; if not, you should go back and double check your stair dimensions with Chapter 6, page 6-25.

46. Click the **green check mark** to recreate the floor element.

**FIGURE 9-1.15** Second floor: sketch lines modified

Now that Revit is recreating the floor, it notices the walls below and at the exterior so you get the "join" prompts.

47. Click **Yes** to the two "join" prompts, if you get them.

Your *Second Floor Plan* view should look like Figure 9-1.16.

**FIGURE 9-1.16** Second Floor: sketch lines modified

**FIGURE 9-1.17** 3D view: cutaway view showing floor elements added

48. Change the second floor's *Visibility* to turn off the floor hatch.

# Turning off Surface Pattern at the Source:

If you do not want a portion of your plan to show a surface pattern, you might want to remove the surface pattern associated with the floor system. That way you could leave the surface pattern setting turned on. Set the *Surface Pattern* to **None** in the *Material Editor.*

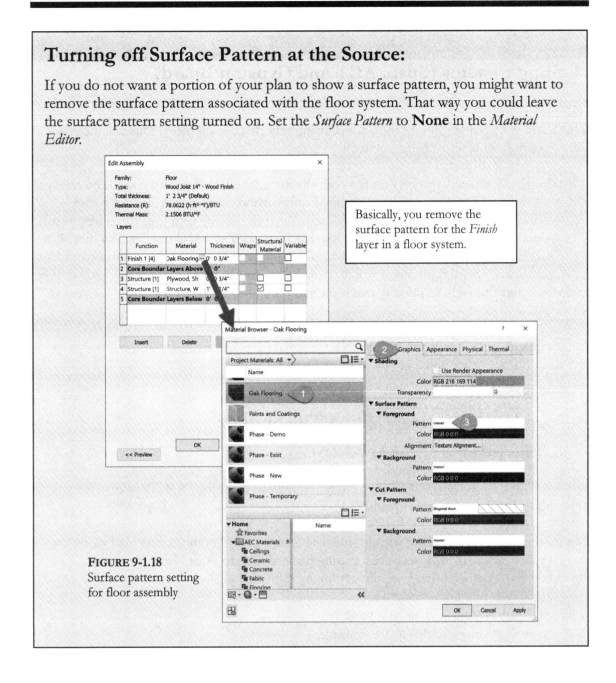

Basically, you remove the surface pattern for the *Finish* layer in a floor system.

**FIGURE 9-1.18**
Surface pattern setting for floor assembly

49. Save your project as **ex9-1.rvt**.

## Exercise 9-2:
## Ceiling Systems (Susp. ACT and Gypsum Board)

This lesson will explore Revit's tools for drawing reflected ceiling plans. This will include drawing different types of ceiling systems.

Traditionally, residential projects do not typically include reflected ceiling plans. The ceilings are generally straightforward, with all required information coming from a *Room Finish Schedule* and *Sections*. However, in Revit you will sketch the ceiling profile in the ceiling plan views, similar to how you drew the floor systems. You want to add the ceilings so they show up in sections. So, seeing as you have ceiling plans, why not include them in the construction documents set? Your design intent will be clearer, and you can make sure the lighting design is coordinated and laid out the way you want it.

The use of suspended acoustical ceiling tile in residential projects is somewhat limited. However, it is occasionally used so it will be covered here. In this lesson you will add it to the second floor office and a family room in the basement.

## Suspended Acoustical Ceiling Tile System:

1.   Open ex9-1.rvt and **Save As ex9-2.rvt**.

2.   Switch to the ***Second Floor Ceiling Plan*** view, from the *Project Browser*; ceiling plans are just below the floor plans.

Notice the doors and windows are automatically "turned off" in the ceiling plan views. Actually, the ceiling plan views have a cutting plane similar to floor plans, except they look up rather than down. You can see this setting by right-clicking on a view name in the *Project Browser* and selecting *Properties*, and then selecting **View Range**. The default value is 7'-6". You might increase this if, for example, you had 10'-0" ceilings and 8'-0" high doors. Otherwise, the doors would show because the 7'-6" cutting plane is below the door height (Figure 9-2.1).

**FIGURE 9-2.1** Properties: View Range settings

3.  Close the *View Range* dialog box, if open, and then select **Architecture → Build → Ceiling**.

Ceiling

You have four ceiling types, by default, to select from (Figure 9-2.2).

**FIGURE 9-2.2** Type Selector: Ceiling: types

4.  Select *Compound Ceiling:* **2′x4′ ACT System**.

Next you will change the ceiling height. The default setting is 8′-0″ above the current level. You will change the ceiling height to 8′-4″; this will give about 6½″ of space above the ceiling to the bottom of the rafters for recessed light fixtures and any required wiring. This setting can be changed on a room by room basis; that is why it is an *Instance Parameter*.

5.  In the *Properties Palette*, set the *Height Offset From Level* setting to **8′-4″** (Figure 9-2.3).

**FIGURE 9-2.3** Ceiling: Properties

You are now ready to place ceiling grids. This process cannot get much easier, especially compared to 2D CAD programs.

6.  Move your cursor anywhere within the office in the lower-right corner of the building. You should see the perimeter of the room highlighted.

7. Pick within the room; Revit places a ceiling grid in the room (Figure 9-2.4).

FYI: Skylights in roof

FYI: Line of roof ridge

2'x4' ACT added

FYI: Roof overhang

**FIGURE 9-2.4**: Second Floor Ceiling Plan view: 2'x4' suspended acoustical ceiling tile added to office

You now have a 2x4 ceiling grid at 8'-4" above the floor, the second floor in this case. Later in the book, when you get to the exercise on cutting sections, you will see the ceiling with the proper height and thickness.

Next, you will add the same ceiling system to the family room in the basement. But, you will notice the ceiling plan section in the *Project Browser* does not have a *Basement* view.

Many residential basements do not have any finished ceilings, so that view was not included in the template from which you started. Next you will create a view for this.

8. Select **View → Create → Plan Views → Reflected Ceiling Plan**.

9. Select the *Basement* view from this list and then click **OK** (see image to the right).

10. You are taken to the ***Basement Ceiling Plan*** view automatically.

Your view should look a little funny, no walls. You will have to adjust the *View Range* settings.

11. Click **Modify** and then set the *View Range* to **6'-6"**.

You should now see the walls and doors. The doors show because the cut plane is lower than the top of the door. You will ignore that for now.

12. Use the *Ceiling* tool to place 2′x 4′ acoustic ceiling tile in the *Family Room*, the large room to the far East. See the following notes (Figure 9-2.5):
    a. You will probably get a symbol at the cross-hairs that indicates you cannot place a ceiling anywhere; the symbol is a circle with a slash through it. This has to do with the ceiling height.
    b. Via the *Properties Palette*, change the ceiling height to **7′-0″**.
    c. You should be able to place the ceiling system now.
    d. Revit automatically rotates and centers the ceiling grid within each room.

**FIGURE 9-2.5**: Basement Ceiling Plan view: 2′x4′ suspended acoustical ceiling tile added to Family Rm.

When you place a ceiling grid, Revit centers the grid in the room. The general rule-of-thumb is you should try to avoid reducing the tile size by more than half of a tile. You can see in Figure 9-2.5 that the East and West sides look OK. However, the North and South sides are small slivers. You will adjust this next.

Looking at Figure 9-2.6, you can see why it was not possible to place a ceiling until the ceiling height was lowered and why the walls did not show up; the foundation wall is only 7′-3″ above the basement floor. Thus, a floor cut plane of 7′-6″ would not show walls and an 8′-4″ ceiling could not find walls to form a perimeter to contain it.

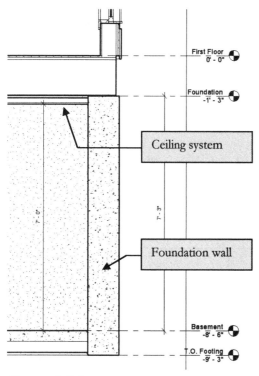

**FIGURE 9-2.6**
Section at basement / foundation wall

13. Select *Modify* from the *Ribbon*.

14. **Select** the ceiling grid. Only one line will be highlighted.

15. Use the **Move** tool to move the grid 24″ to the North (Figure 9-2.7).

**FIGURE 9-2.7**
Basement: Ceiling Grid moved

You should notice that only the grid moved, not the ceiling perimeter.

## Modifying the Suspended Acoustical Ceiling Tile System:

Making modifications to the grid is relatively easy. Next, you will adjust the ceiling height and rotate the grid.

16. In the *Basement* view, select the ceiling grid in the *Family Room*.

17. Within the *Properties Palette*, change the height to **7′-2″**. *(Every inch counts!)*

18. Click **Apply** to accept the new height change (or just move your cursor back into the drawing area).

19. Again, with the grid still selected, use the *Rotate* tool from the *Ribbon* to rotate the grid **30 degrees**.

   *FYI: Notice, while in the Rotate command, the Center of Rotation icon appears, and like in the earlier lessons, this can be dragged to a different location if needed.*

*TIP: When using the Rotate tool you need to pick two points. The first point is your reference line. The second point is the number of degrees off that reference line. In this example, try picking your first point to the right as a horizontal line. Then move the cursor counter-clockwise until 30 degrees is displayed. You can also type the angle rather than clicking the second point.*

Your drawing should look similar to **Figure 9-2.8**. Notice how the perimeter of the room acts like a cropping window when you use *Move* or *Rotate* on a ceiling grid.

**Deleting a Ceiling Grid:**
When selecting a ceiling grid, Revit only selects one line. This does not allow you to delete the ceiling.

To delete: hover cursor over a ceiling grid line and press the TAB key until you see the ceiling perimeter highlight, then click the mouse. The entire ceiling will be selected. Press Delete.

**FIGURE 9-2.8** Basement: Modified Ceiling

Next, you will look at drawing gypsum board ceiling systems. The process is identical to placing the grid system. Additionally, you will create a ceiling type.

# Gypsum Board Ceiling System:

You will create a new ceiling type for a gypsum board (gyp. bd.) ceiling. To better identify the areas that have a gyp. bd. ceiling, you will set the ceiling type to have a stipple pattern. This will provide a nice graphical representation for the gyp. bd. ceiling areas. The ceiling you are about to create would lean more towards a commercial application. However, it will give you a better understanding of how to create custom ceilings. You will add this ceiling to a room in the basement; assume it is being installed below HVAC ductwork, to finish the room.

20. Select **Manage → Settings → Materials**. *This is the list of materials you select from when assigning a material to each layer in a wall system, etc.*

Materials

21. Select *Gypsum Wall Board* in the name list, right-click and then select **Duplicate.** Enter the name **Gypsum Ceiling Board**.

22. In the *Foreground Surface Pattern* area, pick the preview and select **Gypsum-Plaster** from the list, and then click **OK** twice (Figure 9-2.9).

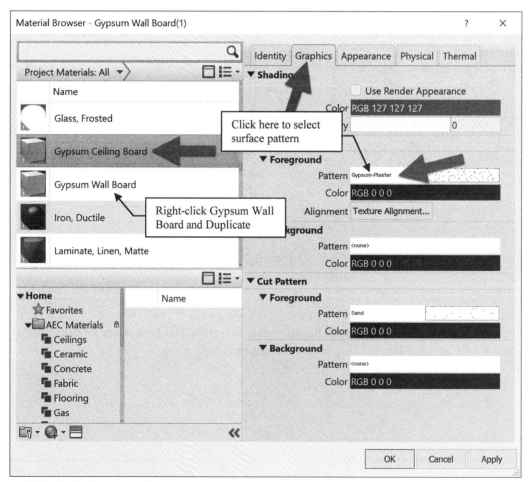

**FIGURE 9-2.9** Materials dialog

The *Surface Pattern* setting is what will add the stipple pattern to the gyp. bd. ceiling areas. With this set to *none*, the ceiling has no pattern, like the basic ceiling type.

Thus, if you wanted "Carpet 1" finish to never have the stipple hatch pattern, you could change the surface pattern to none via the *Materials* dialog and not have to change each view's visibility override.

23. Select the ***Ceiling*** tool from the *Ribbon*.

24. Set the *Type Selector* to **GWB on Metal Stud**.

> *FYI: You are selecting this because it is similar to the ceiling you will be creating.*

25. Click the **Edit Type** button in the *Properties Palette*.

26. Click *Duplicate* and type the name **Susp GB on Metal Stud**.

27. Select **Edit** next to the *Structure* parameter.

28. Create a *Layer* and set the *Values* as follows (Figure 9-2.10):
    a. **1½" Mtl. Stud**
    b. **¾" Mtl. Stud**
    c. **Gypsum Ceiling Board**  *(This is the material you created in Step 21.)*

29. Click **OK** two times.

*FYI: The ceiling assembly you just created represents a typical suspended gyp. bd. ceiling system. The metal studs are perpendicular to each other and suspended by wires, similar to an ACT (acoustical ceiling tile) system.*

You are now ready to draw a gypsum board ceiling.

30. Make sure **Susp GB on Metal Stud** is selected in the *Type Selector* on the *Properties Palette*.

31. Set the ceiling height to **7'-0"**.

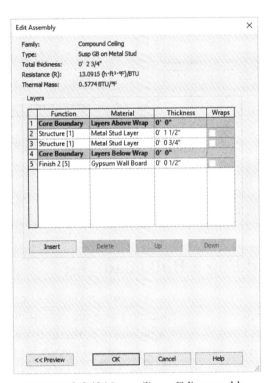

**FIGURE 9-2.10** New ceiling – Edit assembly

32. Pick the lower left room as shown in **Figure 9-2.11**. If you don't see the ceiling, you may have forgotten to change the material to *Gypsum Ceiling Board* back in step 28.

**FIGURE 9-2.11** Gyp. Bd. Ceiling

You now have a gypsum board ceiling at 7'-0" above the basement floor slab.

## Adding a Bulkhead:

Next, you will draw a ceiling in the area at the bottom of the steps. However, you cannot simply pick the room to place the ceiling because Revit would fill in the stair area. First, you will need to draw a bulkhead at the bottom of the steps. A bulkhead is a portion of wall that hangs from the floor above and creates a closed perimeter for a ceiling system to tie into. The bulkhead will create a perimeter that the *Ceiling* tool will detect for the proper ceiling placement.

33. While still in the *Basement Reflected Ceiling Plan* view, select the ***Wall*** tool.

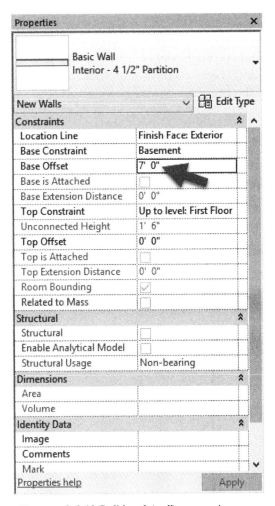

FIGURE 9-2.12 Bulkhead (wall) properties

34. Set the *Type Selector* to **Interior – 4 1/2" Partition**.

35. In the *Properties Palette* set the *Base Offset* to **7'-0"** (Figure 9-2.12).

This will put the bottom of the wall at 7'-0" above the current floor level, the basement in this case.

36. Set the *Top Constraint* to **Up to level: First Floor** (Figure 9-2.12).

*IMPORTANT TIP: The next time you draw a wall you will have to change the Base Offset back to 0'-0" or your wall will be 7'-0" off the floor; this can be hard to remember!*

37. **Draw the bulkhead**; make sure you snap to the adjacent walls (Figure 9-2.13).

Bulkhead added here; a wall with the bottom starting at 7'-0" above the basement floor

FIGURE 9-2.13 Bulkhead drawn

38. Select the *Ceiling* tool.

You could just pick within this room and Revit would automatically create a ceiling; however, you will look at another way to place a ceiling. Next you will sketch the perimeter of the ceiling, just like you did for the floor slabs in the previous lesson.

39. Select **Sketch Ceiling** from the *Ribbon*.

Sketch
Ceiling

40. Sketch a line around the perimeter of the room using *Snaps* (Figure 9-2.14). Settings should be *Susp GB* ceiling at 7'-0".

   *TIP: Remember to use the Chain option.*

41. Click the **green check mark** to finish the sketch.

**FIGURE 9-2.14** Sketching Ceiling

Your ceiling should look like Figure 9-2.15. You will see what is happening here a little better in the sections exercise.

**FIGURE 9-2.15** Ceiling added at bottom of steps

# Modifying a Floor System to Include the Ceiling:

Next you will modify the floor systems, already in place, to have gypsum board attached to the bottom of the joists. This is what is typically done in a residence, unless room is needed above the ceiling for ductwork.

42. Switch to the *Second Floor Plan* view (not the ceiling plan).

43. Select the floor.

> *TIP: Clicking near the stair opening may be the easiest way to select the floor.*

44. Via *Edit Type*, create a *Duplicate* floor from the one selected; name it **Wood Joist 14″ – Wood Finish – Gyp Bd Ceiling**.

45. Edit the floor structure via *Type Properties* (Figure 9-2.16).
    a. Insert a new *Layer* at the bottom of the floor assembly
    b. Set the *Function* to **Finish 1 [4]**
    c. Set the *Material* to **Gypsum Ceiling Board**
    d. Set the *Thickness* to ½″

## Why Did You Create a New Floor Type?

You needed to create a new floor type for the second floor because the first floor does not need gypsum board on the underside. When you modify a *family type*, all instances of that type are changed throughout the project. This is very powerful when you actually want to change several instances of a type. However, if you modify a type and only want the selected one to change, you are in for a big surprise when you look at the other instances of that type elsewhere in your project, because they will all change. That is why you had to create a new floor type, because that same floor type is also placed on the first floor.

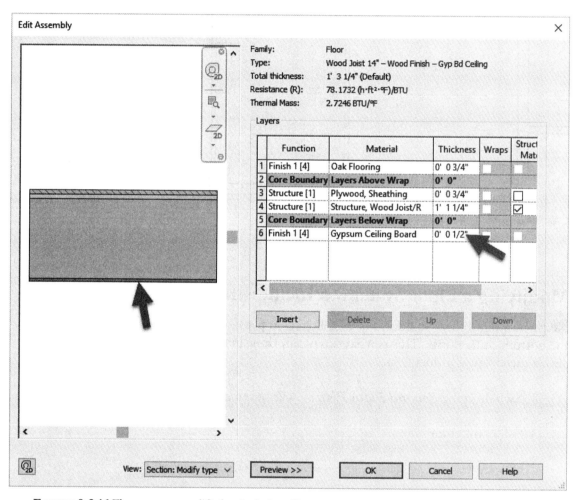

**FIGURE 9-2.16** Floor system modified to include ceiling

46. Close the open dialog boxes.

Now switch to the *First Floor Ceiling Plan* (Figure 9-2.17) and notice that the gypsum ceiling board surface pattern is showing everywhere the floor occurs. If not, make sure the second floor system has been changed to the new type. That takes care of the ceiling for the first floor.

47. Switch to the *Second Floor Ceiling Plan* and add your **Susp GB on Metal Stud** at 8'-0" high to the remaining rooms (Figure 9-2.18).

    *FYI: Once a ceiling is placed you can select it and click Edit Boundary on the Ribbon. Then you can change the perimeter or add an enclosed area within the main perimeter to create a hole. This is how you would accommodate the skylights in the roof: by adding holes to the ceiling to let the light in.*

48. **Save** your project as **ex9-2.rvt**.

**FIGURE 9-2.17** First floor ceiling plan: gypsum board added to bottom of floor structure

## Real-Time Design Validation

Notice how the ceiling, which is a 3D object, covers the roof ridge line and skylights? This is very powerful in that you see all aspects of the design. If you could see ductwork in the view below, that would mean it was added to the model too low and needs to be raised or moved. Being able to see everything in context helps the designers validate their design solution. Also, not seeing the skylights is a problem. This means the light is being blocked by the ceiling and needs to be addressed. However, we will not be doing that in this tutorial.

FIGURE 9-2.18 Second Floor Ceiling Plan: gypsum board ceiling system suspended at 8'-0" AFF

## Exercise 9-3:
## Placing Light Fixtures

In this exercise, you will learn to load and place light fixtures in your reflected ceiling plans.

## Loading Families:

Before placing fixtures, you need to load them into your project.

1. While in the **Second Floor** *Ceiling Plan*, select **Component** from the *Architecture* tab on the *Ribbon*.

2. Select **Load Family** on the contextual *Ribbon* (Figure 9-3.1).

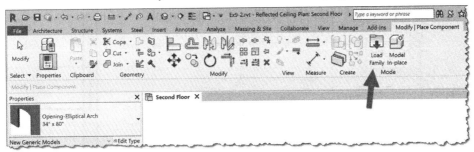

**FIGURE 9-3.1** Component tool active; contextual Ribbon options

3. Double-click the *Lighting\Architectural\Internal* folder, and then double-click **Troffer Light - 2x4 Parabolic.rfa** (Figure 9-3.2).

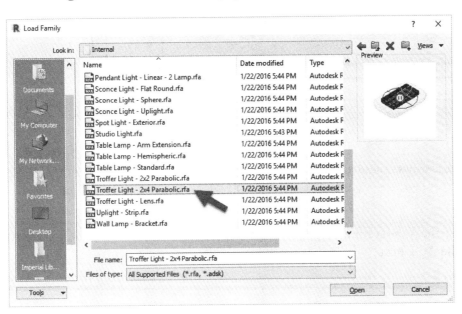

**FIGURE 9-3.2** Load component

## Placing Instances of Components:

You are now ready to place the fixtures in your ceiling plans.

4. With **Component** still selected, pick **Troffer Light – 2′ x 4′ Parabolic: 2′x4′ (2 Lamp) – 120 V** from the *Type Selector* drop-down on the *Properties Palette*.

5. On the ***Second Floor Ceiling Plan*** view, place fixtures as shown in **Figure 9-3.3**.

   *FYI:* Adjust the ceiling grid position if needed.

**FIGURE 9-3.3** Light fixtures added to ceiling

You will have to use the *Move* command, or even better the *Align* tool, to move the fixture so it fits perfectly in the ACT grid.

6.  Switch to the *Basement Ceiling Plan* view.

7.  Now place another **2x4 light fixture** as shown in **Figure 9-3.4**.

**FIGURE 9-3.4** Basement ceiling plan; light fixture added

Notice the fixture does not automatically orient itself with the ceiling grid. There may be an occasion when you want this.

Also, notice the light fixture hides a portion of the ceiling grid. This is nice because the grid does not extend through a light fixture.

8.  Use *Rotate* and *Move* to rotate the fixture to align with the grid (Figure 9-3.5).  The *Align* tool will also work.

    *TIP: You can use the normal* Rotate *and* Move *tools in conjunction with the Snaps.*

FIGURE 9-3.5 Basement Ceiling Plan; light fixture moved/rotated into place

9.  Once you have one fixture rotated, it is easier to use the *Copy* tool and the *Snaps* to add rotated light fixtures. **Copy** the light fixture to match the layout in **Figure 9-3.6.**

    *TIP: Check* Multiple *on the Options Bar when the Copy command is active.*

FIGURE 9-3.6 Basement Ceiling Plan; light fixture copied

10. **Save** your project as **ex9-3.rvt**.

These 2x4 light fixtures have *Rendering* settings already set up. That means the room will automatically have lights when you get to creating a photo-realistic rendering using this built-in feature!

The example image below shows a reflected ceiling plan with supply and return diffusers added. These are not used too often in residential work. They are loaded similarly to the light fixture via component tool.

**FIGURE 9-3.7** Example image; supply and return diffusers added

**Reflected Ceiling Plan Symbols:**
Revit provides many of the industry standard content necessary in drawing reflected ceiling plans (RCP). As shown in Figure 9-3.7, supply air diffusers are represented with an X and return air has a diagonal line. It is typical to have an RCP symbol legend showing each symbol and material pattern and listing what each one represents. The *Legend* feature makes this a snap!

**Component Properties**
If you want to adjust the properties of a component, such as a light fixture, you can browse to it in the *Project Browser* and right click on one of the *Types* listed. *Notice the right click menu also has the option to select all instances of the item in the drawing.* Select *Properties.* You will see the dialog below for the 2x4 (2 lamps)-120V.

You can also click *Duplicate* and add more sizes (e.g., a 4′x4′ light fixture).

| Type Properties | | × |
|---|---|---|
| Family: | Troffer Light - 2x4 Parabolic ∨ | Load... |
| Type: | 2'x4'(2 Lamp) - 120V ∨ | Duplicate... |
| | | Rename... |

**Type Parameters**

| Parameter | Value | = |
|---|---|---|
| Manufacturer | | |
| Type Comments | | |
| URL | | |
| Description | | |
| Cost | | |
| Assembly Description | Lighting - Fluorescent | |
| Type Mark | | |
| OmniClass Number | 23.80.70.11.14.11 | |
| OmniClass Title | Downlights | |
| Code Name | | |
| **Photometrics** | | |
| Light Loss Factor | 0.88 | |
| Initial Intensity | 80.00 W @ 78.75 lm/W | |
| Initial Color | 4230 K | |
| Emit from Rectangle Width | 1' 10" | |
| Emit from Rectangle Length | 3' 10" | |
| Emit Shape Visible in Rendering | ☐ | |
| Dimming Lamp Color Temperature | <None> | |
| Color Filter | White | |
| Light Source Definition (family) | Rectangle+HemiSpherical | |

| << Preview | OK | Cancel | Apply |

You can also select an inserted component and look at the *Properties Palette* for additional properties for that particular instance.

## Exercise 9-4:
## Annotations

This short section will look at adding notes to your RCP.

## Adding Annotations:

1. In the *Basement Reflected Ceiling Plan* view, select the **Annotate → Text → Text** tool from the *Ribbon*.

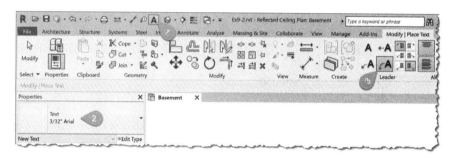

**A**
Text

2. Pick **Text: 3/32″ Arial** from the *Type Selector* (Figure 9-4.1).

3. Select the **Leader** (Curved) button highlighted in **Figure 9-4.1**.

**FIGURE 9-4.1** Text; Ribbon options

Next, you will add a note indicating that a room in the basement does not have a ceiling. First you will draw a leader, and then Revit will allow you to type the text.

4. Add the note "**NO CEILING - TYPICAL**" shown in **Figure 9-4.2**.

**FIGURE 9-4.2** Text with Curved leader

Notice that immediately after adding the text or while it is selected, you see the *Move* icon, the *Rotate* icon and *Grips* to edit the arrow/leader.

When the text is selected you can click the "add leader" tools on the *Ribbon* (shown on the left above) to add additional leaders.

## Adding Text Styles to Your Project:

You can add additional text styles to your project. Some firms prefer a font that has a hand lettering look and others prefer something like the Arial font. These preferences can be saved in the template file so they are consistent and always available. Next, you will add a new style to your Revit project.

5. Click on the *Text* tool.

6. Next, click **Edit Type** in the *Properties Palette*.

7. Select **Duplicate** and enter **1/4″ OUTLINE TEXT** (Figure 9-4.3).

8. Next, make the following adjustments to the *Type Properties* (Figure 9-4.4).
   a. Text Font: **Swis721 BdOul BT**
   b. Text Size: ¼″

   *NOTE: You can use any Windows True-Type font. If you do not have this font, select another that best matches (Figure 9-4.5).*

**FIGURE 9-4.3** New text name

The text size you entered in Step 8 is the size of the text when printed. Revit automatically scales the text, in each view, based on the *View Scale* setting. For example, if you are adding 3/32″ text to a ⅛″ floor plan view, the text placed will be 9″ tall. If you add text to a ¼″ plan view, the text will be 4½″ tall. When both the ¼″ and ⅛″ plan views are placed on a sheet, the text for each is 3/32″ tall. Here is what happens: adding text to the ¼″ plan causes the 3/32″ text to be scaled up 48 times, and when the plan view is placed on a *Sheet*, the entire view, including the text, is scaled down 1/48 times; thus, the text makes a full loop back to being 3/32″ tall.

If you change the *View Scale* of the drawing, the text size will automatically change, so the text is always the correct size when printing. It is best to set the drawing to the correct scale first, as changing the *View Scale* can create a lot of work repositioning resized text that may be overlapping something or too big for a room.

9. Select **OK** to close the open dialog.

You should now have the new text style available in the *Element Type Selector* on the *Ribbon*.

10. Use the new text style to create the text shown below (Figure 9-4.5).

> *TIP: Select the text only option on the Ribbon – i.e., No Leader.*

When typing text, you simply click somewhere in the view to complete the text string; pressing *Enter* just adds more lines.

11. Save as **ex9-4.rvt**.

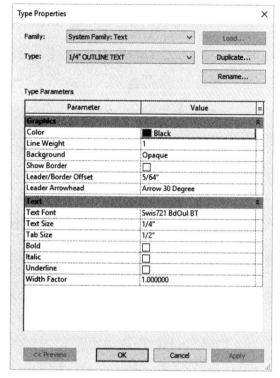

**FIGURE 9-4.4** New text properties

**FIGURE 9-4.5** New text style added

## Self-Exam:

The following questions can be used as a way to check your knowledge of this lesson. The answers can be found at the bottom of the page.

1.  You must pick walls to define floor areas. (T/F)

2.  Use the Ctrl key to cycle through the selection options. (T/F)

3.  When you add a floor element in plan view, the floor does not show up right away in the other views, i.e., 3D, Sections, etc. (T/F)

4.  You use the _____ feature if you need to add a new product, like exterior plaster, so you can add it to wall types and other systems.

5.  You have _____ different types of leader options with the *Text* tool (not including the 6 leader location icons).

## Review Questions:

The following questions may be assigned by your instructor as a way to assess your knowledge of this section. Your instructor has the answers to the review questions.

1.  It is not possible to create new text styles. (T/F)

2.  You can add additional light fixture sizes to the family as required. (T/F)

3.  The light fixtures automatically turn to align with the ceiling grid. (T/F)

4.  You can adjust the ceiling height room by room. (T/F)

5.  Revit allows you to model bulkheads by adjusting the bottom position of the wall. (T/F)

6.  You can use any Windows True Type font in Revit. (T/F)

7.  Use the _____ tool if the ceiling grid needs to be at an angle.

8.  Use the _____ tool to adjust the ceiling grid location if a ceiling tile is less than half its normal size.

9.  Use the _____ tool to adjust whether an element's surface pattern is displayed (i.e., the stipple for the gypsum board ceiling).

10. What is the current size of your project (after completing exercise 9-4)?

_____ MB.

**Notes:**

## Lesson 10
# ELEVATIONS:

This lesson will cover interior and exterior elevations. The default template you started with already has the four main exterior elevations set up for you. You will investigate how Autodesk® Revit® generates elevations and the role the elevation tag plays in that process.

## Exercise 10-1:
## Creating and Viewing Exterior Elevations

Here you will look at setting up an exterior elevation and how to control some of the various options.

## Setting up an Exterior Elevation:

Even though you already have the main exterior elevations set, you will go through the steps necessary to set one up. Many projects have more than four exterior elevations, so all exterior surfaces are elevated.

1.  Open your project, ex9-4.rvt, and **Save As ex10-1.rvt**.

2.  Switch to your *First Floor* plan view.

3.  Select **View → Create → Elevation** *(not the down-arrow)*.

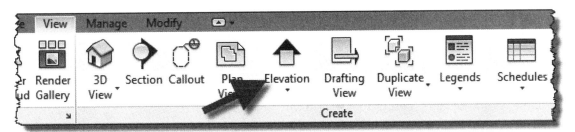

4.  Make sure the *Type Selector* is set to *Elevation:* **Building Elevation** and then place the elevation tag in plan view as shown in Figure 10-1.1.

    *NOTE: As you move the cursor around the screen, the Elevation Tag automatically turns to point at the building.*

You now have an elevation added to the *Project Browser* in the *Elevations* section. **The first thing you should do after placing an elevation is rename it**; the default name is not very descriptive. These generic names would get very confusing on larger projects with dozens of views.

Add this ———→ elevation tag

**FIGURE 10-1.1** Added elevation tag

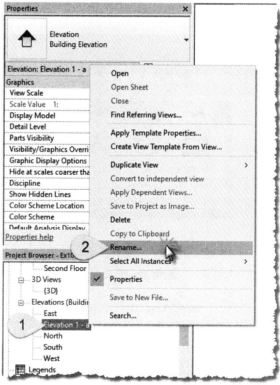

5. **Right-click** on the new view name, in the *Project Browser*, and select **Rename** (Figure 10-1.2).

6. Type: **South – Main Entry**.

The name should be fairly descriptive so you can tell where the elevation is just by the name in the *Project Browser*.

7. Double-click on **South –Main Entry** in the *Project Browser*.

The elevation may not look correct right away (Figure 10-1.3). You will adjust this in the next step. Notice, though, that an elevation was created simply by placing an *Elevation Tag* in plan view.

8. Switch back to the *First Floor Plan* view.

**FIGURE 10-1.2** Renaming new view name

**FIGURE 10-1.3** Initial elevation view

Next, you will study the options associated with the elevation tag. This, in part, controls what is seen in the elevation.

9. The elevation tag has two parts: the pointing triangle and the square center. Each part will highlight as you move the cursor over it. **Select the square center part.**

You should now see the symbol shown on the right.

**View direction boxes:**
The checked box indicates which way the elevation tag is looking. You can check, or uncheck, the other boxes. Do NOT do that at this time. Each checked box adds another view name to the *Project Browser*.

> Rotation Control icon visible when Elevation Tag is selected

**Rotation Control:**
Clicking and dragging on this allows you to look perpendicular to an angled wall in plan, for example.

---

**Interior Elevations:**
When adding an interior elevation tag to the floor plan, you should select *Interior Elevation* from the *Type Selector*. This will use a different symbol to help distinguish the interior tags from the exterior tags in the plan views. Also, the interior and exterior views are separated in the *Project Browser*, making it easier to manage views as the project continues to develop.

---

10. Press the **ESC** key to unselect the elevation tag.

11. Select the "pointing" portion of the elevation tag.

Your elevation tag should look similar to Figure 10-1.4.

**FIGURE 10-1.4** Selected elevation tag

The elevation tag, as selected in Figure 10-1.4, has several features for controlling how the elevation looks. Here is a quick explanation:

- **Cutting plane/extent of view line:** This controls how much of the 3D model is elevated from left to right (i.e., the width of the elevation).

- **Far clip plane:** This controls how far into the 3D model the elevation view can see.

- **Adjustment grips:** You can drag this with the mouse to control the features mentioned above.

12. Next you will take a look at the new elevation's *View Properties*. You can do this in one of the following ways:

   a. Select the "pointing" portion of the elevation tag (which should currently be selected based on the previous step).

   b. Select the view label (South – Main Entry in this example) in the *Project Browser*.

   c. Open the view with nothing in the model selected.

You have several options in the *Properties Palette* (Figure 10-1.5). Notice the three options with check boxes next to them; these control the following:

- **Crop View**: This crops the width and height of the view in elevation.
  *Adjusting the width of the cropping window in elevation also adjusts the "extent of view" control in plan view.*

- **Crop Region Visible**: This displays a rectangle in the elevation view indicating the extent of the cropping window, described above.
  *When selected in elevation view, the rectangle can be adjusted with the adjustment grips.*

- **Far Clipping**: If this is turned off, Revit will draw everything visible in the 3D model, *within the "extent of view."*

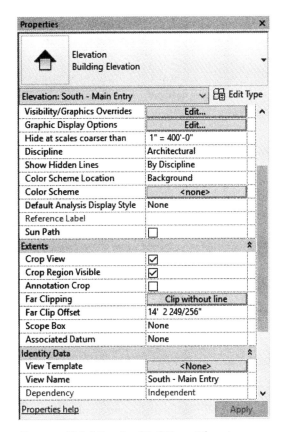

**FIGURE 10-1.5** South – Mail Entry Elev view properties

You will manipulate some of these controls next.

13. With the elevation tag still selected (as in Figure 10-1.4), drag the "cutting plane/ extent of view" line up **into** the main entry as shown in Figure 10-1.6.

**FIGURE 10-1.6** Relocated cutting plane

14. Now switch to the elevation view *South – Main Entry*. Adjust the **Crop Region** so the entire roof is visible; click the *Crop Region* to select it and drag the top grip upward. *FYI:* The roof's ridge line will not be visible yet.

Your elevation should look similar to Figure 10-1.7.

The main entry wall and roof are now displayed in section because of the location of the *cutting plane* line in plan.

**FIGURE 10-1.7** Elevation with cutting plane thru front entry

Notice that the roof is not fully visible. This is not related to the cropping window shown in Figure 10-1.7. Rather, it is related to the *Far Clip Plane* set in the plan view.

15. Adjust the *Far Clip Plane* in the **First Floor Plan** view so that the entire roof shows in the **South – Main Entry** view.

> *TIP: Click on the grip and drag the* Far Clip Plane *North until it is past the ridge line, which is at the middle of the building. You may need to adjust the crop region again.*

Now when you switch back to the **South – Main Entry** elevation view, you should see the entire roof.

Next, you will adjust the elevation tag to set up a detail elevation for the main entry area.

16. In the **First Floor Plan** view, adjust the elevation tag to show only the main entry wall (Figure 10-1.8).
    - The cutting plane/extent of view line is moved South so it is outside of the building footprint.
    - Use the left and right grips to shorten the same line.

17. Switch to the **South – Main Entry** view to see the "detail" elevation you are setting up (Figure 10-1.9).

18. Set the **View Scale** to ½″ = 1′-0″ on the *View Control Bar* at the bottom of the screen.

Notice how the *Level Datum* tags have changed to a smaller size. *Undo* and try it again if you missed it. You did notice the levels were automatically added, right?

19. Click the **Hide Crop Region** icon on the *View Control Bar* to make the *Crop Region* disappear.

1/2″ = 1′-0″

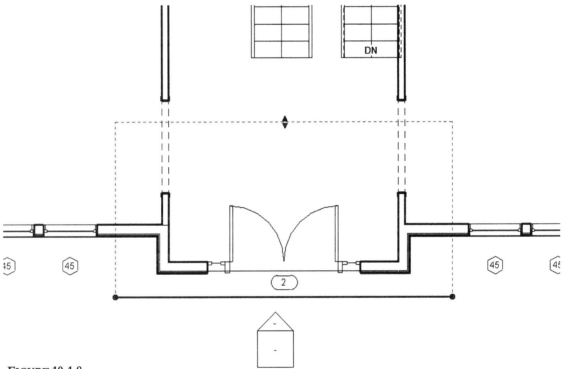

**FIGURE 10-1.8**
Main Entry wall detail elevation

Once you modify the view constraints in plan view (Figure 10-1.8) and you switch to the new elevation view, you can click on the *crop region* and use the grips to make the view wider. You might want to do this to make sure the roof overhang shows.

When you drag the *crop region* to the right, the *Level Datum* tags move so they do not overlap the elevation. This is another example of Revit taking the busy work out of designing a residence!

Crop region; visibility should be turned off in Step 19.

**DETAIL ELEVATION:**
A detail elevation like this might be used to dimension various items like the mail box, sign, special siding/ trim, etc. The scale would typically be larger than the full South elevation so you can fit more notes and dimensions.

This view might be placed on a sheet with the other elevations or any sheet where you can find room.

**FIGURE 10-1.9** Main Entry wall detail elevation; View Scale is set to ¼″ = 1′-0″ so the level labels would be legible in this book

Many designers like to change the line weight around portions of the building which protrude out from the main elevation. This helps the builder and client to more easily read the drawings. However, Revit does not do this automatically. It can be done manually using the **Linework** tool on the *Modify* tab. When the tool is active you can select a line style from the *Ribbon* and then begin clicking lines in the model to override their default settings. These lines will adjust as the model is changed. Selecting **<by category>** for a line style and then clicking an overridden line will set it back to its original state. Give it a try!

20. **Save** your project as **ex10-1.rvt**.

## Exercise 10-2:
## Modifying the Project Model: Exterior Elevations

The purpose of this exercise is to demonstrate that changes can be made anywhere and all other drawings are automatically updated.

## Modify an Exterior Elevation:

1.   Open ex10-1.rvt and **Save As ex10-2**.

2.   Open the *West* exterior elevation view. Adjust the start and end locations of the *Level Datum* lines to be closer to the edge of the building (Figure 10-2.1).

3.   Using the **Ctrl** key, select the two double-hung windows on the right, two of the four windows in the garage wall.

You will delete the two selected windows and move the remaining two windows to the center of the wall.

4.   Press the **Delete** key to erase the selected windows.

5.   Select the remaining two windows and use the *Move* tool to <u>approximately</u> center them on the wall/roof ridge, keeping the vertical alignment unchanged (Figure 10-2.1). The next page will discuss how to center them more precisely.

**FIGURE 10-2.1** Modifying windows on the West elevation

Now you will switch to the *First Floor Plan* view to see your changes.

6.  Switch to the ***First Floor*** plan view and zoom in on the garage area (Figure 10-2.2). Adjust the window position per the information mentioned below.

Notice how the windows in plan have changed to match the modifications you just made to the exterior elevations? This only makes sense seeing as both the floor plan and the exterior elevation are projected 2D views of the same 3D model. Both views are directly manipulating the 3D model.

Also, notice that even the dimensions adjusted! Revit is all about reducing drafting time and maximizing design time. Step 5 had you approximately locate the windows; now you can select the windows in plan and type the exact dimension you want; 12′-3″ centers them on the building.

**FIGURE 10-2.2** Changes automatically made to the floor plan

Next, you will insert a window in elevation. This will demonstrate, first, that you can actually add a window in elevation not just plan view, and second, that the other views are automatically updated.

7. Switch to the **North** exterior elevation view.

8. Select the **Window** tool from the *Architecture* tab.

Notice, with the window selected for placement, you have the usual dimensions helping you accurately place the window. As you move the window around, you should see a dashed horizontal cyan colored line indicating the default sill height, although you can deviate from this in elevation views.

9. From the *Type Selector*, choose *Double Hung with Trim:* **36″x48″**.

10. Place a window as shown in **Figure 10-2.3**; make sure the bottom of the window *Snaps* to the dashed, cyan colored sill line.

   *TIP: The window should be about centered between the existing windows.*

**FIGURE 10-2.3** Placing a window on the North elevation

If you laid out the interior walls as described in Lesson 5, you should get a warning message when inserting the window. This is because the interior wall between the kitchen and the living room conflicts with the exterior window. Revit is programmed to see that conflict and bring it to your attention. You can ignore this error because it is possible to build a wall up to the center of a window; some errors you cannot ignore because they will have a negative impact on Revit's functionality.

11. Click the "X" in the upper-right corner to ignore the wall/window conflict warning (Figure 10-2.4).

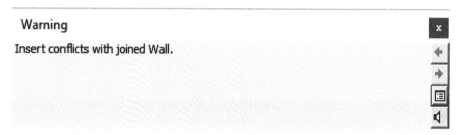

**FIGURE 10-2.4** Conflict warning

12. Switch to the *First Floor* plan view to see the problem (Figure 10-2.5).

**FIGURE 10-2.5** First Floor – kitchen area

13. While in plan view, select the new window and **Delete** it.

Why did the window location dimensions update in Figure 10-9.2 and not in Figure 10-2.5? The first had dimensions associated with the windows and the latter did not. When you dimension something in Revit, the witness lines "remember" what they are dimensioning to and move with that element. Also, notice how the window was tagged in elevation view, but not in plan view like the previously placed windows? The tag is only added in the view the element was placed in but can be manually tagged in any view (even multiple times).

*TIP: When working in the exterior elevation view, you can quickly see where the interior walls are simply by selecting the exterior wall (Figure 10-2.6).*

Whenever something is selected, it turns blue and becomes transparent. Thus, the things behind the element are temporarily visible.

**FIGURE 10-2.6** Transparent selections

## Adding Shutters to the South Elevation:

Next you will add shutters to the South elevation. You will need to load a family from the online Revit Content website.

14. Switch back to the **North** elevation view and notice that the new window is gone, per your plan change.

15. Switch to the **Insert** tab on the *Ribbon*.

16. Using *Load Family*, load **shutter (high-res)** from the provided online files. See the inside front cover of this book for instructions.

17. With the **Component** tool active and **Shutter (high-res): 18″ x 48″** selected in the *Type Selector*, place a shutter in elevation as shown in Figure 10-2.7 (upper-left window on North Elevation).

    *TIP: If the shutter does not land in the correct spot, select it and use the arrow keys (on the keyboard) to nudge it into place, or use the Align tool per the tip below.*

18. Use the same technique to place the remaining shutters shown in **Figure 10-2.8**.

19. Add shutters to the South elevation per **Figure 10-2.9**.

---

**TIP:  USING THE ALIGN TOOL**
*Don't forget about the Align tool. Simply drop your shutter somewhere near the window and use the Align tool to move it into place. After placing the shutter, click Align, select the edge of the window and then select the edge of the shutter to move the shutter into place. If the window moves, you picked in the wrong order – click Undo and try again. Also, immediately after you use Align you can click the Padlock to maintain a parametric relationship; meaning if the window moves, even via a plan view, the shutters will move with it!*

---

**FIGURE 10-2.7** Placing a shutter on the North elevation

The shutter element has been set up so that it can only be placed on a wall (this is called a *wall hosted family*). If you move the cursor over a door or window, you get the (⊘) symbol meaning it cannot be placed there.

**FIGURE 10-2.8** (8) Shutters added to the North elevation

**FIGURE 10-2.9** (4) Shutters added to the South elevation

20. **Save** your Project as ex10-2.rvt.

---

**REMINDER:     ENTERING DIMENSIONS IN REVIT**

As your experience with Revit grows, you will want to learn some of the shortcuts to using the program. One of those shortcuts is how you enter dimensions when drawing. You probably already know, maybe by accident, that if you enter only one number (e.g., 48) and press Enter, Revit interprets that number to be feet (e.g., 48'-0"). So, if you want to enter 48", you may be typing 0'-48" or 48". Both work, but having to press the Shift key to get the inch symbol takes a little longer.

Here are some options for entering dimensions:

| | |
|---|---|
| **0 48** | *Revit reads this as 48" (zero space forty-eight)* |
| **48** | *Revit reads this as 48'-0"* |
| **5.5** | *Revit reads this as 5'-6"* |
| **0 5.5** | *Revit reads this as 5 ½"* |
| **2 0 1/4** | *Revit reads this as 2'-0¼" (two space zero space fraction)* |

---

## Exercise 10-3:
## Creating and Viewing Interior Elevations

Creating interior elevations is very much like exterior elevations. In fact, you use the same tool. The main difference is that you are placing the elevation tag inside the building, rather than on the exterior.

## Adding an Interior Elevation Tag:

1. Open project ex10-2.rvt and **Save As ex10-3.rvt**.

2. Switch to the *First Floor* plan view, if necessary.

3. Select the *Elevation* tool from the *View* tab.

In the next step you will place an elevation tag. Before clicking to place the tag, try moving it around to see how Revit automatically turns the tag to point at the closest wall.

4. Select *Elevation:* **Interior Elevation** and then place an elevation tag, looking East, or to the right, in the living room area (Figures 10-3.1a and b).

FIGURE 10-3.1A Element Type Selector

*REMEMBER: The first thing you should do after adding an Elevation Tag is to give it an appropriate name in the Project Browser list.*

FIGURE 10-3.1B First floor: Elev tag added in Living Rm

5. Change the name of the new elevation to **Living Room – East** in the *Project Browser*.

6. Switch to the ***Living Room – East*** view.

> *TIP: Try double-clicking on the elevation tag, the pointing portion.*

Initially, your elevation should look something like Figure 10-3.2; if not, you will be adjusting it momentarily so do not worry. You will adjust this view next. *Notice how Revit automatically controls the lineweights of things in section versus things in elevations.*

**FIGURE 10-3.2** Living Room - East, initial view

7. Switch back to the ***First Floor Plan*** view.

8. Pick the "pointing" portion of the elevation tag, so you see the view options (Figure 10-3.3).

You should compare the two drawings on this page (Figures 10-3.2 and 10-3.3) to see how the control lines in the plan view dictate what is generated and visible in the elevation view for both width and depth.

Revit automatically found the left and right walls, the floor and ceiling in the elevation view.

Notice the *Far Clip Plane* is also acceptable. If you cannot see the fireplace in the elevation view, that means the *Far Clip Plane* needs to be moved farther to the right.

**FIGURE 10-3.3** Elevation tag selected

*FYI: The elevation tags are used to reference the sheet and drawing number so the client or contractor can find the desired elevation quickly while looking at the floor plans. This will be covered in a later lesson. It is interesting to know, however, that Revit automatically does this, fills in the elevation tag when the elevation is placed on a sheet and will update it if the elevation is moved.*

9. Switch back to the ***Living Room - East*** view.

Just to try adjusting the *crop region* to see various results, you will extend the top upward to see the second floor.

10. Select the *cropping region* and drag the top middle grip upward, to increase the view size vertically (Figure 10-3.4).

**FIGURE 10-3.4** Living Room - East elevation: crop region selected and modified

Here you are getting a sneak peak ahead to the "sections" portion of this book. Notice that additional level datums were added automatically as the view grew to include more vertical information (i.e., second floor, roof).

11. Now select **Undo** to return to the previous view state (Figure 10-3.2).

As you probably noticed, the interior elevation shows the *Foundation* level datum below the *First Floor* level datum. The *Foundation* level datum is not necessary in this view, so you will remove it from this view.

> **IMPORTANT:** You cannot simply delete the level datum because it will actually delete all related views from the entire project (i.e., floor and ceiling plan views). This will delete any model elements that are hosted by that level (walls, doors, windows) and any tags, notes and dimensions in that view.

To remove a level datum, you select it and tell Revit to hide it in the current view. You will do this next.

12. Click on the horizontal line portion of the *First Floor* level datum.

13. Right-click and select **Hide in View** → **Elements** from the pop-up menu.

> *TIP: Selecting Category would make all level datum elements disappear from the current view.*

14. Adjust the bottom of the **crop region** to align with the *First Floor* level (horizontal line).

15. On the *View Control Bar*, make sure the **View Scale** is set to ¼"=1'-0".

Your elevation should look like Figure 10-3.5.

**FIGURE 10-3.5** Living Room - East Elevation

You can leave the *crop region* on to help define the perimeter of the elevation. You can also turn it off; however, some lines that are directly under the *crop region* might disappear. You could use the *Detail Line* tool to manually define the perimeter using a heavy line.

*TIP: If perimeter lines disappear when you print interior elevations, try unchecking* Hide Crop Regions *in the Print dialog, and turn off the ones you don't want to see.*

## Turning off the View Name on the Elevation Tag:

The interior elevation tag currently has the view name showing (in plan view). You will turn this off as it is not required on the construction drawings.

16. Select **Manage** → **Settings** → **Additional Settings** (down-arrow)→ **Elevation Tags**

17. Set the *Type* to ½″ **Circle** (Figure 10-3.6).

18. Select **Elevation Mark Body_Circle: Filled Arrow** from the *Elevation Mark* drop-down list (Figure 10-3.6).

19. Click **OK** to close the dialog box.

The view name is now gone from the *elevation tags* in the floor plan view.

**FIGURE 10-3.6** Adjusting the interior elevation tag

*FYI: If you right-click on an elevation view name in the Project Browser, you will notice you can* Duplicate *the view (via* Duplicate View → *Duplicate). This is similar to how a floor plan is duplicated with one major variation: when an elevation view is duplicated, Revit actually just copies another elevation tag on top of the one being duplicated in the plan view. This is because each elevation view requires its own elevation tag. If two views could exist based on one elevation tag, then Revit would not know how to fill in the drawing number and sheet number if both views are placed on a sheet.*

## Adding Annotation:

Now you will add a note and dimensions to the interior elevation view.

20. Add the (2) dimensions and (1) text (3/32″ text style) with leader shown in Figure 10-3.7.

**FIGURE 10-3.7** Living Room - East elevation: annotation added

It is possible to add *Detail Lines* to this view to represent baseboard or other details such as wall bracing. This is often done for finer details which are not modeled. This approach helps with model performance but will not show up in sections or renderings.

21. On the *View Control Bar*, set the ***View Scale*** to ½″=1'-0″.

Notice the text and dimensions automatically resize to match the new scale. When space permits, most residential interior elevations are ½″ = 1'-0″.

22. Save your project as **ex10-3.rvt**.

## Exercise 10-4:
## Modifying the Project Model: Interior Elevations

This short exercise, similar to Exercise 10-2, will look at an example of Revit's parametric change engine. All drawings are generated from one 3D model.

## Modify the Interior Elevations:

1.  Open ex10-3.rvt and **Save As ex10-4.rvt**.

2.  Open the *Living Room - East* elevation view.

You will move the windows and add an exterior door.

3.  Select both of the windows on the right; use the **Ctrl** key to select multiple objects at one time.

4.  Use the *Move* tool to move the windows 6″ to the right, or South.

5.  Repeat the previous steps to *Move* the other two windows 6″ towards the left, or North.

6.  In the *Living Room - East* elevation view, use the *Door* tool to place a **Single Entry 3: 32″ x 84″** door in the wall to the far left (North). See Figure 10-4.1.

**FIGURE 10-4.1** Living Room - East - modified

You moved the windows out from the mantel so they provide a little more space between them. Revit allows you to design in all views!

You should notice, in Figure 10-4.1, that the door bottom is below the floor level; this is a problem only if your cursor was near the bottom of the wall when you clicked. You will fix it next.

7. Select the new door in the *Living Room – East* view.

8. In *Properties*, change the **level** from *Foundation* to **First Floor** if needed.

The interior elevation should now look correct (Figure 10-4.2).

**FIGURE 10-4.2** Living Room - East elevation: door height adjusted

Notice, back in the *Properties Palette* for the new door, a setting called *Sill Height*. This setting allows you to move the door vertically, relative to the specified level. For example, you might have a second floor door that opens onto a low roof, but the door needs to be 1'-0" above the second floor for this door to work correctly (roof insulation, flashing, etc.). You simply select the door and adjust its *Sill Height* to 1'-0", with the level set to *Second Floor* via the *Properties Palette*.

Now it is time to see the effects to the plan views.

9. Switch to the **First Floor Plan** view (Figure 10-4.3).

When placing a door in elevation, you may have to switch to plan view to verify the door swing is the way you want it. You can control the door swing in elevation: right-click and select "flip hand" or "flip facing."

In elevation, you can adjust many things this way. Some examples are ceiling height, interior and exterior windows, wall locations, perpendicular to the current view, etc.

Notice that the door does not have a door tag like the other doors in the plan view. This is because the door was not placed in this view. You will learn how to add this tag later.

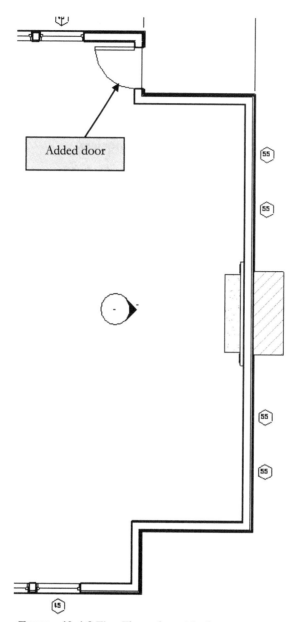

**FIGURE 10-4.3** First Floor plan with changes

10. Save your project as **ex10-4**.

## Exercise 10-5:
## Design Options

This exercise will look at a feature called *Design Options*. This feature allows you to present two or more options for a portion of your design without having to save a copy of your project and end up having to maintain more than one project until the preferred design option is selected.

## Design Options Overview:

A Revit project can have several design option studies at any given time; you might have an (A) entry porch options study, (B) a kitchen options study and a (C) master bedroom furniture layout options study in a project. Each of these studies can have several design options associated with them. For example, the entry porch study might have three options: 1. flat roof, 2. shed roof and 3. shed roof with a dormer type embellishment.

A particular study of an area within your project is called a *Design Option Set*, and the different designs associated with a *Design Options Set* are each called an *Option*. Both the *Design Options Set* and the *Options* can be named (see the examples below).

One of the *Options* in a *Design Option Set* is specified as the *Primary* option (the others are called *Secondary Options*); this is the option that is shown by default in all new and existing views. However, you can adjust the *Visibility* of a *View* to show a different option. Typically you would duplicate a *View*, adjust the *Visibility*, and *Rename* it to have each option at your fingertips.

When the preferred design is selected by you and/or the owner, you set that *Option* to *Primary*. Finally, you select a tool called *Accept Primary* which deletes the *Secondary Options* and the *Design Option Set*, leaving the *Primary Option* as part of the main building model.

### Design Option Set

Option 1                    Option 2

The following images (Figures 10-5.1a and b) provide an overview of the *Design Options* dialog box and *Status Bar* tools. See Step 2 to access this dialog.

**FIGURE 10-5.1A**
Status Bar; Design Options tools

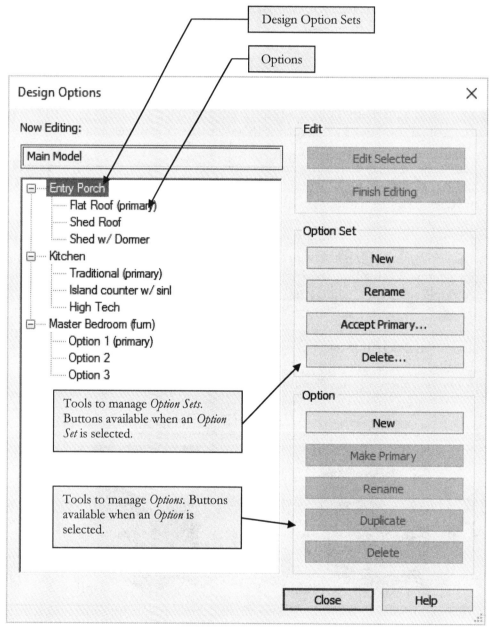

**FIGURE 10-5.1B** Design Options Dialog

Notes about the *Design Options* dialog box:

**Edit** buttons:
You can edit a *Design Option* by selecting an *Option* (in the window area on the left) and then clicking the **Edit Selected** button. Next you add, move and delete elements in that *Design Option*.

When finished editing a *Design Option*, you reopen the *Design Options* dialog and click the **Finish Editing** button.

If you are currently in an *Option Editing* mode, the *Now Editing* area in the *Design Options* dialog displays the *Option* name being modified, otherwise it displays *Main Model*.

**Option Set** buttons:
The **New** button is always available. You can quickly set up several *Option Sets*. Each time you create a new *Option Set*, Revit automatically creates a *Primary Option* named *Option 1*.

The other buttons are only available when an *Option Set* label is highlighted (i.e., selected) in the window list on the left.

The **Accept Primary** button causes the *Primary Option* of the selected set to become a normal part of the building model and deletes the set and secondary options. This is a way of "cleaning house" by getting rid of unnecessary information which helps to better manage the project and keeps the file size down.

**Option** buttons:
These buttons are only available when an *Option* (primary or secondary) is selected within an *Option Set*. You can quickly set up several *Options* without having to immediately add any content (i.e., walls, components, etc.) to them.

The **Make Primary** button allows you to change the status of a *Secondary Option* to *Primary*. As previously mentioned, the *Primary Option* is the *Option* that is shown by default in existing and new views. You can only have one *Primary* option in an *Option Set*.

The **Duplicate** button will copy all the elements in the selected *Option* into a new *Option*; this makes the file larger because you are technically adding additional content to the project. You can then use the copied elements (e.g., walls, furniture, etc.) as a starting point for the next design option. This is handy if the various options are similar.

Now you will put this introductory knowledge to use!

## Setting up a Design Option Set:

In this exercise you will create two *Design Option Sets*: one for the Main Entry Roof and another for the windows above the Entry Door. You will create an alternate roof and window design for your project.

You could just create one *Design Option Set* and have two design options total. However, by placing the roof options in one *Option Set* and the windows in another, you actually get four design options total; you can mix and match the window and roof options.

## Setting up Design Options in Your Project:

First you will set up the *Option Sets* and *Options*.

1.   Open ex10-4.rvt and **Save As ex10-5.rvt**.

2.   Click the **Design Options** icon on the *Status Bar* (Figure 10-5.1a).

You are now in the *Design Options* dialog box (Figure 10-5.2). Your dialog will look like this one, basically empty:

3.   In the *Option Set* area click **New**.

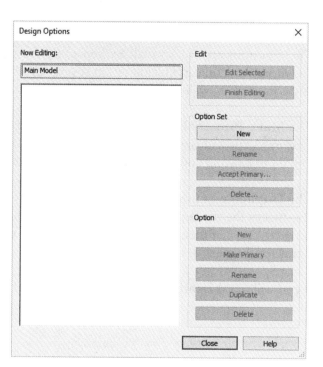

**FIGURE 10-5.2** Design Options Dialog; initial view

Notice an *Option Set* named *Option Set 1* has been created. Revit also automatically created the *Primary Option* named *Option 1* (Figure 10-5.3). Next you will rename the *Option Set* to something that is easier to recognize.

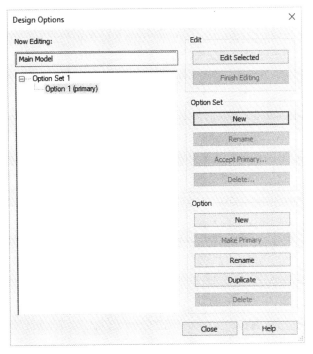

**FIGURE 10-5.3** Design Options dialog; new option set created

4. Select the *Option Set* currently named *Option Set 1* and then click the **Rename** button in the *Option Set* area.

   **WARNING!** *Be sure you are not renaming the* Option *but rather the* Option Set.

5. In the *Rename* dialog type **Entry Windows** (Figure 10-5.4).

6. Click **OK** to rename.

Giving the *Option Set* a name that is easy to recognize helps in managing the various options later, especially if you have several.

Next you will create a *Secondary Option* for the *Entry Windows* option set.

**FIGURE 10-5.4** Rename Option Set dialog

7.  With the *Entry Windows* option set selected, click **New** in the *Option* area (Figure 10-5.5).

Notice a secondary *Option* was created and automatically named *Option 2*. If you have descriptive names for the options in a set, you should apply them. In this example you can leave them as they are.

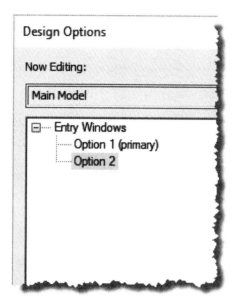

**FIGURE 10-5.5**
Design Options dialog; secondary option created

**FIGURE 10-5.6**
Design Options dialog

8.  Create an *Option Set* for the roof (Figure 10-5.6):
    a.  Name the set ***Entry Roof***
    b.  Create a secondary option

The basic thinking with the *Design Options* feature is that you set up the *Option Set* and *Option*s and then start drawing the elements related to the current *Option*. So, you select the *Option* from the drop-down list on the *Status Bar*, make the additions and modifications relative to that *Design Option*, and finally switch the drop-down back to *Main Model* to finish editing the option and then be able to make changes in the main model.

However, in your case, you want to move content already drawn to *Option 1*. Revit has a feature that allows you to move content to a *Design Option Set*, which means the content gets copied to the *Options* in the *Set* you select.

## Entry Windows Design Option:

You are now ready to set up the different design options.

9. Close the *Design Options* dialog and switch to the *3D* view; adjust the view so you are looking at the main entry (South elevation).

Unfortunately, you cannot just select the windows and add them to a *Design Option Set* because they are hosted elements that require a wall to be inserted in. Therefore, you will also add the entry walls and door to the *Design Option Set*.

10. **Select** the three walls at the main entry, three windows and main entry door; orbit as required.

11. Click the **Add to Set** icon on the *Status Bar*.

12. Select *Entry Windows* from the dialog drop-down and then click **OK** (Figure 10-5.7).

The selected items are now in both *Option 1* and *Option 2* under the option set *Entry Windows* because both options were selected in the previous dialog, Figure 10-5.7.

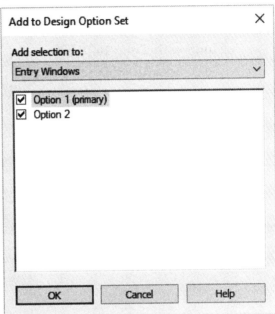

**FIGURE 10-5.7** Add to Design Option Set Dialog

From this point forward you can only modify the entry windows, door and walls when in *Option 1* or *Option 2 Edit* mode. In which case, the tables are turned and you cannot edit the main building model; this is because *Active Only* is checked on the *Status Bar*.

13. In the **Design Options** drop-down list, on the *Status Bar*, select **Entry Windows: Option 2** as shown in the image below.

Now you should notice that the main building model is slightly grey and not editable; it is not editable because *Active Only* is selected on the *Status Bar*. All hosted elements for the wall were also moved into the *Design Option*: three windows and a door in this case. You will change the windows per Figure 10-5.8.

14. Zoom in on the main entry, particularly the second floor window area in your **3D** view.

15. Select the three windows above the main entry door and change their type to **Double Hung with Trim: 16″ x 72″** from the *Type Selector*.

16. Make sure the window head (i.e., top) is at **7′-0″** via the *Properties Palette* for the selected windows.

17. Change the *Design Options* drop-down list, on the *Status Bar*, back to **Main Model**.

**FIGURE 10-5.8** 3D View: second floor windows modified

It now appears like all your changes disappeared, right? Well, if you recall from the introduction to this exercise, the *Primary Option* is displayed by default for all new and existing views. So, when you finished editing *Entry Windows: Option 2* the *3D* view switched back to the *Primary Option*, which is currently set to *Option 1* (Figure 10-5.6).

Next, you will create a new view and adjust its *Visibility* to display *Option 2* of the *Entry Windows* options set.

First you will create a duplicate copy of the *3D* view.

18. In the *Project Browser*, under *3D Views*, right-click on the **{3D}** label.

19. Select **Duplicate View → Duplicate** from the pop-up menu.

You now have a copy of the *3D* view named *Copy of {3D}*.

20. **Rename** the new 3D view to *Entry Windows Option 2.*

21. Switch to your new view, if needed.

22. Select **View → Graphics → Visibility/Graphics** (or type **VV**).

23. Click on the **Design Options** tab at the top of the dialog.

24. Change the *Design Option* parameter for *Entry Windows* to **Option 2** (Figure 10-5.9).

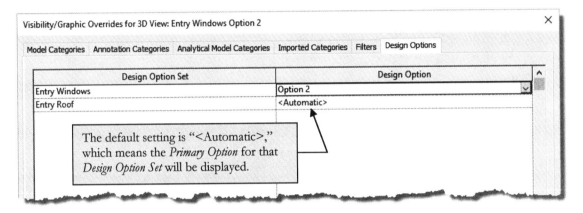

**FIGURE 10-5.9** Visibility/Graphic Overrides dialog: modified Entry Windows design option visibility

25. Click **OK** to close the dialog.

Now, with the *Default 3D* view and the *Entry Windows: Option 2* view, you can quickly switch between design options. Both views could be placed on the same sheet and printed out for a design critique.

## Entry Roof Design Option:

Now you will add an option for a roof over the entry door.

26. Select *Entry Roof:* **Option 2** from the *Design Options* drop-down list on the *Status Bar.*

You will add a roof shortly.

27. Switch to the **South** elevation view.

28. Zoom in to the area below the entry windows, just above the front door.

Next you will create an *in-place family* to represent a curved roof option over the entry area. Basically, you will create a solid by specifying a depth and then drawing a profile of the curved roof with lines.

29. Click **Architecture → Build → Component (down-arrow) → Model In-Place**.

Immediately, you are prompted to select a *Family Category*. This allows Revit to understand how other elements should interact with the object(s) you are about to create and control visibility.

30. Select **Roofs** from the *Family Category* list (Figure 10-5.10).

31. Click **OK**.

Now you are prompted to provide a name for the new *in-place family*.

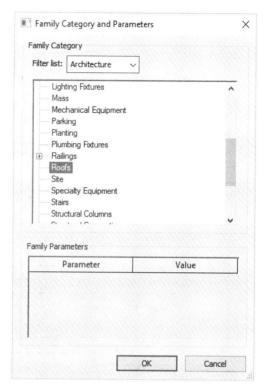

**FIGURE 10-5.10** Family Category and Parameters dialog

32. For the family *Name*, type **Entry Roof** (Figure 10-5.11).

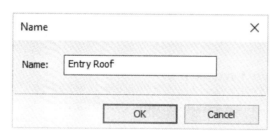

**FIGURE 10-5.11** Family name prompt

You are now in a mode where you draw the *Entry Roof*. Notice that the *Ribbon* has changed to have special buttons on the *Architecture* tab which has all the tools needed to create a family. You are continuously in the *Model In-Place* mode until you select *Finish Model* (green check mark) or *Quit Model* (red x) from the *Ribbon*.

FIGURE 10-5.12 Form Ribbon; select Extrude

You will now select the type of solid you wish to create.

33. Select **Architecture → Forms → Extrusion**.

Finally, you are prompted to select a plane in which to start drawing the profile of the solid to be extruded. Even though the view is a 2D representation of a 3D model, Revit needs to know where you want the 3D solid created so it knows how to show it in other views (both 2D representations and 3D). You will select the entry wall as a reference surface to establish a working plane.

34. Select **Pick a Plane** and click **OK** (Figure 10-5.13).

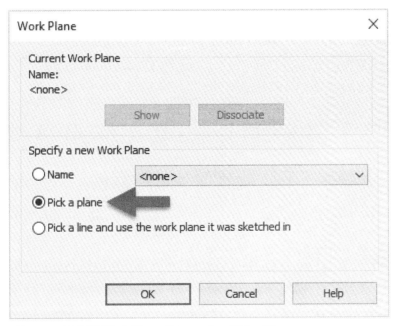

FIGURE 10-5.13 Work Plane dialog; select Pick a Plane

35. Move the cursor near the edge of the entry wall and then click to select it.

*TIP: If needed, click the Tab key until a heavy line appears around the perimeter of the wall. Then click the mouse to select (Figure 10-5.14). Do not hold the Tab key down.*

**FIGURE 10-5.14** South Elevation; select wall to establish work plane

Next, you will draw an arc to specify the bottom edge of the curved roof design option. Notice the *Ribbon* changed again to show tools related to drawing an extruded solid.

36. On the *Options Bar*, enter **2'-0"** for the **Depth** (Figure 10-5.15).

*FYI: A negative number for the depth would cause the solid to project in towards the building from the work plane.*

37. Click the **Start – End – Radius Arc** icon from the *Draw* panel on the contextual tab: *Modify | Create Extrusion.*

38. Pick the three points shown in Figure 10-5.15 to draw the arc. The angle 71.343° is not critical; get as close as possible. The ends of the arc are approximately straight up from the edge of the entry door below.

*TIP: Try typing SO before clicking the third point to temporarily turn off the Snaps for one pick (SO = Snap Off).*

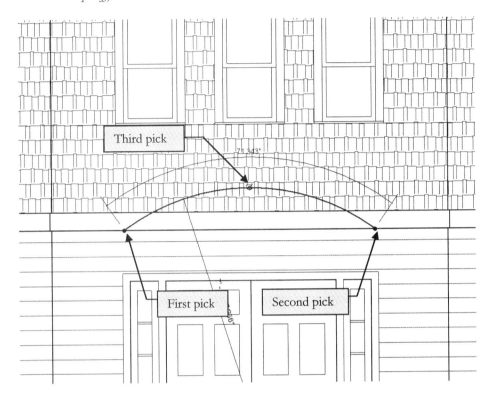

FIGURE 10-5.15 South Elevation; drawing arc to define roof

Now you will draw another arc 7¼" above the previous one.

39. Press **Esc** on the *Options Bar*, and with the *Start-End-Radius Arc* still selected, enter **0 7.25** for the *Offset*.

40. Draw another **Arc** picking the same three points; be sure to snap to the end points and midpoint of the previous arc (Figure 10-5.15).

Notice that an arc is drawn offset 7¼" from the points you picked. If you pick the first two points in the other direction, the arc would be offset in the other direction, downward in this case.

Next, you will draw two short lines to connect the endpoints of the two arcs. This will create a closed area, which is required before finishing the sketch. Think of it this way: you need to completely define at least two dimensions before Revit can create the third.

41. Click the "straight line" icon on the *Draw* panel (see image on previous page); this will switch you from drawing arcs back to drawing straight line segments. Set the *Offset* back to **0″**.

42. Zoom in and sketch a short line on each end of the arc as shown in Figure 10-5.16; be sure to use your *Endpoint* snaps (type SE).

**FIGURE 10-5.16** South elevation; two arcs and two short lines define roof profile

43. Click the **green checkmark** from the *Ribbon*.

> *TIP: If you get any warnings, it may be because one or more of the profile's corners do not create a perfect intersection; zoom in to see and use the Trim tool to close the corners. Delete any stray lines.*

You are still in the *Model In-Place Family* mode. Before you finish you will apply a material to the roof element.

44. Click the roof to select it.

45. In the *Properties Palette*, click in the *Material* value field and then click the "…" icon that appears.

The *Materials* dialog opens.

46. Select **Roofing, Metal** from the list of predefined *Materials* (i.e., the AEC Materials library). See Fig 10-5.17.

> *FYI: Notice the Appearance asset material is set to anodized aluminum with a dark bronze color for Metal – Roofing.*

47. Click **OK** to close the *Materials* dialog.

You are now ready to finish the family.

48. From the *Ribbon* click **Finish Model**.

Material Browser - Gypsum Ceiling Board

roofing, metal

Project Materials: All ▼

Search results for "roofing, metal"

Name

The search term was not found in the document.

Search Res... ▼

**Search Result**
▼ AEC Materials
   Metal  Roofing, Me

Name

Roofing, Me

Roofing, Standing S

**FIGURE 10-5.17** Materials dialog
Step one, in the image, toggles the visibility of the external Autodesk material library. You need to see this library in order to load materials from it into your model.

Finish
Model

Next you will move the roof down a little. At this point, the only "mode" you are in is for editing the *Entry Roof: Option 2*.

49. Click on the roof to select it.

50. Use the arrow keys on the keyboard to nudge the roof element down until it looks similar to Figure 10-5.18.

**FIGURE 10-5.18** South elevation; roof element moved to a lower position

Notice the arrow-grips on each end of the roof element when it is selected? Clicking one of these grips allows you to extend that solid perpendicular to the arrow. Try it; just *Undo* (Ctrl+Z) when you are done experimenting. It works better on rectilinear objects.

You are now ready to finish editing the current design option for the time being.

51. Set the *Design Options* drop-down back to ***Main Model***.

As before, the option you were just working on was not the *Primary Option* in the *Entry Roof* design set, so the current view reverted back to *Entry Roof: Option 1*, which is the primary view.

You will create a 3D view that has *Option 2* set to be visible for both the *Entry Window* option set and the *Entry Roof* option set.

52. Right-click on the ***Default 3D*** view and click **Duplicate View → Duplicate**.

53. Rename the duplicated view to **Entry – Option 2**.

54. Switch to the new view (*Entry – Option 2*); you should already be in that view.

55. Click **Visibility/Graphics** from the *View* tab (or type **VV**).

56. On the *Design Options* tab, set both *Option Sets* to **Option 2** in the *Design Option* column.

57. Click **OK** to close the dialog.

**FIGURE 10-5.19** Entry – Option 2 view with shadows on

You can now see a 3D view of your new entry roof option. The previous image has shadows turned on. This can provide a very dramatic result with almost no extra effort. The shadows can be useful while designing; however, you will probably have them turned off most of the time just to maintain system performance.

To turn on shadows, you simply click the *Shadows* toggle icon on the *View Control Bar* at the bottom of the screen.

Because the new entry roof element is a roof to Revit, you can attach walls to it, meaning a wall top would conform to the underside of the curved roof.

Another entry roof option might be a more traditional shed type porch roof like the one shown above. You might try adding this roof to the *Option 1* place holder. Simply sketch a roof by footprint, with only the South edge set to *Defines slope*.

58. **Save** your project as **ex10-5.rvt**.

*TIP: The Design Options feature can also be used to manage alternates, where both the base bid and the alternate(s) need to be drawn.*

## Self-Exam:

The following questions can be used as a way to check your knowledge of this lesson. The answers can be found at the bottom of the page.

1.  The plan is updated automatically when an elevation is modified but not the other way around. (T/F)

2.  You can use the *Elevation* tool to place both interior and exterior elevations. (T/F)

3.  You can rename elevation views to better manage them. (T/F)

4.  You have to resize the level datums and annotations after changing a view's scale. (T/F)

5.  How do you enter 5½″ without entering the foot or inch symbol? _____

## Review Questions:

The following questions may be assigned by your instructor as a way to assess your knowledge of this section. Your instructor has the answers to the review questions.

1.  The visibility of the *crop region* can be controlled. (T/F)

2.  You **have to** manually adjust the lineweights in the elevations. (T/F)

3.  As you move the cursor around the building, during placement, the elevation tag turns to point at the building. (T/F)

4.  There is only one part of the elevation tag that can be selected. (T/F)

5.  You cannot adjust the "extent of view" using the *crop region*. (T/F)

6.  What is the first thing you should do after placing an elevation tag?

    _____

7.  Although they make the drawing look very interesting, using

    the _____ feature can cause Revit to run extremely slow.

8.  With the elevation tag selected, you can use the _____ icon to adjust the tag orientation to look at an angled wall.

9.  You need to adjust the _____ to see objects, in elevation, that are a distance back from the main elevation.

10. What feature allows you to develop different ideas? _____

## Lesson 11
# SECTIONS:

Sections are one of the main communication tools in a set of architectural drawings. They help the builder understand vertical relationships. Architectural sections can occasionally contradict other drawings, such as mechanical or structural drawings. One example is a beam shown on the section is smaller than what the structural drawings call for; this creates a problem in the field when the duct does not fit in the ceiling space. The ceiling gets lowered and/or the duct gets smaller, ultimately compromising the design to a certain degree.

Autodesk® Revit® takes great steps toward eliminating these types of conflicts. Sections, like plans and elevations, are generated from the 3D model. Thus, it is virtually impossible to have a conflict between the architectural drawings. Many structural, mechanical and electrical engineers are starting to use Autodesk Revit for even greater coordination; this is helping to eliminate conflicts and redundancy in drawing.

## Exercise 11-1:
## Specify Section Cutting Plane in Plan View

Similar to elevation tags, placing the section "graphics" in a plan view actually generates the section view. You will learn how to do this next.

## Placing Section Marks:

1. Open ex10-5.rvt and **Save As ex11-1.rvt**.

2. Switch to the *First Floor* plan view.

3. Select **View → Create → Section**.

   Section

   *TIP: You may also select the Section icon from the Quick Access Toolbar, which would be more convenient.*

4. Draw a **Section** mark as shown in Figure 11-1.1. Start on the left side in this case. Use the *Move* tool if needed to accurately adjust the section after insertion. The section line should go through the stair landings (Figure 11-1.1).

**FIGURE 11-1.1** Section mark (selected)

You can see that the *Far Clip Plane* location in the plan view is out past the building perimeter; this means you will see everything (Figure 11-1.1). Anything passing through the section line is in section; everything else you see is in elevation (Revit calls it "projection"). Also, you can see the roof is shown in section exactly where the section line is shown in plan. Figure 11-1.2 also shows the *crop region*.

The *Section* tool is almost exactly like the *Elevation* tool.

**FIGURE 11-1.2** Longitudinal section view

Notice in the *Project Browser* that a new category has been created: *Sections (building Section)*. If you expand this category, you will see the new section view listed; it is called *Section 1*. You should always rename any new view right after creating it. This will help with navigation and when it comes time to place views on sheets for printing.

5. Rename section view *Section 1* to **Longitudinal Section**.

6. Switch to the new section view, **Longitudinal Section**.

> *TIP: Double-click on the section bubble head to open that view. The section needs to be unselected first; double-click on the blue part.*

7. Change the *View Properties* so the *Detail Level* is set to **Medium**.

Notice how the walls change to show more detail. You can set this on the *View Control Bar* at the bottom of the screen.

8. Zoom in on the portion of the section through the stairs.

You should notice an added level of detail in the section view.

You may also notice a big problem, as first mentioned on page 8-10: in Figure 11-1.3, the stair to the basement is obstructed by the first floor system. You will fix this soon.

The image below lists the additional terms related to the section mark graphics in the plan view, as compared to elevation tags.

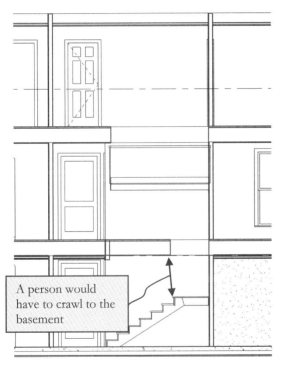

A person would have to crawl to the basement

**FIGURE 11-1.3** Section view – zoomed in

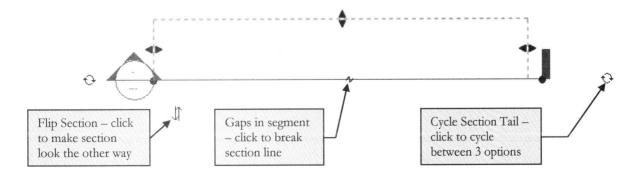

Flip Section – click to make section look the other way

Gaps in segment – click to break section line

Cycle Section Tail – click to cycle between 3 options

9.  Create another **section** in the *First Floor* plan view as shown in **Figure 11-1.4**.

    *TIP: You can use the control arrows to make the section look the other direction.*

**FIGURE 11-1.4** Plan view; Section tag (selected)

10. Rename the new section view to ***Cross Section 1*** in the *Project Browser*.

11. Switch to the ***Cross Section 1*** view.

12. Set the *Detail Level* to ***Medium*** and turn off the ***crop region*** visibility via the *View Control Bar* (Figure 11-1.5).

**FIGURE 11-1.5** Cross Section 1 view

Revit automatically displays lines heavier for elements that are in section than for elements beyond the cutting plane and shown in elevation.

Also, with the *Detail Level* set to *Medium*, the walls and floors are hatched to represent the material in section.

Notice that the *Longitudinal Section* mark is automatically displayed in the *Cross Section 1* view. If you switch to the *Longitudinal Section* view, you will see the *Cross Section 1* mark. Keeping with Revit's philosophy of changing everything anywhere, you can select the section mark in the other section view and adjust its various properties, like its *Far Clip Plane*.

*FYI: In any view that has a section mark in it, you can double-click on the round reference bubble to quickly switch to that section view. However, the section cannot be selected.*

## Modifying the First Floor Stair Opening:

Next, you will fix the problem with the stair opening in the first floor system. Basically, you will switch to the *First Floor Plan* view and select the floor. Then you will click *Edit Boundary* from the *Ribbon* and modify the sketch so the stair opening is larger.

13. Switch to the ***First Floor*** plan view.

14. Select the floor; use *Tab* if required to highlight the floor element for selection.

    ***TIP:*** *You can also toggle on Select Element by Face on the Status Bar and select the floor anywhere within its boundary.*

15. Click **Edit Boundary** on the *Ribbon* (see image below).

16. Use the *Line* and *Edit* tools, such as *Split* and *Trim*, to modify the sketch of the floor opening as shown in Figure 11-1.6.

17. Click the **green check mark** and choose **No** to the *attach walls* prompt.

18. Switch back to the ***Longitudinal Section*** view.

Notice the stair no longer has a problem (Figure 11-1.7).

19. **Save** your project as **ex11-1.rvt**.

**FIGURE 11-1.6** Plan view – Floor, sketch edit

**FIGURE 11-1.7** Longitudinal view – First floor element modified

## Exercise 11-2:
## Modifying the Project Model in Section View

Again, similar to elevation views, you can modify the project model in section view. This includes adjusting door locations and ceiling heights.

## Modifying Doors in Section View:

In this section you will move a door and delete a door in section view.

1. Open ex11-1.rvt and **Save As ex11-2.rvt**.

2. Open *Cross Section 1* view.

Looking back to Figure 11-1.5, you should notice the wall below the basement stair still extends up through the stair. You will move the wall over in the section view and then note that the adjacent wall and ceilings all automatically adjust in other views.

3. Use the *Align* tool to make the wall align with the edge of the floor opening (Figure 11-2.1).

   *TIP: Pick the edge of the floor first and then the face of the wall to align with the selected edge.*

**FIGURE 11-2.1** Cross Section 1 view; wall below stair moved

11-7

4.  Switch to the *Basement* <u>ceiling plan</u> view.

Notice the wall below the stair moved South and the ceiling automatically adjusted as well (Figure 11-2.2).

As long as a wall that defines the perimeter of a ceiling does not get deleted or shortened so that the ceiling perimeter is no longer defined, Revit will automatically update the ceiling. If the perimeter does become undefined, you may have to edit it manually. **Avoid deleting objects** just to redraw them because "hosted" elements, such as lights and dimensions, will be deleted.

Next, looking at Figure 11-2.1, you see that the arched opening in the basement is too tall; you will make it shorter. This will require a new *Type* within the *Opening-Elliptical Arch* family.

5.  Switch back to *Cross Section 1*.

6.  **Select** the **arched opening** in the basement.

7.  Click **Edit Type** on the *Properties Palette* and then **Duplicate**.

8.  Enter **60″ x 80″** for the name.

9.  Change the **Height** *Parameter* to **6′-8″** (Figure 11-2.3).

10. Click **OK** to close the open dialog box.

Your arched opening should now look like Figure 11-2.4 in *Cross Section 1* view. This change would not be apparent in a plan view because the only change was to the opening's height.

**FIGURE 11-2.2** Basement Floor Plan view; notice changes

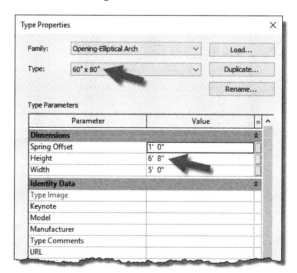

**FIGURE 11-2.3** Changing the arched opening height

**FIGURE 11-2.4** Cross Section 1 view; arched opening modified

Next you will adjust a ceiling height via your *Longitudinal Section* view.

11. Switch to **Longitudinal Section** view.

12. At the basement level, select the suspended acoustical ceiling tile system in the *Family Room* (lower right room).

Notice that while a ceiling is selected in a section view, a temporary dimension appears. This dimension allows you to directly change the ceiling height.

**FYI:** *The dimension may be overlapping a wall.*

13. Change the ceiling height to **6'-8"** using the temporary dimension. If required, adjust the witness lines to go from the top of the basement floor slab to the bottom of the ceiling.

Now, as you can see in the section view (Figure 11-2.5), the ceiling has lowered and there is more room for the recessed light fixtures shown; notice the lights lowered automatically.

**FIGURE 11-2.5** Cross Section 1 view; ceiling height modified

## Adding the Strip Footing Below the Foundation Wall:

A strip footing, in Revit, can be just a wall type set up as concrete. The width of the "wall" is set to be the width of your footing, as is the height. Revit provides a predefined wall and plan view in the residential template; this makes it very easy.

14. Switch to the plan view called *T.O. Footing*.

    **FYI:** *T.O. means "Top Of," i.e., "Top Of Footing."*

15. Select the **Wall** tool and then select *Basic Wall: 24" Footing* from the *Type Selector*.

16. Set the *Location Line* to **Wall Centerline** and make sure the *Depth* is set to **B.O. Footing** (B.O. means Bottom of Footing) on the *Options Bar*.

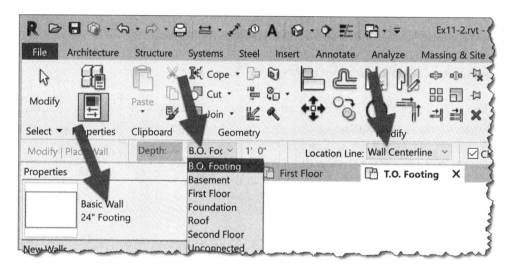

17. Select **Chain** on the *Options Bar*.

18. Start picking the intersection of wall centerlines, working around the perimeter of the building; also add a footing below the wall between the garage and the house. You want the 24" footing to be centered on the foundation wall (Figure 11-2.6).

    **TIP:** *Setting the Location Line to Wall Centerline is for the wall you are about to draw. Revit will automatically "snap" to the centers of walls previously drawn. Hover your cursor over the center of the wall until you see a dashed magenta/purple reference line, letting you know you are snapped to the center of the wall, and then move your cursor towards the end of that wall/purple reference line and click.*

After drawing the footings, you will notice the interior side of the footing will disappear because it is below the basement floor slab; it is visible in the garage area because it is unexcavated.

**FIGURE 11-2.6** T.O. Footing view; 24″ footing added

19. Switch back to the section view *Cross Section 1*.

As you can see (Figure 11-2.7), the footings have been added.

**FIGURE 11-2.7** Cross Section 1 view (modified)

If you look at the properties for the 24″ footing wall type, you can see how the wall was created relative to the *T.O. Footing* view in which you drew it.

Notice the *Base* and *Top Constraints* are selected. The *Base Constraint* is set to *B.O. Footing* and the *Top Constraint* is set to *Up to level: T.O. Footing*. Also notice the *Unconnected Height* is grayed-out, meaning you cannot change this setting, which makes sense seeing as you have defined both the top and bottom of the wall.

The distance between the two levels is 1′-0″, so the footing is 1′-0″ high.

In *Cross Section 1* view, try clicking on the *B.O. Footing* text (i.e., the -10′-3″ text) and change it to -11′-3″ and notice the footing size will automatically change.

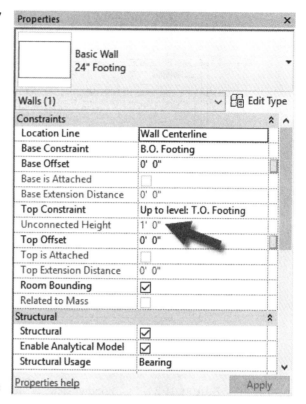

**FIGURE 11-2.8** Properties for 24″ Footing wall

If you try this, make sure you *UNDO* so that when you finish this exercise your footing is only 1′-0″ thick (see image to the right).

## Adding the Strip Footing Using the Foundation Tool on the Structure tab:

Revit offers another tool to add continuous strip footings below your foundation wall. On the *Foundation* panel (on the *Structure* tab) you can select the **Wall Foundation** tool. Then you simply select foundation walls and Revit automatically places a footing, centered, and directly under the wall. If you want to try this option, you can delete a portion of footing and use the *Structure* tool to replace it. If you try this, make sure you *Undo* before proceeding.

# Modifying the Footing Linework in Plan View:

Revit has predefined settings for line styles and lineweights. Most of the time, the developers have selected settings that will be satisfactory to most designers, which is great because this saves much time. However, you will occasionally want to tweak these prescribed settings. As mentioned in the previous chapter, Revit makes this easy with the *Linework* tool on the *Modify* tab. Basically, you select the *Linework* icon, select the desired setting from the *Type Selector* (e.g., lineweight or line style) and then select the lines to change. This change only applies to the current view.

You will try this next, switching the footing lines to dashed.

20. Switch back to the *T.O. Footing* view.

21. Select **Modify → View → Linework**.

22. Select **Hidden** from the *Line Style Panel* on the *Ribbon* (Figure 11-2.9).

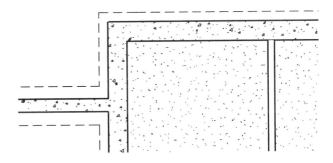

23. Click all the visible footing lines. Click Ctrl+Z if you pick another line by accident; that will *Undo* the previous pick.

**FIGURE 11-2.9** Linework icon selected

The footing lines are now the hidden line style (i.e., dashed) in the current view (Figure 11-2.10).

24. Save your project as **ex11-2.rvt**.

**FIGURE 11-2.10** Footing lines dashed

*FYI: The Linework tool will work on most lines generated by the model that are visible in a view. In the above example, the **Filter** feature of Revit might be more appropriate because you can set up a view to make all the walls with the word "footing" in the name be dashed; this is just one example of how Filter can be used. This will affect current walls and future walls that are visible in the current view. This filter can then be applied to other views if desired.*

# Stepped Footings:

Foundation walls and footings often need to step on sloped sites and around utilities. This is a little more work to set up in Revit but is still very doable. You will not actually do this at this time, but the concept will be covered here to get you started in the right direction when the time comes that you need to implement this type of design.

Basically, you *Split* the footings where the steps occur and edit the vertical position of each section of footing.

You do not need to Split the foundation wall; you will see why in a moment.

- In elevation or plan view, use the **Split** tool to break the footings up where each step needs to occur.

- Modify the *Base* and *Top Constraints* as required for each wall so they are in the correct position vertically (Figure 11-2.11).

**FIGURE 11-2.11**
Footing Split and heights adjusted

- In an elevation or section view, select the foundation wall and pick the **Edit Profile** button on the *Ribbon*.

- Use the **Lines** tool, on the *Ribbon*, and any of the edit tools (*Split, Trim, Mirror,* etc.) to redefine the perimeter of the wall in elevation. Modify the bottom magenta sketch line to follow the tops of the footings. Click **Finish Edit Mode** (i.e., green checkmark) when done (Figure 11-2.12).

**FIGURE 11-2.12**
Foundation wall modified
(via Edit Profile)

- Using the same technique as for the footing "wall" (i.e., *Edit Profile*), you can edit the profile of the footings so they appear correctly in elevation making sure the adjacent edges touch.

- When you **Finish Edit Mode** on the footings, you should see the footings join together and appear monolithic. If not, you can use the *Join Geometry* tool unless the edges do not touch perfectly, in which case you need to use *Edit Profile* again and fix the problem.

**FIGURE 11-2.13**
Footing "wall" modified
(via Edit Profile)

## Exercise 11-3:
## Wall Sections

So far in this lesson you have drawn building sections. Building sections are typically ⅛″ or ¼″ scale and light on the detail and notes. Wall sections are drawn at a larger scale and have much more detail. You will look at setting up wall sections next.

## Setting up the Wall Section View:

1. Open ex11-2 and **Save As ex11-3.rvt**.

2. Switch to the *Cross Section 1* view.

3. From the *View* tab on the *Ribbon*, click the rectangular *Callout* tool and then select *Section:* **Wall Section** from the *Type Selector*.

Callout

4. Place a **Callout** as shown in Figure 11-3.1.

   *TIP: Pick in the upper left and then in the lower right to place the Callout tag; do not drag.*

   *TIP: You can use the control grips for the Callout tag to move the reference bubble if desired; for example, move it away from notes/dimensions.*

**FIGURE 11-3.1** Cross Section 1 view with Callout added

Notice that a view was added in the *Sections (Wall Section)* category of the *Project Browser.* Because *Callouts* are detail references off of a section view, it is a good idea to keep the new callout view name similar to the name of the section.

Additionally, *Callouts* differ from section views in that the callout is not referenced in every related view. This example is typical, in that the building sections are referenced from the plans, and wall sections are referenced from the building sections. The floor plans can get pretty messy if you try to add too much information to them.

5.  Double-click on the reference bubble portion of the *Callout* tag to open the ***Callout of Cross Section 1*** view (Figure 11-3.2).

Notice, down on the *View Control Bar,* that the scale is set to ½″ = 1'-0″. This affects the elevation tags, text, datums and any annotation you add.

6.  On the *View Control Bar* set:
    a)  *View Scale* to **¾″ = 1'-0″**
    b)  *Detail Level* to **Fine**.

Notice the level datum's size changed.

If you zoom in on a portion of the *Callout* view, you can see the detail added to the view. The wall's interior lines are added and the materials in section are hatched (see Figure 11-3.4, at the second floor line).

You can use the *Detail Lines* tool to add more detailed information to the drawing. For example, you could show the truss, wall base, and flashing. Walls can be configured to have wall bases, which are set up as sweeps.

**FIGURE 11-3.2** Callout of Cross Section 1

As before, you can turn off and adjust the *crop region*. If you set the *Detail Level* to **Coarse**, you get just an outline of your structure. The *Coarse* setting is more appropriate for building sections than wall sections. Figure 11-3.3 is an example of the *Coarse* setting.

**FIGURE 11-3.3** Callout view (zoomed in); detail level: Coarse

**FIGURE 11-3.4** Callout view (zoomed in); detail level: Fine

# Refining the Walls:

Now that the residence is more developed, you will modify various wall properties to make them more accurate to what they would be in the real world. Both the main building walls and the garage need a little attention.

In the larger scale wall section you can see a few problems that need to be addressed.

**A** – The siding and sheathing need to extend down and over the edge of the flooring.

**B** – The top of the foundation wall needs to be modified to accommodate a 2x plate for the floor joists to bear on and attach to.

**FIGURE 11-3.5** First floor condition in Wall Section view

7.  In the wall section view, *Callout of Cross Section 1*, click to select the ***Foundation*** datum and then click to select the elevation text **-1'-3"** and change it to **-1'-4 ½"**.

You have now provided space for a continuous 2x board (which is 1 ½" high). This board will be added later.

Note that **all** of the foundation walls in the model have been changed by this one modification!

**FIGURE 11-3.6** Top of foundation wall modified

**11-18**

Next you will adjust the sheathing and siding. Revit provides a way in which specific "layers" (i.e., the sheathing and siding in this example) can extend down farther than the rest of the wall (i.e., the wood studs and gypsum board). You will modify your exterior walls, except at the garage, so that the sheathing and siding extend down to the top of the foundation wall. To do this you need to make one change within the wall type.

8. In the wall section view, select the exterior wall *Basic Wall:* **Exterior - Wood Shingle over Wood Siding on Wood Stud**.

9. Select **Edit Type** on the *Properties Palette* and then click **Edit** next to the *Structure* parameter.

10. Make sure the preview pane is displayed by clicking the **Preview** button in the lower left.

11. Below the preview pane, set the **View** to **Section: Modify type attributes** so the wall is shown in section (Figure 11-3.7).

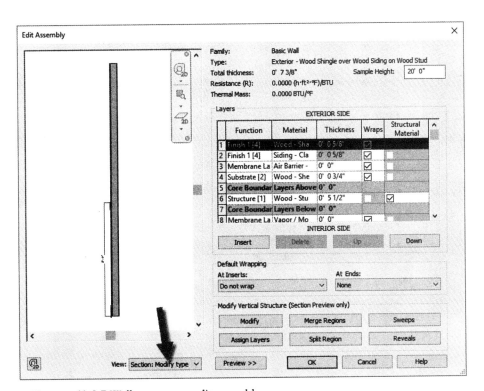

**FIGURE 11-3.7** Wall structure – edit assembly

Next, you will zoom in on the bottom of the wall in the preview pane and unlock the bottom edge of the siding and sheathing layers. This will allow the unlocked material to extend up or down apart from the bottom location of the wall.

12. Click in the preview pane to make sure it is active and then scroll the wheel on your mouse to zoom in on the bottom of the wall; you can also press the wheel button while moving the mouse to pan.

13. Click the **Modify** button (Figure 11-3.8).

14. Click the bottom edge of the siding "layer" (Figure 11-3.8).

Be sure you have the bottom edge of the siding layer selected. You should see a padlock symbol above it. Next you will click that symbol to unlock it. As soon as you make this change you will have a new parameter associated with that wall type named *Base Extension Distance*, which is an *Instance Parameter*, allowing you to change this value on a wall-by-wall basis. Entering a positive number moves the sheathing and siding up that distance from the bottom of the wall and a negative number moves it down.

15. Click the padlock symbol so it is shown in the **unlocked** position.

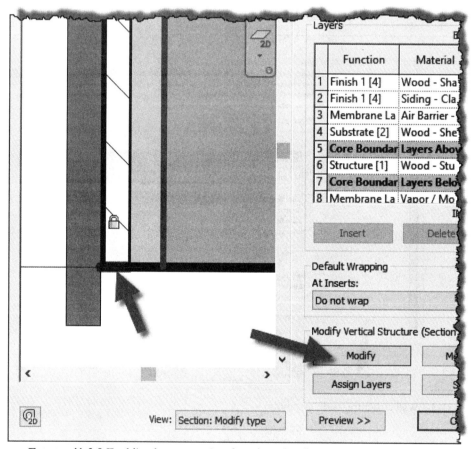

**FIGURE 11-3.8** Enabling base extension for selected wall type

You will repeat the previous two steps for the sheathing layer as well.

16. Click on the bottom edge of the sheathing layer.

17. Click the padlock symbol to unlock it.

*FYI: Only one contiguous section of layers can be set up to move up and down like this. Contiguous means the layers have to touch each other.*

18. **Close** the open dialog boxes.

19. Switch to the *First Floor Plan* view.

In the next step you will select all the exterior walls except the three at the garage. In order to select the three walls at the front entry, you will need to uncheck an option on the *Status Bar*; you will do this next.

20. Uncheck **Exclude Options** on the *Status Bar* (lower right).

21. Hover your cursor over one of the exterior walls to highlight it, but do not click, and then press the **Tab** key, which will highlight all the exterior walls. Click to select the highlighted walls.

*FYI: Alternately you can simply hold down the Ctrl key and individually pick each wall.*

22. Press the **Shift** key and select the <u>four</u> garage walls, one at a time while holding the Shift key down, to un-select them (if they are selected).

23. With all the exterior walls selected, except the <u>four</u> garage walls, draw your attention to the *Properties Palette*.

24. Set the *Base Extension Distance* to **-1'-4"**. Do not forget to add the negative sign at the beginning. See Figure 11-3.9.

This will make the sheathing and siding extend down 1'-4" below the bottom of the wall.

**FIGURE 11-3.9** Base Extension Distance

25. Switch back to *Callout of Cross Section 1* to see the modified wall (Figure 11-3.10).

**FIGURE 11-3.10** Results of 'Base Extension Distance' modification

26. Switch back to plan view and enter edit mode *Entry Windows – Option 2*, via the *Status Bar*, so you can make the same change to the three entry walls located in the second design option for the entry windows. Refer to previous sections for more information on editing *Design Options*.

## Wall Section at Garage:

Next you will set up a wall section view at the garage wall.

27. Switch to the *Longitudinal Section*.

28. Add a "wall section" type **Callout** at the garage wall (Figure 11-3.11).

29. Rename the new view to *Garage Wall Section*.

30. **Open** the *Garage Wall Section* view.

As you can see, the top of the foundation wall is not correct for the garage area. The foundation wall typically comes up to the top of the floor slab or 8-16″ above that. You will make this change next.

**FIGURE 11-3.11** Callout added to longitudinal section

31. Switch to the *Basement Floor Plan* and select the three foundation walls at the garage.

32. In *Properties Palette*, set the *Top Constraint* to **Up to level: First Floor**.

33. Switch back to the *Garage Wall Section* view.

As you can see in the figure below, the foundation wall and floor slab overlap each other. You will fix this next.

**FIGURE 11-3.12**
Garage Wall Section – edge of slab condition

34. Click **Modify → Geometry → Join**.

35. Select the foundation wall and then the floor slab.

Your wall section should now look like Figure 11-3.13. You can use the *Linework* tool if desired to edit any line styles or weights.

36. **Save** your project as **ex11-3.rvt**.

**FIGURE 11-3.13**
Garage Wall Section

**TIP:** *The wall section in Figure 11-3.13 shows two level datums that are not required in this view (Low Roof and Foundation). You cannot delete them, but you can select them; right-click and then pick* Hide in View → Elements *from the pop-up menu. Click* Reveal Elements *on the View Control Bar to see them again.*

## Exercise 11-4:
## Annotation and Detail Components

This exercise will explore adding notes, dimensions and detail components to your wall section.

## Add Notes and Dimensions to Callout of Cross Section 1:

1.  Open ex11-3.rvt and *Save As* **ex11-4.rvt**.

2.  Switch to *Callout of Cross Section 1* view.

3.  Click the **Hide Crop Region** icon on the *View Control Bar*.

4.  Add the three dimensions as show in **Figure 11-4.1**.

    *TIP: Revit lets you dimension to the window opening even though you are not cutting directly through a window in the current view.*

These dimensions are primarily for the carpenters framing the stud wall. Typically, when a window opening is dimensioned in wood stud framing, the dimension has the suffix R.O. This stands for Rough Opening, clearly representing that the dimension identifies an opening in the wall. You will add the suffix next.

5.  Select the dimension at the window opening.

6.  Click directly on the blue dimension text (i.e., 4'-0").

7.  Type **R.O.** in the *Suffix* field and then click **OK**.

FIGURE 11-4.1 Added dimensions

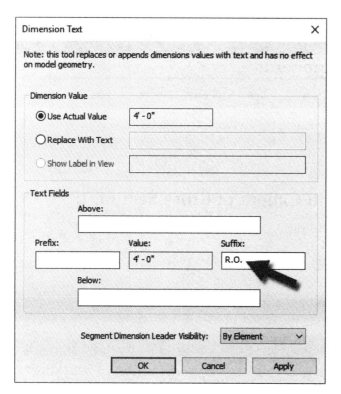

**FIGURE 11-4.2** Selected dimension properties

**FIGURE 11-4.3** Dimension with suffix

Figure 11-4.3 shows the dimension with the added suffix.

8. Use the same process to add the text "WINDOW BEYOND" in the *Below* field (Figure 11-4.4).

**FIGURE 11-4.4** Text added below dimension

9. Turn the *crop region* back on for a moment.

10. Select the ***crop region***.

Notice the dashed line that shows around the *crop region*? It has its own set of positioning grips. This dashed lined area allows you to control the visibility of various elements in the current view, such as text. You will adjust the right-hand side so it will accommodate more text and notes.

11. Drag the control grips for the vertical dashed line on the right as per **Figure 11-4.5**.

12. Turn the *crop region* off again.

**FIGURE 11-4.5** Crop Region Edits

13. Add the notes with leaders shown in Figure 11-4.6 (See Step 14); the text *Type* should be 3/32" Arial.

> *TIP: Select the Text tool and then one of the leader icons on the Ribbon (see image to right).*

**FIGURE 11-4.6** Notes added to wall section

14. The text style should be set to **3/32" Arial**; it may still be set to the last text style you used in this book: ¼" Outline Text.

15. Select the text and use the grips and the justification buttons to make the text look like **Figure 11-4.6**.

## Adding Detail Components:

Revit provides a way in which you can quickly add common 2D detail elements like dimensional lumber in section, anchor bolts, and wall base profiles to "embellish" your sections. These are just a few loaded with your template file (Figure 11-4.7); many others can be created or downloaded from the internet.

Next, you will add just a few *Detail Components* so you have a basic understanding of how this feature is used.

You will add a 2x6 sill plate and double top plate. You will also add the batt insulation symbol in the stud cavity.

16. Select **Annotate** → **Detail** → **Component** → **Detail Component**.

17. From the *Type Selector*, pick *Dimension Lumber-Section* **2 x 6**.

18. Add the sill plates as shown in Figure 11-4.8.

**FIGURE 11-4.7**
Detail Components; Type Selector open

*TIP: When placing the 2x6 you will need to press the spacebar to* Rotate, *and then* Move *to properly position the element. The sill plate should be directly on the ¾" wood sheathing. Note that the horizontal line that extends through the sill plate is the level datum.*

**FIGURE 11-4.8** Callout of Cross Section 1 view; 2 x 6 sill plates added

*Detail Components* can be copied once you have placed one in the view. This saves the step of rotating the stud in this example.

19. Use **Copy** and **Snaps** to add the double top plate (Figure11-4.9).

**FIGURE 11-4.9** Callout of Cross Section 1 view; 2 x 6 dbl. top plate added

Next you will add the batt insulation.

Insulation

20. Select **Annotation → Detail → Insulation**.

21. Pick the midpoint of the sill plate and the top plate to draw a line that represents the center of the batt insulation symbol; you can pick in either direction (Figure 11-4.10).

**FIGURE 11-4.10** Callout of Cross Section 1 view; Insulation added

Next you will change the width of the insulation so it fits the space of the stud cavity (i.e., 5½″ wide).

22. Click **Modify** and then click to select the insulation just drawn.

23. Adjust the **Width** on the *Options Bar* to **5½″**.

Note that this change can also be made via the *Properties Palette* (Figure 11-4.11).

**FIGURE 11-4.11** Insulation properties

**FIGURE 11-4.12**
Insulation width changed

These tools we just used are on the *Annotate* tab of the *Ribbon* because they are 2D graphics and only show up in the current view.

Drawing some elements like this, rather than modeling them three-dimensionally, can save time and system resources. A file could get very large if you tried to model everything. Of course, every time you skip drawing in 3D, you increase the chance of error. It takes a little experience to know when to model and when not to model.

*FYI: Architectural text is typically all uppercase.*

# Loading Additional Detail Components:

In addition to the *Detail Components* that are preloaded with the template file you started with, you can load more from the Revit content folder on your hard drive.

24. Select **Component → Detail Component** from the *Annotate* tab.

25. Click the **Load Family** button from the *Ribbon*.

26. Double-click on the ***Detail Items*** folder and then the following sub-folders: *Div 06-Wood* and *Plastic\064000-Architectural Woodwork\064600-Wood Trim*.

27. Double-click the file named ***Crown Molding-Section.rfa***.

You now have access to the newly imported crown molding. Take a minute to observe some of the other *Detail Components* that may be loaded into the project; for example, in the *Div 05-Metals\05200-Structural Steel Framing* folder you can load a steel beam family which has all the standard shapes contained within it as types (Figure 11-4.13).

28. Add the *Crown Molding* to the intersection between the wall and the ceiling using the ***Component*** tool on the *Annotate* tab (not the *Architecture* tab).

**FIGURE 11-4.13** Load Detail Component dialog, wide flange beams selected

# Using Repeating Details:

Many details and sections have components that occur multiple times, one right after another. Some examples are brick, siding and floor joists in section. Revit provides a tool, called *Repeating Details*, which can basically copy any *Detail Component* the required number of times to fill the space between two pick points you select with the mouse. The spacing of the *Detail Component* being copied has to be predefined when setting up the *Repeating Detail* style.

29. Click **Annotate → Detail → Component → Repeating Detail**.

30. From the *Type Selector*, select *Repeating Detail:* **Lap Siding 6″**.
           Repeating Detail Component

For now, you will draw the siding off to one side just to test this feature. Make sure you are within the *crop window* area or you will not see the results.

31. Pick two points similar to those shown in Figure 11-4.14.

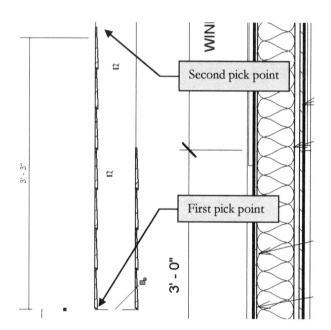

The example to the left shows two *Repeating Details* added. You can adjust them via the grips or the temporary dimensions.

**FIGURE 11-4.14** Repeating Detail added: lap siding

32. Try adjusting the length of the siding by selecting it and clicking on the dimension text.

33. **Delete** the *Lap Siding* repeating detail.

34. **Save** your project as **11-4.rvt**.

## Self-Exam:

The following questions can be used as a way to check your knowledge of this lesson. The answers can be found at the bottom of the page.

1. The controls for the section mark, when selected, are similar to the controls for the elevation tag. (T/F)

2. *Detail Components* added in this lesson were 3D. (T/F)

3. The footings drawn in this lesson were a Revit wall type. (T/F)

4. The *crop region* is represented by a rectangle in the section view. (T/F)

5. Use the _____ tool to reference a larger section off a building section.

## Review Questions:

The following questions may be assigned by your instructor as a way to assess your knowledge of this section. Your instructor has the answers to the review questions.

1. The visibility of the *crop region* can be controlled. (T/F)

2. It is not possible to draw a leader without placing text. (T/F)

3. When a section mark is added to a view, all the other related views automatically get a section mark added to them. (T/F)

4. It is possible to modify elements such as doors, windows and ceilings in section views. (T/F)

5. You cannot adjust the "depth of view" using the *crop window*. (T/F)

6. What is the first thing you should do after placing a section mark?

   _____

7. If the text appears to be excessively large in a section view, the view's

   _____ is probably set incorrectly.

8. The abbreviation R.O. stands for _____.

9. Describe what happens when you double-click on the section bubble:

   _____.

10. Revit provides _____ different leader options within the *Text* command, not including the leader location options.

## Lesson 12
# INTERIOR DESIGN:

This lesson explores some interior design elements of a floor plan, such as toilet room layouts and kitchen cabinets. Additionally, you will look at placing furniture and guardrails into your project.

## Exercise 12-1:
## Bathroom Layouts

Bathroom layouts involve placing toilets, tubs and sinks. You will start with the half bath on the first floor.

1. Open ex11-4.rvt and **Save As ex12-1.rvt**.

The template you started with has everything you need to lay out this room. You will create the layout shown in Figure 12-1.1.

**FIGURE 12-1.1** First Floor plan view: half bath layout

2. Switch to *First Floor* plan view and zoom in on the half bath next to the garage, North of the dining room.

The first step will be to place the toilet.

3. With the *Component* tool selected on the *Architecture* tab, pick **Toilet-Domestic-3D** from the *Type Selector*. Click **No** when prompted to load a *Plumbing Fixture* tag.

4. **Place** the toilet in the middle of the room and then *Move* and *Rotate* into place utilizing *Snaps* (Figure 12-1.2).

   *TIP: Press the spacebar to rotate the toilet before placing it.*

The toilet is 1″ out from the wall, which is typical for floor mounted – tank type toilets.

The overlapping letters, C and L, are the symbol for "centerline." This means that the middle of the toilet is 1′-4″ from the wall. Actually, if you were to add this dimension, Autodesk® Revit® would automatically add this symbol if the *Centerline Symbol* parameter is turned on in the properties of the dimension!

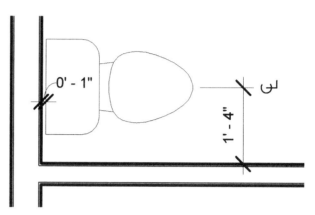

**FIGURE 12-1.2** Toilet location

If you want to make sure the 1′-4″ dimension never changes, you can add the dimension shown and then click the padlock symbol to *Lock* that dimension. Then, anytime the wall moves, the toilet will move with it. If you want the constraint but do not want the dimension, you can delete the dimension and Autodesk® Revit® Architecture will ask you if you want to maintain the constraint after the dimension is deleted.

Next, you will add the sink. This consists of three separate components: a base cabinet, a countertop and a sink, which is similar to what you would have in the "real-world." First you will add the base cabinet.

5. Place a *Vanity Cabinet-Double Door Sink Unit*: **24″** using the *Component* tool (Figure 12-1.3).

   *TIP: Use the spacebar to rotate.*

   *TIP: It is hard to tell which side is the front of the cabinet in plan view; the side the cursor is attached to is the back of the cabinet. If you add it incorrectly you will see the problem when you set up the interior elevation.*

**FIGURE 12-1.3** Vanity base cabinet added

Next, you will add the countertop. Autodesk Revit has one that even has a hole in it for the sink. You will have to adjust the length to fit your cabinet.

6. Using the *Component* tool, place the _Vanity Counter Top w Round Sink Hole:_ **24″** depth in the middle of the room.

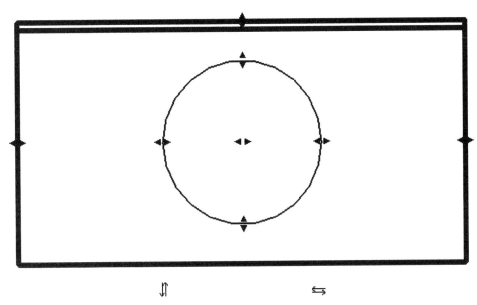

FIGURE 12-1.4 Vanity counter top temporarily placed in middle of room

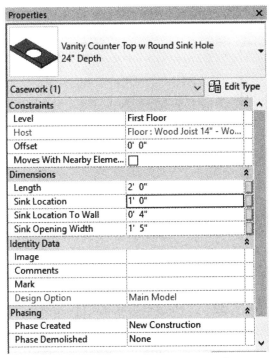

FIGURE 12-1.5 Vanity counter top properties

You will notice that the counter top is 48″ long; you will change this to 24″ in a moment. When selected, you see several arrow-grips which allow you to graphically adjust the size of the selected element.

7. With the countertop selected, note the ***Properties Palette*** options.

8. Change the *Length* to **2′-0″** and the *Sink Location* to **1′-0″** (Figure 12-1.5).

9. Click **Apply**, or just move your cursor back into the drawing window.

The countertop is now the correct size for your base cabinet.

10. Use ***Move*** and ***Rotate*** to position the counter top over the vanity base cabinet; use **Snaps** for accuracy.

11. Again, using the *Component* tool, add _Sink Vanity-Round:_ **19″ x 19″**. Press the spacebar to rotate the sink 90 degrees and then visually place the sink in the center of the hole in the countertop.

Your plan should now look like Figure 12-1.1, less the elevation tag which you will add next.

## Interior Elevation View:

Next, you will set up an interior elevation view for the half bath. You will also add a mirror above the sink in elevation view. As you can see, the tasks in this book are building on previously learned material; refer back to previous chapters if you need a refresher. Using these features multiple times will help you to become more efficient and to better understand the tools.

12. Place an **Elevation** tag, with the *Type Selector* set to **Interior Elevation**, looking towards the "wet" wall, the wall with fixtures on it (Figure 12-1.6).

    *FYI: A "wet" wall is any wall that has plumbing fixtures on it and piping behind it.*

    *TIP: When placing the Elevation Tag, Revit turns the pointer to look at the closest wall, so you will have to place the tag close to the West wall (overlapping the plumbing fixtures) and then move the tag back as a separate step.*

13. Rename the new view to **1/2 Bath** in the *Project Browser*.

**FIGURE 12-1.6** Elevation tag added

14. Switch to the new view; click the *crop region* and drag the bottom up so the floor system does not show. Your view should look like Figure 12-1.7.

FIGURE 12-1.7 ½ Bath elevation

15. Change the *View Scale* to **½″ = 1′-0″**.

16. Load the family named **Mirror** from the families provided with this book, rather than a manufacturer such as Bradley Corp.

17. Create a *Duplicate* of the mirror family just loaded and name the new *Type*: **24″ x 36″**; change the *Width* to **24″** and the *Height* to **36″**.

18. While in the *1/2 Bath* elevation view, place the mirror as shown in Figure 12-1.8.

19. Add the notes and dimensions shown in Figure 12-1.8.

   *TIP: As you are drawing the leaders, Revit will help you align your pick points vertically so the leaders and notes align; just watch for the dashed vertical reference line before picking your points.*

20. Using the same techniques just covered, lay out the two second floor bathrooms per **Figure 12-1.9**; use the tub loaded with the template.

   a. Make the larger vanity cabinet and countertop 4′-0″ wide.

**FIGURE 12-1.8** Interior elevation with mirror and notes added

*FYI:* *Keep in mind that many of the symbols that come with Revit, or any program for that matter, are not necessarily drawn or reviewed by an architect. The point is that the default values, such as mounting heights, may not meet ADA, national, state or local codes. Items such as accessible mirrors have a maximum height off the floor to the reflective surface that Revit's standard components may not comply with. However, as you apply local codes to these families, you can reuse them in the future.*

**FIGURE 12-1.9** Second Floor Bath Rooms

21. **Save** your project as **ex12-1.rvt**.

## Exercise 12-2:
## Kitchen Layout

In this exercise you will look at adding kitchen cabinets and appliances to your project. As usual, Revit provides several predefined families to be placed into the project.

## Placing Cabinets:

You will add base cabinets and appliances first.

1. Open ex12-1.rvt and **Save As ex12-2.rvt**.

2. Switch to the *First Floor* plan view and zoom into the kitchen.

   > *FYI: As with other families (i.e., doors and windows), Revit loads several Types to represent the most valuable and useful sizes available. Cabinets typically come in 3″ increments with different types (i.e., single or double door unit) having maximum and minimum sizes.*

3. With the *Component* tool selected, place the families, cabinets **and appliances**, as shown in Figure 12-2.1; use *Snaps* for accuracy. Remember that the cursor is at the back of the cabinet when placing the component.

   > *FYI: Most of the specified families are already loaded into your project from your template you started with; the others can be loaded manually from the local or online libraries.*

4. Select one of the base cabinets and click **Edit Type** from the *Properties Palette*.

Notice the height is 2′-10½″ which, when combined with a 1½″ standard countertop, gives you a 3′-0″ surface.

Next, you will add the countertops to the base cabinets. You will place three separate countertop elements (Figure 12-2.2). You will adjust the lengths of the countertops to fit the cabinets below.

**FIGURE 12-2.1** First Floor Plan View: base cabinets added to kitchen

5.  Per the steps listed below, add the countertops shown in Figure 12-2.2, using *Snaps* to accurately place them.

    a.  Load the elements not currently loaded in your project from the *Casework* folder.

    b.  Place the bottom-right corner unit (use *Move, Mirror* and *Snaps*) and then, with the unit selected, drag one of the end grips back to align with the edge of the cabinet below.

    c.  Load and place the other corner unit with the sink hole.
        i.   Adjust the edge locations (use *Properties* for accuracy)
        ii.  Adjust sink hole via *Properties Palette: Sink Location:* **5'-4"**

    d.  Add the two straight countertops as shown.

    e.  Verify the *Height* is **3'-0"** via the *Properties Palette.*

**FIGURE 12-2.2** First Floor Plan View: countertops added

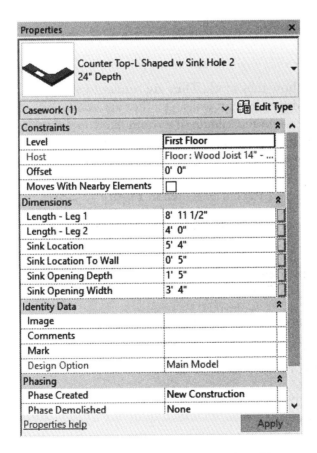

6. Select the countertop with the sink hole and go to the **Properties Palette**.

7. Change the following (Figure 12-2.3):
   a. Sink Location to Wall: **5″**
   b. Sink Opening Depth: **1′-5″**
   c. Sink Opening Width: **3′-4″**

*TIP: Some settings are per instance (i.e., the settings in the palette to the left) and others are per type (i.e., clicking the* Edit Type *button – Type Parameters); the Instant Parameters only affect the selected item. So, if you place another instance of this family in the basement, the sink can be in a different location.*

**FIGURE 12-2.3** Properties for Counter Top with Sink Hole: 24″ Depth

8. Using the *Component* tool, add **Sink Kitchen-Double: 42" x 21"** to your project – centered on the sink hole (Figure 12-2.4).

**FIGURE 12-2.4** Sink placed in countertop, centered on hole

## Placing Wall Cabinets:

Next you will add a couple wall cabinets to see how they work. They are similar to adding base cabinets, with the exception that they are dependent on walls (i.e., they are *wall hosted*). You can only place an upper cabinet on a wall, not in the middle of a room like you did with the base cabinets. The base cabinets are set up to sit on the floor and the upper cabinets are assigned a height above the floor, on the wall, via *Properties*.

9. Using the ***Component*** tool, add the upper cabinets as shown in **Figure 12-2.5**:

   a. Move the cursor close to a wall until you see the cabinet, which means Revit found a wall.

   b. Center the upper cabinet above the range, leaving an equal space on each side of the cabinet; these spaces will get a filler that matches the cabinets.

   c. The numbers (which represent the cabinet width) and Xs in the cabinets are for clarity of this step only; you do not need to add these items.

   d. Use both single and double upper cabinets as necessary.

   e. If you have trouble adding the uppers at the pocket door location, add them to the right and move them into place.

**FIGURE 12-2.5** First Floor plan view: upper cabinets added (Xs added for clarity in this image)

The heights of the cabinets will be adjusted when you get to the interior elevation view.

*FYI: Wall cabinets are typically dashed in plan because they are above the* floor plan cut plane.

## Adding the Interior Elevation Tag:

10. Add an interior **Elevation Tag** as shown in Figure 12-2.6.

   *TIP: Make sure you select* Interior Elevation *from the Type Selector.*

11. Rename the new elevation view to **Kitchen (east)**.

12. Select the **circle** portion of the symbol; the symbol should look like Figure 12-27 when selected correctly.

13. Click the *North* and *South* checkboxes as shown in Figure 12-2.7.

14. **Rename** the two new views to *Kitchen (north)* and *Kitchen (south)*.

The single elevation tag in plan view is associated with the three kitchen elevation views.

15. Double-click the pointer portion of the elevation tag pointing towards the East to open that view.

**FIGURE 12-2.6** Elevation tag added to kitchen

16. Adjust the **crop region** so the floor system is not visible.

17. Set the *View Scale* to **½″ = 1′-0″**; your interior elevation view should look like **Figure 12-2.8**.

Depending on where, exactly, you placed the *Elevation Tag*, you may see the side of the refrigerator or a section through it, as in Figure 12-2.8. In this case you will want to adjust the view so you see the cabinets beyond, which is more important to show. You will switch back to the plan view and adjust the views settings.

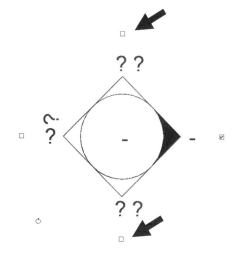

**FIGURE 12-2.7** Elevation tag selected

18. Switch back to the *First Floor* plan view.

19. Click to select the *East view's* pointer portion of the elevation tag so you see the *Extent of View/Far Clip Plane* lines.

**FIGURE 12-2.8** Kitchen (east); initial view

20. Click and drag to adjust the location of the *Extent of View* line as shown in Figure 12-2.9; also adjust the *Far Clip Plane* if necessary.

Notice the *Extent of View* line has been moved to the east of the refrigerator and the *Far Clip Plane* is in the middle of the wall.

21. Switch back to the ***Kitchen (east)*** view and note the changes (Figure 12-2.10).

You will modify one more thing in this view before moving on. The height of the wall cabinets needs a little work (Figure 12-2.10); the corner wall cabinets are too short and the cabinet over the range is too tall. You can adjust these in either the plan or elevation view. You will adjust them in the elevation view so you can immediately see the changes.

**FIGURE 12-2.9** First Floor; elev. tag selected

**FIGURE 12-2.10** Kitchen (east) view; view settings adjusted

22. Select both **corner** upper cabinets and change their height to **2'-6"** and the Elevation to **4'-6"** (2'-6" + 4'-6" = 7'-0" to top). Make these changes via the *Properties Palette* and *Type Properties*.

23. Select the upper cabinet above the range and change its height to **15"** and the elevation so the top stays at 7'-0".

24. Load the **Range Hood** family provided with this book.

**Range Hood**
Library Revit Architecture

Your elevation should now look like Figure 12-2.11. Notice that the cabinets on the right and left, which are actually in section, have heavier lines than the cabinets which are in elevation. Again, Revit saves time by assuming the industry standard. However, you can use the *Linework* tool to change this if you so desire!

**FIGURE 12-2.11** Kitchen (east) view; view settings adjusted

You will add notes and dimensions to the elevation.

25. Add the notes and dimensions per **Figure 12-2.12**.

26. Select the *Linework* tool from the *Modify* tab, and set the *Line Style* (on the *Ribbon*) to **Wide lines**. Select the perimeter lines so they stand out more.

**FIGURE** 12-2.12 Interior elevation with annotations

That is it for the East elevation! Next, you will take a quick look at the other two elevations you set up in the kitchen.

27. Switch to the *Kitchen (north)* view.

28. Adjust the *crop region* and the perimeter lines per the previous elevation (Figure 12-2.13).

29. Change the *View Scale* to **½" = 1'-0"**.

You will notice right away that the windows are in conflict with the cabinets and the countertop does not extend over the dishwasher. Both of these required changes can be made in either the plan or the elevation; again, you will make changes in the elevation view so you can see the results.

First you will fix the windows. An error like this could easily be overlooked using a traditional CAD program because the exterior elevation and the interior elevations are separate/independent drawings files; so you could fix the height of the windows in the interior elevation, but forget to change the exterior elevation, where the windows are specified and ordered from. In Revit, it is not even possible to have one window be two different sizes in the same project file.

**FIGURE 12-2.13** Kitchen (north); initial view

30. Select the *Section* line, right-click and pick **Hide in View → Elements**. You do not need to see that section mark here.

31. Select the two windows in the ***Kitchen (north)*** view.

32. Via *Properties*, create a new window *Type*, via *Edit Type → Duplicate*, named *Double Hung with Trim:* **36″ x 42″**:
    a. Set the *Height* to **3′-6″** (from 4′-0″) – *Type Parameter*
    b. See the *Sill Height* to **3′-6″** (From 3′-0″) – *Instance Parameter*
    c. Click **OK** and then adjust the sill height for the selected windows to **3′-6″**.

Now the windows do not conflict with the countertop's backsplash. Next, you will adjust the countertop.

33. In the ***Kitchen (north)*** view, zoom in on the dishwasher area.

34. Select the **Counter Top** over the **15″** wide base cabinet, to the left of the dishwasher, and press the **Delete** key to erase it.

35. Using the ***Align*** tool, select the left-edge of the 15″ wide base cabinet and then select the left edge of the countertop. The countertop should now align with the edge of the cabinets.

    *FYI: You must pick these items in the order specified.*

36. Edit the perimeter using the ***Linework*** tool and adjust the *Crop Region* to hide the floor.

Your modified *Kitchen (north)* should look like Figure 12-2.14.

**FIGURE 12-2.14** Kitchen (north); modified view

37. Open ***Kitchen (south)***.

38. Modify the ***crop region*** and the perimeter linework.

If you cannot see the refrigerator doors, you would now realize that the refrigerator was inserted backwards (Figure 12-2.15). You will fix this next.

**FIGURE 12-2.15** Kitchen (south); initial view

39. Set the scale to **½″ = 1′-0″** and ***Hide*** the building section mark.

40. If needed, ***Rotate*** the refrigerator (in plan view) 180 degrees (if required – the door handles should be visible if facing the correct way).

41. Modify the upper cabinet above the refrigerator to be **12″** tall, with the top at **7′-0″**.

> *TIP: If this cabinet were used anywhere else in the project, you would have had to make a duplicate before changing the height; otherwise, all the cabinets would have changed as well, because it is a Type Parameter you are changing, not an Instance Parameter.*

Often, you have a portion of a wall that does not have very much on it, so it is not worth elevating. In the *Kitchen (south)* view you will crop a portion of the wall on the right.

42. Click the **crop region** and drag the right side of the *crop region* rectangle towards the left so only the portion of elevation shown in Figure 12-2.16 is visible.

Your *Kitchen (south)* view should now look like Figure 12-2.16.

**FIGURE 12-2.16** Kitchen (south); modified view

The last things you will adjust are the lines in the cabinet elevations that indicate the swing of the cabinet door; these lines are typically dashed lines.

There are two ways to accomplish this. One way will only affect the current view (View → *Visibility/Graphics*) and the other will affect the entire project (Manage → *Settings* → *Object Styles*). You want this change to be applied everywhere, so you want to implement per the latter method.

Object
Styles

43. Select **Manage → Settings → Object Styles**.

44. On the *Model Objects* tab, click the plus symbol next to **Casework** in the *Category* column (Figure 12-2.17).

45. Change the **Line Pattern** for *Elevation Swing* to **Hidden 1/8″** (Figure 12-2.17).

46. Click **OK** to see the results in the three kitchen elevations.

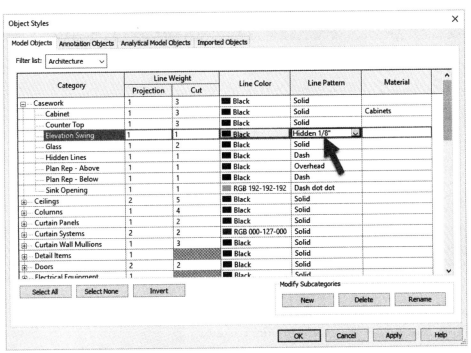

**FIGURE 12-2.17** Object Styles dialog box; controls project wide graphics settings

That is it for the kitchen! With a little practice, you could design a kitchen in very short order.

47. **Save** your project as **ex12-2.rvt**.

*TIP: The North American Architectural Woodwork Standards (https://www.naaws-committee.com/) has Revit families for most of the industry standard cabinets. You can download the cabinets from their website, via the 'Cabinet Design Series' page. You can even print out a small flyer that shows an image of each cabinet that can be downloaded.*

## Exercise 12-3:
## Furniture

This lesson will cover the steps required to lay out furniture. The processes are identical to those previously covered for toilets and cabinets. First you will start with the office on the second floor.

## Loading the Necessary Families:

1. Open ex12-2.rvt and **Save As ex12-3.rvt**.

2. Select the **Load Family** tool, on the *Insert* tab, and load the following items into the current project:

   <u>Local Files</u> *(i.e., on your hard drive)*
   a. **Work Station Desktops**  (Furniture System)
   b. **Chair-Executive**  (Furniture\Seating)
   c. **Sofa-Pensi**  (Furniture\Seating)
   d. **Table-Round**  (Furniture\Tables)

   <u>Provided Files</u> *(see inside front cover of this book)*
   e. **Copier-Floor**

---

*TIP: You can set the* View *mode for the* Open *dialog box, which is displayed when you click* Load from Library. *One option is* Thumbnail *mode; this displays a small thumbnail image for each file in the current folder. Press Ctrl + spin your mouse wheel to adjust preview size. This makes it easier to see the many symbols and drawings that are available for insertion.*

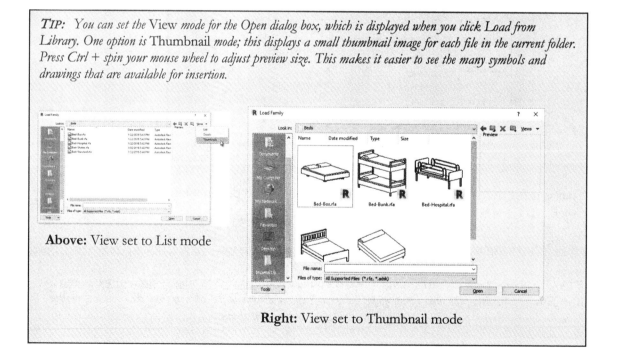

**Above:** View set to List mode

**Right:** View set to Thumbnail mode

# Designing the Office Furniture Layout:

3. Switch to the *Second Floor* plan view.

4. Using the **Component** tool, place the furniture as shown in Figure 12-3.1.

   *TIP: Use Snaps to assure accuracy; use Rotate and Mirror as required.*

**FIGURE 12-3.1** Second Floor – Office furniture layout

Look at the type properties, via *Edit Type*, for the Work Station Desktop to see the *Desktop Height* setting which controls how high the surface is above the current floor.

You may want to browse through the component library and the web library for miscellaneous residential furniture. You can add dining room tables and chairs, bookshelves, washer and dryer, etc. Your instructor may require you to complete this suggested step. An example of a few items placed can be seen in Figure 12-3.2.

**FIGURE 12-3.2** First Floor; one possible furniture layout

# 3D View of Office Layout:

Next, you will look at a 3D view of your office area. This involves adjusting the visibility of the roof and skylights.

5. Switch to the **Default 3D** view via the *QAT*.

6. Click anywhere in the drawing window to activate the view.

7. Type **VV** to access the *Visibility/Graphics Overrides* dialog box. Remember, these settings are only for the current view.

8. Uncheck the *Ceiling* and the *Roof* category then click **OK**.

The ceilings and roof should not be visible now. However, you should still see the light fixtures floating in space. You will make those disappear next.

9. Select one of the 2′ x 4′ light fixtures floating above the office.

10. Click the **Temporary Hide/Isolate** tool from the *View Control Bar.*

You should see the menu shown in **Figure 12-3.3** show up next to the *Hide/Isolate* icon. This allows you to isolate an element, so it is the only thing on the screen. Or you can hide it, so the element is temporarily not visible.

**FIGURE 12-3.3** Hide/Isolate pop-up menu

11. Click **Hide Category** in the menu (Figure 12-3.3).

    *FYI: This makes all the lights temporarily hidden.*

12. Adjust your **3D** view to look similar to **Figure 12-3.4**; try looking at the room from other angles as well.

    *TIP: While pressing the Shift key, also press the wheel button on the mouse and drag the mouse around to "orbit" the model without selecting any icons. Also, selecting an object in the view makes the model pivot about the selected object.*

You will now restore the original visibility settings for the **3D** view. Notice the *Hide/Isolate* icon now has a colored background, which means something in the project is temporarily hidden from view.

13. Click the *Hide/Isolate* icon and then select **Reset Temporary Hide/Isolate** from the pop-up menu.

14. Reset the **3D** view's visibility settings so the ceilings and roof are visible (type VV).

15. Click the *Home* icon via the **ViewCube** to reset the view (Figure 12-3.5).

16. **Save** your project as **ex12-3.rvt**.

**FIGURE 12-3.4** 3D view with ceiling/roof/lights hidden

*FYI: Not all families found online are drawn in full 3D. Some may have been brought over from a CAD program where all the symbols are drawn in 2D only.*

## Online Content:

A few locations on the internet provide additional content for use in Revit; some is free and some is not. Some product manufacturers are starting to provide content based on the products they make. This is making it easier for designers to include that manufacturer's product in their project, both in the virtual and real projects.

Here are just a few examples of sites one might download Revit content from:

- www.revitcity.com *(free content provided by other users)*
- www.turbosquid.com *(buy, sell and trade other user's content)*
- www.arcat.com, www.revit-content.com, bimobject.com, *and* www.smartbim.com

**FIGURE 12-3.5** Home icon next to ViewCube; Home icon is only visible when cursor is over ViewCube.

You should occasionally search the internet to see if additional content becomes available. You can do an internet search for "revit content"; make sure to include the quotation marks. Rendering content, such as that offered by www.archvision.com, will be covered in Chapter 14.

Also, be sure to check out the residential appliances installed with Revit. The image below shows a few examples rendered with Enscape (www.enscape3d.com). This author previously wrote this post when this content first came out:

https://bimchapters.blogspot.com/2017/07/revit-20181-new-content-part-1.html

## Exercise 12-4:
## Adding Guardrails

This lesson will cover the steps required to lay out guardrails. The steps are simple; you select your style and draw its path.

### Adding a Guardrail to the Second Floor Stair Area:

1. Open ex12-3.rvt and **Save As ex12-4.rvt**.

2. Switch to the **Second Floor** plan view.

3. Select **Architecture → Circulation → Railing → Sketch Path**.

4. **Zoom** into the stair area.

At this point you will draw a line representing the path of the guardrail. The railing is offset to one side of the line, similar to walls. However, you do not have the *Location Line* option as you do with the *Wall* tool, so you have to draw the railing in a certain direction to get the railing to be on the floor and not hovering in space just beyond the floor edge.

5. Draw a line along the edge of the floor as shown in **Figure 12-4.1**.

   *TIP: Select* Chain *from the Options Bar to draw the railing with fewer picks.*

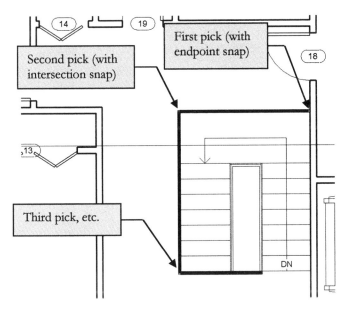

**FIGURE 12-4.1** Second Floor: adding a guardrail

6. Click the **green checkmark** from the *Ribbon* to finish the railing.

The railing has now been drawn. In the next step you will switch to a 3D view and see how to quickly change the railing style. This will also involve changing the height of the railing. Most building codes require the railing height be 42″ when the drop to the adjacent surface is more than 30″; this is called a guardrail.

7. Switch to the **3D** view.

8. Turn off the ceilings and roof as previously reviewed (***TIP:*** *Temp. Hide/Isolate*), and then zoom into the railing just added to the second floor. Notice the railing style shown in Figure 12-4.2.

9. Select the railing. You may have to use the *Tab* key to cycle through the various selection options.

10. With the railing selected, select the other railing types available in the *Type Selector* on the *Properties Palette*. When finished make sure *Railing:* **Handrail – Rectangular** is selected.

**FIGURE 12-4.2** Added railing – 3D view

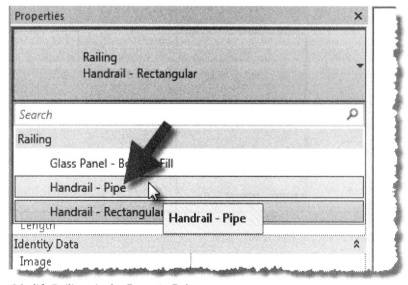

Modify Railing via the *Properties Palette*

When the alternate style was selected, your railing should have looked like Figure 12-4.3. Even the railing for the stair could be changed by a similar step. This style is too contemporary for this design so you will not use it at this time.

*FYI: You can change the height via* Type Properties.

Notice stair handrail buried within the wall; see discussion below.

**FIGURE 12-4.3** Railing with alternate style

## Editing the Sketch Lines for the Stair Railing:

You will notice, in the image above (Figure 12-4.3), that a portion of the railing added with the stair is buried in the wall. You will edit the railing sketch lines to remove this conflict.

**FIGURE 12-4.4** Edit railing sketch lines

11. Switch to the *First Floor Plan* view.

12. Select the outer <u>railing</u> for the upper stair; use the *Tab* key to cycle through your selection options.

13. Click the **Edit Path** button on the *Modify | Railings* tab.

14. Delete the sketch lines on the north and east walls, shown dashed in Figure 12-4.4.

*FYI: The railing added with the stair is simply a separate railing element that was automatically added with the stair.*

15. Select the **green check mark** on the *Design Bar* when finished.

16. Reset the 3D view so the roof and ceiling elements are visible.

Switching back to the *3D* view, you notice the railing lines in the walls are gone (Figure 12-4.5). Revit is consistent in the way many 3D components are defined and edited with 2D sketch linework; editing the stringer extensions is a similar process. This consistency helps reduce the learning curve.

**FIGURE 12-4.5** Railing conflict resolved

The *Railing* tool has the ability to create fairly complex railings. The image below shows the interface for setting up the baluster placement (Figure 12-4.6). This kind of advanced control is beyond the scope of this textbook.

**FIGURE 12-4.6** Dialog to control baluster and newel post placement

Make sure to examine the railing sample file available with the provided content for this book; see the inside front cover for instructions on accessing these files. You can download this file, open it, select a railing and view its properties to see how it works.

**FIGURE 12-4.7**
Railing sample file downloaded
from Revit's website

You can *Copy/Paste* a railing style from this drawing into one of your project files. Then you select your railing and pick the newly imported one from the *Type Selector*. This process was done to achieve the image below (Figure 12-4.8). Notice the traditional balusters and newel post.

**FIGURE 12-4.8** Optional railing configuration

17. **Save** your project as **ex12-4.rvt**.

## Self-Exam:

The following questions can be used as a way to check your knowledge of this lesson. The answers can be found at the bottom of the page.

1. The bathroom fixtures are preloaded in the template file. (T/F)

2. You do not need to be connected to the internet when you want to download content provided with this book. (T/F)

3. Revit content may not always be in compliance with local codes. (T/F)

4. You can use *Crop Region* to crop a portion of wall that is blank. (T/F)

5. Click the _____ tool to modify the path of a railing.

## Review Questions:

The following questions may be assigned by your instructor as a way to assess your knowledge of this section. Your instructor has the answers to the review questions.

1. Revit provides several different styles of vanity cabinets for placement. (T/F)

2. Revit automatically adds a rail to every stair. (T/F)

3. It is not possible to draw dimensions on an interior elevation view. (T/F)

4. Cabinets typically come in 2″ increments. (T/F)

5. Base cabinets automatically have a countertop on them. (T/F)

6. When you create a hole in a floor, Revit automatically adds a railing. (T/F)

7. You can use the _____ to control element visibility.

8. What is the current size of your Revit Project? _____

9. What should you use to assure accuracy when placing cabinets? _____

10. You use the _____ tool to make various components temporarily invisible.

## Lesson 13
# SCHEDULES:

You will continue to study the powerful features available in Autodesk® Revit®. The ability to create parametric schedules is very useful; for example, you can delete a door number on a schedule and Autodesk Revit will delete the corresponding door from the plan.

## Exercise 13-1:
## Room and Door Tags

This exercise will look at adding room tags and door tags to your plans. As you insert doors, Autodesk Revit adds tags to them automatically. However, if you copy or mirror a door, or add one in elevation, you can lose the tag and have to add it.

## Adding Rooms and Room Tags:

You will add a *Room* object, which will also add a *Room Tag* to the current view, to each room on your first floor plan. A *Room* object is not visible by default. It is an object which is used to calculate area, volume and store information about the room (i.e., the I in BIM… **B**uilding **I**nformation **M**odeling).

1.  In the **First Floor** view, select **Architecture → Room & Area → Room**

Placing a *Room* is similar to placing a ceiling in the reflected ceiling plan; as you move your cursor over a room, the room perimeter highlights. When the room you want to place a *Room* element in is highlighted, you click to place it in that room. You are actually placing a *Room* and a *Room Tag*.

2.  Place your cursor within the *Entry* area and place a *Room* (Figure 13-1.1). Make sure *"Tag on placement"* is highlighted on the *Ribbon*.

By default, Autodesk Revit will simply label the space 'Room' and number it '1.' You will change these to something different.

**FIGURE 13-1.1** Room & Room Tag added to entry

**FIGURE 13-1.2** Room tags – First Floor

3. Press **Esc** or select *Modify* to end the *Room* command.

4. Click on the **Room Tag** you just placed to select it.

5. Now click on the room name label to change it; enter **ENTRY**.

6. Now click on the room number to change it; enter **100**.

7. Add *Rooms/Room Tags* for each room on the first floor, incrementing each room number by 1 (Figure 13-1.2). Be sure to change the room names as well.

   *TIP: During placement, pressing the spacebar will toggle the tag between horizontal and vertical orientation.*

## Second and Basement Floors:

8. Add *Rooms/Room Tags* to the *Second Floor*. The numbering should start with 200; place the first room and then change the number to 200. This will make the remaining rooms the correct number. Do **not** change the room names (Figure 13-1.3).

9. Add *Rooms/Tags* to the *Basement Floor Plan*. The numbering should start with 1; **do** change the room names (Figure 13-1.4). Don't worry about the "00" prefix shown for the room numbers.

   *FYI: Room tags can also be added to your building sections, as the Room element will now be there! When the Room element already exists, in plan or section, you use the Room Tag tool, not the Room command.*

**FIGURE 13-1.3** Second Floor – Room tags

**FIGURE 13-1.4** Basement – Room tags

## Adding Door Tags:

Next you will add *Door Tags* to any doors that are missing them. Additionally, you will adjust the door numbers to correspond to the room numbers.

Revit numbers the doors in the order they are placed into the drawing. This would make it difficult to locate a door by its door number if door number 1 was on the first floor and door number 2 was on the second floor, etc. Typically, a door number is the same as the room number the door swings into. For example, if a door swings into a room numbered 104, the door number would also be 104. If the room had two doors into it, the doors would be numbered 104A and 104B.

10. Switch to **First Floor** plan view.

11. Select **Annotate → Tag → Tag By Category** from the *Ribbon* (Figure 13-1.5).

    *TIP: This tool can also be selected from the Quick Access Toolbar or typing TG.*

**FIGURE 13-1.5** Annotate tab

Notice, as you move your cursor around the screen, Revit displays a tag for any element which can have a tag, when the cursor is over it. This includes walls, doors, windows, etc. When you click the mouse is when Revit actually places a tag.

12. **Uncheck** the *Leader* option on the *Options Bar.*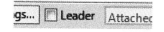

13. Place a *Door Tag* for each door that does not have a tag; <u>do this for each level</u>.

    *TIP: Press the spacebar to Rotate before clicking to place the tag.*

    *TIP: These should mainly be the doors in the Basement and the one added in elevation in the Living Room.*

14. **Renumber** all the *Door Tags* to correspond to the room they open into; do this for each level. Figure 13-1.6 is an example of the first floor and Figure 13-1.7 of the second floor. **FYI:** Revit add-in tools can automatically renumber doors.

    *REMEMBER: Click Modify, select the Tag and then click on the number to edit it.*

*TIP – TAG ALL (Figure 13-1.5): This tool allows you to quickly tag all the elements of a selected category (e.g., doors) at one time. After selecting the tool, you select the category from a list and specify whether or not you want a leader. When you click OK, Revit tags all the untagged doors in that view. This helps to avoid not tagging a door. However, all doors will show up in a schedule whether they are tagged or not.*

**FIGURE 13-1.6** First Floor; door tags (tags enlarged for printing)

**FIGURE 13-1.7** Second Floor; door tags (tags enlarged for printing)

*TIP:* The wall Instance Parameter, via the Properties Palette, must be set to "room bounding" for the Room tool to consider a wall as part of the perimeter within a particular room; this is the default setting. For example, you could set a closet wall so it was not "room bounding" so Revit would ignore it when creating the Room, thus adding the closet square footage to the room total.

15. **Save** your project as **ex13-1.rvt**.

## Exercise 13-2:
## Generate a Door Schedule

This exercise will look at creating a door schedule based on the information currently available in the building model (i.e., the *Room* and *Door* elements). The tags only report information stored within the element being tagged, so it is possible to delete a tag at any time without losing information. The tag can then be added later if required; tags are view specific.

## Create a Door Schedule View:

A door schedule is simply another view of the building model. However, this view displays numerical data rather than graphical data. Just like a graphical view, if you change the view it changes all the other related views. For example, if you delete a door number from the schedule, the door is deleted from the plans and elevations.

1.  Open ex13-1.rvt and **Save As ex13-2.rvt**.

2.  Select **View → Create → Schedules → Schedules/Quantities**.

3.  Select *Doors* under *Category* and then click **OK** (Figure 13-2.1).

*FYI: The template you started with already has a door schedule set up and ready to go, so the first door you added was already scheduled. However, you will go through the steps of setting up a schedule so you understand how a schedule is created.*

**FIGURE 13-2.1** New Schedule dialog

You should now be in the *Schedule Properties* dialog where you specify what information is displayed in the schedule, how it is sorted, and the text format.

4.  On the **Fields** tab, *Add* the information you want displayed in the schedule. Select the following (Figure 13-2.2):
    a.  Mark
    b.  Width
    c.  Height
    d.  Frame Material
    e.  Frame Type
    f.  Fire Rating

As noted in the dialog, the fields added to the list on the right are in the order they will be in the schedule view. Use the *Move Up* and *Move Down* buttons to adjust the order.

5.  Do **NOT** click OK. You need to adjust one more thing.

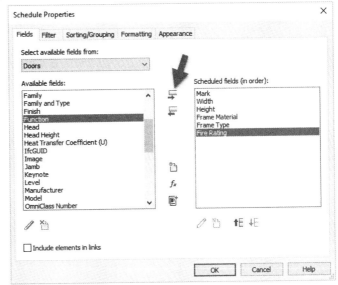

**FIGURE 13-2.2** Schedule Properties; Fields tab

> **TIP:** *If you accidentally clicked OK, click the Edit button next to the Fields parameter in the Properties Palette.*

6.  On the **Sorting/Grouping** tab, set the schedule to be sorted by the **Mark** (i.e., door number) in *Ascending* order (Figure 13-2.3).

> **TIP:** *The Formatting and Appearance tabs allow you to adjust how the schedule looks. The formatting is not displayed until the schedule is placed on a sheet.*

7.  Click the **OK** button to generate the schedule view.

You should now have a schedule similar to Figure 13-2.4.

**FIGURE 13-2.3** Schedule Properties; Sorting tab

**FIGURE 13-2.4** Door schedule view

Next, you will see how deleting a door number from the schedule deletes the door from the plan.

8. Switch to the **_Door Schedule 2_** view, under _Schedules/Quantities_ in the _Project Browser_, if you are not already there.

Next, you will delete door _102_ from the **_Door Schedule_** view; this was the door you added in an interior elevation, the exterior door in the _Living Room_.

9. Click in the cell with the number **102**.

10. Now click the **Delete** [Rows] button from the _Ribbon_ (Figure 13-2.5).

**FIGURE 13-2.5** Ribbon panel for the door schedule view

You will get an alert. Revit is telling you that the actual door will be deleted from the project model (Figure 13-2.6).

11. Click **OK** to delete the door (Figure 13-2.6).

12. Switch back to the *First Floor* view and notice that door 102 has been deleted from the project model (Figure 13-2.7).

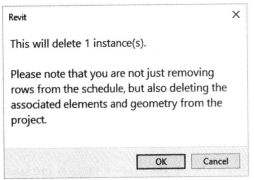

**FIGURE 13-2.6** Revit alert message

**FIGURE 13-2.7** First Floor plan view; door 102 has been removed

13. **Save** your project as **ex13-2.rvt**.

*TIP: You can also change the door number in the schedule and even the size; however, changing the size actually changes the door's Type Property which affects all the door instances of that type.*

## Exercise 13-3:
## Generate a Room Finish Schedule

In this exercise you will create a room finish schedule. The process is similar to the previous exercise.

### Create a Room Finish Schedule:

1.  Open ex13-2.rvt and **Save As ex13-3.rvt**.

2.  Select **View → Create → Schedules → Schedule/Quantities**.

3.  Select **Rooms** under *Category* and then click **OK** (Figure 13-3.1).

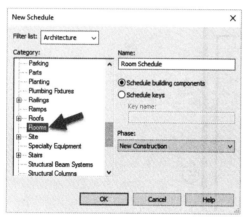

4.  In the *Fields* tab of the *Schedule Properties* dialog, add the following fields to be scheduled (Figure 13-3.2):
    a.  Number
    b.  Name
    c.  Base Finish
    d.  Floor Finish
    e.  Wall Finish
    f.  Ceiling Finish
    g.  Area

**FIGURE 13-3.1** New Schedule dialog

Area is not typically listed on a room finish schedule. However, you will add it to your schedule to see the various options Revit allows.

5.  On the *Sorting/Grouping* tab, set the schedule to be sorted by the **Number** field.

6.  On the *Appearance* tab, set the Title text to 1/8" Arial (Figure 13-3.3).

    *TIP: You can create a new text style that is set to bold or with a different font and then use it here.*

7.  Select **OK** to generate the *Room Schedule* view.

**FIGURE 13-3.2**
Schedule Properties - Fields

**FIGURE 13-3.3**
Schedule Properties - Appearance

Place cursor here to resize the column

| | | | | | | |
| --- | --- | --- | --- | --- | --- | --- |
| A | B | C | D | E | F | G |
| Number | Name | Base Finish | Floor Finish | Wall Finish | Ceiling Finish | Area |
| 001 | HALLWAY | | | | | 271 SF |
| 02 | Room | | | | | 39 SF |
| 003 | FAMILY ROOM | | | | | 754 SF |
| 004 | SHOP | | | | | 271 SF |
| 005 | MECH | | | | | 84 SF |
| 006 | Room | | | | | 36 SF |
| 007 | CRAFT | | | | | 304 SF |
| 100 | ENTRY | | | | | 282 SF |
| 101 | COAT CLOSET | | | | | 39 SF |
| 102 | LIVING ROOM | | | | | 786 SF |
| 103 | KITCHEN | | | | | 280 SF |
| 104 | MUD ROOM | | | | | 87 SF |
| 105 | BATH | | | | | 38 SF |
| 106 | DINING | | | | | 312 SF |
| 107 | GARAGE | | | | | 749 SF |
| 200 | Room | | | | | 345 SF |
| 201 | Room | | | | | 241 SF |
| 202 | Romm | | | | | 343 SF |
| 203 | Room | | | | | 44 SF |
| 204 | Room | | | | | 41 SF |
| 205 | Room | | | | | 80 SF |
| 206 | Room | | | | | 207 SF |
| 207 | Room | | | | | 272 SF |

**FIGURE 13-3.4** Room Schedule view

Your schedule should look similar to the one to the left (Figure 13-3.4).

8. Resize the **Name** column so all the room names are visible. Place the cursor between *Name* and *Base Finish* and drag to the right until all the names are visible.

*FYI: If you right-click on a column, you can select to hide it. Why add a column if you are just going to hide it? Well, for Revit to do calculations on data, the required parameters must be "in" the schedule, not just the project.*

## Modifying and Populating a Room Schedule:

Like the door schedule, the room schedule is a tabular view of the building model, so you can change the room name or number on the schedule or in the plans.

9.  In the *Room Schedule* view, change the name for room **201** (lower right corner of floor plan) to **OFFICE**.

    *TIP:* Click on the current room name and then click on the down-arrow that appears. This gives you a list of all the existing names in the current schedule; otherwise you can type a new name.

10. Switch to the *Second Floor* plan view to see the updated *Room Tag*.

You can quickly enter finish information to several rooms at one time. You will do this next.

11. In the *Second Floor* plan view, select the **Rooms** (not the *Room Tags*) for all bedrooms (three total); move the cursor near the *Room Tag* until you see the room highlight with an "X" (Figure 13-3.5).

    *REMEMBER:* Hold the Ctrl key down to select multiple objects.

**FIGURE 13-3.5** Second Floor Plan – Rooms selected

The parameters listed here are the same as the *Fields* available for display in the *Room Schedule*. When more than one room is selected and a parameter is not the same (e.g., different names), that value field is left blank. Otherwise, the values are displayed for the selected room. Next, you will enter values for the finishes.

12. In the *Properties Palette*, change the *Name* field; enter **BEDROOM**.

13. Enter the following for the finishes (Figure 13-3.6):
    a. *Base Finish:*     **WOOD**
    b. *Ceiling Finish:*  **GB**        *(Gb = gypsum board)*
    c. *Wall Finish:*     **PAINT-1**
    d. *Floor Finish:*    **CARPET-1**

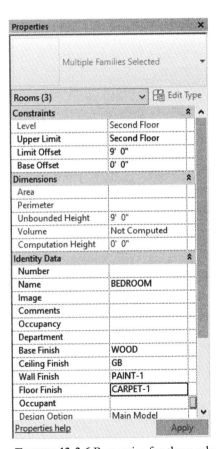

**FIGURE 13-3.6** Properties for three selected rooms

14. Click **Apply**.

15. Switch back to the ***Room Schedule*** view to see the automatic updates (Figure 13-3.7).

You can also enter data directly into the *Room Schedule* view but only one room at a time.

Hopefully, in the near future, Revit will be able to enter the finishes based on the wall's *Material* settings, as well as floor and ceiling types previously created in the project!

***TIP:*** *For the schedule, you can add fields and adjust formatting anytime by clicking on one of the edit buttons in the Properties Palette. This gives you the same options that were available when you created the schedule.*

| <Room Schedule> | | | | | | |
|---|---|---|---|---|---|---|
| A | B | C | D | E | F | G |
| Number | Name | Base Finish | Floor Finish | Wall Finish | Ceiling Finish | Area |
| 001 | HALLWAY | | | | | 271 SF |
| 02 | Room | | | | | 39 SF |
| 003 | FAMILY ROOM | | | | | 754 SF |
| 004 | SHOP | | | | | 271 SF |
| 005 | MECH | | | | | 84 SF |
| 006 | Room | | | | | 38 SF |
| 007 | CRAFT | | | | | 304 SF |
| 100 | ENTRY | | | | | 282 SF |
| 101 | COAT CLOSET | | | | | 39 SF |
| 102 | LIVING ROOM | | | | | 786 SF |
| 103 | KITCHEN | | | | | 280 SF |
| 104 | MUD ROOM | | | | | 87 SF |
| 105 | BATH | | | | | 38 SF |
| 106 | DINING | | | | | 312 SF |
| 107 | GARAGE | | | | | 749 SF |
| 200 | Room | | | | | 345 SF |
| 201 | OFFICE | | | | | 241 SF |
| 202 | BEDROOM | WOOD | CARPET-1 | PAINT-1 | GB | 343 SF |
| 203 | Room | | | | | 44 SF |
| 204 | Room | | | | | 41 SF |
| 205 | Room | | | | | 80 SF |
| 206 | BEDROOM | WOOD | CARPET-1 | PAINT-1 | GB | 207 SF |
| 207 | BEDROOM | WOOD | CARPET-1 | PAINT-1 | GB | 272 SF |

**FIGURE 13-3.7** Room Schedule; new data added

If you have trouble finding a room in the *Floor Plan* view, you can click the room number in the *Schedule* view and then click the **Highlight in Model** button on the *Ribbon*.

16. **Save** your project as **ex13-3.rvt**.

*FYI: When the* Room Tag *is selected, not the* Room *element, you can change its type from the* Type Selector. *The other option available, by default, is one without the square footage listed below the room number. For the cubic footage to show up, the* Area and Volumes Computations *dialog must be set to calculate volumes – see image to right.*

**FIGURE 13-3.8** Room Tag options in current project

## Self-Exam:

The following questions can be used as a way to check your knowledge of this lesson. The answers can be found at the bottom of the page.

1.  Doors are automatically numbered based on the room number. (T/F)

2.  The area for a room is calculated when a *Room*, and tag, is placed. (T/F)

3.  Revit can tag all the doors not currently tagged on a given level with the *Tag All* tool. (T/F)

4.  You can add or remove various fields in a door or room schedule. (T/F)

5.  Click Delete on the *Ribbon* to delete a door from a schedule. (T/F)

## Review Questions:

The following questions may be assigned by your instructor as a way to assess your knowledge of this section. Your instructor has the answers to the review questions.

1.  You can add a door tag with a leader. (T/F)

2.  You can add a fire rating by selecting a door, then *Properties Palette*. (T/F)

3.  A door can be deleted from the door schedule. (T/F)

4.  The schedule formatting only shows up when you place the schedule on a sheet. (T/F)

5.  It is not possible to add the finish information (i.e., base finish, wall finish) to multiple rooms at one time. (T/F)

6.  To modify the schedule view, click Edit in the *Properties Palette*. (T/F)

7.  Use the _____ palette to adjust the various fields associated with each Room in a plan view.

8.  Most door schedules are sorted by the _____ field.

9.  You can select a different *Room Tag* via the *Type Selector*. (T/F)

10. A schedule is just another way of looking at the building information model, a tabular view of the project database. (T/F)

**Notes:**

## Lesson 14
# Site Tools and Photo-Realistic Rendering:

You will take a look at the site design tools and the photo-realistic rendering abilities of Autodesk® Revit®. Revit uses a rendering technology called **Autodesk Raytracer®**. Revit also has a Cloud Rendering feature, which is free to students and can generate Stereo Panorama images to be used with Google® Cardboard®.

## Exercise 14-1:
## Site Tools

This exercise will give the reader a quick overview of the site tools available in Revit. The site tools are not intended to be an advanced site development package. Autodesk has other programs much more capable of developing complex sites such as AutoCAD Civil 3D 2019. These programs are used by professional Civil Engineers and Surveyors. The contours, or surface tin, generated from these advanced civil CAD programs can be used to generate a topography object in Revit.

In this lesson you will create a topography object from scratch rather than using imported CAD geometry; you will also add a driveway and sidewalk.

Once the topography object (the topography object, or element, is a 3D mass that represents part *or* all of the site) is created, the grade line will automatically show up in building and wall sections, exterior elevations and site plans. The sections even have the earth pattern filled in below the grade line.

As with other Revit elements, you can select the object after it is created and set various properties for it, such as surface material, phase, etc. One can also return to *Sketch* mode to refine or correct the surface; this is done in the same way most other sketched objects are edited: by selecting the item and clicking *Edit Sketch* on the *Ribbon*.

## Autodesk Site Designer

Autodesk recently made a new Revit add-in available to Subscription customers. The add-in, called Site Designer (see image below), has several tools intended to allow the building designer to create a more realistic surface with curbs, sidewalks and more. These features are all intermediate to advanced and thus will not be covered here. However, the reader may want to explore these tools on their own.

# Overview of Site Tools on the Ribbon:

Below is a brief description of what the site tools are used for. After this short review you will try a few of these tools on your residence project.

Toposurface: Creates a 3D surface by picking points, specifying the elevation of each point picked, or by using linework within a linked AutoCAD drawing that were created at the proper elevations.

Subregion: Allows an area to be defined within a previously drawn toposurface; the result is an area within the toposurface that can have a different material than the toposurface itself. The subregion is still part of the toposurface and will move with it when relocated. If a subregion is selected and deleted, the original surface and properties for that area are revealed.

Split Surface: This tool is similar to the *Subregion* tool in every way except that the result is separate surfaces that can intentionally, or accidentally, be moved apart from each other. If a split surface is selected and deleted, it results in a subtraction or a void relative to the original toposurface.

Merge Surfaces: After a surface has been split into one or more separate surfaces you can merge them back together. Only two surfaces can be merged together at one time. The two surfaces to be merged must share a common edge or overlap.

Graded Region: This tool is used to edit the grade of a toposurface that represents the existing site conditions and the designer wants to use Revit to design the new site conditions. This tool is generally only meant to be used once; when used it will copy the existing site conditions to a new phase and set the existing site to be demolished in the new construction phase. The newly copied site object can then be modified for the new site conditions.

Property Line: Creates property lines in plan views only.

Building Pad: Used to define a portion of site to be subtracted when created below grade, and added when created above grade. An example of how this might be used is to create a *pad* that coincides with a basement floor slab which would remove the ground in section above the basement floor slab; otherwise the basement would be filled with the earth fill pattern. Several pads can be imposed on the same toposurface element, but they cannot overlap.

<u>Parking Component</u>: This is a parking stall layout that can be copied around to quickly lay out parking lots. Several types can be loaded which specify both size and angle.

<u>Site Component</u>: Items like benches, dumpsters, etc., that are placed directly on the toposurface at the correct elevation at the point picked.

<u>Label Contours</u>: Adds an elevation label to the selected contours.
*FYI: Contours are automatically created based on the toposurface.*

## Site Settings:

The *Site Settings* dialog controls a few key project-wide settings related to the site. Below are brief descriptions of these settings.

The **Site Settings** dialog is accessed from the *arrow* link in the lower-right corner of the *Model Site* panel.

<u>Contour Line Display</u>: This controls if the contours are displayed when the *toposurface* is visible, via the check box, and at what interval. If the *Interval* is set to 1'-0" you will see contour lines that follow the ground's surface and each line represents a vertical change of 1'-0" from the adjacent contour line. The contour lines alone do not tell you what direction the surface slopes in a plan view; this is where contour labels are important. The *Passing Through Elevation* setting allows control over where the contour intervals start from. This is useful because architects usually base the first floor of the building on elevation 0'-0" (or 100'-0"), and the surveyors and civil engineers will use the distance above sea level (e.g., 1009.2'). So this feature allows the contours to be reconciled between the two systems. The *Additional Contours* section allows for more contour detail to be added within a particular area (vertically); on a very large site you might want 1'-0" contours only at the building and 10'-0" contours everywhere else. However, this only works if the building is in a distinctive set of vertical elevations. If the site is relatively level or an adjacent area shares the same set of contours, you will have undesirable results.

<u>Section Graphics</u>: This area controls how the earth appears when it is shown in section, for example, exterior elevations, building sections, wall sections, etc. Here is where the pattern is selected that appears in section; the pattern is selected from the project *Materials* similar to the process for selecting the pattern to be displayed within a wall when viewed in section. The *Elevation of poche base* controls the depth of the pattern in section views relative to the grade line.

Property Data: This section controls how angles and lengths are displayed for information describing property lines.

## Creating Topography in Revit

1. Open your Revit project ex13-3.rvt and **Save As ex14-1.rvt**.

2. Switch to the **Site Plan** view via the *Project Browser*.

Here you will basically see what appears to be a roof plan view of your project (Figure 14-1.1). This view has its visibility set such that you see the project from above and the various site categories are turned on so they are automatically visible once they are created. Next you will take a quick look at the *View Range* for this view so you understand how things are set up.

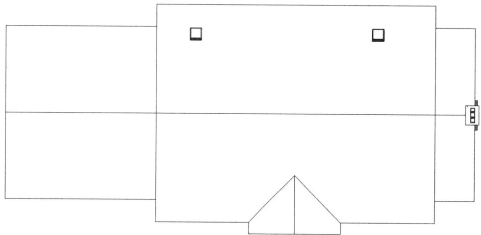

**FIGURE 14-1.1** Initial Site Plan view

3. Make sure nothing is selected in the view so you have access to the view properties in the *Properties Palette*.

4. In the *Properties Palette*, scroll down if necessary, and select **Edit** next to *View Range*.

Here you can see the site is being viewed from 200′ above the first floor level, so your building or roof would have to be taller than that before it would be cut like a floor plan. The *View Depth* could be a problem here: on a steep site, the entire site will be seen if part of it passes through the specified *View Range*. However, items completely below the *View Range* will not be visible.

5.  In the *View Depth* section, set the **Level** to **B.O. Footing**.

This change will ensure everything shows up on a steeper site, as you will now be looking deeper into the model.

6.  Click **OK** to close the open dialog.

When creating the topography, you will want to be able to see the exterior walls so you can pick points on those walls to define the grade at the building. At the moment, the roof obscures the view of the exterior walls. Next, you will modify the view so the roof elements are transparent and dashed; this will reveal the perimeter of the building while still indicating where the roof overhangs are.

7.  Select one of the roof objects in the *Site Plan* view.

8.  Right-click and select **Override Graphics in View → By Category** (Figure 14-1.2).

    *FYI: As the menu name implies, the graphics will only be modified in the current view. Also, by selecting "By Category" rather than "By Element" you will be modifying all roof elements, not just the selected one.*

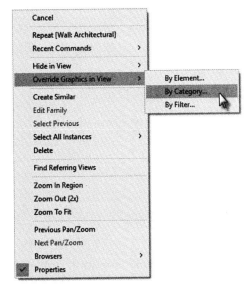

**FIGURE 14-1.2** Graphics override by view

9.  Click the **Open the Visibility Graphics dialog** and make the changes shown in Figure 14-1.3:

    a.  Set the *Projection* lines for "Roofs" to **Dash 3/32"**.

    b.  Check the box in the ***Transparent*** column for "Roofs."

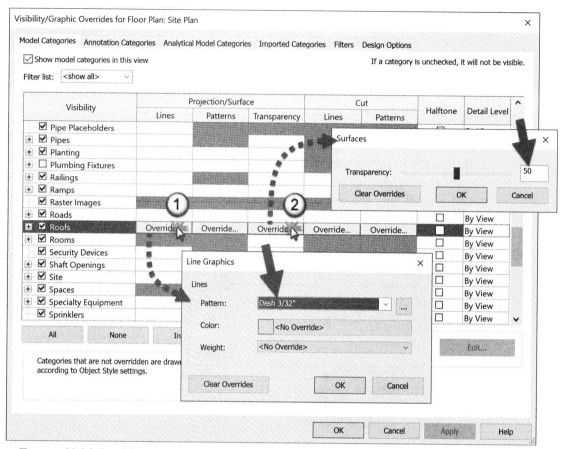

**FIGURE 14-1.3** Graphics override by view

Your *Site Plan* should now look similar to Figure 14-1.4.

**FIGURE 14-1.4** Site plan with dashed roof

Next, you will make the floating skylights hidden in the *Site Plan* view as well. In addition to controlling the graphics by view, you can also control object visibility by view via the right-click menu. You will do this next to hide the skylights.

10. Select one of the skylights and then right-click (Figure 14-1.5).

11. From the pop-up menu, select **Hide in view → Elements**.

12. Repeat the previous two steps to hide the other skylight.

*TIP #1: This method is the only way to hide individual items (e.g., if you want to hide just one of the skylights) whereas the entire category can be hidden here or via the Visibility Graphics dialog for the current view.*

*TIP #2: The only way to see these skylights again, in this view, is to click the Reveal Hidden Elements icon at the bottom of the screen (the lightbulb icon).*

**FIGURE 14-1.5**
Right-click with skylight selected

The skylights are now hidden; however, the hole in the roof is still visible.

*TIP: You could use the Linework tool set to <Invisible Lines> to hide the opening if needed.*

You are now ready to create the site object. The element in Revit which represents the site is called *toposurface*.

13. Select **Massing & Site → Model Site → Toposurface** from the *Ribbon*.

By default the *Place Point* tool is selected on the *Ribbon*; you are now in *Sketch* mode. This tool allows you to specify various points within the view at various elevations. Revit will generate a 3D surface based on those points, so the more points you provide, the more accurate the surface. Notice on the *Options Bar* (Figure 14-1.6) that you can enter an elevation for each point as you pick them on the screen.

**FIGURE 14-1.6** Options Bar for Toposurface tool

**FIGURE 14-1.7** Partial South Elevation

*What elevation should I enter on the Options Bar?*

The elevation you enter for each point should relate to the *Level* datums set up in your project. For example, look at your *South Exterior* elevation (Figure 14-1.7). Recall that the first floor is set to 0′-0″ and the top of foundation is set to -1′-3″.

As you can see in the *South Elevation*, the only place you would want to add Points at an elevation of 0′-0″ would be at the garage doors. Everywhere else should be at about
-1′-6″ so the grade does not rise higher than the top of the foundation wall and come into contact with any wood.

14. With the *Elevation* set to **0′-0″** pick the two points shown in Figure 14-1.8.

    *TIP: You should be able to Snap to the edge of the garage doors even though you cannot see them.*

15. Change the **Elevation** to **-1′-6″** (do not forget the minus sign) on the *Options Bar* and then pick the **points** as specified in Figure 14-1.9 on the next page.

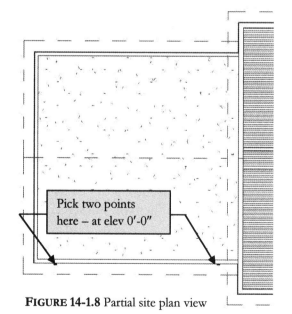

Pick two points here – at elev 0′-0″

**FIGURE 14-1.8** Partial site plan view

**FIGURE 14-1.9** Site plan view – 16 points to be selected (elev -1′-6″)

16. Set the **Elevation** to **-2′-6″** and select the ten points shown in Figure 14-1.10 which will define the extents of the toposurface.

   *FYI:* *The elevations selected will generally provide a positive slope away from the building; this will be visible in elevations and sections.*

Points to be added in Step 16

**FIGURE 14-1.10** Site plan view – 10 points to be selected (elev – 2′-6″)

17. Select the **green check mark** on the *Ribbon* to finish the surface.

Revit has now created the toposurface based on the points you specified. Again, the more points you add, the more refined and accurate the surface will be.

Ideally you would use the *Toposurface* tool to create a surface from a surveyor's points file or contour lines drawn in an AutoCAD file; Revit can automatically generate surfaces from these sources. This process is beyond the scope of this tutorial. See Revit's *Help System* for more information.

18. Switch to the *3D* view to see your new ground surface (Figure 14-1.11). *TIP:* Type **VV** and turn on the *Roof* category if needed.

**FIGURE 14-1.11** 3D view showing new ground surface

Unfortunately, the toposurface object cannot tell the difference between the inside and the outside of the building. So if you were to cut a section through the building, you would see the earth poche, or fill pattern, both inside and outside the building (Figure 14-1.12a). Therefore, you will need to create a *building pad* object that will "stamp" an area out of the ground (Figure 14-1.12b).

19. Switch to the *Basement Floor Plan* so you can see the foundation walls which will be used to define the perimeter of the pad.

20. Select **Massing & Site → Model Site → Building Pad**.

Building
Pad

**FIGURE 14-1.12A** Section BEFORE Building Pad is added

**FIGURE 14-1.12B** Section AFTER Building Pad is added

By default, the *Building Pad* object is created 12″ thick which is deeper than the basement floor slab and would show. Thus, you will edit the properties of the pad so it is only ½″ thick and does not interfere with any other model elements. The floor slab will hide the pad object.

21. In the Properties Palette, click the **Edit Type** button.

22. Click **Edit** next to the *Structure* parameter.

23. Change the *pad* thickness from 1′-0″ to **1/2″**.

24. Close the open dialog box.

25. With *Pick Walls* selected on the *Ribbon*, select each of the foundation walls  in the basement area (Figure 14-1.13).

*FYI: Do not select the three exterior walls of the garage. There is no basement below the garage so the fill pattern should show up below the garage floor which is at elevation 0'-0".*

**FIGURE 14-1.13** Basement floor plan – walls selected to define the building pad

26. Click the **green check mark** to finish the pad.

You now have a *pad* object that "stamps" a portion of the ground surface down and out of the way for sections through the building.

If you had a basement with multiple levels, maybe a tuck-under garage at the basement level that dropped 8″ lower than the rest of the basement, you would need to create multiple *pads* to "stamp" the ground down in different amounts.

Next, you will quickly create a driveway and sidewalk to wrap up this lesson.

You can use the *Subregion* tool or the *Split Surface* tool to create the driveway and sidewalks. The *Subregion* tool defines an area that is still part of the main site object; the *Split Surface* tool literally breaks the toposurface into separate elements. Splitting a surface can create problems when trying to move or edit the site, so you will use the *Subregion* tool.

27. Switch back to the ***Site Plan*** view.

Subregion

28. Select the ***Subregion*** tool and sketch the lines for the driveway (see Figure 14-1.14).

*TIP: The sketch lines can extend out past the edge of the toposurface. The final subregion will actually still stop at the edge of the toposurface.*

29. Click the **green check mark** on the *Ribbon* to finish the subregion.

Select the first line or wall to trim/extend.  (Click on the part you want to keep)

FIGURE 14-1.14 Partial site plan – closed sketch lines for subregion

30. Switch to **3D** view to see your driveway (Figure 14-1.15). Notice the 2D lines sketched in the *Site Plan* view have been projected down onto the surface of the 3D site object!

FIGURE 14-1.15 Driveway added

Notice that the material is still the same as the main ground surface. You will learn how to change this in a moment.

Notice, also, how the grade slopes up at the garage doors because the two points that were placed on either side of the doors are at elevation 0′-0″.

When you select the toposurface and click *Edit Surface* on the *Ribbon*, you can select existing points and edit their elevations to refine the surface. You can also delete points or add new ones.

31. Use techniques previously covered to add a sidewalk as shown in Figure 14-1.16 below. You can also add a stair up to the front door (Figure 14-1.17).

**FIGURE 14-1.16** 3D view with driveway and sidewalk added; trees added later in this chapter

32. In the **Default 3D** view, select the *driveway* subregion.

33. Via the *Properties Palette*, set the *Material* parameter to **Site – Asphalt**. Close open dialogs. *FYI: Be sure to select this from the* Materials *tab.*

34. Set the sidewalk *Material* to **Concrete – Case-in-place concrete**.

35. Set the main site element's *Material* to **Site – Grass**.

36. Make sure the *View Properties*, via the *Properties Palette* when nothing is selected, for your **3D** view is set to **Shaded, Consistent Colors or Realistic** so you can see a presentation version of the materials.

   *TIP: Set via the View Control Bar at the bottom of the Drawing Window.*

**FIGURE 14-1.17** Stair and railing added at front entry – railing shown from "sample railing" model

That concludes this overview of the site tools provided within Revit.

## Exercise 14-2:
## Creating an Exterior Rendering

The first thing you will do is set up a view. You will use the *Camera* tool to do this. This becomes a saved view that can be opened at any time from the *Project Browser*. Several cameras can be added to a project.

## Creating a Camera View:

1. Open the **First Floor** plan view and **Zoom to Fit** so that you can see the entire plan (or type ZF).

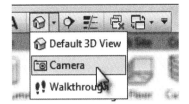

2. On the *QAT*, select the down-arrow next to the 3D view and then select **Camera**. See image to the right.

3. Click the mouse in the lower right corner of the screen to indicate the camera eye location (Figure 14-2.1).

   *NOTE: Before you click, Revit tells you on the Status Bar it first wants the eye location, and you can set the eye level on the Options Bar.*

4. Next, click near the entry doors (Figure 14-2.1).

Autodesk Revit will automatically open a view window for the new camera. Take a minute to look at the view and make a mental note of what you see and do not see in the view (Figure 14-2.2).

5. Switch back to the **First Floor** plan view.

6. Adjust the camera, using its grips, to look similar to Figure 14-2.3.

   *TIP: If the camera is not visible in plan view, right click on the 3D view name in the Project Browser (3D View 1) and select Show Camera; do all this while still in the first floor plan view.*

Depth of view, also relates to Crop Region

Second pick point

First pick point

**FIGURE 14-2.1** Placing a Camera in plan view

Crop Region window

**FIGURE 14-2.2** Initial Camera view

FIGURE 14-2.3 Revised camera – plan

7. Now switch to **3D View 1** and adjust the **Crop Region** to look similar to **Figure 14-2.4**.

   *FYI: You may need to adjust the Camera location back in the plan view as well.*

This will be the view you render later in this exercise.

FIGURE 14-2.4 Revised camera – 3d View 1

## Assigning Materials to Elements:

Materials are high quality images which represent the materials your building will be made of.

Typically, materials are added while the project is being modeled. For example, when you create a material using the *Materials* command on the *Manage tab*, you can assign it to elements in the model at that time. Of course, you can go back and add or change it later. Next, you will change the material assigned for the brick chimney.

8.   Switch to **First Floor** plan view.

9.   Select the fireplace, not the mantel.

10.  Click **Edit Type** on the *Properties Palette*.

11.  Click on the **Exterior Material** *value*; notice the material selected for the exterior finish is **Masonry – Brick** (Figure 14-2.5).

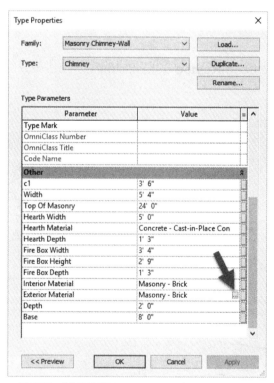

FIGURE 14-2.5 Chimney properties

12. Click the icon to the right of the label **Masonry – Brick**.

Now you will take a look at the definition of the material *Masonry – Brick*.

*FYI: From the* Manage *tab you can also select* **Materials**.

You are now in the *Material Browser* dialog. You should notice that a material is already selected on the left. Next, you will select a different brick material.

**FIGURE 14-2.6** Materials Browser dialog

13. In the *Material Browser* dialog, select the *Appearance* tab and then click the **Replace this asset** link (Steps 1 and 2, Figure 14-2.6).

You can browse through the thumbnails and select any appearance in the list to be assigned to the *Masonry – Brick* material in Revit. The material does not have to be brick but would be confusing if something else were assigned to the *Masonry – Brick* material name.

14. Select the *Appearance Library* category and then *Masonry\Brick* (Steps 3 and 4), locate the **Non-Uniform Running – Red** and then click the Replace link (Step 5) (Figure 14-2.6).

Notice the material preview is now updated.

15. Click **OK** to close the *Material Browser* and *Properties* dialog boxes.

Now, when you render any object (wall, ceiling, etc.) that has the material "Masonry – Brick" associated with it, it will have the red brick on it.

If you need more than one brick color, you simply create a new material in the *Material Browser* dialog and assign that material to another element.

## Project Location:

A first step in setting up a rendering is to specify the location of the project on the earth. This is important for accurate daylight studies.

Location

16. Select **Manage → Project Location → Location**.

17. In the *Project Address* field, enter **Minneapolis, MN**.

    a. You may also enter your location if you wish.

    b. It is even possible to enter the actual street address.

18. Press **Enter**.

**FIGURE 14-2.7** Location Weather and Site dialog

You should now see an internet based map of your project location, complete with longitude and latitude (Figure 14-2.7).

19. Click **OK**.

## Sun Settings:

Another step in preparing a rendering is to define the sun settings. You will explore the various options available.

20. Select **Manage → Settings → Additional Settings** (*drop-down list icon*) **→ Sun Settings**.

Sun Settings

21. Make the following changes (Figure 14-2.8):

    a.  Solar Study: **Still**
    b.  **Uncheck** *Ground Plane at Level.*
    c.  Select **Summer Solstice** on the left.
    d.  Change the year to **2016**.

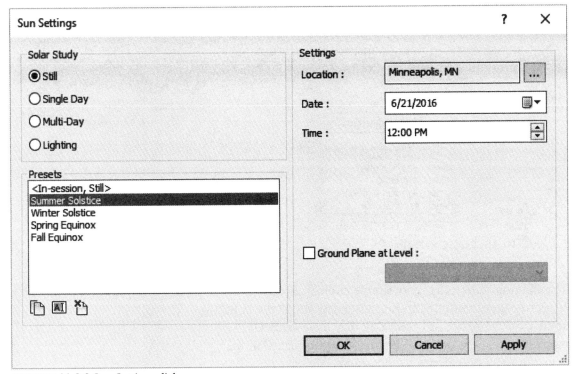

FIGURE 14-2.8 Sun Settings dialog

22. Click **OK** to close the dialog

## Setting Up the Environment:

You have limited options for setting up the building's environment. If you need more control than what is provided directly in Revit, you will need to use another program like Autodesk 3DS Max 2019, which is designed to work with Revit and can create extremely high quality renderings and animations; it even has daylighting functionality that helps to validate LEED® (Leadership in Environmental and Energy Design) requirements.

23. Switch to your camera view:
    **3D View 1**.

24. Select the **Show Rendering Dialog** icon on
    the *View Control Bar*; it looks like a teapot
    (Figure 14-2.9).

**FIGURE 14-2.9** Render dialog icon

> *FYI: This icon is only visible when you are in a 3D view,
> which is the same with the* NavigationWheel *and*
> ViewCube.

The *Rendering* dialog box is now open (Figure 14-2.10).
This dialog box allows you to control the environmental
settings you are about to explore and actually create the
rendering.

25. In the *Lighting* section, click the down-arrow next
    to *Scheme* to see the options; select **Exterior:
    Sun and Artificial** (Figure 14-2.11).

**FIGURE 14-2.11** Lighting options

**FIGURE 14-2.10** Rendering dialog

The lighting options are very simple choices: is the
rendering an interior or exterior rendering and is the light
source *Sun*, *Artificial*, or both? You may have artificial
lights, that is, light fixtures like the ones you placed in the
office but still only desire a rendering solely based on the
light provided by the sun.

26. Also in the *Lighting* section, set the *Sun* to **Summer Solstice**.

> *FYI: In the Sun Settings dialog box, Revit lets you set up various "scenes" which control time of day. Two
> examples might be:*
> * *Daytime, summer*
> * *Nighttime, winter*

Looking back at Figure 14-2.8, you would click *Duplicate* and provide a name. This name
would then be available from the *Sun* drop-down list in the *Render* dialog box.

27. Click on the **Artificial Lighting** button.

You will now see a dialog similar to the one shown to the right (Figure 14-2.12). You will see several 2x4 light fixtures. The light fixtures relate to the fixtures you inserted in the reflected ceiling plans. It is very convenient that you can place lights in the ceiling plan and have them ready to render whenever you need to (i.e., render and cast light into the scene!). Here you can group lights together so you can control which ones are on (e.g., exterior and interior lights).

28. Click **Cancel** to close the *Artificial Lighting* dialog.

**FIGURE 14-2.12** Scene Lighting dialog

29. Click the down-arrow next to *Style* in the *Background* area (Figure 14-2.13).

    a. Notice the options; click **Sky: Few Clouds** to keep that option selected.

30. Click the "**X**" to close the Rendering dialog box for now. Your settings will be saved.

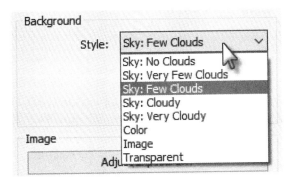

**FIGURE 14-2.13** Background options

Notice that for the background, one option is Image. This allows you to specify a photograph of the site or one similar. It can prove difficult getting the perspective just right, but the end results can look as if you took a picture of the completed building.

Next, you will place a few trees into your rendering. You will adjust their exact location so they are near the edge of the framed rendering, so as not to cover too much of the building.

31. Switch to the **First Floor** plan view and select **Component** from the *Architecture* tab.

32. Pick **RPC Tree – Deciduous : Largetooth Aspen 25'** from the *Type Selector* on the *Properties Palette*.

    *FYI: If the tree is not listed in the Type Selector, click Load Family and load the RPC Tree - Deciduous tree family from the Plantings folder.*

33. Place four trees as shown in **Figure 14-2.14**; you will make one smaller in a moment.

**FIGURE 14-2.14** First Floor – with trees added

34. Adjust the trees in plan view, reviewing the effects in the *3D View 1* view, so your 3D view is similar to Figure 14-2.15.

    *TIP: Adjust the crop region if required.*

35. In the **First Floor** plan view, select the tree that is shown smaller in **Figure 14-24**.

36. Click **Edit Type** on the *Properties Palette*.

37. Click **Duplicate** and enter the name **RPC Tree – Deciduous : Largetooth Aspen 18′**.

38. Change the *Height* to **18′** (it is currently 25′), and then click **OK** to close the open dialog boxes.

The previous three steps allow you to have a little more variety in the trees being placed. Otherwise they would all be the same height, which is not very natural.

**FIGURE 14-2.15** 3D View 1 – with trees

39. Open the **3D View 1** camera view.

40. Open the *Rendering* dialog.

41. Make sure the *Quality* is set to **Draft**.

> *FYI: The time to process the rendering increases significantly as the quality level and resolution are raised.*

42. Click **Render** from the *Rendering* dialog box.

You will see the following progress bar while Revit is processing the rendering (Figure 14-2.16).

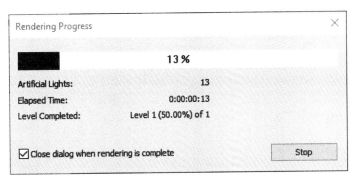

**FIGURE 14-2.16** Rendering progress

After a few minutes, depending on the speed of your computer, you should have a rendered image similar to Figure 14-2.17 on the next page. You can increase the quality of the image by adjusting the quality setting in the *Render* dialog. However, these higher settings require substantially more time to generate the rendering. The last step before saving the Revit project file is to save the rendered image to a file.

*FYI: Each time you make changes to the model that are visible from that view, you will have to re-render the view to get an updated image. Depending on exactly how your view was set up, you may be able to see light from one of the light fixtures in the second floor office or see the stair and railing through the window. Revit can have the glazing in windows set to be transparent! Renderings with artificial lighting can take a lot longer to render.*

**FIGURE 14-2.17** Rendered view – low resolution draft setting

43. From the *Rendering* dialog select **Export**.

*FYI: The 'Save to Project' button saves the image within the Revit Project for placement on Sheets; this is convenient but does make the project size larger so you should delete the old ones when they are not needed anymore!*

44. Select a *location* and provide a *file name*.

45. Set the *Save As* type to **JPEG**.

46. Click **Save**.

The image file you just saved can now be inserted into MS Word or Adobe Photoshop for editing or it can be emailed to your client.

## Design Options can also be rendered:

You can render your design options in addition to the primary options. As mentioned before, you can copy a view and change its visibility settings to show specific design options or you can just change the settings for the current view. You will do that next.

47. In the **3D View 1** view, adjust the **View Properties** so the curved entry roof and taller entry windows are visible. Refer back to the *Design Options* section if necessary – page 9-25.

48. Switch to plan view and change the tree in front of the house to another option available from the *Type Selector* or the Library.

49. **Render** the image, adjusting these settings:

   a.  Quality: **Medium**
   b.  Output Settings: **Printer @ 300dpi**
   c.  Lighting: **Exterior: Sun only**

50. **Save** your project as **ex14-2.rvt**.

**FIGURE 14-2.18** Rendered view with design options adjusted

Notice the large tree casts shadows on the ground; you can also see reflections of the tree in the windows when the angle and lighting are right. Remember, the angle and location of the shadows are based on the time, date and location on the earth; if you change those settings, the shadows will change accordingly. You also need to set true North for the given site! This can be done via **Manage → Project Location → Rotate True North**.

As you can imagine, an image like this could really "sell" your design to the client. Revit makes the process to get to this point very easy compared to legacy CAD programs and techniques used prior to Revit.

## Exercise 14-3:
## Rendering an Isometric in Section

This exercise will introduce you to a 3D view tool called *Section Box*. This tool is not necessarily related to renderings, but the two features used together can produce some interesting results.

## Setting up the 3D View:

1. Open file ex14-2.rvt and **Save As ex14-3.rvt**.

2. Switch to the **Default 3D** view via the icon on the *QAT (not the 3D View 1 from Exercise 14-2)*.

3. Make sure nothing is selected so the *Properties Palette* shows the current view's properties. If something is selected, you can still see the current view's properties by selecting **3D View: {3D}** from the drop-down list below the *Type Selector*.

4. Activate the **Section Box** parameter and then click **Apply**.

You should see a box appear around your building, similar to Figure 14-3.1. When selected, you can adjust the size of the box with its grips. Anything outside the box is not visible. This is a great way to study a particular area of your building while in an isometric view. You will experiment with this feature next.

Section Box (shown selected)

Six grips to manipulate the Section Box – only visible while the *Section Box* is selected

**FIGURE 14-3.1** 3D view with Section Box activated

5. To practice using the **Section Box**, drag the grips around until your view looks similar to Figure 14-3.2.

   *TIP: This may require the ViewCube tool as well, or hold Shift + drag the Wheel button on the mouse.*

   a. Click and drag the grip from the top downward.

   b. Click and drag the grip for the East (right) face toward the West (left).

**FIGURE 14-3.2** 3D view with adjusted Section Box

Did you notice the grips look different? One grip looks like two arrows rather than a small square. You can still click on any part of the grip and drag it, but you can also single-click on one of the arrows to slightly adjust the section box in the direction the arrow points. This is similar to the nudge feature, when an element is selected and you use the arrows keys to move it just a little bit.

This creates a very interesting view of the First Floor plan. What client would have trouble understanding this drawing?

6. Now readjust the **Section Box** to look similar to **Figure 14-3.3**.

**FIGURE 14-3.3** 3D view

7. From the *Manage* tab, select **Sun Settings** and change the following *Sun* settings (Figure 14-3.4): ***TIP:*** *Set* Solar Study *to* Still *first and then click any named preset.*

   a. New name: **28 February 8am** (via Duplicate)

   b. Month: **2** (February)

   c. Day: **28**

   d. Time: **8:00am**

*FYI: Do not forget, without doing any rendering in Revit you can turn on the shadows in any view. You can even turn on shadows in your 2D exterior elevation view (see below) for a great effect with little effort!*

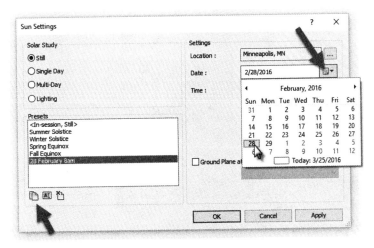

**FIGURE 14-3.4** Modified Sun Settings

8. Select the **Render** icon, select the *Scheme*: **Exterior: Sun only**, and then set *Sun* to **28 February 8am**.

9. Set the options as shown in the image to the left, including setting the *Background Style* to **Color**.

10. Select the **Region** option and then adjust the "render region crop" that appears in the view to indicate the area to be rendered.

   *TIP: This tool is nice for checking a material before rendering the entire building, which takes longer.*

11. Click the **Render** button.

The image will take a few minutes to render, again depending on the speed of your computer. When finished it should look similar to **Figure 14-3.5**. The image looks much better on the screen or printed in color.

As mentioned previously, you can increase the rendering quality settings to get much better results, though it simply takes more time. Also, the higher quality images can be printed larger without pixilation. If you have time, try changing the Quality to High or Best and the Resolution to 300dpi. Note the difference in the time to complete.

## Adjusting an Element's Material:

As previously mentioned, most elements already have a material assigned to them. This is great because it allows you to quickly render your project to get some preliminary images. However, they usually need to be adjusted. You will do this next.

**FIGURE 14-3.5** Rendered isometric view - draft settings selected

12. In the *Render* dialog, click the *Show Model* button at the bottom; the rendered view disappears. Close the *Render* dialog.

13. Select one of the cabinets in the kitchen.

14. Click the **Edit Type** button in the *Properties Palette*.

Notice the Cabinet Material parameter is set to **<By Category>** (Figure 14-3.6). You could change the material here for just the selected cabinet type; however, by setting a material to be *By Category* you can quickly change the material for all the cabinets at one time, without having to select every cabinet.

**Sun Path**

It is possible to turn on the feature called Sun Path. This shows the path of the sun over a day and a year. This is accessed from the View Control Bar while in a 3D view.

Once on, you can click and drag the sun along its daily or yearly path!

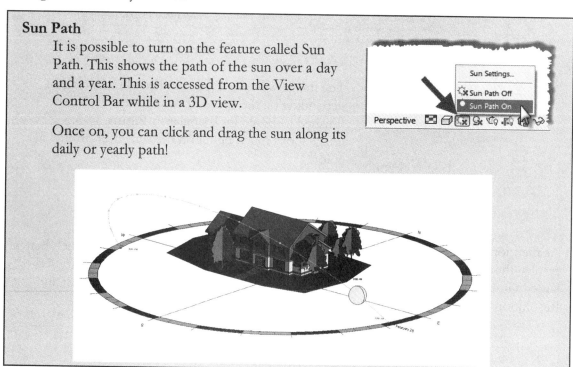

15. **Close** the *Type Properties* dialog.

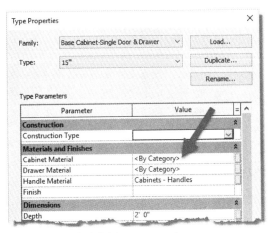

FIGURE 14-3.6 Cabinet properties

The next step will open the dialog box which controls color, line weight, line pattern and material, for both hatching and rendering representations. This is for the entire project, with the exception of any overrides added per view via VV.

16. Select **Manage → Settings → Object Styles**.

17. Expand the **Casework** category (Figure 14-3.7).

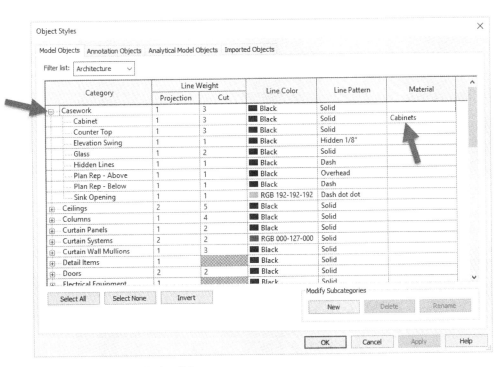

FIGURE 14-3.7 Object Styles dialog

The *Cabinet* subcategory has a material assigned to it called **Cabinets**.

18. Click on **Cabinets** in the *Material* column, and then click the "**...**" button that appears to the right.

You are now in the *Material Browser* dialog box, where you can create and edit *Materials*.

19. Open the *Asset Browser* by clicking the **Replace this asset** link on *Appearance* tab as previously covered (Figure 14-3.8).

20. Change the *Appearance* material to
**Cherry - Natural Low Gloss** (Figure 14-3.8).

> **TIP:** *Select the category label* Wood *under* Appearance Library *first.*

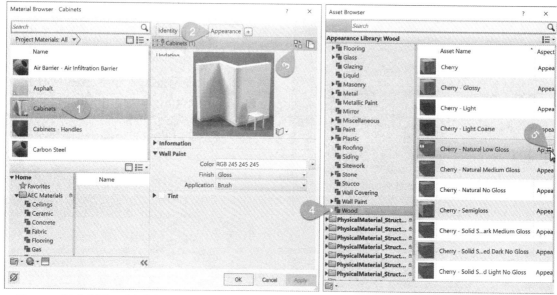

**FIGURE 14-3.8** Material dialog – with *Asset Browser* open

21. Click **OK** to close the open dialog boxes.

22. You can now re-render the 3D view and see the results.

23. **Save** your project as ex **14-3.rvt**.

> **TIP:** *While in the 3D view with the Section Box active, you can zoom in to an area, just like you can in other views, and render that enlarged area (just check the "Region" option in the Render dialog). Similarly, you can change the material for the counter top, faucet, dishwasher, etc.*

## Exercise 14-4:
## Creating an Interior Rendering

Creating an interior rendering is very similar to an exterior rendering.
This exercise will walk through the steps involved in creating a high quality interior rendering.

## Setting Up the Camera View:

1. Open ex14-3.rvt and **Save As ex14-4.rvt**.

2. Open the **First Floor** plan view.

3. Select the **Camera** tool from the *QAT*.

4. Place the *Camera* as shown in **Figure 14-4.1**.

**FIGURE 14-4.1** Camera placed – Kitchen

Revit uses default heights for the camera and the target. These heights are based on the current level's floor elevation plus the eye height of an average height person. These reference points can be edited via the camera properties.

Revit will automatically open the newly generated camera view. Your view should look similar to **Figure 14-4.2**.

**FIGURE 14-4.2** Initial interior camera view

5.   Using the **Crop Region** rectangle, modify the view to look like **Figure 14-4.3**; select it and then drag the grips.

6.   Uncheck **Far Clip Active** in the *Properties Palette*. Copy the two trees in the back of the house into a position so they can be seen through the window over the sink.

   *TIP: You will have to switch to plan view to adjust the camera's depth of view to see the trees. REMINDER: If the camera does not show in plan view, right-click on the camera view label in the Project Browser, while in plan view, and select Show Camera. You may need to switch between the plan and camera views several times to adjust the trees so they are visible through the windows.*

7.   Switch back to **First Floor** plan to see the revised *Camera* view settings.

Notice the field of view triangle is wider based on the changes to the **Crop Region** in the camera view (Figure 14-4.4).

**FIGURE 14-4.3** Modified interior camera

**FIGURE 14-4.4** Modified camera – First Floor

14-37

**FIGURE 14-4.5** Camera properties

8. Select the *Camera.*

9. Make sure the **Eye Elevation** is **5′-6″** (Figure 14-4.5).

Notice the other settings for the camera; these are the properties for the 3D view itself. Changing the *Target Elevation* would cause the camera to look up at the ceiling or down at the floor depending on the value entered.

10. Click **Apply** if any changes were needed.

The vertical lines are distorted due to the wide field of view, crop region. This is similar to what a camera with a 10-15mm lens would get in the finished building.

## Creating the Rendering:

Next you will render the interior kitchen view.

11. In the interior camera view, create a new item in *Sun Settings* dialog as shown below (Figure 14-4.6).

> *Name*: **Kitchen**
> *Azimuth*: **302.00**
> *Altitude*: **34.00**

You just created a "fake" sun angle to make the rendering look better for presentation purposes. This may be useful if the exact

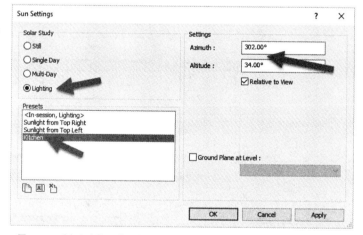

**FIGURE 14-4.6** Sun Settings

north is not known or the designer wants to leverage a little artistic freedom.

12. Select **Show Rendering Dialog** from the *View Control Bar.*

13. Settings should be **Medium** *quality and* **150 dpi.**

14. Set the *Scheme* to **Interior: Sun only**; be sure to select "interior:" as it makes a big difference.

15. Click **Render** to begin the rendering process.

This will take several minutes depending on the speed of your computer. When finished, the view should look similar to **Figure 14-4.7**.

16. Click **Export** from the *Rendering* dialog box to save the image to a file on your hard drive. Name the file **Kitchen.jpg** (jpeg file format).

You can now open the *Kitchen.jpg* file in Adobe Photoshop or insert it into a MS Word type program, or equivalent, to manipulate or print.

To toggle back to the normal hidden view, select **Show the Model** from the *Rendering* dialog box.

There are many things you can do to make the rendering look even better. You can add interior light fixtures and props (e.g., pictures on the wall, items on the countertop, and lawn furniture in the yard). Once you add interior lights, you can adjust the Sun Setting to nighttime and then render a night scene.

> *TIP: Setting the Output to Printer rather than Screen allows you to generate a higher resolution image. Thus, between the Quality setting and the Output setting you can create an extremely high quality rendering, but it might take hours if not days to process!*

Revit also gives you the ability to set a material to be self-illuminating. This will allow you to make a button on the dishwasher look like it is lit up or, if applied to the glass on the range door, like the light in the oven is on! You can also set a lamp shade to glow when a light source has been defined under it so it looks more realistic.

**FIGURE 14-4.7** Rendered view

You can quickly add another camera view to look at the other half of the kitchen. The ability to stretch the *Crop Region* allows you to create interesting views like the one below, which is really more like a panoramic view than a traditional camera view (Figure 14-4.8).

**FIGURE 14-4.8** Another rendered view

17. **Save** your project as **14-4.rvt**.

# Realistic Display Setting:

In addition to *Shade* and *Hidden Line* display settings you can also select *Realistic*. This will show the *Render Appearance* materials on your building without the need to do a full rendering. However, the shades and shadows are not nearly as realistic as a full rendering.

This is a great way to get an idea on how the materials look but you will find it best to minimize the use of this setting as Revit will run much slower.

# Duplicating a Material:

It is important to know how to properly duplicate a *Material* in your model so you do not unintentionally affect another *Material*. The information on this page is mainly for reference and does not need to be done in your model.

If you **Duplicate** a *Material* in your model, the **Appearance Asset** will be associated to the new *Material* AND the *Material* you copied it from! For example, in the image below, we will right-click on Carpet (1) and duplicate it. Before we duplicate it, notice the *Appearance Asset* named "RED" is not shared (arrow #3 in the image below).

Once you have duplicated a *Material*, notice the two carpet materials in this example; now indicate they both share the same *Appearance Asset*. Changing one will affect the other. Click the **Duplicate this asset** icon in the upper right (second image).

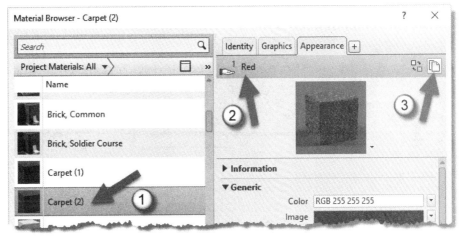

Once the *Appearance Asset* has been duplicated (third image), you can expand the information section and rename the asset. You can now make changes to this material without affecting other materials.

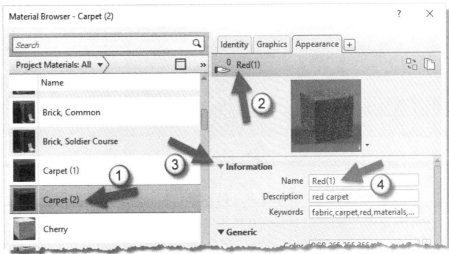

## Exercise 14-5:
## Adding People to the Rendering

Revit provides a few free RPC people to add to your renderings; RPC stands for Rich Photorealistic Content. These are files from a popular company that provides 3D photo content for use in renderings (http://www.archvision.com). You can buy additional content in groupings such as college students or per item. In addition to people, they offer items like cars, plants, trees, office equipment, etc.

## Loading Content into the Current Project

1. Open ex14-4.rvt and **Save As 14-5.rvt**.

2. Switch to the **First Floor** plan view.

3. Select the **Component** tool from the *Architecture* tab.

4. Click the **Load Family** button on the *Ribbon*.

5. Browse to the **Entourage** folder and select both the **RPC Male** and **RPC Female** files, using the Ctrl key to select both at once, and click **Open** to load them.

6. Place one **Male** and one **Female**, specified via the *Type Selector*, as shown in **Figure 14-5.1**.

FIGURE **14-5.1** Kitchen – RPC people added

The line in the circle (Figure 14-5.1) represents the direction a person is looking. You simply *Rotate* the object to make adjustments. The image below shows the RPC people that can be placed in your project. **Notice the two families each have multiple types.**

**FIGURE 14-5.2**
Type Selector – Properties Palette

7. Switch to your interior kitchen camera view.

8. Set the *Quality* setting to **Medium**.

9. Set the *Scheme* to **Kitchen**.

10. Click **Render**.

Additional RPC content can be purchased from ArchVision via their website: www.archvision.com. They also have a yearly subscription option which provides hundreds of trees, cars and people to add to your renderings.

Your rendering should now have people in it and look similar to **Figure 14-5.4**. Notice how the people cast shadows; remember the only light source is the sunlight coming through the two windows and the glass door. If you want to change the people, simply select them and pick from the *Type Selector*.

Adding people and other "props" gives your model a sense of scale and makes it look a little more realistic. After all, architecture is for people. These elements can be viewed from any angle. Try a new camera view from another angle to see how the people adjust to match the view and perspective; see Figure 14-5.3, front of the female model versus the side view below.

**FIGURE 14-5.3** Interior kitchen view with people added

**FIGURE 14-5.4** Interior kitchen view with people added

11. **Save** your project as **ex14-5.rvt**.

The image below shows all the transportation content available through Archvision. When using their subscription option, you have access to all of their content (including people, trees and more). Using the Archvision Dashboard program, you simply drag and drop content into Revit. Students should contact Archvision about special student options. These elements work in Realistic views, renderings and A360 Cloud renderings.

# Sketchy Lines

Be sure to Check out the **Sketchy Lines** options available via View Properties → **Graphic Display Options**. Tip: Also turn on **Smooth lines with anti-aliasing** when using the *Sketchy Lines* feature.

## Self-Exam:

The following questions can be used as a way to check your knowledge of this lesson. The answers can be found at the bottom of the page.

1. Creating a camera adds a view to the *Project Browser* list. (T/F)

2. Rendering materials are defined in Revit's *Materials* dialog box. (T/F)

3. After inserting a light fixture, you need to adjust several settings before rendering to get light from the fixture. (T/F)

4. You can adjust the season, which affects how the trees are rendered. (T/F)

5. Use the _____ tool to hide a large portion of the model.

## Review Questions:

The following questions may be assigned by your instructor as a way to assess your knowledge of this section. Your instructor has the answers to the review questions.

1. Draft renderings can be printed very large with no pixilation. (T/F)

2. You cannot get accurate lighting based on day/month/location. (T/F)

3. Adding components, i.e. families, to your project does not make the project file bigger. (T/F)

4. Creating photo-realistic renderings can take a significant amount of time for your computer to process. (T/F)

5. The RPC people can only be viewed from one angle. (T/F)

6. The RPC components do not cast shadows. (T/F)

7. Adjust the _____ to make more of a perspective view visible.

8. You use the _____ tool to load and insert RPC people.

9. You can adjust the Eye Elevation of the camera via the camera's _____.

10. What is the file size of (completed) Exercise 14-5? _____ MB

## Lesson 15
# Construction Documents Set:

This lesson will look at bringing everything you have drawn thus far together onto sheets. The sheets, once set up, are ready for plotting. Basically, you place the various views you have created on sheets. The scale for each view is based on the scale you set while drawing that view, which is important to have set correctly because it affects the text and symbol sizes. When finished setting up the sheets, you will have a set of drawings ready to print individually or all at once.

## Exercise 15-1:
## Setting up a Sheet

### Creating a Sheet View:

1. Open ex14-5.rvt and **Save As** 15-1.rvt.

2. Select **View → Sheet Composition → Sheet**.

Next Autodesk® Revit® will prompt you for a *Titleblock* to use. The template file you started with has two *titleblock families* from which to choose: 11 x 17 and 22 x 34 (Figure 15-1.1).

**FIGURE 15-1.1** Select a Titleblock

3. Select the **D 22x34 Horizontal** titleblock and click **OK**.

That's it; you have created a new sheet that is ready to have views and/or schedules placed on it!

*NOTE: A new view shows up in the Project Browser under the heading* Sheets. *Once you get an entire CD set ready, this list can be very long.*

Autodesk Revit also lets you create placeholder sheets which allow you to add sheets to the sheet index without the need to have a sheet show up in the *Project Browser*. This is helpful if a consultant, such as a food service designer, is not using Autodesk Revit. This feature allows you to add those sheets to the sheet index. Placeholder sheets can only be added in the sheet list schedule by using the *New Row* tool on the *Ribbon*. Once a placeholder sheet exists, it can be turned into a real sheet by selecting from the lower list in the dialog to the left.

**FIGURE 15-1.2** Initial Titleblock view

4. **Zoom in** to the sheet number area (lower right corner).

5. Adjust the text to look similar to **Figure 15-1.3**. Click on the text and edit it; make sure *Modify* is selected first.

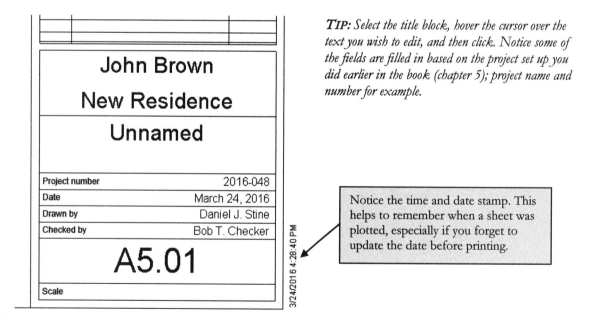

*TIP: Select the title block, hover the cursor over the text you wish to edit, and then click. Notice some of the fields are filled in based on the project set up you did earlier in the book (chapter 5); project name and number for example.*

Notice the time and date stamp. This helps to remember when a sheet was plotted, especially if you forget to update the date before printing.

**FIGURE 15-1.3** Revised Titleblock data

6. **Zoom out** so you can see the entire sheet (type ZF).

7. With the sheet fully visible, click and drag the **Living Room - East** label, under *Elevations (Interior elevations)*, from the *Project Browser* onto the sheet view. Let go of the mouse button once it is within the drawing window; do not click yet.

You will see a box that represents the extents of the view you are placing on the current sheet. If the box is larger than the sheet, this means the *View Scale* is to a scale that is too large. You would need to open the view and adjust the *View Scale*.

8. Move the *Viewport* around until the box is in the upper-right corner of the sheet (this can be repositioned later at any time) and click to place.

Your view should look similar to **Figure 15-1.4**.

**FIGURE 15-1.4** Sheet with Living Room view placed on it

9. Click the mouse in a white area, not on any lines, to deselect the *Living Room - East* view. Notice the extents box goes away.

**FIGURE 15-1.5** Drawing title

10. **Zoom in** on the lower left corner to view the drawing identification symbol that Revit automatically added (Figure 15-1.5).

*NOTE: Each drawing placed on a sheet automatically gets a number, starting with one. The next drawing you add will be number two.*

The view name, from the *Project Browser*, is listed as the drawing title. This is another reason to rename the elevation and section views as you create them.

Also notice that the drawing scale is listed. Again, this comes from the *View Scale* setting for the *Living Room - East* view.

As you can see, if you added furniture to the living room, the furniture shows up; normally this would be turned off. You can turn these off using the same technique covered later in this chapter for the trees in the exterior elevations.

## Setting up the Floor Plans:

Setting up floor plans is easy; actually, they are already set up from the template you started with.

11. From the *Sheets* section in the *Project Browser*, double-click on the sheet named **A1 – First Floor Plan** to open it.

As you can see, the floor plan is already set up on a sheet. Again, a few things can be turned off (i.e., trees, RPC People) per the techniques covered next. You would also want to move the exterior elevation tags closer to the building so they are within the title block if they are not already.

12. Adjust the location of the plan view on the sheet if needed. Click and drag to move it.

13. Change the sheet number to **A2.01**, and then close the First Floor Plan, *Sheet*.

## Setting up the Exterior Elevations:

Next you will set up the exterior elevations. Again, the sheets are already set up but the views have not been placed on the sheets like the floor plans have.

14. Open Sheet **A6 – Elevations**, and drag the *South* elevation view onto the sheet. Place the drawing near the bottom and centered on the sheet.

Your drawing should look similar to Figure 15-1.6.

**FIGURE 15-1.6** South exterior elevation

Next, you will turn off the trees in the *South* view. Normally you would turn them off in all views. However, you will only turn them off in the *South* view to show that you can control visibility per view on a sheet.

15. In the sheet view, click on the *South* exterior elevation view to select it; the outer extents rectangle is called the *viewport* (Figure 15-1.6).

16. Now **right-click** and select **Activate View** from the pop-up menu. *TIP: You can also double-click within the view to activate it.*

At this point you are in the viewport and can make changes to the project model to control visibility, which is what you will do next.

17. Turn on **View Cropping** and **Show Crop Region** on the *View Control Bar*; adjust the crop region to minimize the space needed by the view on the sheet. When finished, hide the crop region.

18. Make sure nothing is selected. With nothing selected in the view, the *Properties Palette* is displaying the activated view's properties, just as if you were in the view and not the sheet.

19. Click the **Edit** button next to *Visibility/Graphics Overrides*. *TIP:* Or type VV.

20. In the *Visibility* dialog **uncheck Planting**.

21. Close the open dialog box.

22. Right-click anywhere in the drawing area and select **Deactivate View** from the pop-up menu. *TIP: Double-clicking outside of view also will deactivate the view.*

Now the trees are turned off for the *South* elevation; if you would have had another elevation view on this same sheet, the trees would still be visible for that view.

23. Add the ***North*** elevation to the **A7 – Elevations** *Sheet.*

> *TIP: You may need to switch to the North view and turn on the* Crop *and* Crop Display *icons on the View Control Bar to make the area placed on the sheet smaller so it will fit; when finished, turn off* Crop Display *but leave* Crop View *turned on. Or use the* Activate View *option just covered.*

Now you will stop for a moment and notice that Revit is automatically referencing the drawings as you place them on sheets.

24. Switch to ***First Floor*** (Figure 15-1.7).

Notice in Figure 15-1.7 that the number A6 represents the sheet number that the drawing can be found on. The number one (1) is the drawing number to look for on sheet A6. The empty tag is the enlarged elevation view you set up earlier in the book; it has not been placed on a sheet yet so it is not filled in.

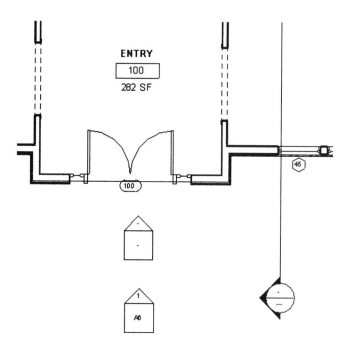

**FIGURE 15-1.7** First Floor – elevation tag filled-in

## Setting up Sections:

25. Open *Sheet* **A8 – Building Sections** and place *Cross Section 1.*

26. Open *Sheet* **A9 – Building Sections** and place the *Longitudinal Section* view on the *Sheet.*

27. Switch to *First Floor* plan view and zoom into the area shown in Figure 15-1.9.

**FIGURE 15-1.8** A9 – Building Sections sheet

Notice, again, that the reference bubbles are automatically filled in when the referenced view is placed on a sheet. If the drawing is moved to another sheet, the reference bubbles are automatically updated.

You can also see in Figure 15-1.8 that the reference bubbles on the building sections are filled in.

**FIGURE 15-1.9** First Floor – Section ref's filled in

## Set up the Remaining Sheets:

Next you set up sheets for the remaining views that have yet to be placed on a sheet, except for the 3D views.

28. Add the remaining views to the appropriate sheets; if one does not exist you can create a new sheet.

**Question:** On a large project with hundreds of views, how do I know for sure if I have placed every view on a sheet?

**Answer:** Revit has a feature called *Browser Organization* that can hide all the views that have been placed on a sheet. You will try this next.

Take a general look at the *Project Browser* to see how many views are listed.

29. Select **View → Windows → User Interface** (*drop-down*) **→ Browser Organization.**

30. On the *Views* tab, click the checkbox next to **not on sheets** (Figure 15-1.10).

31. Click **OK**.

32. Notice the list in the *Project Browser* is now smaller (Figure 15-1.11).

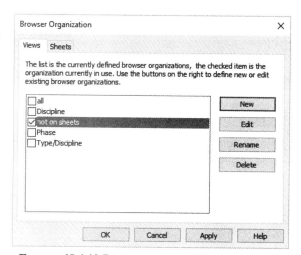

FIGURE 15-1.10 Browser Organization dialog

The *Project Browser* now only shows drawing views that have not been placed onto a sheet. Of course, you could have a few views that do not need to be placed on a sheet, but this feature will help eliminate errors. Also notice the label at the top: *Views (not on sheets)*; this tells you what mode or filter the *Project Browser* is in.

Next you will reset the *Project Browser*.

33. Open *Browser Organization* again and check the box next to **all** and click **OK** to close the dialog box.

*TIP: You can also select the title* Views *at the top of the Project Browser and toggle between filter types via the Type Selector.*

FIGURE 15-1.11 Project Browser

## Sheets with Design Options:

Finally, you will set up a sheet to show the two *Design Options*.

34. Create a *Sheet* named ***Entry Options*** and number it **A100**.

35. Place both *Entry – Option 2* 3D views on the new sheet and change the scale to **⅛″ = 1′-0″**.

   ***TIP:*** *Select the placed view and change the scale in the Properties Palette.*

36. **Save** your project as **ex15-1.rvt**.

Each 3D view has its *Visibility* modified to show the desired *Design Options*. When a view is placed on a sheet, those settings are preserved.

FIGURE 15-1.12 Entry Options Sheet; two views with Design Options added

# Exercise 15-2:
# Sheet Index

Revit has the ability to create a *Sheet List* (or sheet index) automatically. This feature uses the same schedule creation interface previously covered. Whenever a sheet is added or removed from the project, this *Sheet List* will automatically update. You can even use the *Sheet List* to make changes to the sheet. For example, if you noticed a few sheets were not all uppercase you could change them in the *Sheet List* and the sheet itself would update as it represents the same information. You will study this feature now.

## Creating a Sheet List View

 Sheet List

1. Open ex15-1.rvt and **Save As** ex15-2.

2. Select **View → Create → Schedules** *(down-arrow)* **→ Sheet List**.

You are now in the *Sheet List Properties* dialog box. Here you specify which fields you want in the sheet index and how to sort the list (Figure 15-2.1).

3. Add **Sheet Number** and **Sheet Name** to the right (click *Add* →).

4. Click **OK**.

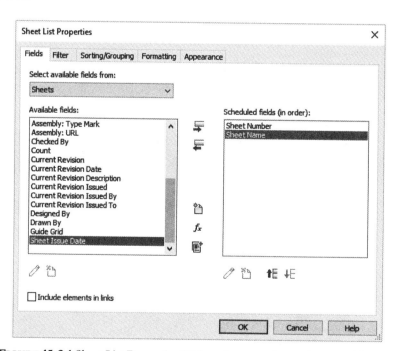

**FIGURE 15-2.1** Sheet List Properties Dialog; sheet number and name added

Now you should notice that the *Sheet Names* are cut off because the column is not wide enough (Figure 15-2.2). You will adjust this next.

5. Move your cursor over the right edge of the *Sheet List* table and click-and-drag to the right until you can see the entire name (Figure 15-2.2).

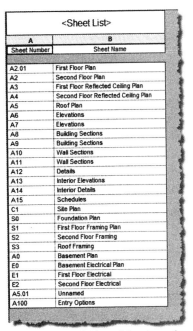

**FIGURE 15-2.2** Sheet List view; notice sheet names are cut off in right column

**FIGURE 15-2.3** Sheet List view; sheet names are now visible

## Adjusting Which Sheets Show Up in the List:

Looking at the *Sheet List* (Figure 15-2.3), you decide to remove the *Entry design options* sheet (i.e., sheet A100) from the list as it is not part of the construction document set.

As with other schedules, this is live data which is directly connected to the model. If you change a sheet number here, the number will change throughout the project. If you delete a number (i.e., a row), Revit will delete the sheet from the project.

You will look at the option that allows you to remove a sheet from the list without deleting the sheet.

6. Right-click on sheet **A100** in the sheet list and select **Delete Row**. You will NOT actually delete this sheet, so <u>do not click **OK**</u>.

You will get a warning stating the sheet will be deleted and what you should do if you only want to remove the sheet from the *Sheet List*.

7. Click **Cancel**.

8.  Select *Sheet* **A100 – Entry Options** in the *Project Browser* and click **Properties**.

9.  Uncheck **Appears In Sheet List** (Figure 15-2.4) and then click **Apply**.

**FIGURE 15-2.4** Properties for sheet A100

Notice the *Sheet* was removed from the *Sheet List* view but is still in the project.

10. In the *Sheet List*, right-click on sheet **A13 Interior Elevations** and select **Delete Row(s)** from the menu.

11. Click **OK**.

Not only was the sheet removed from the *Sheet List*, it was also deleted from the project. However, any views placed on a sheet are not deleted from the project. Next, you will renumber a sheet via the *Sheet List*.

12. Click in the cell with the sheet number **A5.01** and change the number to read **A13**.

Now an existing sheet has been renumbered and so has all the detail, elevation and section bubbles that point to this sheet.

13. In the *Properties Palette*, click the **Edit…** button next to **Sorting/Grouping**.

14. Set *Sort By* to **Sheet Number**.

15. Click **OK** to close the open dialog box.

Now the sheets should be sorted correctly, including the sheet you just renumbered.

*TIP: It is possible to create a custom parameter and sort the sheets using the information entered there. This allows you to place the sheets in any order you wish. Usually the "C" (i.e., civil) sheets are before the "A" (i.e., architectural) sheets. So, for example, all the "C" sheets could have the value "02" entered in the custom parameter, and the "A" sheets could all have the value "03" entered. Then, in sorting and grouping, you would sort by your custom parameter and then by sheet number. You can create the custom parameter on the* Fields *tab in the* Sheet List *schedule (Figure 15-2.1) by clicking the* Add Parameter *button.*

## Setting up a Title Sheet:

Now you will create a title sheet to place your sheet index on.

16. Create a new sheet:
    a. *Number:* **T1**
    b. *Name:* **Title Sheet**

17. From the *Schedules/Quantities* category of the *Project Browser*, place the view named **Sheet List** on the *Title Sheet* via drag-and-drop.

18. With the schedule selected on the sheet, drag the column grips so each row is only one line. (Figure 15-2.5).

19. Create a new text style named **1″ Arial**, and adjust the settings accordingly.

    *TIP: Select the* Text *tool, click* Edit Type *and then* Duplicate.

| Sheet List | |
|---|---|
| Sheet Number | Sheet Name |
| A2.01 | First Floor Plan |
| A2 | Second Floor Plan |
| A3 | First Floor Reflected Ceiling Plan |
| A4 | Second Floor Reflected Ceiling Plan |
| A5 | Roof Plan |
| A6 | Elevations |
| A7 | Elevations |
| A8 | Building Sections |
| A9 | Building Sections |
| A10 | Wall Sections |
| A11 | Wall Sections |
| A12 | Details |
| A13 | Interior Elevations |
| A14 | Interior Details |
| A15 | Schedules |
| C1 | Site Plan |
| S0 | Foundation Plan |
| S1 | First Floor Framing Plan |
| S2 | Second Floor Framing |
| S3 | Roof Framing |
| A0 | Basement Plan |
| E0 | Basement Electrical Plan |
| E1 | First Floor Electrical |
| E2 | Second Floor Electrical |
| A5.01 | Unnamed |
| A100 | Entry Options |

**FIGURE 15-2.5** Adjusting column width

20. Add large text across the top of the sheet that reads "NEW RESIDENCE FOR JOHN BROWN" (Figure 15-2.6).

Next, you will place one of your rendered images that you saved to file, which is a raster image. If you have not created a raster image, you should refer back to Lesson 13 and create one now. Otherwise, you can use any PNG or JPG file on your hard drive if necessary.

If you used the *Save to Project* feature, you can simply drag one of the images listed under *Renderings* from the *Project Browser*. The interior kitchen rendering was added to the title sheet using this method. Here you can see Revit has added a *Drawing Title* tag beneath the image, which would allow you to reference this image from another location.

21. Select **Insert → Import → Image**.

Image

22. Browse to your JPG or PNG raster image file, select it and click **Open** to place the Image.

23. Click on your *Title Sheet* to locate the image; use the corner grips to resize the image.

Your sheet should look similar to Figure 15-2.6.

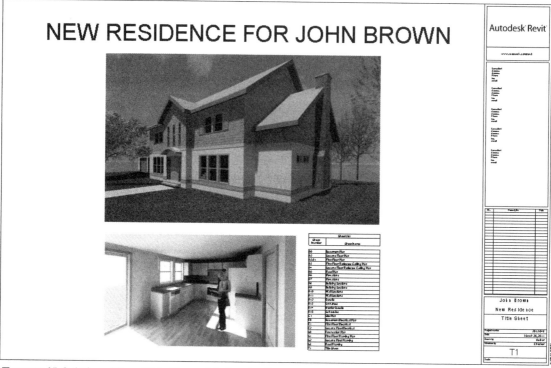

FIGURE 15-2.6 Sheet View: Title Sheet with drawing list, text and image added

24. Select **Insert → Import → Manage Images**.

You are now in the *Raster Image* dialog which gives you a little information about the image and allows you to delete it from the project (Figure 15-2.7).

*FYI: You can delete a view from a Sheet without deleting the view from the project. Also, you can only place a view on one sheet; you would have to duplicate the view in order to have that view repeated.*

*TIP: You can use the standard modification tools on raster images (e.g., Move, Copy, Rotate and Resize). You can also control the draw order to make sure your leaders pointing at the image show up.*

FIGURE 15-2.7 Manage Images dialog

25. Click **OK** to close the *Manage Images* dialog.

# Exporting a 3D DWFx File:

The *3D DWFx* file is an easy way to share your project file with others without the need to give them your editable Revit file or the need for the recipient to have Revit installed.

> *NOTE: You can download Revit from Autodesk's website and run it in* viewer mode. *It's free – full Revit with no save functionality.*

The 3D DWFx file is much smaller in file size than the original Revit file. Also, *Autodesk Design Review* is a free DWF viewer which can be downloaded from www.autodesk.com.

26. Switch to your *Default 3D* view.

You must be in a 3D view for the 3D DWF feature to work. If you are not in a 3D view, you will get 2D DWF files:

27. Select **File Tab → Export → DWF**.

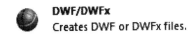

**DWF/DWFx**
Creates DWF or DWFx files.

28. Click the **Next** button in the lower right (Figure 15-2.8); specify a file name and location for the DWF file and then click **Save**.

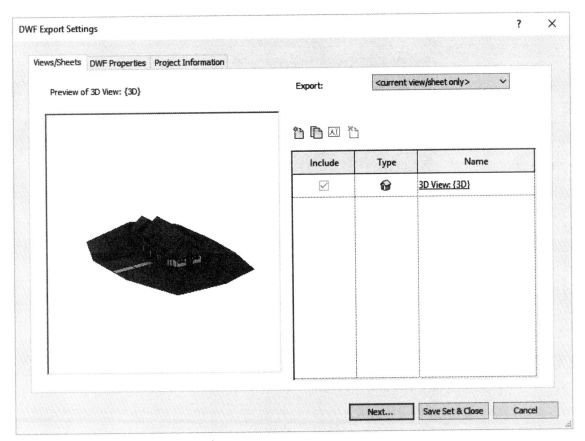

FIGURE **15-2.8** DWF export options

That's all you need to do to create the file. Now you can email it to the client or a product representative to get a cost estimate on windows, for example.

The 3D DWF file is about 2mb, whereas the Revit project file is 13 MB. Your file sizes will vary slightly based on factors like the number of families loaded. In many cases, networks and servers are set up so they cannot receive large files via email, so the 3D DWF is very useful.

The DWF viewer can be downloaded from http://usa.autodesk.com/design-review/. Once installed, you can access it from *Start → All Programs → Autodesk → Autodesk Design Review 2017*. You can zoom, orbit and select objects. Notice the information displayed on the left when the front door is selected (see image below). Also notice, under the *Windows* heading the sizes and quantities are listed.

> **TIP:** *Autodesk Design Review 2017 is a free download from Autodesk. This is their full-featured DWF viewer and markup utility!*

This DWF file can also be used in conjunction with **Autodesk Quantity Takeoff** to develop cost estimates for your project. See Autodesk's website for more information.

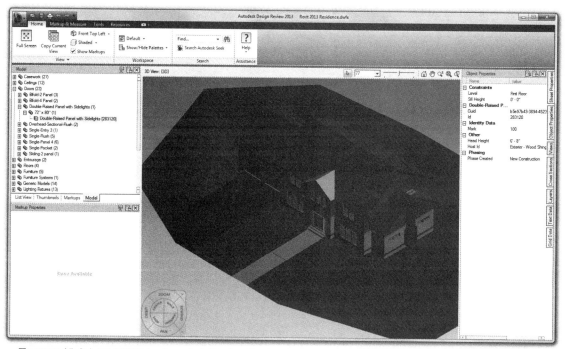

**FIGURE 15-2.9** 3D DWF in Autodesk Design Review

29. **Save** your project as **ex15-2.rvt**.

## Exercise 15-3:
## Printing a Set of Drawings

Revit has the ability to print an entire set of drawings, in addition to printing individual sheets. You will study this now.

### Printing a Set of Drawings:

1. **Open ex15-2.rvt.**

2. Select **File Tab → Print → Print.**

3. In the *Print Range* area, click the option **Selected views/sheets** (Figure 15-3.1).

4. Click the **Select…** button within the *Print Range* area.

**FIGURE 15-3.1** Print dialog box

You should now see a listing of all *Views* and *Sheets* (Figure 15-3.2).

Notice at the bottom you can show both *Sheets* and *Views*, or each separately. Because you are printing a set of drawing you will want to see only the sheets.

**FIGURE 15-3.2** Set tool for printing

5.  **Uncheck** the **Views** option.

The list is now limited to just *Sheets* that have been set up in your project.

6.  Select all the drawing sheets except **A100**.

7.  Click **OK** to close the *View/Sheet Set* dialog.

8.  IF YOU ACTUALLY WANT TO PRINT A FULL SET OF DRAWINGS, you can do so now by clicking OK. Otherwise click **Cancel**.

9.  You do not need to save the file at this time.

> *FYI: Once you have selected the sheets to be plotted and click OK, you are prompted to save the list. This will save the list of selected drawings to a name you choose. Then, the next time you need to print those sheets you can select the name from the drop-down list at the top (Figure 15-3.2). On very large projects (e.g., 20 floor plan sheets) you could have a Plans list saved, a Laboratory Interior Elevations list saved, etc.*

If you have software on your computer to create PDF files, you can check the "combine sheets" option in the *Print* dialog (15-3.3). Many design firms create a multi-sheet PDF file to send to a print shop so they can produce the final printed sheets for the contractors to bid from. It is also possible to do the same thing with a multi-sheet DWF file, but fewer people have Autodesk's Design Review installed than Adobe's PDF Reader. However, both viewers are free; the PDF format is used by virtually everyone, not just the design industry. Another interesting option is 3D PDF files. Check out **Tetra4D.com** or **Bluebeam.com** for information on an add-in they sell for Revit. A 3D PDF can be viewed by anyone with the free Adobe Reader installed. **Check out the 3D PDF appendix via the online files.**

# Good Luck!

You should now have a basic understanding of the Autodesk Revit software. **Good luck with your future Revit projects!** Be sure to visit www.augi.com to share knowledge with other Revit users.

## Self-Exam:

The following questions can be used as a way to check your knowledge of this lesson. The answers can be found at the bottom of the page.

1. You have to manually fill in the reference bubbles after setting up the sheets. (T/F)

2. You cannot control the visibility of objects per *viewport*. (T/F)

3. It is possible to see a listing of only the views that have not been placed on a sheet via the *Project Browser*. (T/F)

4. You only have to enter your name on one titleblock, not all. (T/F)

5. Use the _____ tool to create another drawing sheet.

## Review Questions:

The following questions may be assigned by your instructor as a way to assess your knowledge of this section. Your instructor has the answers to the review questions.

1. You need to use a special tool from the *Ribbon* to edit text in the titleblock. (T/F)

2. The template you started with has two titleblocks to choose from. (T/F)

3. You only have to enter the project name on one sheet, not all. (T/F)

4. The scale of a drawing placed on a sheet is determined by the scale set in that view's *Properties*. (T/F)

5. You can save a list of drawing sheets to be plotted. (T/F)

6. Use the _____ tool to edit the model from a sheet view.

7. The reference bubbles will not automatically update if a drawing is moved to another sheet. (T/F)

8. On new sheets, the sheet number on the titleblock will increase by one from the previous sheet number. (T/F)

9. DWF files can consist of an entire set of drawings which a client/owner can view with a free download, similar to Adobe PDF files. (T/F)

10. It is not possible to remove a sheet from the *Sheet List* without deleting that sheet from the project. (T/F)

**Notes:**

# Lesson 16
# Introduction to Phasing and Worksharing:

This chapter will start a small new exercise designed to explore two important features in Revit: Phasing and Worksharing. Unless a project is brand new, it will be using Revit's phasing feature. Additionally, if a project needs to be worked on by more than one person at a time, it will be utilizing Revit's Worksharing feature.

**Note: This tutorial can be done at any time separate from the rest of the book.**

## Exercise 16-1:
## Introduction to Phasing

Any project that involves remodeling or an addition should use the **Phases** feature in Revit. Revit is often referred to as three-dimensional modeling software. However, Revit's ability to manage elements over time is considered a fourth-dimension. This section will provide an introduction to Revit's phasing feature.

The **Phasing** dialog (Figure 16-1.1) is accessible from the Manage tab.

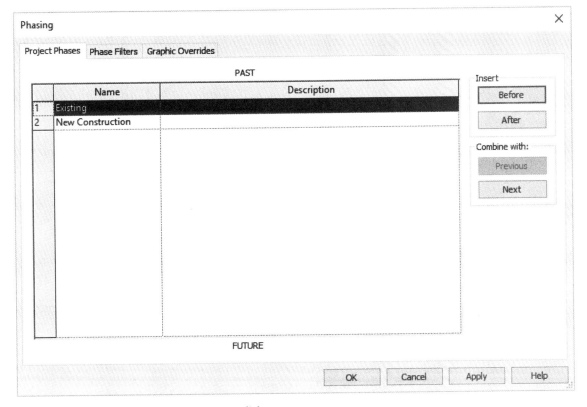

**FIGURE 16-1.1** Project Phases tab; Phasing dialog

Most existing/remodel projects have two phases (Figure 16-1.1):
- Existing
- New Construction

Additional phases can be created, such as Phase 2 and Phase 3 (in this case, New Construction might be renamed to Phase 1). There should never be a phase called "Demolition," as Revit handles this automatically (more on this later).

Revit manages Phases with two simple sets of parameters:
- **Elements:**
  - Phase Created
  - Phase Demolished
- **Views**
  - Phase
  - Phase Filter

Among these four parameters, Revit is able to manage elements over time and control when to display them.

### Element Phase Properties

As just mentioned, every model element in Revit has two phase-related parameters as shown for a selected wall in Figure 16-1.2.

The **Phase Created** parameter is automatically assigned when an element is created—the setting matches the phase setting of the view the element is created in. Put another way, in a floor plan view with the Phase set to *New Construction*, all model elements created in that view will have their Phase Created parameter set to *New Construction*.

FIGURE 16-1.2 Element phase properties

The **Phase Demolished** parameter is never set automatically. Revit has no way of knowing if something should be demolished.

## View Phase Properties

Every view has two phase-related parameters, as shown for the floor plan view in Figure 16-1.3. Any elements added in this view would be designated as existing.

The **Phase** parameter can be set to any Phase that exists in the project. This setting can be changed at any time; however, it is best to have one floor plan view for each phase—thus, the Phase setting is not typically changed.

This setting represents the point in time the model is being viewed.

**TIP:** Create existing and demolition views in a company/personal template.

**FIGURE 16-1.3** View phase properties – nothing selected

## Phase Filters:

The **Phase Filter** setting controls which model elements appear in the view based on their phase settings.

To understand how the Phase Filter setting affects the view, look at **Manage → Phasing → Phase Filters** (See Figure 16-1.4).

Elements will appear in one of three ways:

- **By Category**    - Displayed as normal, no changes
- **Overridden**    - Modified based on Graphic Overrides tab settings
- **Not Displayed**    - These elements are hidden

Be careful not to confuse the *Phase Filter* column headings, New, Existing, Demolished and Temporary, as literal phases—they are not. Rather, they are a 'current condition' (aka **Phase Status**) based on a view's Phase setting and the element's Phase Created & Phase Demolished settings.

For example, the 'current condition' of an *Existing* wall in an *Existing* view is considered <u>New</u> because the phases are the same. Think of it as if you are standing in the year 1980, looking at a wall built in 1980—it is a new wall. Similarly, a *New Construction* wall in a *New Construction* view is also considered <u>New</u> in terms of how the Phase Filters work (now all *Existing* walls are considered <u>Existing</u>). You are now standing in the year 2015 looking at a wall built in 1980.

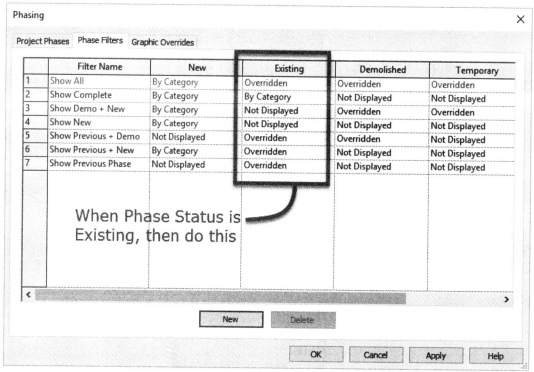

**FIGURE 16-1.4** Phase Filters; Phasing dialog

The three images below are of the same model as seen in three different views—each with a different combination of Phase and Phase Filter settings. Each condition will be explained in depth on the next pages.

**View Settings:**

| | | | |
|---|---|---|---|
| *Phase:* | Existing | New Construction | New Construction |
| *Phase Filter:* | Show Complete | Show Previous + Demo | Show Previous + New |

**Existing Conditions:**
When modeling an existing building, create a
**Level 1 – Existing** plan view; do this for each
level in the building. This view will have the
following phase-related settings:

- Phase: **Existing**
- Phase Filter: **Show Complete**

Any model element created in this view will
automatically have Phase Created set to Existing.

Everything in the drawing to the right has the
Phase Created set to Existing. FYI: One wall and
both doors have their Phase Demolished set to
New Construction—however, we cannot visually
see that here.

**The Phase Status is actually considered New
in this view.** The phase of the element matches
the phase of the view. Thus, because the Show
Complete Phase Filter has New set to By
Category, there are no overrides applied to this
view. We see the normal lineweights and fill
patterns.

**FIGURE 16-1.5** Existing view

**Demolition Conditions:**
When demolition is required, create a **Level 1 –
Demo** plan view; do this for each level in the
building. This view will have the following phase-
related settings:

- Phase: **New Construction**
- Phase Filter: **Show Previous + Demo**

Often, new Revit users think it strange that the
demo view needs to be set to New
Construction—given no new elements appear in
this view. However, looking at the existing view
just covered—all existing elements (even ones set
to be demolished) are considered "new."
Therefore, the "time slider," if you will, needs to
be moved past Existing to invoke the Phase
Demolished setting. If this is still confusing, it
should make more sense in the tutorial.

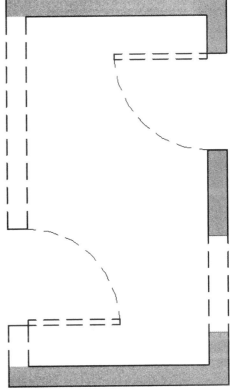

**FIGURE 16-1.6** Demolition view

In Figure 16-1.6, the wall and two doors which appear dashed have their Phase Demolished set to New Construction. Recall that the view's phase is set to New Construction. In the lower right, a new door (i.e. Phase Created = New Construction) automatically demolishes the existing wall.

Notice the Phase Filter **Show Previous + Demo** has the <u>Demolished</u> *Phase Status* set to **Overridden**. So if any element with the Phase Created setting is set to a phase which occurs prior to the Phase setting of the current view, **and** the same element has a Phase Demolished setting that matches the current view's Phase setting, then it will show demolished.

**FYI:** If this project had a Phase named Phase 2, no existing elements set to be demolished in Phase 1 (i.e., New Construction in our example) could be shown in a view that's phase is set to Phase 2. Those elements simply do not exist anymore, and there is no reason to ever show them in this future context.

One final note on this demolition view: because Revit inherently understands the need to demolish elements, **it is never necessary to have a Demolition phase**.

**New Conditions:**

All Revit templates come with the default plan views set to New Construction. For projects with existing and demolition conditions, it might be helpful to rename these views to something like **Level 1 – New** (similar for each level). This view will have the following phase-related settings:

- Phase:  **New Construction**
- Phase Filter:  **Show Previous + New**

The door and curtain wall shown in the Figure 16-1.7 have their Phase Created set to New Construction. The existing walls are shaded due to the Phase Filter having an override applied to existing elements (more on this later).

Demolished openings present a unique situation in Revit. When an opening, e.g., door or window, is demolished, Revit automatically infills the opening with a wall. By default, this wall is the same type as the host wall (this can be selected and changed to another type). This special wall does not have any phase settings and it cannot be deleted. If an opening in the wall is required, then the wall needs to be hidden or an opening family added. If the demolished door is deleted this special wall will also be deleted.

**FIGURE 16-1.7** New construction view

The Phase Filter used here has the Demolished items set to Not Displayed. Also, the Existing items are set to Overridden, which is why the existing walls are filled with a gray fill pattern. The overrides will be covered next.

**TIP:** Smaller projects might show the demo in the new construction plans, in which case the <u>Show All</u> Phase Filter might work better.

### Phase Related Graphic Overrides

When the Phase Filter has a **Phase Status** set to **Overridden**, we need to look at the Graphic Overrides tab in the Phasing dialog to see what that means (Figure 16-1.8).

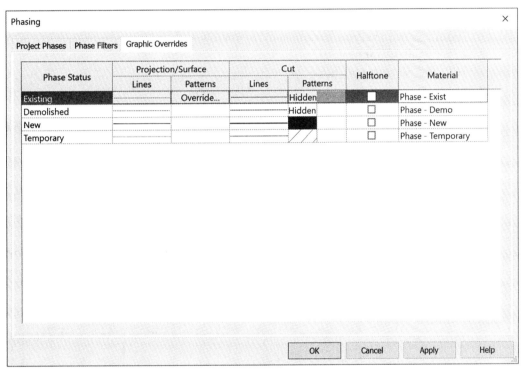

**FIGURE 16-1.8** Graphic Overrides tab; Phasing dialog

In the context of a given view, if elements are considered Existing, and the selected Phase Filter has existing set to Overridden—then the settings for the Existing row shown above are applied.

All the walls being cut by the View Range in plan will have **black** lines with a lineweight of **3** (Figure 16-1.9). Simply click in the box below Cut/Lines to see these settings.

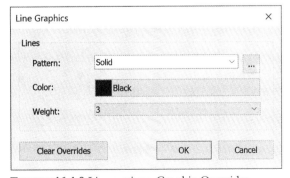

**FIGURE 16-1.9** Line settings; Graphic Overrides

Existing walls, in this example, will also have a solid fill [background] pattern set to gray (Figure 16-1.10). This convention is helpful to clearly delineate existing walls from new walls in printed bidding and construction documents.

**FYI:** Phase state overrides will override nearly all other graphic settings in the view (view Filter being an exception.)

In Figure 16-1.8, Graphics Overrides tab, the **Hidden** setting for the Demolished row (Phase Status) means that the Visibility option has been unchecked (compare Figure 16-1.10). Any blank boxes have no overrides and Revit will still use the By Category equivalent.

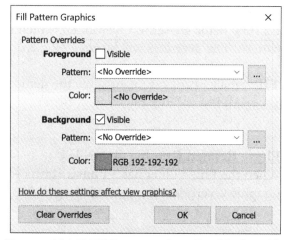

**FIGURE 16-1.10** Fill Pattern settings; Graphic Overrides

Also in Figure 16-1.8, Graphics Overrides tab, notice there are several overrides applied to the New phase status. However, notice in Figure 16-1.4, Phase Filters tab, nothing in the New column is set to Overridden. Thus, the overrides for New do not apply to anything in the entire project currently.

**Phasing and Rooms**

The Room element has only one phase parameter: Phase. This parameter is set based on the Phase setting of the view it is placed in. However, this parameter is read-only and cannot be changed.

**FIGURE 16-1.11** Phase setting for Room elements in existing view

In the image above, the view phase is set to Existing. If the view's phase is changed to anything other than existing, the Rooms and Room Tags will be hidden. Rooms are not really model elements that are built in the real world, so they are handled a little differently. As we will see in a moment, when walls are set to be demolished, Revit would not be able to maintain to existing Room elements in the new, larger area in the building. Thus, Rooms only exist per phase. The unfortunate side effect to this is that existing Rooms which have no changes need to have another Room element added for each Phase in the project. The room name and number are manually entered each time and are not connected in any way between phases.

> **TIP:** It is possible to Copy/Paste existing Rooms with no changes into a new view. This will save time retyping room names and numbers. However, there is still no connection between the two phases.

In the image below, we see the same model with a wall and door demolished. The Rooms and Room Tags shown are completely separate elements from those shown in the existing view.

**FIGURE 16-1.12** Phase setting for Room elements in new construction view

### Phasing and Annotation

Most annotation elements are not affected by phasing; they are view specific and can tag an element whether it is New Construction or Existing. However, beware of a few exceptions.

View tags such as Sections, Elevations and Callouts all have Phase and Phase Filter settings. Actually, when these elements are selected, the properties presented in the Properties Palette are the same as the view properties seen when that item's view is active. The tag and view are connected—that is why the view is deleted when the section tag is deleted.

If a View's Phase setting is changed from New Construction to Existing, all the view tags will be hidden in that view (not deleted).

One more exception is that tags will disappear if the element they are tagging disappears due to phase-related view setting adjustments.

## Exercise 16-2:
## Introduction to Worksharing

When a Revit project requires more than one person to work on it, the Worksharing feature must be used. The feature is fairly simple, but everyone with access to the project must know a few basic rules to ensure things go smoothly.

Projects started from a template do not have Worksharing enabled. These projects can only have one person working in them at a time—just like most other files, e.g., a Word, Excel, AutoCAD, etc. file.

### Worksharing Concept

The basic concept of Worksharing can be described with the help of the graphic below. When a regular Revit project file has Worksharing enabled, it becomes a **Central File**. The Central File is stored on the server where all staff have access (normal Read/Write access). **Once a Central File is created, it is typically never opened directly again.** Individual users work in what is called a **Local File**, which is a copy of the Central File, usually saved on the local C drive of the computer they are working on. When modifications are made to the Local File, the Central File is NOT automatically updated. However, the modified elements ARE checked out in that user's name—other users cannot modify those elements until they are checked back in. When a Local File is **Synchronized with Central**, the delta changes are saved; that is, only changes the user made are 'pushed' to the Central File, and then only changes found in the Central File, since the last Sync, and 'pulled' down (thus, the two way arrow). All elements checked out are typically relinquished during a Sync with Central. There is no technical limit to the number of users, though when there are more than 10 users the project can become sluggish.

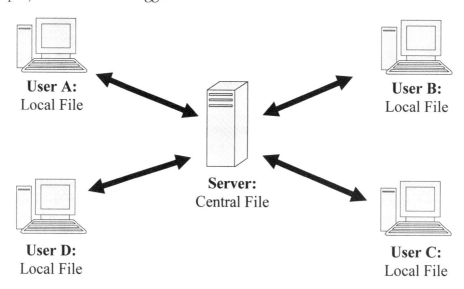

FIGURE 16-2.1 Revit project Worksharing concept

Overall, this system is very stable and has very few issues.

> **FYI:** Revit Worksharing does not work on cloud storage services such as Dropbox. There is too much latency in the network and several problems will be created including possible file corruption. There have been recent developments in using Revit Worksharing over the internet, but they involve Revit-specific software and/or hardware.

### Enabling Worksharing

In just a few clicks of the mouse, Revit's Worksharing feature can be enabled; this section will describe how.

The main Worksharing tools are conveniently located on the Status Bar (Figure 16-2.2). These same tools, plus a few others, are located on the Collaboration tab in the Ribbon. The average user can get by with just the Status Bar tools, but we have to start on the Ribbon.

**FIGURE 16-2.2** Worksharing tools on the Ribbon

To enable Worksharing do this:
- Ensure project file is in a shared location on a server
- Open the Revit project
- Click **Collaborate** on the Ribbon shown in Figure 16-2.2
- With **Collaborate with your network** selected, click **OK** (Figure 16-2.3)
- **Save** the project
- Click **Yes** (Figure 16-2.4)

**FIGURE 16-2.3** Enabling Worksharing (Collaboration)

The project file now has Worksharing enabled. **At this point the project file should be closed and all users will create a Local File** (covered in the next section). There is typically no reason to ever open this file again, even if only one person will be working on the project. It is not necessarily bad for someone to open the Central File, even with others working in Local Files, but following this rule will help minimize issues.

The option to collaborate using A360, shown in Figure 16-2.3, is a paid cloud service offered by Autodesk to allow design firms from different offices to work on the same Revit model.

Once Worksharing is enabled, two folders are created next to the Central File—one contains the same name as the project file (Figure 16-2.5). The "temp" folder only exists while the Central File is open.

**Important: The Central File cannot be moved and the folders defining the path to the file cannot be changed.**

There is a special set of steps required if the Central File needs to be moved. This involves opening the Central File, or a Local File, **Detached From Central**—which is discussed more later on.

**FIGURE 16-2.4** Worksharing related notice

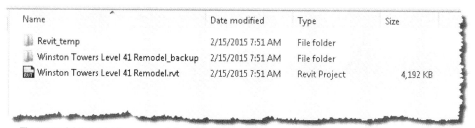

**FIGURE 16-2.5** Folder created for Worksharing

## Creating a Local File

Once a Central File has been created there is really no reason to ever open it directly again. Rather, each user creates a Local File to work in. This section describes how to do that.

The steps to create a Local File are simple:

- Open Revit
    - Use the desktop icon or start menu
    - <u>Do not</u> double-click on the Central File from Windows Explorer
- Click **Open**
- Browse to, and select, the Central File
- Ensure **Create New Local** is <u>checked</u> (Figure 16-2.6)
    - This should be checked by default when a Central File is selected
- Click the **Open** button

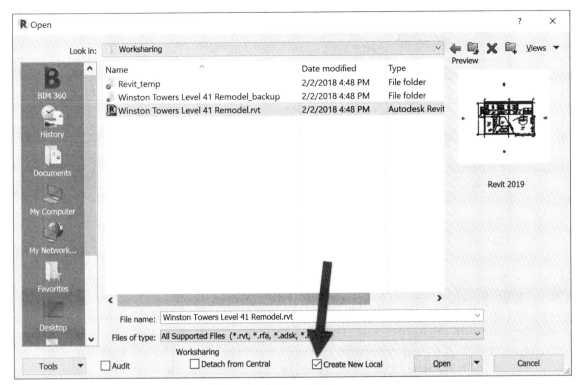

**FIGURE 16-2.6** Create New Local check box; Revit Open dialog

The **Create New Local** option copies the Central File to the user's local hard drive (Figure 16-2.7). The file is located based on the "Default path for user files" setting in the **Options → File Locations** dialog. The local file has a slightly different name: **Central Filename + Username**. Once the open process is done, this user is in the newly copied Local File.

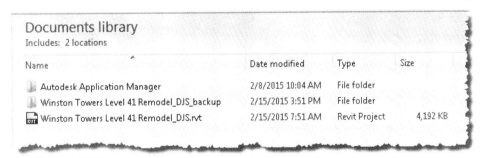

**FIGURE 16-2.7** Local file created on user's hard drive

Each local file has one **Username** associated with it; the local filename includes the username on the end to help keep this straight. The Username is specified in the Options dialog (Figure 16-2.8). This is initially set to match the username of the Windows login/username. The username can be changed—in fact, Revit will change it to match your **Autodesk A360** username when you log into the Autodesk Cloud Services (the username will not change if you are in a Local File).

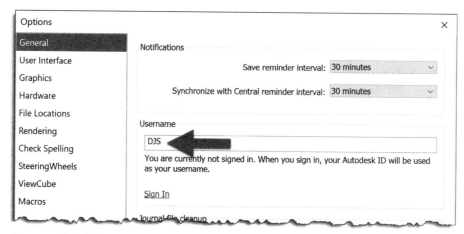

**FIGURE 16-2.8** Username setting in Options dialog

If the Username saved within the Local File (which does not really have anything to do with the filename) does not match the current username specified in the Options dialog, Revit will warn you that this situation is not acceptable. In this case, the Local File will not be able to synchronize with the Central File. This problem can arise if/when Revit changes the username to match the Autodesk A360 account as just mentioned. In this case, the file should be closed and a new Local File created per the steps previously covered.

The Revit Username is the designator used to track who has what checked out. No two users may have the same username. Duplicate usernames, either at the same time or at different times, would cause corruption in the Revit database.

**Saving; Local versus Central**
Once Worksharing is enabled there are two ways in which each user working in their Local Files may save their work: **Local Save** and **Synchronize with Central** (Fig. 16-2.9). These two options will be covered here.

**FIGURE 16-2.9** Save icons on QAT

While in a Local File, the user has two save options on the Quick Access Toolbar.

- **Save Local**
  The first one is the normal **Save** icon (looks like a floppy disk). Every time this is selected, the Revit project is saved to the local hard drive. This ensures data will not be lost if Revit crashes or if the power goes out. A local save is fast as it does not involve the network and should be done often while working actively in the Local File.

- **Synchronize with Central**
  The second option is only available when Worksharing is active in the current project file. This command saves all the delta changes between the user's Local File and the Central File. This save takes more time as data is being saved across the network. This type is performed less frequently: once an hour, at the end of the day and when someone needs access to elements you have checked out.

The **Synchronize with Central** (SWC) command opens the dialog shown below (Figure 16-2.10). <u>Avoid using the **Synchronize Now**</u> option listed in the drop down as this option may not relinquish rights to items you have checked out.

While in the SWC dialog, **it is important to check all of the 'relinquish' boxes** which are not grayed out (except Compact Central). If this is not done, elements will remain checked out in your name even when you are not working on the project. This can be a big problem for teammates working in the evenings or while you are on vacation/holiday!

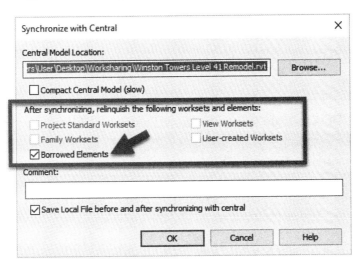

FIGURE 16-2.10 Synchronize with Central dialog

<u>Relinquish</u>
In the image above, only one category has elements checked out for the current user: User-created Worksets. Checking this box will ensure all the checkout elements are available to others on the project team.

<u>Save Before and After SWC</u>
The Save local before and after SWC is checked by default. This is good practice, as Revit can sometimes crash during SWC (especially on large projects on 32bit computers). Saving local before SWC helps prevent data loss. Saving local after SWC ensures the new local file is up to date.

<u>Compact Central</u>
This option is often used once a week on large, complex projects. It only needs to be performed by one person. Doing this database management helps to keep the file optimized for performance and file size. When selected, the SWC takes significantly longer.

<u>Comment</u>
This allows the user to add a brief note about what changes they made. This is helpful if the central file needs to be rolled back to a previous version; the comments are listed in the related dialog.

> **TIP:** This author recommends users create a new Local File each day. The existing local file does not benefit from the Compact Central command, so creating a new

Local File allows the user to work in the more optimized file. This also ensures the user is working on the latest version of the model, e.g., there are changes in the Central File which have not been downloaded yet—maybe another user worked all night on the project.

### Detach from Central

Whenever a new Central File is needed or a user wants to look at a file without making changes, then **Detach from Central** should be used.

If a Central File becomes corrupt, any Local File can be used to replace the Central File. To do this:

- Open Revit (do not double-click on the project file)
- Click **Open**
- Browse to and select the Local File
- Check the **Detach from Central** option (Figure 16-2.11)
- Click **Open**
- Select **Detach and Preserve Worksets**

You are now in an unnamed, unsaved Central File. Simply save the file to the server and it will be a Central File. At this point, everyone will need to make new Local Files.

If someone wants to look at a Revit Project file without making changes, they need to open the file Detached from Central. When this is done, there is no way to save any changes back to the original Central File as Revit does not know about it. It is important to understand that even copying a Central File to your desktop will automatically turn it in to a Local File when opened. Some make this mistake, thinking they will copy a file to see how others have created a Revit model—not realizing they are checking things out with their username! The consequence of this mistake is that staff working on the project can no longer edit parts of the model until the elements are checked back in.

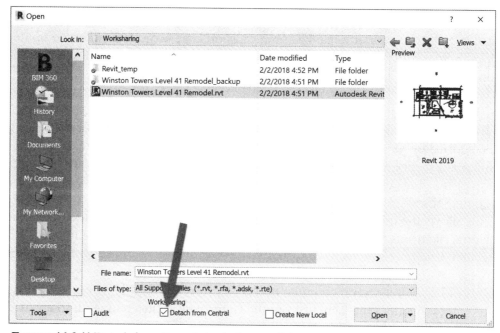

**FIGURE 16-2.11** Detach from Central checked; open dialog

Know the Red Flags

While in the Open dialog, if you select what you think is a Central File and the Create New Local is not checked, that is a red flag! There are two reasons why this would not be checked:

- The file is actually a Local File
  - You may have accidently selected the Local File rather than the Central File
  - Someone may have accidentally saved a local file over the Central File
    - In this case, they need to do a Save As; in Options check 'Make New Central' and save the file to the same location. Everyone needs to make a new Local File.
- The file is a different version of Revit
  - A Revit project should not be upgraded unless everyone on the team is ready to do so
  - If the file is saved in a newer version of Revit, that version must be used

**Worksets**

Once Worksharing has been enabled in a Revit project, every element, view and family is associated with a Workset. Here are a few things Worksets are used for:

- The underlying mechanism allowing multiple people to work in same file/model
- Opening specific Worksets limits geometry loaded, conserving computer resources
- Controlling visibility project-wide or per view

Looking back at Figure 16-2.3, notice that modeled elements, if any exist, are divided up between two default Worksets when Worksharing is activated:

- **Shared Levels and Grids**
- **Workset1**

All the Levels and Grids in the model are associated with the same named Workset. FYI: when creating new Levels or Grids, the user needs to make sure they go on the correct workset.

All other elements in the model are placed on Workset1. Additionally, each view and family is associated with its own Workset—that is, one unique Workset per view and per Family.

This default setup is all that is ever needed on many projects. On large, complex projects additional Worksets are created. For Example:

- Core and Shell
- Level 1
- Level 1 Furniture
- Level 2
- Level 2 Furniture
- Etc.

**FIGURE 16-2.12** Specify worksets; Open dialog

Segregating model elements on separate Worksets is mainly done to conserve computer resources. For example, in the Open dialog, a user can choose to open only the <u>Level 1</u> and <u>Level 1 Furniture</u> worksets (Figure 16-2.12). For a 30 story building this can save a significant amount of RAM/Memory.

The Worksets in the current Revit project are listed in the Worksets drop-down list on the status bar (Figure 16-2.13). The selected Workset is what all new elements will be placed on. In this example, all model elements would go only on Workset1.

If elements are created on the wrong Workset, it is simple to change. Once Worksharing is enabled all elements have a Workset parameter (Figure 16-2.14). Simply select a different workset from the list in the Properties palette.

**FIGURE 16-2.13** Worksets drop-down on status bar

**FIGURE 16-2.14** A selected elements workset; properties palette

## Worksets Dialog

The Worksets dialog (Figure 16-2.15) can be accessed from the Worksets icon on the status bar (Figure 16-2.13).

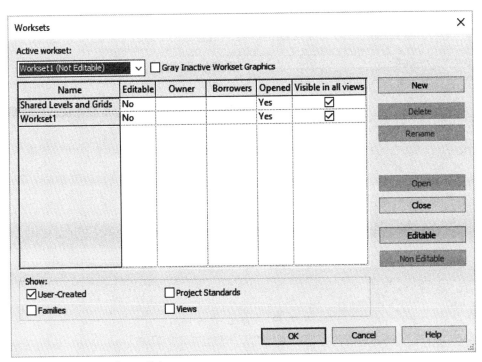

**FIGURE 16-2.15** Worksets dialog

Clicking the **New** button allows additional Worksets to be created. Worksets can also be opened and closed when selected using the buttons on the right. The two default Worksets cannot be deleted. When deleting Worksets, which contain elements, Revit prompts to select which Workset to move the elements to – deleting a Workset will not delete elements.

The **Editable** column should typically be set to **No**. This allows individual elements to be checked out by multiple people. When the Editable column is set to Yes, then only that person listed may edit anything on that Workset. This is sometimes done to limit who can change certain elements in the model. For example, if the structural model is in the same model as architectural and interior design, the structural engineer/designer might leave the structural Worksets checked so no one on the design team can accidentally move a column.

Unchecking the **Visible in all views** option will hide those elements in the entire project.

## Workset visibility by View

Once Worksharing is enabled, each view's visibility/graphics override dialog has a Worksets tab (Figure 16-2.16). This allows elements to be hidden based on which Workset they are on. The default setting for visibility is to rely on the Worksets dialog (i.e., Use Global Setting). Two other options, Show and Hide, allow for a view specific setting independent of the global setting.

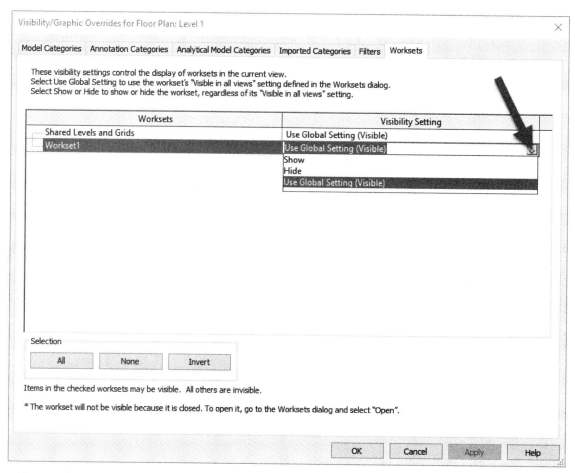

**FIGURE 16-2.16** Workset options per view

## Worksharing Display

One of the toggles on the View Control Bar provides a way to highlight a few Worksharing items (Figure 16-2.17). Revit is able to highlight, with different colors, which Workset elements are on, or who has what checked out at any given time. Clicking the **Worksharing Display Off** turns the highlights off.

**FIGURE 16-2.17** Worksharing display visual toggles

## Making Worksets Editable

It was already mentioned that an entire Workset should not be made editable, as no one else can edit any element on that Workset.

Most of the time, Revit will automatically check out elements when you begin to edit/modify them. However, some edits are more indirect and require the user to manually make the elements editable before changes may be made. When an element, or elements, is selected and a right-click is performed, there are two related options (Figure 16-2.18):

- Make Worksets Editable
- Make Elements Editable

Typically, only the second option is used—which checks out just the selected elements rather than the entire workset.

**Worksets and linked models**

If a linked model and the host model have the same named Workset, then Revit automatically connects the two. For example, if the structural grids in the structural model are on a Workset called <u>Struct Grids</u>, and the architectural model also has a Workset called Struct Grids, then they will be connected. Turning off the global visibility of <u>Struct Grids</u> in the architectural model will turn off the structural grids, leaving the architectural grids visible. This would be done when the architects have used Copy/Monitor to create

**FIGURE 16-2.18** Making worksets editable

their own semi-independent copy of grids they can adjust lengthwise. Structural engineers might also want to do something similar for the architects' levels.

Each linked Revit model will also have a separate list of Worksets contained with the linked model itself. This provides granular control over Workset visibility per linked Revit model. For example, the structural model sometimes contains duplicate walls, compared to the architectural model, to highlight just the structural/bearing walls in their model. If those duplicate walls are placed on a separate Workset, then the other disciplines may turn them off.

To see the Worksets in linked models:

- In any view, type **VV**
- Click the **Revit Links** tab (Figure 16-2.19)
- Click the *Display Settings* button for the desired link
- Click the **Workset** tab

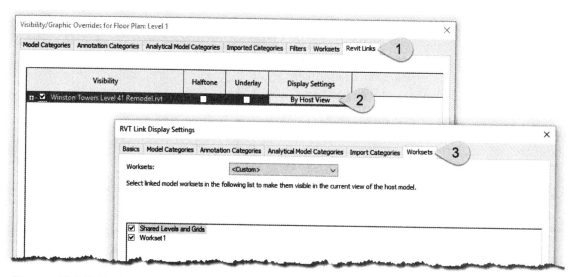

**FIGURE 16-2.19** Worksets in linked models

While a Central file is being accessed others cannot access it – this includes Syncing with Central or opening the file. Sometimes prompts will appear during opening that need to be closed before the file is finished opening. Ideally each user should not walk away from the computer while the file is opening.

### Logging into A360

When logging into Autodesk A360, to access cloud services, Revit requires the A360 username and the Revit username match. If the Revit username is changed, via Options, then the user needs to create a new Local File.

### Conclusion

This concludes the introduction to Worksharing. It is important that everyone working on a Worksharing project understands this information to have a successful project without significant issues and/or downtime.

## Exercise 16-3:
## Phasing Exercise

This section will provide a hands-on tutorial of Revit's **Phasing** functionality. The exercise involves remodeling an existing building.

1.  Open the Revit project file, from the online content (see inside front cover of book), called **Existing Widget Engineering Building.rvt** – this file is in the **Phasing and Worksharing** folder. There is another file with a similar name, so be sure you have the correct file.

2.  Ensure the **Level 1** floor plan view is open (Figure 16-3.1).

Notice the Phase setting for this view is set to Existing. Thus, any elements added in this view will be existing. In this tutorial, the boxed rooms will be converted to a conference room. Level 2 will also have some modifications, which will be discussed next.

**FIGURE 16-3.1** Level 1 floor plan with Phase set to existing

3.  Switch to the **Level 2** floor plan view (Figure 16-3.2).

On this level, the goal is to add offices, with walls and doors, in the boxed area.

**FIGURE 16-3.2** Level 2 floor plan with Phase set to existing

The next step will be to set up separate views for the Existing and New Construction phases.

4. In the Project Browser, right-click on **Level 1** and select **Rename**.

   a. Change the view name to **Level 1 – Existing**.

   b. Click **No** to rename the corresponding level and views.

5. Repeat the previous step for Level 2, creating a new plan named **Level 2 – Existing**.

Next you will duplicate the two plan views and adjust their Phase setting for New Construction.

6. Right-click on *Level 1 – Existing* and select **Duplicate View → Duplicate**.

7. Rename the newly created view to **Level 1 – New**; click **No** to rename the levels.

8. With nothing selected in the *Level 1 – New* plan view, change the following in the Properties Palette (16-3.3):

   a. Phase Filter:  **Show Previous + New**
   b. Phase:  **New Construction**

9. Repeat the previous three steps to create **Level 2 – New**.

Due to the selected Phase Filter, the existing walls appear filled in the new views. Next, we will adjust the solid fill to be a shade of gray, rather than solid black.

FIGURE 16-3.3 Level 1 – New floor plan with Phase settings adjusted

10. Select **Manage → Phasing**.

11. Select the **Phase Filter** tab (Figure 16-3.4).

Notice the Phase Filter we set for Level 1 – New, which is **Show Previous + New**. The existing items will be **Overridden**. This is what is causing the walls to be filled in black. Next we will adjust the overrides on the next tab.

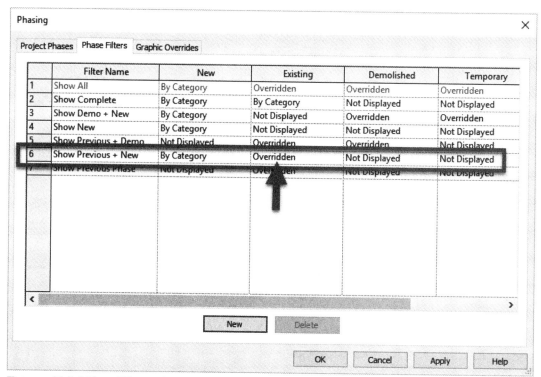

**FIGURE 16-3.4** Phase Filters tab; Phasing dialog

12. Select the **Graphic Override** tab.

13. Follow the steps shown in Figure 16-3.5 to change the fill color to gray.

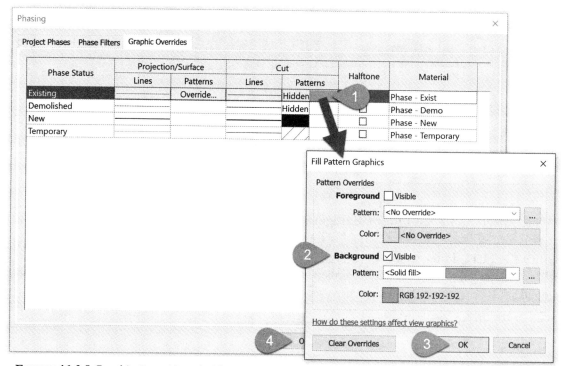

**FIGURE 16-3.5** Graphic Overrides tab; Phasing dialog

You should notice, in ALL of the 'new' views, that the walls are now filled in gray rather than black. However, the wall lines are also gray and would be better black. You will also make that change.

14. Make the following change in the Phases dialog to adjust the lines to black for existing elements (Figure 16-3.6).

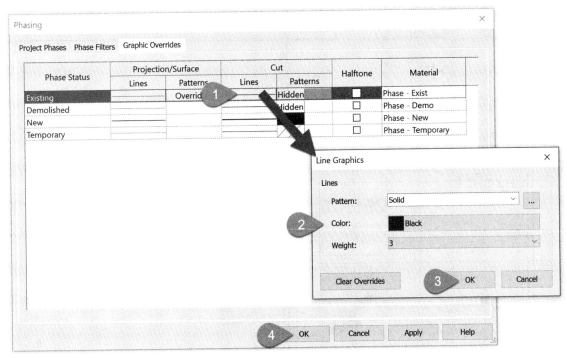

FIGURE 16-3.6 Graphic Overrides tab; Phasing dialog

Notice the existing walls are now filled with a solid gray pattern but the lines are solid black (Figure 16-3.7). This will make the existing elements contrast well next to new elements.

Now that the views are set up the original existing conditions can always be viewed in the 'existing' views and the new work in the 'new' views.

FIGURE 16-3.7 Existing walls shaded with black lines

## Demolition

Next, some elements will be set to be demolished, and a third set of views will be created to see the demolition work.

15. Switch to the **Level 1 – Existing** floor plan view.

16. Zoom into offices 104 and 105 as shown in Figure 16-3.8.

**FIGURE 16-3.8** Level 1 – Existing floor plan view – wall and two doors to be demolished

17. Holding the Ctrl key, select the wall and two doors pointed out in Figure 16-3.8.

18. With the three elements selected, set the Phase Demolished to **New Construction** (Figure 16-3.9).

Notice, with the wall and two doors selected, that the Type Selector says 'Multiple Categories Selected' and the drop-down list below (aka Properties Filter) indicated three elements are currently selected. When multiple items are selected, only the Common properties between those elements are displayed. In this case there are only five common parameters, two of which are related to phasing.

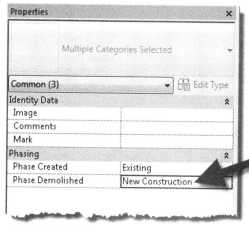

**FIGURE 16-3.9**
Phased Demolished set to New Construction

19. Move your cursor back into the drawing area and press **Esc**, or the Modify button, to unselect the elements.

Because you are in the existing view, nothing has changed graphically in the view.

20. Switch to **Level 1 – New** floor plan view (Figure 16-3.10).

Notice, due to the phase settings of the New view, the wall and two doors are hidden in this view. The Phase Filter **Show Previous + New** is set to hide demolished elements. One interesting thing that happened is Revit automatically infills demolished openings, both doors and windows, with a wall that matches the host wall type. This wall can be selected and adjusted to another wall type, but it cannot be deleted. If a "plain" opening is needed, with no door or frame, the infill wall needs to be manually hidden via right-click → hide element or using a view filter.

**FIGURE 16-3.10** Level 1 – New floor plan view – wall and two doors hidden

21. Select one of the infill walls pointed out in Figure 16-3.10.

22. Notice the following in the Properties Palette:
    a. The default wall Type matches the demolished door's host
    b. The Type Selector allows different types to be selected
    c. There are no phase parameters
    d. This wall may not be deleted without deleting the door

Next you will demolish the furniture. First, we will see that existing items may be set to be demolished in the New Construction views. Second, a problem related to demolishing elements within Groups will be reviewed.

23. While still in the **Level 1 – New** floor plan view, select one of the chairs at the desk in Office 105.

24. Set the Phase Demolished to **New Construction**.

The chair instantly disappears in the 'new' floor plan view.

25. Switch back to the Level 1 – Existing view to see the chair is still there.

26. In either Level 1 floor plan view, select one of the round tables with chairs in Office 105.

Notice the selected element is a Group and no phase properties are listed. The group can be edited and elements within the group changed to be demolished, but that would affect all instances of the Groups—which is not what we want. Thus, there are two options: create another Group for demolition or just un-group the elements to be demolished. For this smaller project we will do the latter.

27. With the Group still selected, click **Ungroup** on the Ribbon.

28. With the table and four chairs selected, set the Phase Demolished parameter to **New Construction**.

29. Repeat these steps to demolish all furniture in Offices 104 and 105. Do not delete the furniture tags in the existing views.

**FYI:** Sometimes it is easier to demolish elements in a 'new' view as things will disappear as they are set to be demolished. This way you know you have everything once all elements are hidden in the view. This is especially helpful with things like system furniture which has smaller elements hidden under larger elements.

### Adding New Elements

The next step in converting the two offices to a larger conference room is to add a door.

30. In the Level 1 – New floor plan view, add a **Door** as shown in Figure 16-3.11.

31. Press **Esc** to end the door command, and then **select** the door.

**FIGURE 16-3.11** Door added in Level 1 – New floor plan view

Notice, in properties for the selected door, that its Phase Created is New Construction, which matches the Phase setting of the current view. Also, the Phase Demolished is set to none.

32. Looking at the **Level 1 – Existing** view, nothing has changed graphically at the new door location.

Next a view will be created to document the demolition work. This is a view, placed on a sheet, which indicates the elements to be demolished. Contractors need to know this for bidding and during construction.

33. Right-click on the **Level 1 – New** view and select **Duplicate View → Duplicate**.

34. **Rename** the newly created view to **Level 1 – Demolition**.

35. Change the Phase Filter to **Show Previous + Demo** for Level 1 – Demolition; the Phase setting should already be set to New Construction.

**FIGURE 16-3.12** Level 1 – Demolition floor plan view

This new view shows all the elements to be demolished with dashed lines—this is an industry standard convention (Figure 16-3.12). Often, movable items such as furniture are not shown. Notice the opening for the new door is also identified. This tells the contractor that a portion of the existing wall needs to be removed; dimensions should be added to the demolition view so the new door is accurately positioned.

In the demolition view, notice the Phase is set to New Construction. The view phase must be past Existing in order for the demolish setting to kick in. Also, due to the Phase Filter (Show Previous + Demo), only Existing and Demo elements appear. All new elements are hidden, even though the view's phase is set to New Construction.

36. Using the information just covered, create a **Level 2 – Demolition** plan view.

37. In the **Level 2 – New** floor plan view, demolish the eight desks shown dashed in Figure 16-3.13.

Next, new walls and doors will be added.

**FIGURE 16-3.13**
Level 2 – Demolition floor plan view

38. In the **Level 2 – New** floor plan view, add the walls and doors shown in Figure 16-3.14; center the two walls on the exterior curtain wall mullions.

All the walls and doors just created in the 'new' view are set to New Construction for Phase Created. These elements do not appear in the existing view or the demolition views.

**Room Elements**
The final thing to consider for this introduction to phasing is the Room elements.

39. In the **Level 1 – Existing** view, select the **Room** element for Office 105.

**FIGURE 16-3.14**
Level 2 – New floor plan view

In the Properties Palette, notice the Phase is set to Existing and that it cannot be changed. Existing Rooms only appear in existing views and new Rooms only appear in new views. The phase is set based on the view the Room was placed in.

40. Switch to **Level 1 – New** and zoom in on the new conference room.

Notice there are no Room elements in this entire view. Given our specific remodel project, this logic starts to make sense. When two rooms become one larger room, Revit cannot automatically make the two existing rooms become one – especially without affecting the fidelity of the existing view.

Thus, Room elements must be added separately in the 'new' floor plan view.

41. In the **Level 1 – New** view, add a **Room** to the new conference room.

42. Edit the name to **CONFERENCE ROOM** and the number to **105**.

43. In the **Level 1 – New** view, add **Rooms** as shown in Figure 16-3.15; name and number as shown.

**FIGURE 16-3.15** Rooms added; Level 1 – New floor plan view

The four Rooms just added have their Phase set to New Construction. These Rooms do not appear in the 'existing' views. Given these steps, it should be noted that the existing rooms have no connection to the new rooms in the same location. Thus, any changes to existing room names and/or numbers must be carefully coordinated.

> **TIP:** For existing room elements that don't change, i.e., the room name and number are the same in both 'existing' and 'new' views, they can be copied and then pasted from one view/phase to another. This is a quick way to transfer the name and number data.

44. Add three **Rooms** to the **Level 2 – New** floor plan as shown in Figure 16-3.16.

**FIGURE 16-3.16** Rooms added, Level 2 – New floor plan view

## Room Tags in Demolition Views

The demolition views will only be able to show the 'new' Rooms because the view's phase is set to New Construction. This is a challenge as we want to show the existing rooms to make sure the contractor enters the correct area and removes the right stuff!

One trick, or workaround, is to create another 'existing' view and hide everything in the view except the Room and Room Tag categories. This new special view can be placed on top of the demolition view on the sheet. In fact, Revit will allow you to snap the two models together when placing one on top of another (you will see an alignment snap for both the X and the Y axis).

## No Demolition Phase

It is important to reiterate that Revit handles the demolition phase automatically. There should never be an actual demolition phase in the Phases dialog.

## Conclusion

This concludes the introduction to Phasing. There is more that can be covered on this topic, but the material presented should be enough to get started with Phasing in any project.

## Exercise 16-4:
## Worksharing Exercise

This section will provide a hands on application to worksharing, more than one person working in the project at one time. The tricky thing about this tutorial is that it is best followed with two people, at the same time, with access to the same network.

**FYI:** Worksharing does not work over the internet, using file sharing tools such as Dropbox, A360, Google Drive or Microsoft One Drive.

If this tutorial cannot be performed by two people, <u>at the same time</u>, on the same network, there is a way to simulate this on one computer, by one person. As mentioned at the beginning of this chapter, Revit tracks each user based on their Username set in Options. Thus, opening two sessions of Revit on one computer and changing the Username for each allows Revit to 'see' two different users accessing the Central file.

### Steps to simulate two users:

<u>User A:</u>
- Open Revit
- Application Menu → Options
  - Change Username to **User A**
- Open project starting at step #1 below
- Continue following steps as User A

<u>User B</u>
*Important:* don't follow these steps until second user instructions begin – starting on page 16-40:
- Open a second session of Revit
  - This does not mean open another Revit project file
  - Double-click the desktop icon
  - This starts a second session of Revit on your computer
- Application Menu → Options
  - Change Username to **User B**
- Open the project file as instructed for User B
- Follow steps for User B using this session of Revit
  - Notice the Local File name, seen on the Title Bar, contains 'User B' as a suffix

**Before Closing The Revit Sessions**
- Application Menu → Options
  - Restore your original Username

*FYI: Do not log into A360 as that will change your username.*

The steps just listed, allowing Revit to 'see' two users on the same computer, must be performed each time Revit is used. So, if this entire tutorial cannot be completed in one sitting, these steps must be followed each time. The reason has to do with how Revit stores the username. When the username is changed, a text file (Revit.ini) is adjusted. Each time Revit is opened, it reads this file to determine what the username is. Obviously there can only be one username, and it is based on the last session of Revit to change it.

**Warning: Be Patient and Take Turns**

The steps MUST be followed in the order listed by BOTH users or this tutorial will not work. When User A has a step, User B should be idle—not doing anything. There are no steps where both users are working at the same time. Once the basics are understood, students are encouraged to "go at it" with multiple users working at the same time. However, to highlight the way Worksharing actually works, we need to have one user make a change and then, after that, have another user do something so the sequence of events can be clearly seen.

**Enabling Worksharing**

The first step is to enable Worksharing. **This is only done by one person.** If a second person is involved in this tutorial, that person is encouraged to watch User A perform these steps.

> **TIP:** It might be best to work through this tutorial twice—switching roles the second time.

1. <u>**USER A**</u>: Open the completed phasing project **Existing Widget Engineering Building.rvt** from the previous exercise.

    a. Make sure the file is on the network first, if two people will be following this tutorial.

    b. While in the **Open** dialog, notice the Worksharing options at the bottom— they are grayed out because the selected file does not have Worksharing enabled (Figure 16-4.1).

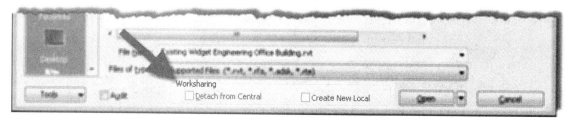

FIGURE 16-4.1 Worksharing options in the Open dialog

The process to enable Worksharing starts by simply opening the Worksets dialog.

2. <u>**USER A**</u>: Click the **Collaborate** tool on the Ribbon (Figure 16-4.2).

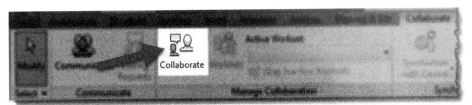

**FIGURE 16-4.2** Collaborate tool on Ribbon

This process can take a minute or two, depending on the speed of your computer (and the size of the project).

The Collaborate dialog is now open (Figure 16-4.3).

3. **USER A**: With **Collaborate within your network** selected, click **OK** to close the dialog.

At this point the Worksharing file has not been saved yet, so no one else can work in it.

4. **USER A**: Click the **Save** icon on the Quick Access Toolbar (Fig. 16-4.4).

    a. Notice the icon just to the right of the Save icon… this is currently grayed out.

5. **USER A**: Click **Yes** to the final worksharing related prompt (Figure 16-4.5).

The file, in the location you opened it from, is now a Central File. Be careful not to edit, move or rename the folders created next to the central file.

On the Quick Access Toolbar, notice the regular Save icon is now grayed out and the icon to the right, **Synchronize with Central**, is active (Figure 16-4.6). In the future, keep in mind that this is a clue that you are in the Central File— which you should not be in. **In fact, once this file is closed, you typically never need to open it directly again.**

6. Click **Synchronize with Central** on the QAT (Figure 16-4.6).

**FIGURE 16-4.3**
Enabling collaboration options dialog

**FIGURE 16-4.4** Save icon

**FIGURE 16-4.5** Final prompt for worksharing

7. Check all checkable boxes, except the *Compact Central Model*; ignore the grayed out boxes and then click **OK** (Figure 16-4.7).

8. **USER A**: Close the project <u>and</u> close Revit.

FIGURE 16-4.6 Sync with Central

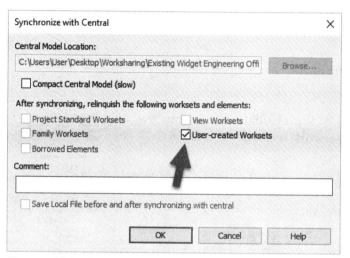

FIGURE 16-4.7 Synchronize with Central dialog

The Revit project has officially been converted into a Worksharing file. User A did not really have to completely close Revit to continue with the next step. However, to clearly delineate the Central File setup steps from the multiple workers in the Central File, the application was closed.

9. **USER A**: Open Revit – do not open the project file yet; **do not** double-click on the file via *Windows Explorer*.

10. **USER A**: Select the **Open** icon on the Quick Access Toolbar.

11. **USER A**: Browse to and select the Central File, which is the same file and location from which this section was started (See Figure 16-4.8). **Do not double-click or open the file yet.**

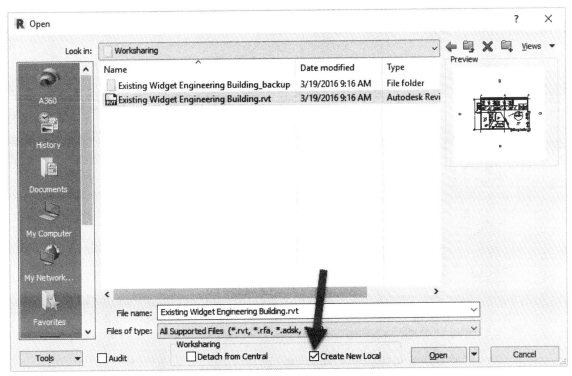

**FIGURE 16-4.8** Central file selected; Open dialog

In the Open dialog (Figure 16-4.8) Revit can detect that the selected file is a Central File. When a Central File is selected, and the file version matches the version of Revit you are using, the **Create New Local** option is automatically checked. This is good—each user will always work in a Local File.

    12. **<u>USER A</u>**: With the Central File selected and **Create New Local** checked, click **Open**.

User A is now in a Local File, which has a special connection back to the Central File. In the background, the Central File was copied to the local Documents folder and renamed to include the username as a suffix (Figure 16-4.8).

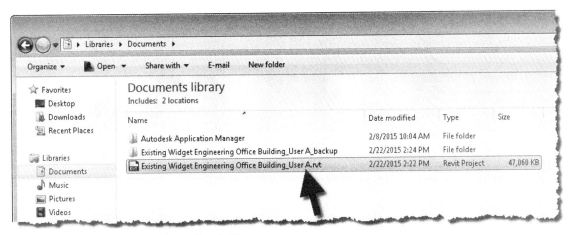

**FIGURE 16-4.9** Windows Explorer; Local File

**Warning:** If the Central File is copied manually using Windows Explorer and then opened, it will also become a Local File with a connection to the Central File.

Notice while in a Local File, that both save icons are active on the Quick Access Toolbar (Figure 16-4.10). Click on the one on the left for a quick save to the Local File on your hard drive (Save once every 15 minutes). Click the Sync with Central (maybe once an hour) when someone needs access to elements you have checked out and for sure before closing Revit.

**FIGURE 16-4.10**
Save Local and Sync w/ Central

Now User B will also open a Local File.

13. **USER B**: Open Revit – do not open the project file yet.

   a. Important: If the same person is simulating a second user, refer to the steps at the beginning of this section on opening a second session of Revit and adjusting the username in Options.

   b. If a second user will be following these steps on a second computer there is nothing extra to do.

14. **USER B**: Select the **Open** icon on the Quick Access Toolbar.

15. **USER B**: Browse to the Central File and select it; **Do not double-click or open the file yet.**

16. **USER B**: With the Central File selected and **Create New Local** checked, click **Open**.

User B is now in a Local File. Similar to User A, the Local File has a connection to the Central File on the server. Changes made to the Local File do not automatically change the Central File—however, modified elements are marked as checked out in the Central File. This prevents more than one person from making changes at the same time. We will see an example of this next.

17. **USER B**: Switch to the **Level 2 – New** floor plan view.

18. **USER B**: Zoom into the new offices in the Southwest corner of the building.

**FIGURE 16-4.11** Wall adjusted by user B

19. Adjust the wall shown in Figure 16-4.11 from 18' – 0" to **14' – 0"**.

The adjusted wall has been checked out in the Central File, but the wall has not changed in the Central File yet. In fact, the wall has not changed in the Local File either. The modification only exists in your computer's memory (i.e., RAM). Next User B will do a Save Local so their work is committed to the hard drive.

20. **USER B**: Click the **Save** icon on the Quick Access Toolbar; see image to right.

The change is now saved to User B's hard drive. However, the Central File is still out of date and User A does not have access to the modification to the model.

21. **USER B**: Click the **Synchronize and Modify Settings** icon to the right of the Save icon.

> **TIP:** <u>Never</u> click the sub-option 'Synchronize Now' as elements may remain checked out.

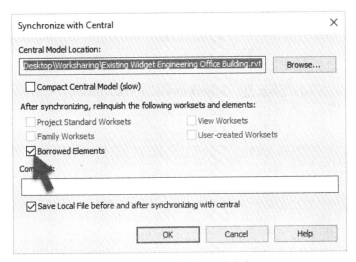

FIGURE 16-4.12 Synchronize with Central dialog

22. **USER B**: Make sure all checkable boxes **are checked** except 'Compact Central Model' (Figure 16-4.12).

23. **USER B**: Click **OK**.

The Central File now has the updated wall; however, User A still cannot see the change as their Local File is still based on the original Central File and any changes they have made. (User A should not have made any changes yet in this tutorial.)

24. **USER A**: Click the **Synchronize and Modify Settings** icon to the right of the Save icon.

25. **USER A**: Make sure all checkable boxes **are checked** except 'Compact Central Model'.

User A can now see the changes User B made. Every time a Sync with Central (SWC) is done, the delta changes are saved between the Local and Central models. Designers are often working on different parts of the building so it is not necessary to see each other's changes in real-time (plus the computers are not really that powerful, yet!).

Next we will look at what happens when users "step on each other's toes" and try to edit the same elements. There are really only two warnings anyone will ever see.

Two Worksharing-related warnings (paraphrased):
- Another user has this element checked out
- The element you are trying to change is outdated in your Local File

The first warning requires BOTH users to SWC—the user who changed the element(s) must SWC first. The second only requires the person who received the warning to SWC.

26. **USER A**: In the **Level 2 – New** floor plan, <u>change the door</u> swing in Office 203 as shown in Figure 16-4.13.

   a. **Do not save**

27. **USER B**: In the **Level 2 – New** floor plan, <u>try moving the door to the center</u> in Office 203.

The warning in Figure 16-4.14 immediately appears. This warning indicates that User A has this element checked out. User B must ask User A to SWC, which can be done manually (by calling or talking to them) or clicking the Place Request button.

The next steps will walk through the resolution to this issue.

28. **USER B**: Click **Cancel** and ask USER A to SWC.

**FIGURE 16-4.13** User A changed door swing

**FIGURE 16-4.14** Worksharing warning

29. **USER A**: Perform a **Synchronize with Central**.

30. **USER B**: DO NOT do an SWC yet!!!

The Central File is up to date; however, User B's Local File still has the door shown with the wrong swing. Next, you will see the second and last Worksharing-related warning.

31. **USER B**: Try moving the door in Office 203 to the center of the room again.

The warning, shown in Figure 16-4.15, indicates User B now has the element checked out. However, Revit will not let the element(s) be changed until User B is seeing the elements in the correct location; the correct location being the most recent change to the element among all users.

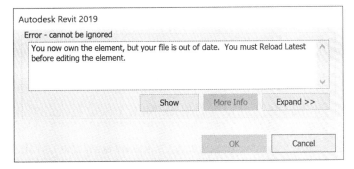

**FIGURE 16-4.15** Worksharing warning

32. **USER B**: Click **Cancel** and then perform an **SWC**.

User B's Local File has now been updated and they can now freely edit the door.

33. **USER B**: Try moving the door to the center of the room (Figure 16-4.16).

That is all there is to know about Worksharing! These same steps work for any number of users; however, project performance can suffer when more than about 8-10 users are in the model at one time.

The only thing left to discuss is what to do at the end of the day and what to do the next day.

**FIGURE 16-4.16** User B moved door

We will assume the end of day has come and the design team is ready to go home.

34. **USER B**: Perform an SWC and then close Revit.

    a.  For a single user simulating two users, change the Username, in Options, to User A before closing Revit.

35. **USER A**: Perform an SWC and then close Revit.

Now we will assume it is the next day and User A is ready to start working on the project. This author recommends creating a new Local File each day.

36. **USER A**: Open Revit.

    a.  Ensure the Username is set to User A via Options.

37. **USER A**: Click the **Open** icon.

38. **USER A**: Browse to the **Central File** (not the Local File).

39. **USER A**: Select the file, and with **Create New Local** checked, click **Open**.

User A is prompted to either overwrite yesterday's file or copy the old file and add a 'timestamp' to the file name—and then create a new Local File. If you are sure you synced your changes at the end of the day yesterday, then use the first option. If you want to be safe, you can use the second option. However, the second option can fill your hard drive up pretty quickly.

40. **USER A**: Click **Append timestamp to existing filename** (Figure 16-4.17).

User A is now in a 'fresh' Local File which will have any changes which may have been made by others working last night. This new Local File will also benefit from **Compact Central** having been run by another user.

The old Local File has now been renamed and is accessible if needed (Figure 16-4.18).

FIGURE 16-4.17 Cannot Create Local File dialog

As mentioned previously in this chapter, any Local File can replace the Central File if needed. Also, if you want to just 'look' at a Revit model, be sure to open it with Detach from Central checked in the open dialog. This will open an unnamed file with no connection to the original central file – keep in mind no changes can ever be saved from the detached file to the original central.

FIGURE 16-4.18 Time stamped local file in Documents folder

41. **USER A**: SWC and then close Revit.

This concludes the brief introduction to Worksharing in Revit. Students are encouraged to continue experimenting in the sample project, making several changes by all users at the same time.

### Autodesk Collaboration for Revit

A newer development in Revit Worksharing is Autodesk Collaboration for Revit. This technology allows multiple users or companies to work in the same Revit model over the internet. This is not available for students yet; however, it may be in the future so be sure to visit the Autodesk student portal for more information.

See this location for commercial access: http://www.autodesk.com/products/collaboration-for-revit/overview

## Self-Exam:

The following questions can be used as a way to check your knowledge of this lesson. The answers can be found at the bottom of the page.

1. Phasing makes Revit a 4D modeling program. (T/F)

2. More than one person can work in any Revit project file. (T/F)

3. For a Worksharing project, users work in their Local File. (T/F)

4. A Demolition phase should be created for remodel projects. (T/F)

5. The author recommends creating a new Local File each day. (T/F)

## Review Questions:

The following questions may be assigned by your instructor as a way to assess your knowledge of this section. Your instructor has the answers to the review questions.

1. Elements to be demolished can just be deleted. (T/F)

2. Worksets can be used to optimize computer resources. (T/F)

3. Additional Worksets can be created. (T/F)

4. A Revit project can only have two phases: Existing and New Construction. (T/F)

5. To casually look at a Revit project set up for Worksharing, simply copy it to the Desktop using Windows Explorer. (T/F)

6. The Phase setting for a demolition view is New Construction. (T/F)

7. For a Worksharing project, everyone will see all changes in real-time. (T/F)

8. Compact Central should be run once a day. (T/F)

9. Every element in Revit has a Phase Filter parameter. (T/F)

10. Revit requires the A360 username and the Revit username match. (T/F)

## Lesson 17
# Introduction to Revit Content Creation:

This chapter will introduce you to many of the basic concepts which relate to using and creating families. The reader will benefit from learning to create custom content as the need often arises. An entire book could be written just on creating *Families*. This chapter is intended to provide a very basic introduction to help get you started.

## Exercise 17-1:
## Basic Family Concepts

## Kinds of Families:

Autodesk Revit has three primary types of *Families*:
- *System Families*
- *Loadable Families*
- *In-Place Families*

This book will mainly focus on the second, that being loadable families. Below is a brief explanation of each, followed by a graphic to help tell the story.

<u>System Families:</u>
Autodesk describes *System Families* generally as the portion of the building that is **constructed on site**. Things like walls, floors, ceilings, roofs, stairs, wiring, ductwork and piping are system families. These families can only be defined and exist within the *Project Environment*.

Unlike loadable families (doors, windows, furniture), System families cannot exist separately outside the project environment. This image shows a wall in plan with its various layers of material.

*System Families* have the ability to **host** *Loadable Families*. The concept of *Hosted Families* will be covered in more detail later in this section, but here is a simplified explanation: a wall hosted *Family*, such as a window, can only exist within a wall; it automatically moves with the wall and is deleted when the wall is deleted.

It is too bad that *System Families* cannot exist outside the project in individual files as it would be helpful to have several construction types predefined and load them when needed, as opposed to having them predefined within the Revit project template. Therefore, your options are to have the *System Family* predefined in a template file or Copy/Paste them between projects. This author prefers to load relevant content and not have extraneous items cluttering the selection lists. There are always tricks and workarounds to facilitating this concept but it is not as simple as *Loadable Families* which are described next.

Loadable Families:

Building components which are **constructed in a factory** and shipped to the project site are what mainly make up *Loadable Families*. These are typically just referred to as *Families* rather than "Loadable" Families; this book will mainly use the term *Family* and mean "*Loadable*" *Family*. Building elements such as doors, windows, furniture, casework, columns, beams, appliances, electrical devices (i.e., outlets and switches), electrical panels, mechanical equipment (i.e., VAV boxes, air handling units and water heaters), duct fittings and plumbing fixtures (i.e., toilets and sinks) constitute *Loadable Families*.

Plumbing fixtures, such as this toilet, are "loadable," that is, they can exist in a file outside of the project environment.

*Image credit: Stabs, Wingate*

As the name implies, these *Families* can be stored outside of the *Project Environment* within individual files (*.rfa is the family extension, versus *rvt which is the project file extension). Using a "Load Family" command (found on the Insert tab), one is able to bring one or more Families into the Project Environment for placement.

In-Place Families:

Using a special command (*Architecture* → *Build* → *Component* → *Model In-Place*) within the *Project Environment* it is possible to create what is called an *In-Place Family*. This feature allows you to create a *Family* within the context of your project.

The *In-Place Family* has a couple of rather significant warnings that go along with it. First, it is meant for one-off items like a reception desk or a unique built in cabinet. If you copy an *In-Place Family* it is really just making another independent instance of the family – which makes the Revit project file grow in size. If you know something will occur more than once, it should be created as a *Loadable Family*, not

Stone trimmed opening created as an in-place family to interface with project conditions.
*Image courtesy of LHB, Inc.*

an *In-Place Family*. Second, *In-Place* families cannot ever exist outside the *Project Environment*, similar to System Families, so the item may not be added to your firm's library for use on another project. One last point is from Autodesk's "Revit Platform Performance Document": *In-Place Families* tend to reduce system performance within the Project Environment, especially on larger projects.

So with these points in mind it is best to use *Loadable Families* whenever possible. However, they are still acceptable in some situations.

Creating *In-Place Families* will not specifically be covered in this book. However, the process is almost identical in several ways to creating *Loadable Families* so you should be able to create them without too much trouble when needed.

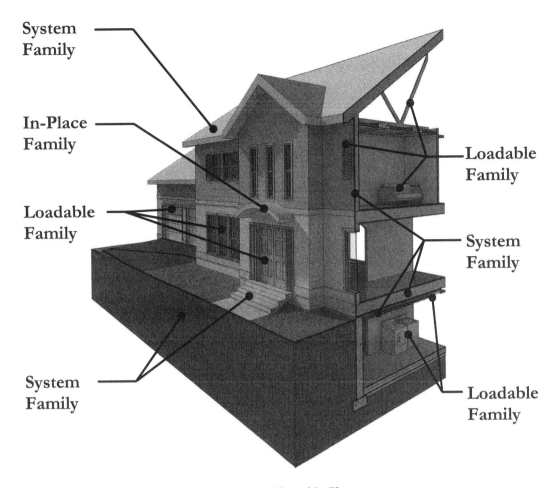

**FIGURE 17-1.1** Types of Families; System, Loadable and In-Place

## Nested Families:

It is possible to insert one or more *Families* into another *Family*; this is called nesting a family. One way in which this is useful might be two double-hung windows, as shown in the image above. Although it is possible to simply place the two windows close to each other in the project, this does not represent the reality of how the window will need to be documented in the project and how it will be delivered to the job site. The two windows would typically be mulled together by the window manufacturer and shipped and installed as one unit. By nesting one family into another and then copying it, you can quickly create a two window unit, which can also be tagged as one window. Lastly, nested families can typically have their position controlled more easily by parameters because they act as one element rather than several, or even hundreds.

## Hosted Families:

*Loadable Families* can be created to be Hosted or Non-hosted. As briefly mentioned above, the host is a *System Family* (e.g., a wall, floor, ceiling or roof) and when the host is moved, copied or deleted the Hosted Family is moved, copied or deleted.

Wall hosted family - Window.
*Image credit: Stabs, Wingate*

This feature helps solve some coordination problems but also creates a few new problems.

*Problems solved:*
When a wall is moved, things like cabinets, toilet fixtures, windows, specialty equipment (e.g., paper towel dispensers, grab bars, mirrors, etc.), doors and electrical devices (e.g., light switches and outlets) all move with the wall. This significantly helps with last minute coordination.

Roof hosted family – Solar
Conforms to slope of roof.
*Image credit: Stabs, Wingate*

*Problems created:*
A few problems have surfaced when using hosted content. For example, when designing a kitchen the wall cabinets are hosted. It is difficult to quickly mirror one's kitchen design. Also, when a supply air diffuser is hosted by a ceiling there is occasionally a problem with the ductwork when the ceiling is moved vertically.

Ceiling hosted family – Light Fixture
*Image credit: Stabs, Wingate*

Oftentimes the benefits outweigh the problems created.

> **TIP:** *One technique is creating your content initially as non-hosted and then nest that family into a hosted family, giving you access to both types, which is convenient as it is not possible to convert from one type to the other. Quick examples of why you would want to do this: wall cabinets in a kitchen are sometimes hung from rods above a peninsula countertop. Also, light fixtures which are attached to a ceiling are sometimes suspended within mechanical rooms or basements which do not have ceilings.*

Face based family – FE Cabinet
*Image courtesy of LHB, Inc.*

# Family Types:

Revit *Families* have the ability to hold information in placeholders called parameters. These parameters are defined, when created, to hold a specific kind of information; for example, text, integer, number, length, currency, yes/no, etc. This helps to validate data when it is entered. You cannot type text into a parameter that is set to currency. Finally, some of the parameters, such as lengths, can be associated with actual dimensions in the *Family*. Adjusting a length parameter value actually changes the size of the *Family*.

*Wall Cabinet*:
With the information from the previous paragraph in mind, it is time to discuss how slight variations are dealt with for content that is geometrically the same; that is, for example, a wall cabinet is a rectangular box that has four different heights, two different depths and several widths.

It is possible to create 100 individual *Families*, each of which represents one wall cabinet. However, this would be very cumbersome to manage; if one change was required you would have to open 100 files and make the same change 100 times. This is where *Family Types* are employed.

A single *Family* can have several *Types* defined. A *Type* is simply a saved state of all the parameter settings. For example, the wall cabinet may have two *Types* defined as follows:

| **Type A** | | **Type B** | |
|---|---|---|---|
| *Parameter* | *Value* | *Parameter* | *Value* |
| Width | **24"** | Width | **27"** |
| Depth | 14" | Depth | 14" |
| Height | 24" | Height | 24" |
| Model | **W241424** | Model | **W271424** |
| Manufacturer | Merillat | Manufacturer | Merillat |
| LEED – 500mi | Yes/No | LEED – 500mi | Yes/No |

Normally the *Type* name would be more meaningful than Type A and Type B. As you can see, the various parameters can be edited within each type. Therefore, one wall cabinet Family can represent 100 different sizes.

Some of the information in the table above has a direct impact on the 3D geometry; the Width, Depth and Height parameters can be associated with dimensions in the *Family*. When the parameter is changed the size of the *Family* actually changes. So one only has to change the *Family* type in a *Project Environment* to change the size of the placed *Family*. And, of course, some of the information has no effect on the 3D geometry. Rather it is used to track design decisions and for scheduling purposes. Shared parameters can show up in schedules.

There are always exceptions to the rule, but generally speaking, anytime the geometry changes you need to create a new *Family*. For instance, one Family can represent all the wall cabinets with a single door. But when the cabinet width dictates two doors a new *Family* is required. This change in geometry cannot easily be managed within a single *Family*.

When the geometry changes a new Family is typically required.
The example above has different handle, door and drawer locations.

*Family Types within the Project Environment*:

When utilizing content within the *Project Environment*, the *Family* and *Types* are presented as shown in the image below (Figure 17-1.2). Notice <u>*Chair-Desk*</u> only has one *Type* defined within that *Family* whereas <u>*Cook Top-2 Unit*</u> has three. Within the project anyone on the design team can manually add or delete *Types* associated with any *Family*.

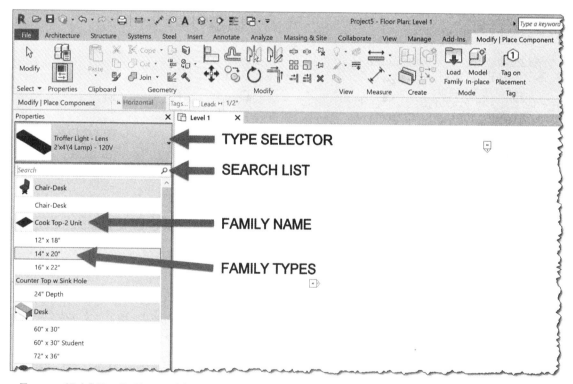

**FIGURE 17-1.2** Family Types within the Project Environment

*Type Catalog:*
There is one last concept to point out about *Family Types* before moving on. When a *Family* is loaded into a project all of its *Types* are automatically loaded. Sometimes this is good and other times it is not. The image on the previous page (Figure 17-1.2) shows manageable lists of *Families*. However, you can imagine how this list would get rather long if you loaded the wall cabinet *Family*, described on the previous pages, that had 100 types. Not only would the list be long, but you are likely only using one depth and two heights.

To better manage this situation Revit has a feature for *Families* called a *Type Catalog*. Rather than loading all of the *Types* into the project with the *Family*, the user is prompted to select the *Types* desired. This process could be repeated until all of the *Types* are ultimately loaded for a specific *Family*.

The image below (Figure 17-1.3) shows the dialog box the user is presented with when loading the steel wide flange beam *Family*.

| Type | W | A | d | bf | tw | tf | |
|------|-----|-------|--------------|---------------|--------------|---------------|----|
| (all) | (all) | (all) | (all) | (all) | (all) | (all) | |
| W44X335 | 335 | 0.68 SF | 3' 8" | 1' 3 115/128" | 0' 1 1/32" | 0' 1 197/256" | 0' |
| W44X290 | 290 | 0.59 SF | 3' 7 77/128" | 1' 3 205/256" | 0' 0 221/256" | 0' 1 37/64" | 0' |
| W44X262 | 262 | 0.53 SF | 3' 7 77/256" | 1' 3 205/256" | 0' 0 201/256" | 0' 1 27/64" | 0' |
| W44X230 | 230 | 0.47 SF | 3' 6 115/128" | 1' 3 205/256" | 0' 0 91/128" | 0' 1 7/32" | 0' |
| W40X593 | 593 | 1.21 SF | 3' 7" | 1' 4 179/256" | 0' 1 101/128" | 0' 3 59/256" | 0' |
| W40X503 | 503 | 1.03 SF | 3' 6 13/128" | 1' 4 51/128" | 0' 1 69/128" | 0' 2 195/256" | 0' |
| W40X431 | 431 | 0.88 SF | 3' 5 77/256" | 1' 4 51/256" | 0' 1 87/256" | 0' 2 23/64" | 0' |
| W40X397 | 397 | 0.81 SF | 3' 5" | 1' 4 13/128" | 0' 1 7/32" | 0' 2 51/256" | 0' |
| W40X372 | 372 | 0.76 SF | 3' 4 77/128" | 1' 4 13/128" | 0' 1 41/256" | 0' 2 13/256" | 0' |
| W40X362 | 362 | 0.74 SF | 3' 4 77/128" | 1' 4" | 0' 1 31/256" | 0' 2 3/256" | 0' |
| W40X324 | 324 | 0.66 SF | 3' 4 51/256" | 1' 3 115/128" | 0' 1" | 0' 1 207/256" | 0' |

Specify Types

Family:
W-Wide Flange.rfa

Types:

Select one or more types on the right for each family listed on the left

OK    Cancel    Help

**FIGURE 17-1.3** Selecting specific *Types* when loading a *Family* via the *Type Catalog*

The implementation and use of *Type Catalogs* will be covered later in the book.

The first *Family* you create, in the next lesson, will not even have a *Type* as they are optional.

# Instance and Type Parameters:

When creating *Parameters* for use in a *Family* you need to decide if it is an *Instance* or a *Type* parameter. Remember, parameters are placeholders for information in which some of them can be linked to geometry size and visibility.

An **Instance Parameter** only impacts the one or more *Families* that are selected, or about to be created within the *Project Environment*, whereas the **Type** parameter affects all instances of the *Family* within the project.

A good example to describe how Instance/Type parameters are used in a project is to consider a window. Looking at the image below you can see this window *Family* has been set up so that the width and height parameters are *Type* and the <u>Sill Height</u> is an *Instance* parameter. *FYI: You only know this here by the labels and arrows provided in the image (Figure 17-1.4).*

This works with the standard industry convention where all windows that are the same size (i.e., width and height) are labeled with a common mark or tag. For example, the 2'x4' window below might be referred to as "W1" in a project. Thus, if it was determined that all W1 window types need to increase in size to let in more natural light, changing one window's *Type Properties* would change the size of all "W1" windows in the project. On the other hand, the <u>Sill Height</u> dimension needs to be an *Instance* parameter. The "W1" windows might be 2'-4" above the first floor and 2'-8" above the second.

It is possible to edit a family and change a parameter from a *Type* to an *Instance*, with one exception: some parameters that are predefined in the template files are not editable. You cannot even change the name.

Final thought: a table *Family* might have its width and depth parameters set as *Type* or as *Instance* depending on how the design team wanted to use it in the project.

**FIGURE 17-1.4** Exterior view of a window in the Family Editor

## Family Templates:

When starting a new *Family* you need to know what it is and how it will be used in a project. With this information you can then select a *Family Template* from which to begin the content creation process.

Selecting the correct template saves time setting up the most basic parameters and in some cases is critical to the *Family* working. For example, the door and the window templates have the following parameters setup:

| Door Template | | | Window Template | |
|---|---|---|---|---|
| *Parameter* | *Value* | | *Parameter* | *Value* |
| Width | 3'-0" | | Width | 3'-0" |
| Height | 7'-0" | | Height | 4'-0" |
| **Frame Width** | 3" | | **Sill Height** | 3'-0" |
| Model | *blank* | | Model | *blank* |
| Manufacturer | *blank* | | Manufacturer | *blank* |

Other templates, such as **Generic Model**, do not have a <u>Width</u> and <u>Height</u> parameter predefined. Additionally, the door and window templates are wall hosted whereas the *Generic Model* is not.

Revit comes with over 70 template files. This book will only provide a discussion on a handful of them, but many are self-explanatory and it should be possible to discern what most of them are for after completing this book.

## Family Categories:

Another item that needs to be covered at an overview level is the concept of a *Family Category*. Each *Revit Family* needs to be assigned to a specific category. This is done automatically by way of the template files for most *Families*. For example, starting a new *Family* from the window template file, the category has been set to window as shown in Figure 17-1.5.

The category setting does two basic things: it controls which command is used to place the *Family* and it relates directly to manipulating visibility within the project; turning off the window category for a specific view makes all the windows disappear in that view.

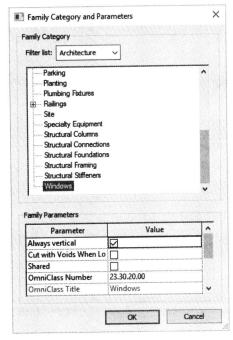

**FIGURE 17-1.5** Family categories

## Custom Family Libraries:

Whether you are creating content for personal use or for a large firm, you should have a plan on how and where to store your custom content. There are probably an infinite number of solutions to this problem, but a relativly simple one will be suggested here.

It is best to store your custom Revit content in a separate folder and not in the folders that contain the Revit OOTB content (OOTB = out of the box, meaning the content that comes with the software). It is best to segregate the content that has been created or edited to comply with your firm's graphic or design standards. Additionally, each year, when a new version of Revit is released you would need to sift through all the OOTB content folders to find your custom content.

Revit has a specific set of folders created to house the OOTB content (see Figure 17-1.6). One suggestion is to create those same folders in a parallel folder and place your content there. Then, when content is needed, a user might first look through the OOTB location and then the firm location. At some point your custom content may be sufficient enough to reverse the order in which you look for content (i.e., Firm folder and then OOTB folder).

Of course, in a firm setting, the content should be located on a server so everyone has access to the same content, and so it gets backed up!

## Naming Families:

The name of the *Family* file (.rfa files) on your hard drive, or server, is also the name the users see in Revit. The following information is offered as a suggestion, as there is no hard and fast rule on *Family* naming.

The *Family* name should be concise and as short as possible, and it should not contain information that will appear in the *Type* name, or vice versa. For example:

| *Family name* | *Type name* |
|---|---|
| Metal Locker – **Tall** | **Tall** 18″ x 18″ |

Annotations
Boundary Conditions
Cable Tray
Casework
Columns
Conduit
Curtain Panel By Pattern
Curtain Wall Panels
Detail Items
Doors
Duct
Electrical
Entourage
Fire Protection
Furniture
Furniture System
Lighting
Mass
Mechanical
Openings
Pipe
Planting
Plumbing
Profiles
Railings
Site
Specialty Equipment
Structural Columns
Structural Connections
Structural Foundations
Structural Framing
Structural Rebar Shapes
Structural Retaining Walls
Structural Stiffeners
Structural Trusses
Sustainable Design
Titleblocks

**FIGURE 17-1.6**
OOTB Family Folders

The *Family* name should be as generic as possible so others on the design team, or in the firm, can quickly ascertain what the various *Families* are. If only one type of locker is used then the *Family* name can be more generic. Similarly, the *Type* name within the *Family* should be easy to understand if possible; show the size of the locker rather than the model number. For example:

**Generic naming convention:**

<u>*Family name*</u>                          <u>*Type name*</u>
Metal Locker – Tall              18″ x 18″

**Detailed naming convention:**

<u>*Family name*</u>                          <u>*Type name*</u>
Arrow Locker – Tall              ALT181860

Locker family shown
in perspective.

Remember, a *Family* often has several types defined within it. Thus, the example above would have several similarly named types which define several locker sizes.

The detailed naming convention above would be appropriate if a design firm used several locker manufacturers depending on the project type; maybe they specialize in sports facilities and design various types of locker rooms.

Another option, based on the example above, is to have a detailed *Family* name and a generic *Type* name:

<u>*Family name*</u>                          <u>*Type name*</u>
Arrow Locker – Tall              18″ x 18″

A good naming convention will help promote efficiency in the project environment. Many of the *Families* are added to the Revit model via the catch-all tool: **Component: Place a Component** (on the *Architecture* tab). When the *Component* tool is active, the *Element Type Selector* lists all the *Families* that are loaded into the project; that is, all the *Families* that do not have their own insertion tool, as windows and doors do.

These *Families* are listed in alphabetical order in the *Element Type Selector,* within the project environment. Therefore, if the *Families* are not named properly, you might have a toilet at the bottom of the list, a Bathtub near the top and many other types of content sprinkled in between.

One solution to this problem would be to implement some sort of abbreviation or prefix naming system.

- Families
  - Annotation Symbols
  - Casework
  - Ceilings
  - Columns
  - Curtain Panels
  - Curtain Systems
  - Curtain Wall Mullions
  - Detail Items
  - Doors
  - Floors
  - Furniture
  - Lighting Fixtures
  - Parking
  - Pattern
  - Planting
  - Plumbing Fixtures
  - Profiles
  - Railings
  - Ramps
  - Roofs
  - Site
  - Specialty Equipment
  - Stairs
  - Structural Beam Systems
  - Structural Columns
  - Structural Foundations
  - Structural Framing
  - Walls
  - Windows

**FIGURE 17-1.7** Project Browser within the Project Environment showing Family Categories

Each *Family* falls within a *Family Category* as previously discussed. These categories are listed within the *Project Browser*; note the list varies depending on the content currently loaded into the project. Creating a two letter prefix would sort the content by category within the *Element Type Selector*. For example:

| CW | = Casework |
|----|------------|
| FN | = Furniture |
| PF | = Plumbing Fixtures |
| SE | = Specialty Equipment |

This naming convention would cause all the related content to be grouped together within the *Element Type Selector*.

**FIGURE 17-1.8** Element Type Selector within the Project Environment showing loaded Families available for placement via the Component tool. **Left**, default naming; **right**, prefix added to control sort order.

Utilizing a naming convention like this means a firm's name or initials cannot appear at the beginning of the name.

Family and Type naming is highly subjective so one firm's solution may be completely different from another's. But, in any case, some sort of standard should be developed and agreed upon within each design firm.

## Exercise 17-2:
## The Box: Creating the Geometry

The emphasis will be placed on Revit features and techniques related to *Families* and not so much on geometry. A simple box will be created and then utilized to show many of the things that can be done with, and within, a *Family*. So, to keep things simple early on, a basic box will be used.

This exercise demonstrates how to start a *Family* and develop a 3D box that can be adjusted in size; i.e., a **parametric box**. Note that more detailed steps and graphics will be provided the first time a subject is covered. The subsequent steps for the same subject will be less detailed and may not contain graphics. It is therefore beneficial to work through the lessons in order.

## Creating a New Family:

1. Open Revit

   a. There is no difference to the user between 32bit and 64bit versions of the software. Therefore it does not matter which one is used with this book.

2. **File Tab → New → Family**
   (Figure 17-2.1)

Assuming Revit was installed properly you should see a large list of files from which to choose. If not, you may download the *Family* template files from Autodesk's website.

The template names make it rather obvious as to what each template file is intended to be used for. When a template is selected, Revit makes a copy of the file and then opens it as an unnamed *Family* called **Family1** until saved.

**FIGURE 17-2.1** Starting a new Family

3. Select **Generic Model.rft** and then click **OK** (Figure 17-2.2).

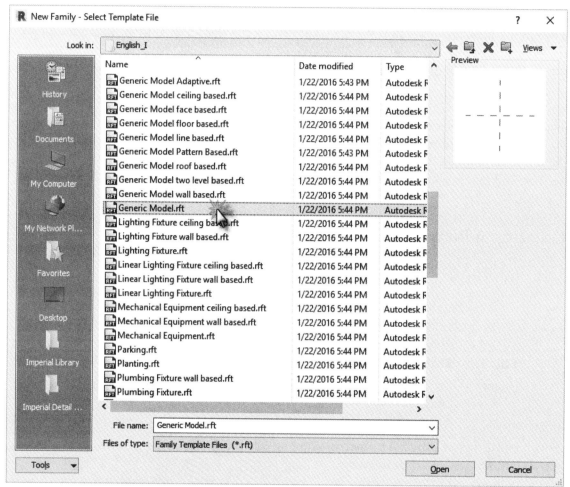

**FIGURE 17-2.2** Selecting a Family template file

The initial view is a plan view from the top (Figure 17-2.3). As seen in the *Project Browser*, the following views have been established, via the template file:

- Floor Plan
- Ceiling Plan
- 3D View
- Elevations
  - ○ Back
  - ○ Front
  - ○ Left
  - ○ Right

**FIGURE 17-2.3** Initial view shown reference planes

In the initial plan view, Figure 17-2.3, are two *Reference Planes*: one horizontal and one vertical. These two *Reference Planes* define the center of the content about to be created, in each direction. The intersection of the two also defines the origin. The origin is the insertion point, relative to your cursor, when placing the *Family* in a project. Ultimately the box to be created needs to be centered on the intersection of the reference planes.

The *Reference Planes* do not appear in the *Project Environment*. However, Revit is aware of them and can use them when dimensioning and aligning to other elements; this depends on how a few properties for the *Reference Planes* are set, but in any case the *Reference Planes* are never visible.

## Creating the Framework for a New Family:

A common method used when creating Revit content is to first add *Reference Planes*, make them parametric and then create the 3D geometry and lock its edges to the *Reference Planes*. This allows complex *Families* to be broken down into more manageable elements and makes controlling multiple 3D objects easier (i.e., moving one reference plane moves several 3D objects).

In the next few steps you will create *Reference Planes* that ultimately will control the size and location of a 3D box.

4. Select **Create** → **Datum** → **Reference Plane**.

To add a *Reference Plane* one simply picks two points in a view. A *Reference Plane* is a 3D plane that will appear in all views which cut through it, on end (or perpendicular to), or are within the Select/Elevation/Plan "view range." The edges of the *Reference Planes* are typically only visible unless "show" is toggled on under the *Create* tab on the *Ribbon*, and then only the current *Work Plane* is shown.

5. Add a horizontal *Reference Plane* as shown in Figure 17-2.4.

   a. The exact location and length does not matter at this time; it will be adjusted later.
   b. Make sure the *Reference Plane* is snapped to the horizontal plane before picking the second point. Watch for the cyan-colored dashed line and a *tooltip* which displays the word horizontal.

   *FYI: The use of the word "horizontal" above is in reference to the computer screen.*

The first *Reference Plane* has now been added to the new *Family*. Later in the book, a dimension will be added between the two parallel *Reference Planes* shown in Figure 17-2.4. This dimension can be locked so it does not move, or made to be parametric in which case the end user in the project environment can edit a value in the properties of a selected element, causing the *Reference Plane* to move accordingly.

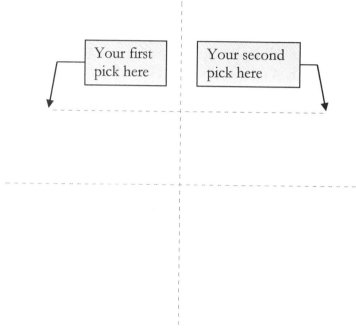

**FIGURE 17-2.4** Adding a "horizontal" reference plane

6. Switch to the **Right** elevation view by double-clicking on it in the *Project Browser*.

Notice that the newly added *Reference Plane* is visible in this view, as well as the <u>Left</u> view. Again, this is because the *Reference Plane* is a 3D element.

**FIGURE 17-2.5** Newly created *Reference Plane* visible in the "side" views

7.  Close the **Right** elevation view and switch back to the **Plan** view.

8.  Draw three more *Reference Planes* approximately as shown in Figure 17-2.6.

9.  Select **Modify**, on the *Ribbon*, to finish the *Reference Plane* command.

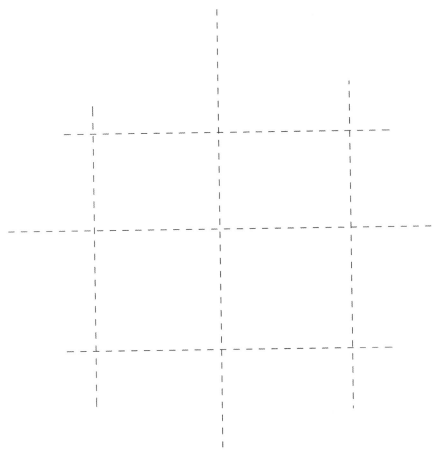

**FIGURE 17-2.6** Three more reference planes added

The four *Reference Planes* just drawn will ultimately serve as the guides for the edge of the 3D box. The top and bottom edges of the box will be controlled by *Reference Planes* not visible in the current view.

Next, the newly added *Reference Planes* position will be adjusted relative to the center or origin *Reference Planes* that came with the template file. This can be done simply by selecting one *Reference Plane* at a time and editing the on-screen temporary dimension which appears.

10. Select the top horizontal *Reference Plane* (Figure 17-2.7).

11. Edit the *Temporary Dimension* to be **2'-0"** (Figure 17-2.7).

    a. If needed, adjust the ends of the *Reference Planes* so they cross each other and form a corner as shown below. Procedure: select a *Reference Plane* and then click and drag on the visible endpoint grip.

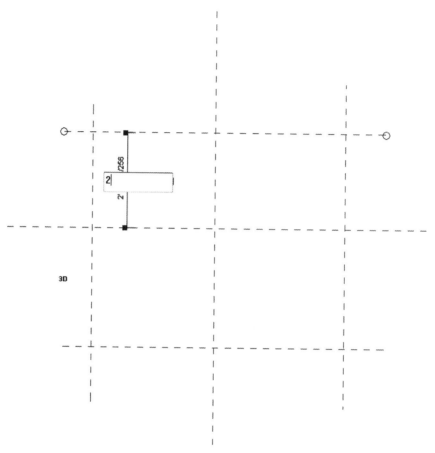

**FIGURE 17-2.7** Top "horizontal" reference plane selected

12. Modify the remaining three *Reference Planes* to have the same **2'-0"** dimension off of the original centerline/origin *Reference Planes* that came with the template.

The four *Reference Planes* now define the extents of a 4'-0" x 4'-0" box. This only defines the sides of the box. Next the top and bottom of the box will be defined.

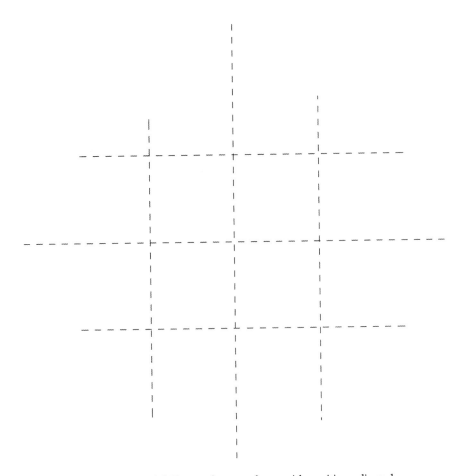

**FIGURE 17-2.8** Four reference planes with position adjusted

13. In the *Project Browser,* double-click **Front** under *Elevations.*

The Front (or South elevation) shows two of the four *Reference Planes* created in this exercise. All *Reference Planes* that are perpendicular to the view are visible, as long as they are within view range. Additionally, the center (left/right) *Reference Plane* and one in line with the **Ref. Level** is visible, both of which came from the template.

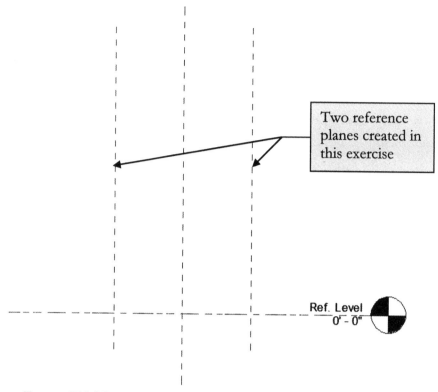

**FIGURE 17-2.9** Front view

Next, a *Reference Plane* will be drawn as a guideline for the top of the 3D box. A *Reference Plane* is always drawn perpendicular to the "plane" that is being defined.

14. Draw a *Reference Plane* **2'-0"** above the Ref. Level (Figure 17-2.10).

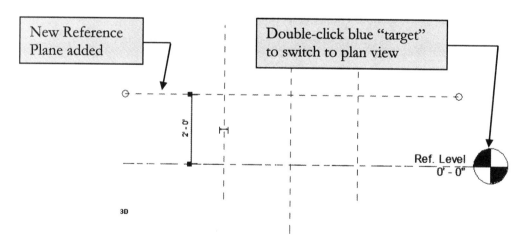

**FIGURE 17-2.10** Front view; relocated ref. level

15. Switch back to the plan view, double-click **Ref. Level** under *Floor Plans* in the *Project Browser*, or Double-click the blue target; see Figure 17-2.10.

## Creating the 3D Geometry:

Now that the framework, or guidelines, have been established using Reference Planes, the 3D geometry can be created. A simple box will be created.

16. Select **Create → Forms → Extrusion** from the *Ribbon*.

17. Draw a square within the outer *Reference Planes* (Figure 17-2.11).

   a. Select "rectangle" on the *Ribbon* in the *Draw* panel.

   b. Notice the depth is set to 1'-0" on the *Options Bar*; this is fine.

   c. The exact size does not matter here.

**FIGURE 17-2.11** Sketch lines for 3D extrusion

When creating a *Solid Extrusion*, a simple 2D outline is sketched as in Figure 17-2.11. This defines the perimeter of the extrusion. When "finish extrusion" is selected, the 2D outline is extruded perpendicular to the sketch lines to a thickness (or depth) specified on the *Options Bar*.

The 2D sketch must be "clean," meaning no gaps or overlaps occur at the corners. Because the rectangle option was selected, the outline will automatically be "clean."

18. Select the **green check mark** on the *Ribbon*.

With the previous three simple steps a 3D box was created. This box will now serve as our "test subject" for an introduction on many of the basic options and settings that can be done with a *Family*.

The last step, in this exercise, is to align and lock the 3D geometry to the *Reference Planes*. Thus, whenever the *Reference Planes* move, so will the geometry. Revit provides a tool to easily do this; it is called **Align**. The tool brings two lines and/or surfaces into alignment. Once the *Align* tool has been employed, the opportunity to "lock" the relationship is available. This lock creates a parametric relationship within the *Family*. This is just one of the tools in which a *Family* can be made parametric.

> 19. Select **Modify** → **Align** on the *Ribbon*.

> 20. Select the vertical *Reference Plane* on the right (Figure 17-2.12).

> 21. Select the right-hand side of the box.

The right side of the box should now be aligned with the *Reference Plane* (Figure 17-2.12). If the *Reference Plane* moved rather than the edge of the box, click **Undo**. When using the *Align* tool, the element that does not move is selected first.

> 22. Click the **Padlock** icon that appears to lock the relationship between the edge of the box and the *Reference Plane*.
>
>> a. Figure 17-2.12 shows the icon in its initial position, unlocked.
>>
>> b. Clicking the "unlocked" icon will change it to a "locked" icon.
>>
>> c. When a *Reference Plane* is selected the "locked" icon will appear.
>>
>>> i. This lets the users know a "lock" exists.
>>>
>>> ii. Clicking the "locked" icon will unlock the relationship.
>>
>> d. Selecting the 3D box does not reveal the locked icon (except when in "edit sketch" mode).

**FIGURE 17-2.12** Aligning 3D geometry to reference planes

23. **Align** and **Lock** the other three sides of the box (Figure 17-2.13).

    a.   Remember to select the *Reference Plane* first.

    b.   Select *Undo* on the *Quick Access Toolbar* if you select things in the wrong order.

The four sides of the 3D box now have a parametric relationship to the four *Reference Planes* created in the plan view.

Next, the top and bottom of the 3D box will be *Aligned* and *Locked* to *Reference Planes*.

24. Switch to the **Front view** via the *Project Browser*.

**FIGURE 17-2.13** Side of 3D box aligned with *Reference Planes*

25. **Align** and **Lock** the top of the box, which is 1'-0" high, to the top *Reference Plane* (Figure 17-2.14).

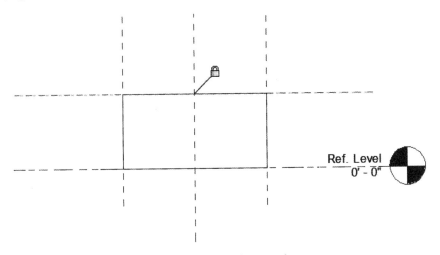

Ref. Level
0' - 0"

**FIGURE 17-2.14** Aligning 3D geometry to reference planes

26. **Select the 3D box** to reveal the edit grips (Figure 17-2.15).

Notice the four triangle shaped grips on each side of the box. These grips can be dragged, which repositions the selected side. The one limitation with editing geometry with these grips is that there is no way to control the distance in which the edge is moved.

Ref. Level
0' - 0"

2' - 0"

**FIGURE 17-2.15** 3D geometry selected, edit grips revealed

In the next step, the bottom of the box will be raised to make it easier to *Align* and *Lock* it to the bottom *Reference Plane*. It is not required that this be done. However, it is easier to select things in the correct order and assure the desired things are selected, which can be challenging when several things overlap.

27. Click and drag the bottom grip up as shown in Figure 17-2.16; the exact position does not matter.

**FIGURE 17-2.16** Bottom of 3D box repositioned

28. *Align* and *Lock* the bottom edge of the 3D box with the bottom *Reference Plane*.

29. Switch back to the **Plan View**.

## Flexing the Family:

Now that the 3D box has been tied to the *Reference Planes*, any time the *Reference Planes* are moved the 3D box will move with it. This will be tested next.

30. Select the *Reference Plane* on the right and use the **Move** tool to move it **1'-0"** more to the right (Figure 17-2.17).

    a. The *Move* tool is only visible when something is selected.
    b. The exact distance here does not matter.

31. Notice the 3D box moves with the *Reference Plane* (Figure 17-2.17).

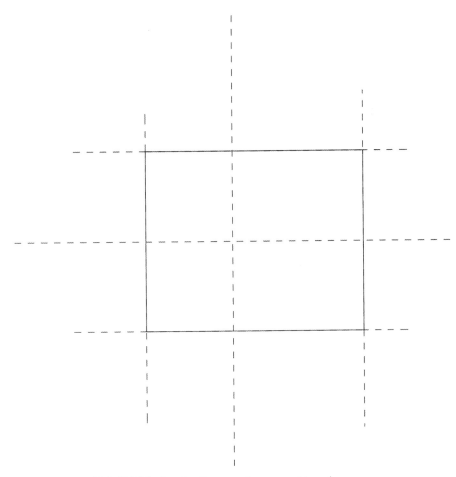

**FIGURE 17-2.17** Right-hand reference plane repositioned

32. Click **Undo** on the *Quick Access Toolbar* to undo the previous step.

Now the *Family* will be loaded into a project to show how that process works. Once in the project, the content does not have any direct connection to the external *Family* created in this lesson.

33. Open a **new project**; see chapter one if needed.

   a. Use the default template.

34. Switch back to the **Family Editor** by pressing **Ctrl + Tab**.

   a. Ctrl+Tab cycles through open projects and views.

Before loading the *Family* into a project, it should first be saved to a file. The main reason is to establish the *Family's* name. The *Family's* file name becomes the name of the content within a Revit project.

35. Save the *Family* to your hard drive as **Box.rfa**.

    a. The location where the file is saved does not matter; however, it would be a good idea to create a folder in which all the files created in this text are stored.

    b. It is highly recommended that all data files be backed up regularly. If a Revit file becomes corrupt a backup may be the only solution; another option would be to send the file to Autodesk support and they may be able to salvage it.

36. Click the **Load into Project** button on the *Ribbon*.

Load into Project

Revit automatically switched back to the Revit Project.

37. *In the project:* Select **Architecture → Build → Component**.

38. With the *Box* family current in the *Element Type Selector*, click somewhere within the floor plan view to place an instance of the box.

39. Click the **3D** icon on the *Quick Access Toolbar* to see the 3D box.

40. **Save** the *Family* as **Box** and the *Project* as **Box Project**.

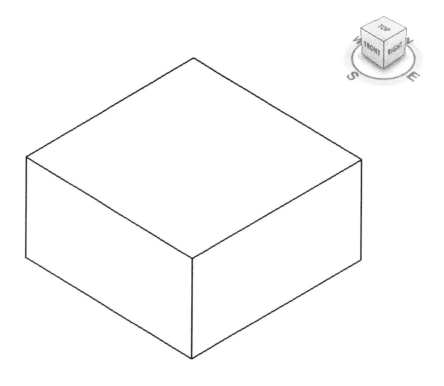

## Exercise 17-3:
# The Box: Adding Parameters

In this exercise the steps required to make the box parametric will be covered. Parametric, in this case, means that certain parameters control the size of the box. Thus, in the project environment it is possible to select the box, go to its properties, edit a few parameters (e.g., width and height) and then the box will change size accordingly. This is a very powerful feature and can save time creating content, as a *Family* is not required for every size.

All parameters are either a ***Type*** parameter or an ***Instance*** parameter. An introduction to this concept was presented on page 17-8 of this chapter. This exercise will help to better explain the differences and how to implement them.

1.  Open the ***Box*** *Family* created in the previous exercise.

    a.  It is recommended that a copy of the "Box" *Family* be saved for each exercise in case problems arise and an older file is needed to revert back to. Maybe copy the "Box" *Family* file and rename it to Box 17-2 to save a copy of the *Family* from the previous exercise.

## Adding Dimensions:

The first step in making 3D geometry parametric is to add dimensions in a view. Two dimensions will be added in plan view, which will eventually be tied to parameters to control the width and depth of the 3D box.

2.  In the *Ref. Level* plan view, select **Annotate → Dimension → Aligned**.

3.  Click the vertical left and right *Reference Planes*, and then click a third point to position the dimension line (Figure 17-3.1).

    *TIP: The third click needs to be in a blank area, as clicking on something will add another segment to the dimension string.*

    *TIP: Be careful to select the reference plane and not the 3D box.*

4.  Similar to the two previous steps, add another dimension for the other side of the box (Figure 17-3.2).

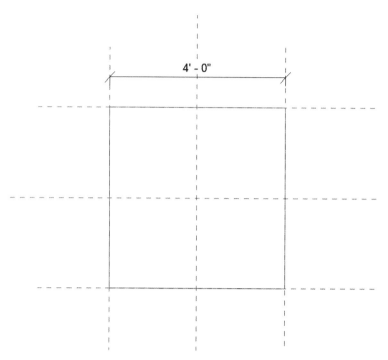

**FIGURE 17-3.1** Dimension added to reference planes

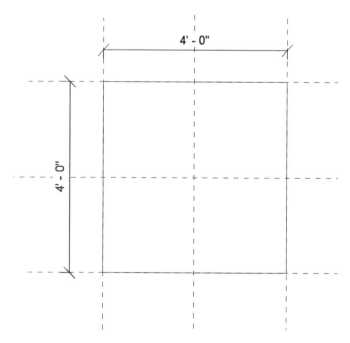

**FIGURE 17-3.2** Second dimension added

# Creating Parameters:

Now that the dimensions are placed, they can be tied to parameters. The dimensions can be tied to previously created parameters or a new parameter can be created based on the selected dimension. The latter will be employed, that is, selecting a dimension and then creating a parameter for it.

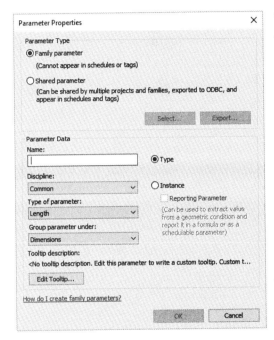

When defining a parameter, the user must specify the following:

- Name
- Parameter Type
  - Family Parameter
  - Shared Parameter
- Group parameter under
- Instance or Type
- Discipline
- Type of Parameter

You will gain a better understanding of how these various settings work once you start using them, but the following descriptions are offered as a primer for what is about to be covered in the next few steps.

**Name**: The *Parameter Name* should be descriptive. It can have spaces and symbols. However, dashes and other mathematical formula symbols should be avoided as they will confuse Revit when using them to do calculations. The name IS case sensitive. One common naming convention is to name all custom parameters with all uppercase letters to distinguish the Revit default parameters from the custom ones. The name can be changed at any time.

**Parameter Type**: The *Parameter Type* concept takes a little time to fully understand. A simple explanation will be provided here so as not to get too bogged down in the details early on.

*Family parameters*: cannot appear in schedules (e.g., a door schedule or a furniture schedule) or be used in tags (e.g., a door tag or a furniture tag). Thus, if one were to create a *Family Parameter* to keep track of the recycled content, that value (e.g., 80%) could not appear in a schedule, nor could it appear in a tag (e.g., a tag that listed the item number and directly below it the 80% value). This is the option that will be used initially in this book.

*Shared parameters*: can be shared by multiple projects and families, and appear in schedules and tags. This method requires the use of an external text file to manage the parameters.

**Group parameter under**: The *Group parameter under* setting simply specifies which section to place the parameter in when displayed in the properties dialogs in the project (see Figure 17-3.3). This setting can be changed at any time after the parameter has been created.

**Instance vs. Type**: The *Instance* vs. *Type* parameter has already been discussed; see page 17-8. This setting can be changed at any time after the parameter has been created.

**Discipline**: This setting is simply a way to manage the large number of value types as can be seen in the information below.

**FIGURE 17-3.3** Instance Properties dialog for box family (in a project environment)

**Type of Parameter**: The *Type of Parameter* is how Revit knows what type of information will be stored in a specific placeholder, or parameter.

Looking at the images to the left, one can see the various disciplines and parameter types that can be used.

Setting this properly has the following benefits:

- *Input validation*: when a *Parameter* is set to the type *Integer*, a user working with the family in a project cannot enter a decimal number.

- *Proper formatting*:
  - o   Common, Currency = 1.50
  - o   Electrical, Wattage = 60 W
  - o   Structural, Force = 2.45 kip

*FYI: Additional formatting can be done in the project via Project Units and also within the scheduling functionally.*

This setting cannot be changed once the parameter has been created; it would have to be deleted and recreated.

5.   Select the horizontal dimension (see Figure 17-3.4).

Notice one of the options on the *Ribbon* is **Label Dimension**, and it has a drop-down list next to it. This might better be titled "Parameter" because the drop-down list presents *Parameters* that can be tied into the selected dimension and ultimately used to drive the dimensions from the *Properties* dialog from within a project. However, once a parameter has been tied into a dimension a *Label* does show up next to the dimension text as will be seen in a moment, so the *Label* title is not totally inappropriate.

6.  Click the **Create Parameter** icon on the *Ribbon* (see Figure 17-3.4).

**FIGURE 17-3.4** Adding a parameter to a previously drawn dimension

The information on creating parameters, covered on the previous two pages, can now be put to use. Notice, in Figure 17-3.5, that the *Discipline* and *Type* of *Parameter* have been automatically selected because there are no other options when tying a parameter into a dimension. Therefore, creating a parameter for a dimension using this method saves a little time.

7.  Enter the following in the *Parameter Properties* dialog (Figure 17-3.5):

a.  *Parameter Type:*  **Family parameter**
b.  *Name:*  **Width**
c.  *Group under:*  **Dimensions**
d.  *Instance vs. Type:*  **Type**

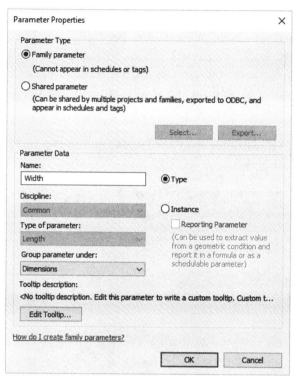

**FIGURE 17-3.5** Creating the *Width* parameter

8. Repeat the previous steps to add a **Depth** parameter, or label, to the vertical dimension in the *Ref. Level* view.

Notice, on the *Options Bar*, that previously created parameters are listed in the *Label* drop-down list. If the <u>Width</u> parameter were selected for the vertical dimension, one parameter would drive both the width and depth of the box.

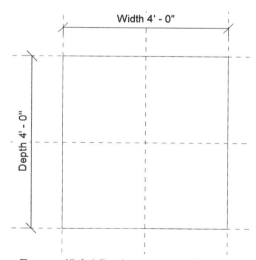

Looking at Figure 17-3.6, notice both dimensions have a *Label* associated with the dimension. This *Label* helps keep track of which dimensions are parametric. Another use for dimensions in a family is to "lock" it in order to maintain a relationship or spacing.

Even though the *Reference Planes* show up in the elevation views (front, left, etc.), the dimensions do not. So it is not visually obvious in the <u>Left</u> view that the *Depth* parameter has been created.

**FIGURE 17-3.6** *Depth* parameter added

Next, an *Instance Parameter* will be created for the height of the box. Once the box family is loaded into a project, the height can vary from box to box (i.e., per instance). However, if the width (or depth) is changed, all boxes in the project will change. You will test this in a project momentarily.

9. Switch to the **Front** view.

Notice the *Width* dimension is not visible in this view.

10. Add a **dimension** from the *Reference Level* to the *Reference Plane* at the top of the box.

11. Add a **Height** parameter to the dimension (see Figure 17-3.7 and 17-3.8).

   a. Be sure to select the **Instance** option.

**FIGURE 17-3.7** Creating the *Height* parameter

As can be seen in Figure 17-3.8, the Height parameter has been successfully added. This dimension can be seen in opposite views, the <u>Back</u> view in this case, but it cannot be seen in the side views, Left and Right in this case.

**FIGURE 17-3.8** Front view; *Height* parameter added

## Flexing the Family:

Now that parametric dimensions have been added to the *Family* it is necessary to flex them and make sure they work as intended before loading into a project.

12. Switch to the **3D view** via the *Quick Access Toolbar*.

13. Click the **Types** tool on the *Ribbon*.

> ***FYI:*** *Notice the last two tools on the* Ribbon *are repeated for each tab; this is for convenience within the Family Editor.*

The *Family Types* dialog is now open (Figure 17-3.9). Notice the three parameters created are showing up under the specified *Dimensions* heading. The easiest way to "flex" the *Family* is to move this dialog off to one side, adjust the dimension(s) and then press *Apply*. When *Apply* is selected, the changes are applied to the *Family* without the need to close the dialog box.

Also, notice the Height parameter has "(default)" next to its name. This is because it is an Instance parameter. The Height can vary, but when the Family is initially placed, the "default" value will be used.

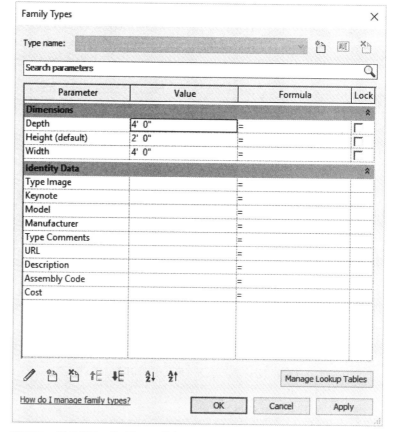

**FIGURE 17-3.9** Family Types dialog

14. In the *Family Types* dialog, make the following adjustments:

    a. Height:    **6"**

    b. Width:    **1'-0"**

    c. See Figure 17-3.10.

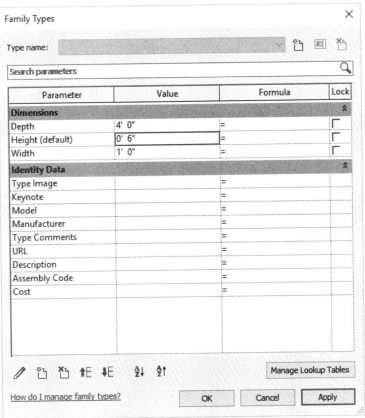

**FIGURE 17-3.10** Family Types dialog - Modified

15. Move the dialog box off to one side, so the 3D view of the box can be seen, and drag on the dialog title bar; this will allow the changes to the box to be seen.

16. Click **Apply**.

*TIP: Clicking* Apply *within a dialog box commits the changes to the model. This allows the user to see if the modification looks correct before closing the dialog box and possibly needing to reopen it. If the changes do not need to be visually inspected first, the* OK *button can simply be selected – it is not necessary to click* Apply *first.*

The size of the box should now be modified as shown in Figure 17-3.11 below. When flexing the family, the size was changed by a large enough amount to make it unmistakable that a change occurred. Just changing the numbers by an inch or two might make it hard to notice the adjustment visually.

Next the box will be loaded into the Project environment; there it will be shown how the family can be adjusted via the properties.

Because the *Width* and *Depth* are **Type Parameters**, any change will affect all instances of the box. On the other hand, with the *Height* being an **Instance Parameter** – one change will only affect the selected objects.

**FIGURE 17-3.11** 3D Box - Modified

17. Open the *Project* from the previous exercise **Box Project**. Do <u>not</u> close the **Box Family**.

18. Press **Ctrl + Tab** until the **Box** *Family* is current (Ctrl + Tab switches between the currently open views).

Load into Project

19. Click the **Load into Project** button on the *Ribbon*.

The **Box Project** is a Revit *Project* that already contains a *Family* named **Box**, which was loaded at the end of the previous exercise. When Revit notices that a *Family* is being loaded with the same name as one previously loaded, it will present the user with the **Family Already Loaded** dialog, see Figure 17-3.12, which provides a few options in which to choose from. Revit will not assume that the file being loaded is a replacement for the previously loaded *Family*. Rather, the user must decide by selecting one of two overwrite options or clicking *Cancel* to not load the *Family* at all. It could be that a totally different box was created or downloaded and should not replace the currently loaded box; in this case you would click *Cancel* and rename the *Family* so it does not conflict with the previously loaded one.

Most of the time the first overwrite option should be selected, as the second may overwrite project specific changes to the *Family* such as the **Cost** parameter.

20. Click **Overwrite the existing version.**

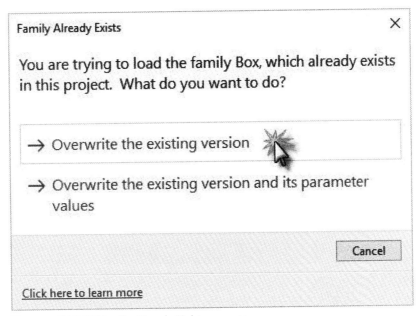

**FIGURE 17-3.12** Family Already Exists prompt

*TIP: Revit will only display the "Family Already Exists" prompt if the Family file being loaded has been modified as compared to the version already in the Project file.*

If the user has more than one Revit project open, a dialog displays in which the user selects which project(s) to load the *Family* into.

The **Box Project** file becomes the current view on the computer screen and the **Box** *Family* changes size to match the values of the newly added *Parameters*.

21. In any view (i.e., Level 1, Elevations, 3D), **select** the previously placed **Box** within the *Drawing Window*.

Notice the selected element temporarily turns blue and the *Modify Generic Models* contextual tab is displayed on the Ribbon.

22. With the Box selected, notice the *Properties Palette*.

Of the three parameters created in this exercise, only one shows up under the *Instance Parameters* (see Figure 17-3.13). The other two parameters, <u>Width</u> and <u>Depth</u>, will be visible in the *Type Parameters* dialog which will be explored next.

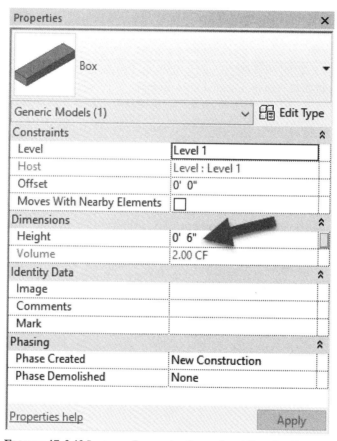

**FIGURE 17-3.13** Instance Properties for updated Box family

23. In the *Properties Palette* dialog box, click **Edit Type**.

The two *Type Parameters* show up here in the *Type Properties* dialog; see Figure 17-3.14. An example will be shown next on exactly what the difference is between an *Instance Parameter* and a *Type Parameter*. However, it may be helpful to go back, at this time, and review the **Instance and Type Parameters** discussion earlier in this chapter (see page 17-8) before proceeding.

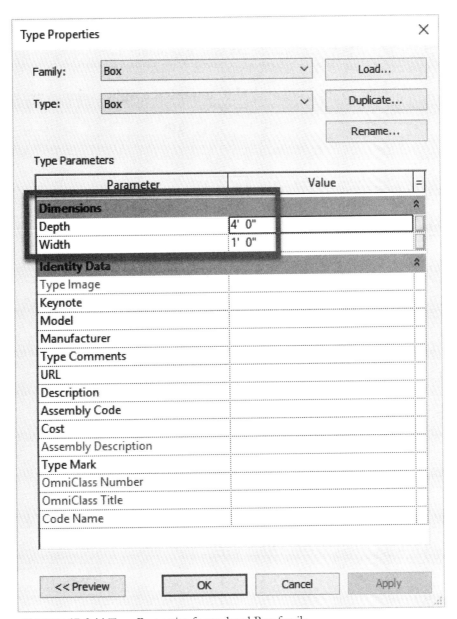

**FIGURE 17-3.14** Type Properties for updated Box family

24. Close the dialog box by selecting **Cancel**.

Next, two additional boxes will be placed to show the difference between *Instance and Type Parameters*. This can be accomplished by clicking the *Place a Component* button on the *Architecture* tab, as was done to place the first box, or by simply copying the existing box.

25. Select the box, if not already selected, and then click **Copy** on the *Ribbon*.

> **WARNING:** *Do not click the* Copy *command in the* Clipboard *panel; this is for copies between views or projects! Rather, use the* Copy *command on the* Modify *panel.*

26. Make two copies of the *Box Family* **6'-0"** towards the **right** as shown in Figure 17-3.15 below.

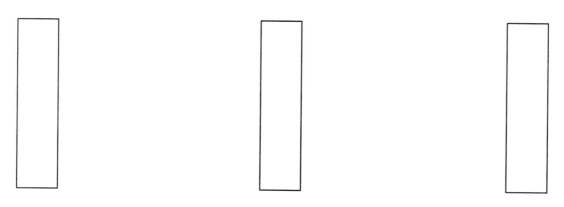

**FIGURE 17-3.15** Box family copied for *Type* versus *Instant* study

27. Select the *Box* instance on the far left, and then view its *Type Parameters*; click **Edit Type** on the *Properties Palette*.

28. Change the **Width** *Parameter* from 1'-0" to **4'-0"**.

29. Click **OK** to close the *Type Parameter* dialog.

Because the <u>Width</u> *Parameter* is a *Type Parameter*, all instances of the type <u>Box</u> are updated instantly; see Figure 17-3.16 below. The <u>Depth</u> and <u>Height</u> for each remain unchanged. It makes no difference which box is selected anywhere in the *Project*. If this box existed on 20 different floors and in multiple phases, they would all have been updated. This is an important concept to understand because, just as it is easy to make several corrections or revisions with this technique, it is just as easy to make several errors in the design.

If additional widths are needed, either an additional *Type* would need to be added to the *Family* or a totally new *Family* would need to be created. ***FYI:*** *If the geometry is the same, and just the dimensions need to change, one would typically make a new* Type *within an existing* Family *rather than a new* Family.

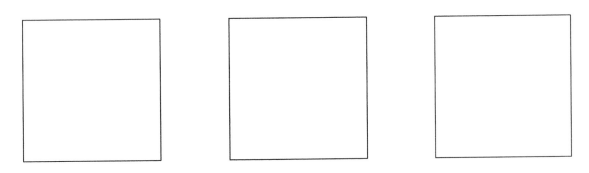

**FIGURE 17-3.16** Type parameter <u>Width</u> changed

Next, the *Instant Parameter* <u>Height</u> will be studied. To see this change, a vertical (i.e., elevation) or 3D view needs to be opened.

30. Switch to the **South** exterior elevation via the *Project Browser*.

**FIGURE 17-3.17** South exterior elevation

Notice the Boxes are all **6″** tall (Figure 17-3.17) which was set previously in the *Family Editor*, prior to being loaded into the current *Project*.

31. Select the box in the middle and view its *Instance Properties* via the *Properties Palette*.

32. Change the **Height** from 6″ to **2′-3½″**.

Notice that just the selected instance was changed.

**FIGURE 17-3.18** South exterior elevation middle box modified

***TIP:*** *It is possible to change multiple instances at once if they are all selected prior to editing the* Properties Palette *dialog. Additionally, if EVERY instance in the entire Project needs to be modified, simply select one and then right-click and pick the "Select all instances" option. Caution should be used when employing the second tip as things change in ALL views and on ALL levels, and in ALL phases of the current Project when the "entire Project" option is selected.*

33. **Save** both the *Project* and the *Family* as they will be further developed in the next exercise.

## Revit Model Content Style Guide:

A number of years ago Autodesk released a document intended to help standardize how Revit content is made. This will help when sharing projects between offices and when downloading content from manufacturer's websites. Specifically, adding tags and scheduling will be greatly streamlined. This file is not readily available from Autodesk anymore but can be found by searching "Revit Model Content Style Guide" in your web browser.

## Exercise 17-4:
## The Box: Formulas and Materials

The ability to add formulas and materials will be covered in this exercise.

The ability to add **formulas** means that the <u>Width</u> *Parameter* could be "programmed" such that it is always half the size of the depth *Parameter*; this is the example that will be explored in this exercise. Additionally, one could control the spacing of shelving brackets based on the length of the shelf, or the size of a lintel based on the width of the window below it; the lintel would need to be in the window family in this case. As should be obvious, the possibilities are many.

Defining **materials** in the *Family Editor* means that the component is ready to be rendered the moment it is placed in the project. It may not always be possible to anticipate what the material should be, but it is often more convenient to have something selected rather than nothing, which renders a flat gray color.

*Cabinets with different materials applied (same family)*

## Adding a formula:

The following steps show how to add a formula to a parameter.

1.  Open the **Box** *Family* created in the previous exercise.

    a.  It is recommended that a copy of the **Box** *Family* be saved for each exercise in case problems arise and an older file is needed to revert back to. Maybe copy the **Box** *Family* file and rename it to **Box 17-3** to save a copy of the *Family* from the previous exercise.

2.  Click the **Types** button on the *Ribbon* (see image to right).

Notice in the *Family Types* dialog below that a column named "*Formula*" exists. *Whenever* something is entered in this column the *Value* is grayed out for that *Parameter* (i.e., row); the result of the formula becomes the *Value* for that *Parameter*. A preliminary example is shown below.

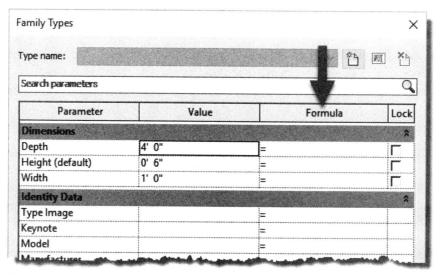

**FIGURE 17-4.1** Family Types dialog

It is often helpful to open and explore the various *Families* that come with Revit; this can provide much insight on how to do certain things. The image below shows several formulas used to define a pipe elbow *Family* that comes with Revit. The values next to the formulas are the result of the adjacent formula; it is not possible to manually enter a value in this case, when a formula is present. Notice how other parameters can be used in formulas; this is case sensitive.

| Parameter | Value | Formula | ▲ |
|---|---|---|---|
| **Dimensions** | | | ⌄ |
| Tick Size (default) | 115/256" | = Fitting Outside Diameter * 0.4 * tan(Angle / 2) | |
| Nominal Radius (default) | 1/2" | = | |
| Nominal Diameter (default) | 1" | = Nominal Radius * 2 | |
| Insulation Radius (default) | 9/16" | = Fitting Outside Radius + Insulation Thickness | ≡ |
| Fitting Outside Diameter (default) | 1 1/8" | = text_file_lookup(Lookup Table Name, "FOD", Nominal Dia | |
| Center to End (default) | 13/16" | = Center Radius * tan(Angle / 2) | |
| Angle (default) | 90.000° | = | |

**FIGURE 17-4.2** Sample Family showing complex formulas

3. For the *Width* parameter, in the *Formula* column, enter the following: **Depth/2** (see Figure 17-4.3).

4. Click into a different cell within the *Family Types* dialog to see the *Value* update.

Notice the <u>Width</u> *Value* is now half of the <u>Depth</u>, i.e., 2'-0" (see Figure 17-4.3).

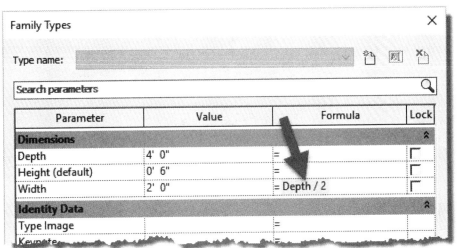

**FIGURE 17-4.3** Adding formula to control the width

***TIP:*** *When using parameters in a formula, keep the following in mind:*

- *Parameters in formulas must match the case (i.e., uppercase, lowercase, mixed) of the Parameters being referenced. Typing "depth" rather than "Depth" in the example above would not work – Revit would show an error message.*
- *A Parameter used in a formula must exist in the Family before it can be used.*
- *If a Parameter is deleted, any formulas that use that Parameter will also be deleted. Revit will present a warning first.*
- *If a Parameter is renamed, Revit will automatically rename the Parameter in all formulas in which it is used.*

Below are a few of the basic symbols Revit can use in formulas. See Revit's *Help System* for a full list:

- *Addition*: **+**
- *Subtraction*: **-**
- *Multiplication*: **\***
- *Division*: **/**
- *Tangent*: **Tan**
- *Cosine*: **Cos**
- *Sine*: **Sin**

Conditional Formatting

It is also possible to use conditional statements in a formula such as IF, AND, OR, <, >, =

Here are a few examples:

- if(Depth > 3', 2', 1')
- if(and(Depth > 3', Height = 1'), 2', 1')
- See Revit's *Help* for more info.

Next the *Family* will be loaded into the *Project Environment* to see the formula in action.

5. Open the project file **Box Project**, and then switch to the **3D view**.

6. Press **Ctrl + Tab** until the **Box Family** file is current.

7. Click the **Load into Project** button on the *Ribbon*.

Notice the size of the box changes. When the <u>Depth</u> is now changed, the <u>Width</u> will automatically be updated. This will be tested next.

8. Select one of the boxes and, via its *Type Properties*, change the **Depth** to **6'-0"** and then

   a. Click in an adjacent cell.

   b. Notice the <u>Width</u> instantly updates.

9. Click **OK** to close the dialog and accept the changes.

All three boxes change size: 6'-0" depth and 3'-0" width. The height is still an *Instance Parameter* so it remained unchanged.

10. Switch back to the box family.

Next, a brief look at a few variations.

The following revisions will not be saved; the Cancel button will be selected to discard the next two steps.

11. Change the formula for *Width* to simply read **Depth** (see Figure 17-4.4).

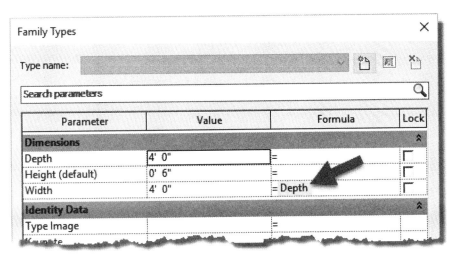

**FIGURE 17-4.4** Modifying formula to control the width

Thus, it is possible to have one *Parameter* simply equal another one.

12. Click **Cancel** to discard the formula change.

Another way to achieve the results shown in the previous image and steps is to have one *Parameter* control two dimensions. This would reduce the number of *Parameters* from three to two as the *Family* currently stands. The image on the next page (see Figure 17-4.5) shows an example of this. Simply select a previously drawn dimension and then select the desired *Parameter* from the *Label* drop-down list on the *Options Bar*. This is only visible when a dimension is selected.

One *Parameter* could control several dimensions. A *Parameter* has to be of type *Length* (versus *Text, Currency, Volume, Yes/No,* etc.) to work with a *Dimension*. The *Label* drop-down list will automatically filter the list.

It is best if the dimensions reference the *Reference Planes* rather than the 3D geometry.

**FIGURE 17-4.5** One Parameter controlling multiple dimensions

This concludes the brief introduction to adding formulas to a *Family*. The remainder of this exercise will shift gears a bit and look at adding materials to the box family.

## Adding a Material:

Adding a *Material* in the *Family* can save time for the design teams using the content when it comes to creating renderings.

13. Select the 3D extrusion that represents the box in the *Family Editor*.

14. View the *Properties Palette* dialog box.

Notice, in Figure 17-4.6, that the *Material* is set to *By Category*. This will be changed to something specific to this *Family*.

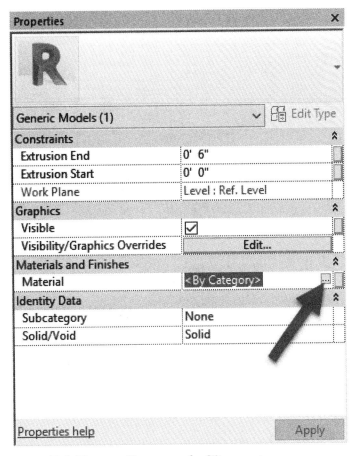

**FIGURE 17-4.6** Instance Parameters for 3D geometry

15. Click in the cell with *<By Category>* to reveal the small link button to the right; see Figure 17-4.6.

16. Click the **link-button** to open the *Materials* dialog.

Notice the *Family* has a limited number of *Materials* loaded; see Figure 17-4.7. The following sequence of steps will show how to create a new *Material* and define it.

**FIGURE 17-4.7** Materials for the Box Family, not the Box Project

17. Click the **Create New Material** icon in the lower left corner; see arrow in Figure 17-4.7.

18. Right-click the new *Material* and **Rename** it to **Box Material**; see Figure 17-4.8.

19. Click the **Foreground Surface Pattern** preview area (currently set to "none"); see Figure 17-4.9.

> *TIP: Make sure the Graphics tab is selected to see the Surface Pattern area.*

**FIGURE 17-4.8** Naming new material

**FIGURE 17-4.9** Setting surface pattern

A new "Model" *Surface Pattern* will be created. A "Model" pattern will not change scale with the *View Scale* in the *Project Environment*; this is meant for real-world items like siding, tile, CMU, etc. as seen in elevation. Conversely, the "Drafting" patterns do change scale with the *View Scale* and are meant for representative patterns typically used in sections to imply a certain material.

20. Select **Model** for *Pattern Type* and then follow the steps shown in Figure 17-4.10 to create a new "Model" based *Fill Pattern* named **3″ Tile**.

**FIGURE 17-4.10** Creating a new model based surface pattern

21. Click **OK** to close the *Fill Patterns* dialog but not the *Materials* dialogs!

Next you will add an *Appearance* asset so you can control how the material will appear in a rendering.

22. Click to add an **Appearance** asset (Figure 17-4.11).

23. Set the *Render Appearance* to **3in Square - Terra Cotta** (from the *Appearance Library*).

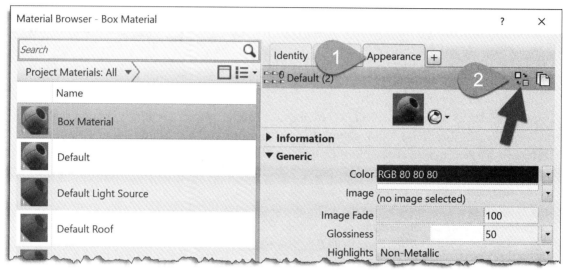

**FIGURE 17-4.11** Selecting rendering appearance

24. Click **OK** to close the *Materials* dialog box.

The fill pattern is now visible, Figure 17-4.12. However, the render appearance is not visible until loaded and rendered in a project. Per steps previously covered in the textbook, load the family into the project and do a rendering in a 3D view.

*TIP: When loading a Family, if the project already has a material named "box material," per the above example, the material definition in the project will take precedence if the two are not identical.*

25. **Save** the Box *Family.*

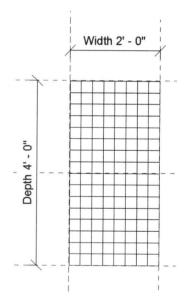

**FIGURE 17-4.12** Family Editor

26. Load the updated *Family* into the **Box Project** (*Project* file).

When the newly updated *Family* is loaded into the project, the **Fill Pattern** shows up right away (Figure 17-4.13). The fill pattern can be selected on each face of each box and be rotated and reposition as desired in the *Project Environment*.

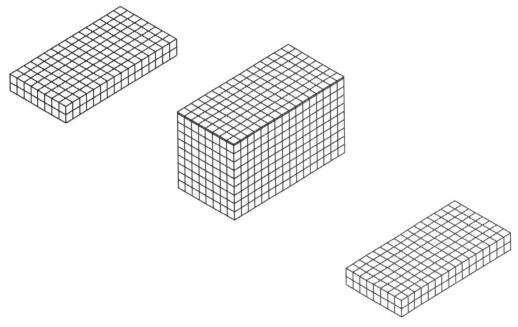

**FIGURE 17-4.13** Box family in project environment

27. Switch to a 3D or Camera view and create a **rendering** to see the *Render Appearance* material.

    a.  Adding a floor below the boxes will allow the shadows to show up as in the image to the right.

28. **Save** the *Project*.

**FIGURE 17-4.14** Rendered in project environment

## Changing the Material in the Project Environment:

So far, the *Material* for the Box has been "hard wired" within the *Family* and cannot be changed once in the *Project Environment*. In this last set of steps, the techniques required to achieve this goal will be covered.

Just to make things more clear: it is possible to create several 2D shapes in a single *Family*. For example, a door has a solid for the frame, the door panel and a vision panel; see the image to the right (Figure 17-4.15).

Therefore, it would not make sense for Revit to provide one built-in parameter that controls the *Material* for everything in the *Family*.

**FIGURE 17-4.15** Door family with multiple materials defined

In the door example, a parameter is created for each *Material* needed in the *Family*. Next, each solid in the *Family* is mapped to one of the three *Parameters*. It is possible for one *Parameter* to control the *Material* of several 3D elements, e.g., a "glass material" *Parameter* controls the *Material* for all seven pieces of glass in Figure 17-4.15.

29. In the Box *Family* click the **Types** button.

30. Click the **Add…** button to make a new *Parameter*.

31. Modify the *Parameter Properties* dialog as shown in Figure 17-4.16.

    a. *Name*:
       **Finish Material**

    b. *Group parameter under*:
       **Materials and Finishes**

    c. *Type*:
       **Material**

32. Click **OK**.

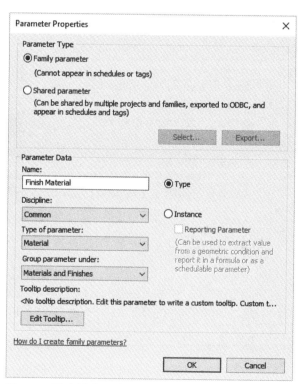

**FIGURE 17-4.16** Creating a new parameter

33. In the *Family Types* dialog, change the "value" for **Finish Material** to **Box Material**. (See Figure 17-4.17.)

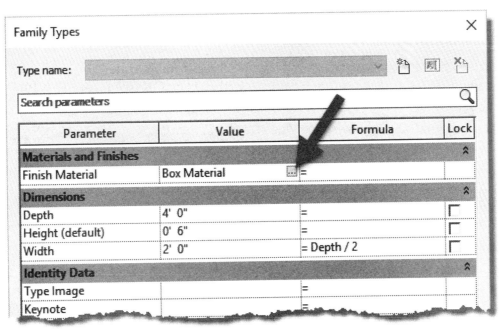

**FIGURE 17-4.17** Setting material for new parameter

At this point, a new *Parameter* has been created but does not control anything yet. In the next few steps you will map the *Material* for the 3D box to the *Material* parameter just created in the previous steps. After this, the *Family Types* parameter will be the only way to change the *Material* for the box.

34. Click **OK** to close the *Family Types* dialog box.

35. Select the box and then look at the **Properties Palette**.

36. Click the small mapping icon to the far right of the **Material** *Parameter* (see Figure 17-4.18).

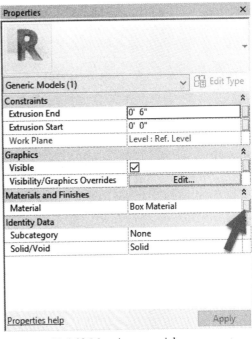

**FIGURE 17-4.18** Mapping material to parameter

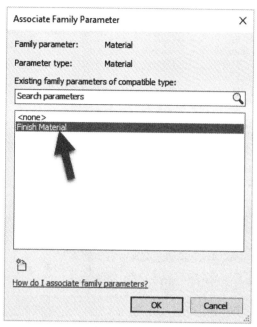

**FIGURE 17-4.19** Mapping material to parameter

The *Associate Family Parameter* dialog is now displayed. Revit presents the user with a list of *Parameters* that are of the *Type* "material" (versus text, currency, etc.). At this point, the only option is the *Parameter* just created.

37. Select **Finish Material** from the list and then click **OK** (see Figure 17-4.19).

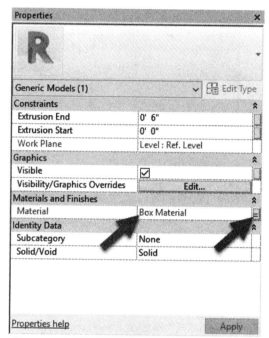

**FIGURE 17-4.20** Mapped material

Now that the *Material* is mapped to a *Parameter*, notice that the mapping icon now has an **equal** sign in it and the rest of the row is grayed out; see Figure 17-4.20. The grayed out *Material* means that the *Family Type Parameter* is now controlling this *Instance Parameter*.

38. **Save** the **Box** *Family* again.

39. **Load** the *Family* into the box Project.

40. Select one of the boxes and view its **Type Parameters**.

41. Notice **Finish Material** is now an option.

42. **Save** the **Box Project** file.

## Exercise 17-5:
## The Box: Family Types and Categories

This exercise will study *Family Types*. A *Type* is simply the ability to save various parameter settings in a *Family* so they do not need to be entered manually within each Project.

Thus far, in this chapter, a *Family* with just a single *Type* has been created. Any new *Family* automatically has one *Type* if none are specifically created; the *Type* name is the same as the *Family* name once loaded into the *Project Environment*. This exercise will look at how to create several predefined *Types* within the *Family Editor* and how to create additional *Types* on the fly within the *Project Environment*.

**Why use Types?** Let us say a "Box" manufacturer offers several standard sizes. When creating the *Family* for the "Box," it would be most expedient to create a *Type* for each standard option. This would save the end-user(s) time in more ways than one. If a design firm had trusted custom Revit content, an end-user could load the "Box" *Family* and pick a size from the predefined *Types* knowing that they are real options. Maybe some rarely used or overpriced options are intentionally omitted. However, just not having to enter the data manually can be a great benefit.

The reader may wish to turn back to the first exercise in this chapter and review the information initially presented on this topic; see page 17-5.

Finally, the use of **Categories** will be studied. Revit uses *Categories* to control visibility and to determine which command will be used to place a *Family* (e.g., Door tool, Window tool, Mechanical Equipment tool, Component tool).

1. **Open** the *Family* named **Box**.

2. Click the **Types** button on the *Ribbon*.

Notice, in Figure 17-5.1, that the *Name* drop-down at the top is blank. Clicking the *New* button on the right allows one or more named *Types* to be created.

Once *Types* exist, all the *Parameter* **Values** below relate specifically to the selected named *Type*.

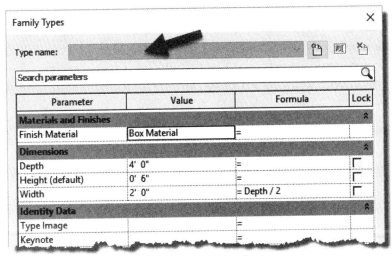

FIGURE 17-5.1 Family Types – no types created yet

Next, four *Types* will be created in the <u>Box</u> *Family*. Each *Type* will have a different <u>Depth</u> assigned to it.

3. In the *Family Types* dialog, click the **New...** button.

4. Enter **2'-0" x 4'-0"** for the name of the first *Type* (Figure 17-5.2).

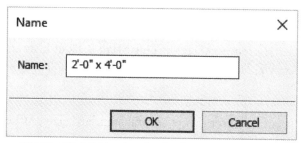

**FIGURE 17-5.2** Naming the family type

*Type* names should be descriptive and not duplicate any part of the *Family* name (i.e., the name of the file on the hard drive). In this example the exact size will be used as the *Type* name. In other cases it might be more useful to list the model number or some other descriptive wording.

5. Click **OK**.

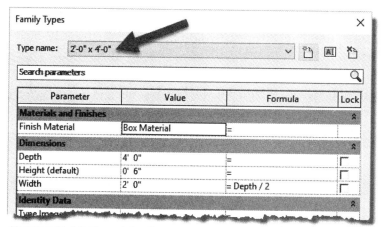

**FIGURE 17-5.3** Named family type

Now, one *Type* exists in the *Name* drop-down list. Note that the *Type* name matches the values below; this was intentional. However, it should be stated that the name and values could be inconsistent. The name has no direct control over any of the *Parameter* values, i.e., the name 2'-0" x 4'-0" does not automatically make the <u>Depth</u> and <u>Width</u> *Values* match. Thus, the person creating the *Family* needs to do some QA (quality assurance) checking. This will be made clear in the next few steps.

6. Click the **New...** button again.

7. Enter the name **3'-0" x 6'-0"**.

   a. Remember, because of the formula added in the previous exercise, the <u>Width</u> is always half the <u>Depth</u>.

The **Box** *Family* now has two *Types* created; each can be easily selected within the *Project Environment*.

**Revit is now managing two complete lists of** *Parameters*, **one for each** *Type*.

As will be proven momentarily, the *Values* (i.e., <u>Width</u> and <u>Depth</u>) can vary from one list to the other.

As seen in Figure 17-5.4, the new *Type* did not change the *Parameter Values* below. Next this will be changed.

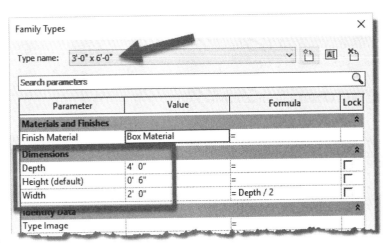

**FIGURE 17-5.4** Second named family type

8. With the *Type* 3'-0" x 6'-0" current, change the <u>Depth</u> to **6'-0"**.

**FIGURE 17-5.5A** First type settings

**FIGURE 17-5.5B** Second type settings

9. Using the *Name* drop-down list, switch back and forth between the two options; notice the *Parameter Values* change (Figures 17-5.5A and B).

10. Create two more *Types* per the information below:
    a. *Name*: **4'-0" x 8'-0"**          **5'-6" x 11'-0"**
    b. *Depth*: **8'-0"**                 **11'-0"**

Now that several *Types* have been defined in the **Box** *Family* it will be loaded into the *Project Environment* to see how they work.

11. **Open** the **Box Project** file, if not already open.

12. In the <u>Box</u> *Family* file, click the **Load into Project** button.

13. Select **Overwrite the existing version**.

14. Select the **Component** tool from the *Architecture* tab on the *Ribbon*.

15. Select the **Type Selector** (Figure 17-5.6).

**FIGURE 17-5.6** *Type Selector* in the project environment

Looking at Figure 17-5.6, notice all the *Types* created in the *Family Editor* are now available under the *Family* name **Box**. A *Type* named **Box** is also listed because the *Family* was previously loaded without any specific *Types* created, and as mentioned previously, when no *Types* exist Revit will create one with the same name as the *Family*. This can be deleted or renamed in the *Project Browser* within the *Families* section.

## Selecting a Category:

Selecting a *Category* is actually one of the first things typically done when starting a new *Family*. However, this change was left until now to make it perfectly clear what this setting does.

*NOTE: Some* Family *templates will already have the correct* Category *selected (e.g., door, window, casework templates). However, the* **Box** *Family was started with the* **Generic Model** *template, so the* Category *needs to be set manually as this template can be used for many things.*

16. **Open** the **Box** *Family* (if not already open).

17. On the *Create* tab, click **Category and Parameters**.

This list represents all the *Categories* used by Revit to control visibility and determine which tool inserts any given *Family*. *Categories* are also used by *Filters* and for scheduling. This list is "hard wired" and cannot be modified in any way.

This list is filtered for Architecture categories. However, clicking the drop-down list at the top allows each discipline to be toggled on individually.

At this point we will pretend that our **Box** *Family* is *Furniture*. Once set to be "furniture," the **Box** will show up in the *Furniture* schedule(s) and be visible (or not visible) based on the visibility and filter settings for any given view.

18. Click **Furniture** and then click **OK**.

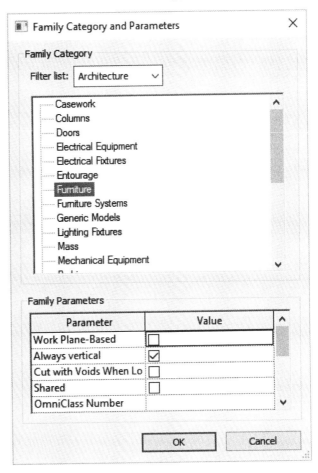

**FIGURE 17-5.7** Family Category and Parameters dialog

*TIP:*
*The* **Furniture** *category is generally for freestanding items that are not fastened to the building. Examples might be chairs, tables, desks, beds, etc.*

*The* **Furniture Systems** *category is for modular desks, often called cubicles. These can be fastened to the wall and/or have power and data hardwired to them. Thus they are different enough from regular furniture to warrant a separate section.*

19. **Save** the **Box** *Family*.

Next the modified *Family* will be loaded into the project and tested.

20. Load the *Family* into the **Box Project** file per steps previously covered.

21. In the **Box Project**, switch to the default **3D view**.

The next few steps will show how the visibility of the furniture category now affects the <u>Box</u> family.

22. Type **VV** to control visibility settings for the current view.

23. Uncheck *Furniture* on the *Model Categories* tab (Figure 17-5.8).

Notice there is a category for "Generic Models" as well. This would have allowed control of the **Box** *Family* previously. However, this category should be used sparingly due to its ambiguity.

24. Click **OK**.

The three boxes should have been hidden from the 3D view. They should still be visible in other views as long as the view's *Visibility Graphics Override* dialog did not have the *Furniture Category* turned off.

25. Per the previous steps, **turn the Furniture Category back on** in the *3D view*.

26. **Save** the **Box Project** file.

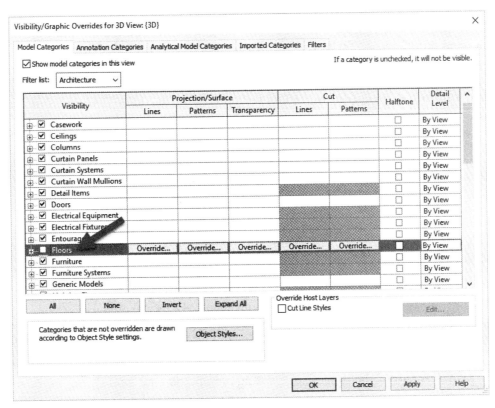

**FIGURE 17-5.8** VISIBILITY control in the project

Revit does not have a specific *Furniture* tool on the *Ribbon* so new instances of the **Box Family** would still be placed using the *Component* tool.

Care should be taken to select the correct *Category* for Revit *Families*. If someone is in a hurry they may hastily select a wrong *Category* which could have a huge negative impact on a project in terms of budget and completion time.

For example, a "smart board" for a classroom might be placed on the *Furniture Category* when it should have been placed on *Electrical Equipment*. Near the end of the project the design team decides to turn off all the *Furniture* for the construction documents set, as it was laid out for design only and is not part of the bid set. Now, the final set is missing all of the "smart boards" in the floor plans, ceiling plans and interior elevations.

Much more could be said and taught about *Family* creation but is beyond the introductory scope of this text.

Smart board family with materials

## Self-Exam:

The following questions can be used as a way to check your knowledge of this lesson. The answers can be found at the bottom of this page.

1.  *Loadable Families* can be imported into a project as needed. (T/F)

2.  How a *Family* is named is not important. (T/F)

3.  The <u>sill height</u> of a window is usually an *Instance* parameter. (T/F)

4.  Use the _____ tool to create the framework for a new *Family*.

5.  The solid tool, used in this chapter, to create the 3D box: _____.

## Review Questions:

The following questions may be assigned by your instructor as a way to assess your knowledge of this section. Your instructor has the answers to the review questions.

1.  The 3d box, drawn in this chapter, was aligned and then locked to the reference planes as part of the process of creating parametric content. (T/F)

2.  *Loadable Families* are typically preferred over in-place *Families*. (T/F)

3.  A <u>family name</u> and a *Family's* <u>type name(s)</u> should not have redundant information. (T/F)

4.  It is possible to specify if a parameter is an <u>instance</u> or <u>type</u> while in the process of creating it. (T/F)

5.  When the geometry changes, a new *Family* is typically required, rather than being able to use named *Types*. (T/F)

6.  The tool used to get a completed family into a project (while in the family editor environment): _____.

7.  Of the two types of *Fill Patterns*, only the _____ type patterns do not change size when the view scale changes.

8.  A *Family's* _____ setting controls/determines its visibility and which tool is used to place the item in the project environment.

9.  When a *Parameter* is associated to one or more dimensions, the *Parameter's* value controls the length of the dimension (and object being dimensioned). (T/F)

10. It is not possible to make one parameter to always be one half the size of another. (T/F)

# INDEX

## A

| | |
|---|---|
| Activate View | 15-5 |
| Align | 5-11, 5-26, 11-7, 17-23 |
| Annotation | 2-11, 9-36 |
| Appears in Drawing List (sheet index) | 15-12 |
| Arc, Detail Lines | 4-18, 4-25 |
| Array | 4-27, 8-2 |
| Attach | 8-20 |

## B

| | |
|---|---|
| Bath Room | 12-1 |
| Browser Organization | 15-8 |
| Bulkhead | 9-24 |

## C

| | |
|---|---|
| Cabinets | 12-2, 12-7 |
| Callout | 11-15 |
| Camera | 14-15, 14-35 |
| Camera; Eye Elevation | 14-38 |
| Ceiling height | 9-17 |
| Ceiling Properties | 9-23 |
| Ceiling tool | 9-17 |
| Ceiling; Bulkhead | 9-24 |
| Ceiling; Deleting | 9-21 |
| Chain (option) | 5-9 |
| Circle (detail line) | 3-13 |
| Close Revit project | 1-30 |
| Component | 9-31, 10-13, 12-21 |
| Component, Load | 11-29 |
| Conditional Formatting | 17-48 |
| Context Menu | 1-22 |
| Contextual Tab | 1-15 |
| Control Arrows | 8-7 |
| Copy | 3-24 |
| Copy to Clipboard | 4-23, 6-7, 6-20, 9-11 |
| Counter Top | 12-3, 12-9 |
| Crop Region | 10-5, 12-18, 14-17, 14-36 |
| Crossing Window | 3-22 |

## D

| | |
|---|---|
| Deactivate View | 15-5 |
| Default 3D View | 1-36, 5-21 |
| Delete | 3-20 |
| Design Options | 10-25, 15-9 |
| Detach from Central | 16-16 |
| Detail Components | 11-29 |
| Detail Level (view) | 5-19, 8-1, 11-3 |
| Detail Lines | 3-3, 3-10, 3-11, 3-18, 4-14 |
| Dimension tool | 2-14, 3-6, 7-16, 7-18 |
| Dimensions; Activate | 8-31 |
| Dimensions; Locking | 3-8, 5-13, 7-27 |
| Dimensions; Masonry | 5-11, 5-24, 5-36 |
| Dimensions; Suffix | 11-25 |
| Dimensions; Witness Line | 5-27 |
| Dimension Snaps | 3-16 |
| Door Tag | 5-39-40, 13-4 |
| Door tool | 2-5, 5-35, 6-10 |
| Door; Load Family | 5-37 |
| Door; Properties | 5-40 |
| Door Schedule | 13-6 |
| Drafting View | 3-3, 4-2, 4-4 |
| Drop-down Button | 1-13, 1-14 |
| 3D DWF | 15-15 |

## E

| | |
|---|---|
| Element Properties | 5-46 |
| Elevation | 1-8, 10-1, 10-16, 12-4, 12-12 |
| Ellipse | 4-21 |
| Export Image | 14-26, 14-39 |
| Extrusion | 17-21 |

## F

| | |
|---|---|
| Families | 17-1 |
| Family Types | 17-5, 17-59 |
| Far Clip Plane | 10-5, 11-2 |
| Fillet Arc | 4-14 |
| Fill Pattern, New | 17-53 |
| Filter | 5-19, 6-19 |
| Fireplace | 5-51 |
| Flip Symbol (element control) | 5-20, 5-46 |
| Floor tool | 9-1 |
| Furniture | 12-20 |
| Footing, Continuous | 11-10 |
| Formula | 17-45 |

**H**

Hide / Isolate      6-13, 12-22

**J**

Join Geometry      6-9
Join/Unjoin Roof      8-32, 8-33

**K**

Kitchen Layout      12-7
Keynoting      7-46

**L**

Length (entering)      4-3, 10-15
Level      1-6, 6-34, 8-24
Light Fixture      9-31, 9-35
Linework      11-13, 12-16
Load Family      5-36
Local File      16-13, 16-39

**M**

Materials      9-15, 9-22
Measure      2-14
Mirror      4-26
Modify      3-5
Move      3-26, 4-6, 4-9, 4-23, 5-20

**N**

New (project)      1-31, 5-2

**O**

Offset      4-15
Open      1-26
Open Documents      1-28
Openings      5-43, 11-8
Options bar      1-11, 1-20

**P**

Parameter, Material      17-56
Parameter, New      17-31
Paste Aligned      6-7, 6-20
Phase Created/Demo      16-2, 16-28
Phasing Dialog      16-1, 16-26
Phase Filter      16-3
Print      2-15, 15-17
Project Browser      1-21, 5-4, 5-38
Project Browser      5-50, 15-8
    Organization

Project Information      5-5

**Q**

Quick Access Toolbar      1-11, 1-13

**R**

Railing (guardrail)      12-25, 12-29
Raster Images      15-14
Rectangle (dtl. line)      3-12
Redo      3-5
Reference Plane      1-6, 17-15
Rendering      14-25
Rendering material      14-18, 14-32
Rendering;      14-42
    RPC People
Repeating Detail      11-34
Ribbon      1-11, 1-13-1-19
Roof tool      2-9, 8-1
Roof; Flat      8-9
Roof; Gable      8-4, 8-16, 8-21
Roof; Hip      8-3, 8-31
Roof; Join/Unjoin      8-32, 8-33
Roof; Shed      8-6
Room Schedule      13-10
Room Tag      13-1
Room Tag; Properties      13-13
Rotate      3-26, 9-20

**S**

Save      1-30
Schedule/Quantities      1-10, 13-6, 13-10
Scale      3-30, 4-22
Scroll Wheel      1-37
Section      11-1
Section Box      14-28
Section; Far Clip Plane      10-4
Selection Window      3-22
Shadows      14-30
Shared Parameters      7-39
Sheet      5-6, 15-1
Sheet Index      15-10
Show the Model      14-39
Skylight      8-35
Sketchy Lines      14-45
Snap      2-8, 3-15
Solid Form      10-35
Split (wall)      5-29
Split Button (UI)      1-13
Stair      6-22
Stair Width      6-26
Status bar      1-11, 1-21, 5-11

Sun Path                     14-32
Sun Settings                 14-21, 14-30
Surface Pattern              9-22
Sweeps                       5-32
Synchronize with             16-15
  Central

## T

TAB key                      2-8, 9-12
Tag                          7-31
Tag all                      13-4
Template                     1-32, 5-2
Text Properties              9-38
Text Tool                    2-11, 3-34, 7-2, 9-36,
                             9-37, 11-28
Titleblock                   15-1
Trim                         5-29
Type Catalog                 17-7
Type Parameters              5-40

## U

Underlay                     6-1, 6-15
Undo                         3-5
User Interface               1-11
Username                     16-14, 16-35

## V

View Control Bar             1-11, 1-22
View Range                   5-50
View Scale                   2-12, 6-9, 10-7, 10-
                             21, 11-16
Viewport                     15-3
Visibility Graphics          9-5, 12-22, 16-19
  Overrides

## W

Wall; Footing                11-10
Wall Height                  5-22, 6-3
Wall tool                    2-2, 5-9, 5-14, 5-15,
                             5-18, 6-15
Wall tool; Base              9-25
  Offset
Wall tool; Chain             5-9
Wall tool; Edit              5-16, 5-31
  Assembly
Web Library                  5-38, 5-39
Worksets                     16-17
Worksets Dialog              16-18, 16-19
Worksharing                  16-10, 16-36

**Sections** *Sample image from page 15-7*

**Renderings** *Sample image from page 14-44*

**3D Views** *Sample image from page 14-29*

**Interior Elevations** *Sample image from page 10-23*

## Z
Zoom                         1-33

**Notes:**